Advance Praise for *Comes a Horseman*

"Read this book with the lights on! Gory and ghastly, yet with a gripping plot, these pages will literally tremble in the hands of readers! *Comes a Horseman* is a chilling ride into a horrifying possibility!"

— www.inthelibraryreview.com

". . . Comes A Well-Crafted Page Turner Mindful Of *The Da Vinci Code*"

— Tampa Bay Tribune

"Frightening and fiendishly smart, *Comes a Horseman* is a must-read! Robert Liparulo's intense thrill ride will keep your nerves frayed and your lights on."

— David Morrell, author of *Creepers* and
The Brotherhood of the Rose

"Not for the faint of heart, this is quality writing that deserves a lofty niche within the action/suspense genre. It is well-researched and meticulously detailed, and the characters are fascinating and 'real,' the dialogue clever and altogether human, the plot compelling. What I'm trying to say is, I love it!"

— Frank Peretti, author of *Monster* and
This Present Darkness

"Take *The DaVinci Code*, throw in a dash of *Left Behind*, pair it with the intrigue of a Tom Clancy thriller, and you've got this chilling debut thriller from journalist Robert Liparulo."

— *Christianity Today*

"Liparulo has crafted a diabolical thrill ride of a novel that makes the roller coaster at Magic Mountain seem like a speed bump. Part serial killer procedural, part global techno-thriller, part spiritual suspense epic, *Comes a Horseman* has enough plot twists and action to decode *Da Vinci*! Highly recommended!"

— Jay Bonansinga, author of *Frozen,*
The Killer's Game, and *The Sinking of the*
Eastland

"A riveting thriller that spins effortlessly off great writing and a demonic villain real enough to have you looking over your own shoulder."

— David H. Dun, author of *The Black Silent*

"*Comes a Horseman* is an ambitious and original debut thriller by a fine new writer. Robert Liparulo deserves an audience, because he has something meaningful to say."

— C.J. Box, Anthony Award winning
author of *Out of Range*

"This book is a true page-turner, with wonderfully developed characters who have all-too-human strengths and weaknesses. This story is frighteningly real and insidious in a way that makes me hope our two FBI agents really are on the job. Robert Liparulo's writing is refreshingly good, especially for a first-time novelist. I hope there's a sequel!"

— Terri Lubaroff, Senior Vice President,
Humble Journey Films

"*Come a Horseman* is chalk-full of unbelievable excitement and credible research. My nails got shorter with each page—I could not put it down. This incredibly real-to-life thriller envelops the epic battle of good versus evil with a new depth. It is the thriller of thrillers! I can't wait for the next book."

— Dwight Cenac, President, Welcome
Home Care and HCMC Properties

"Liparulo's book takes the reader across the globe in a riveting story of murder and Church intrigue. A quick, compelling read."

— W.H. Watford, Edgar-nominated author
of *Mortal Strain* and *Lethal Risk*

"Robert Liparulo has burst onto the thriller scene with a ferociously original page-turner. *Comes a Horseman* takes religious conspiracy to the next, frightening level. Cutting-edge forensics, horrifying villains, and a slam-bang race to the finish all come together to make one of the most exciting and satisfying reads of the year"

— J.A. Konrath, author of *Bloody Mary*

"Fasten your seat belt; *Comes a Horseman* is a wild ride! With great skill and prophetic clarity, Robert Liparulo knows how to tell an exciting story and boost a reader's adrenaline level. You won't want to put this one down!"

— Angela Hunt, author of
The Novelist and *Unspoken*

"*Comes a Horseman* has a powerful sense of doom from the first pages on. Though the story is global, some of its best writing is surprisingly intimate: a boy and his father besieged in their house, two good people, a man in the middle, and one very bad man in a dark room on an empty floor in a hotel. There's some fresh role-reversal in the two leads. The sense of doom yields to a downhill, no brakes, runaway pace, an inevitable clash of complicated Good and uncomplicated Evil. Liparulo knows more than you and I do about some dark corners of history."

— Dan Vining, author of *The Quick*

COMES A HORSEMAN

A NOVEL

ROBERT LIPARULO

WestBow
PRESS

A Division of Thomas Nelson Publishers
Since 1798

visit us at www.westbowpress.com

Published in Nashville, Tennessee, by WestBow Press, a division of Thomas Nelson, Inc.

WestBow Press books may be purchased in bulk for educational, business, fund-raising, or sales promotional use. For information, please e-mail SpecialMarkets@ThomasNelson.com.

Publisher's Note: This novel is a work of fiction. Names, characters, places, and incidents are either products of the author's imagination or used fictitiously. All characters are fictional, and any similarity to people living or dead is purely coincidental.

Library of Congress Cataloging-in-Publication Data

Liparulo, Robert.
     Comes a horseman / by Robert Liparulo.
     p. cm.
     ISBN 0-7852-6176-1 (hard cover)
     ISBN 1-5955-4179-9 (trade paper)
     1. Government investigators—Fiction. 2. Americans—Jerusalem—Fiction. 3. Serial murders—Fiction. 4. Jerusalem—Fiction. 5. Colorado—Fiction. I. Title.
PS3612.I63C66 2005
813' .6—dc22   2004026692

Printed in the United States of America

06 07 08 09 10 RRD 5 4 3 2 1

For the ladies who have always made my life sweeter:
My wife, Jodi;
My daughter, Melanie;
My mother, Mae Gannon;
And my sister Lynda, who went Home way too early.

PART i

COLORADO

To die will be an awfully big adventure.
—*J. M. Barrie,* Peter Pan

Oh, how I wish I were the Antichrist!
—*Percy Bysshe Shelley*

Five years ago
Asia House, Tel Aviv, Israel

He waited with his face pressed against the warm metal and his pistol gouging the skin at his lower back. He thought about pulling the weapon from his waistband, setting it beside him or even holding it in his hand, but when the time came, he'd have to move fast, and he didn't want it getting in his way. He'd been there a long time, since well before the first party guests started arriving. Now it sounded as though quite a crowd had gathered on the third floor of the big building. Their voices drifted to him through the ventilation shaft, reverberating off its metal walls, reaching his ears as a jumble of undulating tones, punctuated at times by shrill laughter. He would close his eyes for long periods and try to discern the conversations, but whether by distortion or foreign tongue, even single words eluded him.

Luco Scaramuzzi lifted his cheek out of a pool of perspiration and peered for the hundredth time through the two-foot-square grille below him. He could still see the small spot on the marble floor where a bead of sweat had dropped from the tip of his nose before he could stop it. If that spot were the center point of a clock face, the toilet was at noon, the sink and vanity at two o'clock, and the door—just beyond Luco's view—at three. Despite the large room's intended function as a lavatory for one, modesty or tact had prompted the mounting of walnut partitions on the two unwalled sides of the toilet. It was these partitions that would allow him to descend from the air shaft without being seen by a person standing at the sink—by his target.

A gust of pungent wind blew past him, turning his stomach and forcing him to gasp for air through the grille. The building was home to several embassies, an art gallery, and a restaurant—enough people, food, and trash to generate some really awful effluvia. When the cooling system was idle, the temperature in the ventilation shafts quickly soared into summer-sun temperatures, despite the nighttime hour, and all sorts of odors roamed the ducts like rabid dogs. Then the air conditioner would kick in, chasing away the smells and freezing the perspiration to his body.

Arjan had warned him about such things. He had explained that covert operations necessitated subjecting the body and senses to elements sane men avoided: extreme heat and cold; long stretches of immobility in the most uncomfortable places and positions; contact with insects, rodents, decay. He had advised him to focus on a single object and think pleasant thoughts until equilibrium returned.

Luco shifted his eyes to a perfume bottle on the vanity. He imagined its fragrance, then thought of himself breathing it in as his fingers lifted hair away from the curve of an olive-skinned neck and felt the pulse with his lips.

He heard the bathroom door open and pulled his face back into the darkness. He held his breath, then exhaled when he heard the click of a woman's heels. Her shoes came into view, then her legs and body. Of course she was elegantly dressed. Not only did the nature of the gathering demand it, but this room was reserved for special guests—the target, his family, and his entourage: people who were expected to look their best. The woman stopped in front of the vanity mirror, glanced at herself, and continued into the stall. Turning, she yanked up her dress. Hooked by two thumbs, her hosiery came down as she sat.

The top of the partition's door obstructed Luco's view of her lap, and during the bathroom visits of two other lovely ladies, he had found that no amount of craning would change that fact. So he lay still and watched her face. She was model-beautiful, with big green eyes, sculpted cheekbones, and lips too full to be natural. She finished, flushed, and walked to the sink, where she was completely out of view. This reassured him that the plan had been well thought through. She fiddled at the sink for a minute after washing her hands—applying makeup, he guessed—and left.

He waited for the click of a latch as the door settled into its jamb. It didn't come . . . Someone was holding the door open. Masculine shoes and pant legs stepped silently into view. Luco's breath stopped.

Watch for a bodyguard, Arjan had told him. *He'll come in for a look. He may flush the toilet and run the water in the sink, but he won't use anything himself. The next man in is your guy.*

He would recognize his target, of course, but getting these few seconds of warning allowed his mind to shift from vigilance to readiness.

He could see the bodyguard in the bathroom now, a square-jawed brute packed into an Armani. The guard stepped up to the vanity to examine each of the bottles and brushes in turn. He dropped to one knee, with more grace than seemed possible, and examined under the countertop and sink. The bathroom had been thoroughly checked once already, earlier in the day, but nobody liked surprises. Luco smiled at the thought.

Standing again, the guard glanced around, his eyes sweeping toward the grille. Luco pulled back farther, fighting the urge to move fast, which might cause the metal he was on to pop, or the gypsum boards that formed the bathroom's ceiling to creak. He imagined the guard's eyes taking in the screws that seemed to hold the grille firmly in place. In reality, they were screw heads only, glued in place after Luco had removed the actual screws. Now, a solitary wire held up the grille on the unhinged side.

The guard inspected the toilet, the padded bench opposite the sink, and the thin closet by the door, bare but for a few hand towels and extra tissue rolls. Every move he made was quick and efficient. He had done this count-less times before—probably even did it in his dreams—and never expected to find anything that would validate his existence. He didn't this time either. After all, his boss was the benign prime minister of a democratic country with few enemies. A grudge would almost have to be personal, not political.

Or preordained, thought Luco. *Preordained.*

The guard spoke softly to someone in the hall.

The door closed, latching firmly. Someone set the lock. The target walked into view. He drained a crystal glass of amber fluid, almost missed the top of the vanity as he set down the glass, and belched loudly. He fumbled with his pants, and Luco saw that his belly had grown too round to let him see his own zipper, which could present a problem with the super-fluous hooks and buttons common to finely tailored slacks. The target left the stall door open. He stood before the toilet with his pants and boxers crumpled around his ankles, his hips thrust forward for better aim, the way a child pees.

A confident assassin may have done the deed right then, just pulled back and shot through the grille into the target's head. And, certainly, he could have hired such professionalism. Arjan would have done it; had even requested the assignment.

But it has to be me. If I don't do this myself, then it is for nothing.

Given that requirement, Arjan had set about preparing his boss for this moment, arranging transportation and alibis, securing timetables and blue-prints. Arjan had made him train for five weeks with *Incursori* loyalists. They had worked him physically and filled his mind with knowledge of ballistics and anatomy, close-quarters combat, the arts of vigilance and stealth—at least to the extent that time allowed. Arjan had explained that using a sniper's rifle and scope was infeasible, considering the deadline.

Shooting a man from three hundred yards is a skill! he had snapped. *It's not like the movies, man. It takes years of training to guarantee a kill. And you'll have only one chance, right?*

Right.

So somewhere in Arjan's dark mind, a switch labeled "close kill" had been thrown, sending Luco down a track that led to this ventilation shaft and his hand on the wire that held the grille in place. Slowly, he unwound it from an exposed screw. Then he recalled Arjan's instructions and relooped the wire.

The target's unabated flow told him he had at least a few more seconds. Luco removed a moist washcloth from a Ziploc baggy. He rubbed it over his face, removing sweat and dust from around his eyes, letting the water refresh him. Arjan had told him that countless missions failed because of haste and machismo myths about warriors fighting despite handicaps. "Perspiration in your eyes is a disadvantage you can avoid, so do it!" he had ordered.

Luco dried himself with a washcloth from another Ziploc. His fingers felt clammy inside the tight dishwashing gloves he wore, but that was better than trying to handle the wire and pistol with sweaty hands. Surgical gloves, he had learned, were too thin to prevent leaving fingerprints. And Arjan had been clear about wearing the gloves from ingress to egress—so clear, in fact, that he'd made Luco wear them the entire last week of his training.

The target was tugging his pants up, running a hand around to tuck in his shirt. As soon as he rounded the partition to step in front of the sink, Luco whipped the wire off the screw and let the grille swing down. A string that was attached to the wire slid between his thumb and forefinger until a knot stopped it, halting the grille inches from the wall.

The water at the sink came on.

He used his strong arms to position himself directly above the opening. His legs pistonned down, and he dropped to the floor. By bending his knees as soon as the toes of his rubber-soled boots touched the marble, he managed an almost-silent landing. Still crouched, he pulled the pistol from his waistband. It was a China Type 64, old but especially suited for the job at hand. Its barrel was no longer than any handgun's, but included a silencer; its breech slide was lockable—and was now locked, he noted—to prevent the noises of cartridge ejection and round rechambering inherent to semiautomatic pistols. With its subsonic 7.65mm bullets, it was the quietest pistol ever made.

He stepped behind the target, who was bent over the sink, splashing water on his face. Perfect. The gun's locking slide meant he had only one quick shot. The next shot would take at least five seconds to prepare—an eternity if a wounded victim was screaming and thrashing around and bodyguards were kicking in the door. His goal was instant incapacitation . . . instant death. And that meant the bullet had to sever the brain stem, which was best achieved from behind. He pointed the pistol at the approximate spot where the man's head would be when he straightened.

But, still bent, the man reached for a hand towel, knocked it to the floor, and turned to retrieve it. Catching Luco in his peripheral vision, he stood to face him. His eyes focused on the gun, and he raised his hands in surrender. His attention rose to Luco's face. Puzzlement made his eyes squint, his mouth go slack.

He knows he's seen me before, Luco realized.

"*Ti darò qualsiasi cosa oppure,*" the man pleaded. *I will give you everything.*

His voice was hushed, obviously believing that cooperation would forestall his death.

"*Sono sicuro che lo farai,*" Luco said. *I know you will.* Stepping forward, he touched the barrel to the indentation between the man's lips and nose— lightly, as if anointing him—and pulled the trigger. The man's head snapped back. Brain and blood and bone instantly caked the mirror behind him, as a dozen fissures snapped the glass from a central point where the bullet had struck. Miraculously, none of the shards came loose. The noise had been barely audible above the sound of the faucet. Luco caught the body as it crumpled and laid it gently on the floor.

Then the smell hit him, like meat shoved into his sinuses. He stood, tried to breathe. Something fell from the mirror and landed wetly on the countertop. Vomit rose in his throat. He slapped his palm over his mouth and willed it back down. Hand in place, he forced himself to survey the slaughter—the brain matter on the mirror and counter; the blood there, as well as spreading in a pool under the head, a rivulet breaking away and snaking toward a floor drain near the toilet; the face contorted in terror, mouth open, tongue protruding, eyes wide.

He wanted to remember.

Back below the ventilation opening, he jumped and pulled himself into the shaft. He could have used the bench for a boost up, but the idea was to slow his pursuers, even by mere seconds. It wasn't the time it would take the guards to move the bench into place that mattered, but any confusion produced by not having an obvious escape route to follow. First, they'd call for a screwdriver (or shoot away the screw heads). Then they'd tug at the grille, which the high-tensile wire would hold firm. Ultimately they'd get into the shaft, glance at the false metal wall he would place behind him, and head the other way.

Six minutes after the assassination, he clambered out of the shaft behind a stack of boxes in a storage room. Through the door, two steps down a hall-way, and he was descending the narrow and dark servants' staircase, rarely used since the installation of elevators in the 1970s. He came out in a kitchen three floors below. Hands were immediately on him, pulling at his blood-spattered overalls.

"Hurry," a young man whispered in Italian. His head moved in all directions as he peeled the clothes away.

Luco stripped off the rubber gloves, then vigorously rubbed his hands together. He opened a pocketknife and ran the blade over the laces of his boots. The young man—Antonio, Luco remembered—tugged off the boots and pushed on a pair of expensive oxfords to match his suit. Everything went into an attaché case. Antonio scrubbed at his neck, face, and hair with a wet towel.

"Ah," Luco complained, wiping at his eye.

"Dishwasher soap. Nothing better for blood." Antonio tossed the towel into the attaché, produced a comb, and ran it through Luco's hair. "Come." He led Luco to a heavy fire door at the rear of the building and signaled for him to wait. He opened it and slipped through. Fifteen seconds later he was back, beckoning Luco outside.

A long alley ran away from the Asia House, cutting a canyon between two tall buildings. The only illumination appeared to be the glow of a mercury-vapor lamp on the far street where the alley ended. Everything else was submerged in blackness. Propping the door open with his foot, Antonio pointed down the alley. "The car is parked on Henriata Sold."

Luco gripped the young man's shoulder and gave it a shake. He leaned closer. *"Grazie."*

Antonio whispered back, "Anything for you."

Luco stepped into the dark alley, the click of his heels echoing quietly. The door closed behind him. He smiled.

It was finished.

And it had just begun.

2

The boy had his mother's hair, dark and fine and shining. Brady Moore ran a hand over his son's head, feeling the soft strands slip through his fingers like water. Zach's face was turned away; his breathing was deep and rhythmic. Asleep, or almost. Sitting next to Zach on the bed, his back against the headboard, Brady gently scooted away and shifted his legs over the edge.

What at first glance might have been a tan wig lying on the bedspread at Zach's feet stirred. Then a head popped up from one side of the clump and swiveled toward him. This was Coco, the most loving Shih Tzu to grace the breed, Brady was sure, and Zach's ever-present companion since the boy was in diapers. Brady raised a finger to his lips. Coco, pink tongue protruding from a mouth-shaped part in his fur, simply watched Brady with eyes that were slightly bulging and slightly crossed. After a moment, the dog's head disappeared back into the collective whole.

Brady closed the book in his lap and set it on the nightstand, pushing aside a G.I. Joe and the accoutrements of make-believe warfare: a tiny canteen, a plastic M16, something that looked like a field radio. When they clinked against a picture frame, Brady let his eyes linger on the woman looking out from it. Pretty. No . . . *beautiful*. In that grand genetic crapshoot, her father's Chickasaw lineage had mixed with her mother's Teutonic ancestry to create a stunning progeny. Not just physically, though certainly her appearance was the first thing that had attracted Brady's attention. Dark, sultry. High cheekbones, narrow nose, doe eyes. The shape and composition of her features invited lingering scrutiny, the way some foods—Swiss chocolate came to mind—demanded to be savored. Then her personality revealed itself, along with her intelligence and wry humor . . . Some people seemed to have it all, and the best of them had no clue about the effect they had on other people.

That's Karen. She's so . . .

Brady stopped himself. Even eighteen months after her death, he thought of Karen in the present tense. A familiar ache pinched his heart, tightened his throat.

"Thinking of Mom?"

The voice was sleepy, so ethereal it took Brady a second to realize it had not originated in his own head.

He turned to see his son looking over his shoulder at him. The boy was all Karen. Besides the hair, his eyes, like hers, were the dark brown of polished coffee beans. Zach also possessed her not-quite-full lips that made a sudden jaunt upward at the corners, forming a smile even when it wasn't intended. It was that faux smile—on the mother, not the son who was at the time still seven years from conception—that had caused Brady to break away from his friends in line for a movie to ask the dark beauty if she'd mind if he held down the seat next to hers, seeing that he was a great movie companion, laughing in all the right places and sharing his popcorn. Never mind that she was in line to see something other than *The Untouchables*; he didn't know what and didn't care. It was only after they were engaged that he learned she hadn't been smiling at him after all. But his boldness in approaching a girl without the slightest hint of an invitation had made her say, *Sure, who in her right mind would turn down free popcorn?* Funny how things work. They had both been seventeen.

Brady leaned over the boy, propping himself up with one arm. "Hey, I thought you were asleep," he whispered.

"Do you think she thinks of us?"

"All the time." He leaned closer. "More than that. She watches us."

Zach smiled. A real smile, not a trick of his lips. Brady didn't know how the boy did it. Here Brady was, thirty-three and feeling constantly on the brink of some chasm, some breakdown whose torments he couldn't imagine and from which he probably wouldn't return. At nine, Zach was

holding it together much better. Lots of tears, sure, and times of melancholy no kid should experience. For the most part, however, he was func-
tioning well, with healthy bouts of giggles and curiosity about babies and
electronics and airplanes and only an occasional, if precocious, question
concerning death, dying, and the afterlife. Ignorance is bliss? Or was it
something else that enabled Zach to get on with his life? Whatever it was,
Brady was glad for it.

"She watches me when you can't? Like when I'm at school and when
you . . . go away?"

Brady's business trips were a painful subject. In fact, Zach's eyes were still
red-rimmed from an earlier bout of tears over the trip Brady was going on
the next day.

"Right," Brady said. "All the time."

"If she sees something bad happening, can she stop it?"

Brady thought for a moment. "I think she sort of whispers in our ears.
'Don't step off the curb yet. Wait for that car to pass.' And 'Don't climb that
tree. There's a broken branch up there.'"

Zach nodded. Well, of course Mom would do that. He said, "Will you
pick me up from school tomorrow?"

"No, Mrs. Pringle will do that."

Zach made a sour face. At the foot of the bed, Coco whined in his sleep,
as if agreeing with his master's opinion.

"What? You like Mrs. Pringle."

"Yeah . . ." He hesitated. "It's just that she drives so slow, by the time
we get home, *Scooby-Doo's* over."

"You should be doing your homework then anyway. Or playing outside
while the sun's hot."

"Yeah, but, Dad . . . *Scooby-Doo.*"

Brady knew how the boy felt. Time was when he and Zach would rent
old episodes and spend an evening cracking up at Scooby and Shaggy's mis-
adventures with ghosts, goblins, and other assorted spookies. Karen never
saw the attraction, and since her death, Brady hadn't felt like yukking it up,
even with Zach. So the boy watched reruns on his own and always got
down to the business of being an energetic fourth grader after the show was

over. Before Brady could respond, Zach continued: "And she's so *old*, like a hundred and something."

"Not quite, but even if she were, what does it matter?"

He wrinkled his nose. "She smells funny."

True enough. Mrs. Pringle was a widow in her seventies who smelled as if she stored herself in mothballs when she wasn't baby-sitting Zach. But she had no problem in the mental acuity department, and despite operating at half speed, she seemed perfectly capable of doing all the things required to look after the boy. Weekday mornings, Brady saw his son off to the bus stop. After school, Zach went to a day-care center with several other schoolkids whose parents both worked or who had a single parent. Until a year and a half ago, Brady had never imagined that he'd fall into the latter category.

He knew some parents let their children stay home alone for the few hours between the end of school and the end of their work. He'd been in law enforcement long enough, however, to know latchkey kids were more likely to expose themselves to danger—by being careless or naive on the Internet, with fire, around strangers—and become victims of accidents or crime. During the infrequent times Brady worked late, Mrs. Pringle filled in. She may have been slow and odorous, but to Brady, the woman was a godsend.

"Look," Brady said, "when I get home, we'll rent some *Scooby-Doo*s and watch them till our eyes fall out, okay?"

Zach brightened. "The two of us?"

A brief pause. "You bet."

"You too?"

Brady let out a chuckle, as if it was a silly question, but of course it wasn't. "Me too," he said.

"All right!" Instantly wide-awake, Zach scooted into a sitting position. "How long will you be gone?"

"A few days, at least. Maybe a week."

The boy's face fell. "That long? Why do you have to go? Can't someone else do it?"

"It's my job, Zachary. Other people are doing their jobs."

"Will Miss Wagner be there?"

Brady knew that Zach liked his partner, Alicia Wagner.

"She's there already. The Bureau decided to send us too late to get to the crime scene before the local police . . . processed it."

"You mean before they contaminated it."

Brady wasn't sure he liked his son so steeped in the ways of the FBI, its parlance and procedures.

He said, "That's right. So, anyway, there's no real hurry getting there. We'll do what we can, review the evidence, and hope to be there sooner the next time."

Zach said, "Hope for the next time?"

The kid was quick.

"I don't mean hope there *is* a next time. Of course not. I mean, if the bad guy strikes again, we hope to get there sooner so we can help."

Zach nodded.

Brady leaned over, parted his bangs, and kissed him on the forehead. "Now get to sleep, big guy," he said. "I'll see you in the morning."

As he rose, Zach gripped his arm. "Can we pray?"

Brady paused. It was a ritual Karen had started. Sinking back down onto the bed, he said, "You do it."

The boy closed his eyes and began speaking in the gentlest of tones.

Brady noticed how the bedside lamp cast a warm glow over Zach's face. He never tired of observing his son, and now his eyes absorbed every detail, his mind storing it for instant recall while he was away. Between his entwined hands, Zach held his "blankie," a threadbare infant blanket that he had originally given up at age four. Shortly after Karen's funeral, he'd had a number of bed-wetting incidents and had begun crying for his blankie. Fortunately, Karen, as organized as she was sentimental, had stored it in a box marked Zachary's Baby Things. The nighttime accidents had stopped, but Zach was now more attached to that raggedy cloth than he had been as a toddler. Mrs. Pringle kept stitching it back together, especially its silk trim, which Zach absently rubbed between forefinger and thumb when wearied or worried.

Wetting the bed, needing the blankie, clinging to Brady—these were Zach's telltale signs of distress. Brady's were anger and sullenness. He'd also developed a rigid skepticism of the so-called ordered universe. Man's notion that he could somehow shape his future was bunk. How many Ivy League grads wound up flipping burgers? Brady personally knew of one, and not because the guy was flaky, but because the universe was. Brady also remembered being shown the extensive security of a house from which a baby had just been kidnapped. And was a lifetime of exercise and healthy eating able to stop a drunk from plowing his car into you? Karen had discovered the answer to that one herself. "Fair" implied order, and life wasn't fair.

Zach's face leaned into his field of vision. "Dad?" he said.

Brady's eyes—and attention—refocused on his son. "That was great," he said. "Thank you."

Zach appeared skeptical but said only, "I'll miss you."

Brady pulled him into his arms and squeezed. "Me too, son. Me too." He laid the boy's head down on the pillow and switched off the lamp. At the door, he looked back. Light from the hallway spilled in, climbed the bed, and fell in a wide rectangle across the covered figure. Everything from the chest up was in darkness.

"Dad?" came Zach's voice from nowhere.

"Hmm?"

"Who are you after this time? What did he do?"

Brady considered his response. "Very bad things, Zach. Whoever it is needs to be caught."

Silence. Brady pulled on the door, then stopped. He walked to the bed and resumed his position on it, eliciting another noisy exhalation from Coco. Here, he could make out Zach's face. "Don't worry," Brady said. "I'll be extra safe. I *will* come home."

It was a careless promise, he realized. No one could be 100 percent sure of surviving a stroll across a country road, let alone the pursuit of a serial killer. Still, Zach's experience with losing his mother made him especially aware of death's randomness and suddenness. Anything Brady could do to alleviate the boy's natural concerns, he would do. A family friend had given him a book about guiding a child through the loss of a parent. It had firmly recommended telling the child that indeed the surviving parent could also be "called home" anytime. Brady had dropped it in the trash.

Zach reached up to pull Brady in for one more hug. "You'd better," he said.

3

Palmer Lake, Colorado

The beast moved through the woods like the falling of night. It crossed the rough terrain effortlessly and skimmed past branches that snagged at its thick fur. Through the trees, the moon became a strobe of flittering light and shadow, but the beast's vision was unaffected, always keen. It sensed everything: a rabbit scampered into its hole a meadow away; a doe had left dung here recently but was now long gone. The beast's companions, one on either side, kept pace, agile and powerful. Thirty paces behind, their master crunched over twigs and veered around obstacles, following. The beast smelled their destination before seeing it, a human odor, a human den. Fire. It had known they were heading toward fire but only now realized the smoke also marked their objective. It opened its mouth to let cool air fill its lungs, then exhaled in a low, hungry growl.

———

BREATHING DEEPLY from the fireplace's flue, the flames bit into the wood, found an especially dry section, and flared briefly. The blaze warmed Cynthia Loeb's bare arms as she sat on the rug in her living room, dressed in a summer blouse and shorts. She added the final strokes to what would be listed on eBay as a "hand-painted wastebasket by world-famous artist." Well, *famous* was a stretch, she conceded to herself as she swirled her brush through two globs of paint on her palette. Her mouth skewed with the admission. At least it was true that her artwork could be found in bathrooms all over the world, thanks to the propagation of on-line trading. So what if that claim represented only a few hundred sales, each barely enough to purchase a decent meal? Fewer people knew her name than, say, Julia Roberts's, but now you were talking about matters of degree. She nodded at that and dabbed splotches of orange around bloodred flames.

Her head jerked up at a sound from the back bedrooms. She listened but heard only the crackle of the fire. Outside noises were rare this far back from the road, which itself was dirt and infrequently traveled. Occasionally a salesman would find his way to the secluded homes that dotted the wooded foothills west of town, but not at—she looked at the clock on the mantel—not at 11:20 at night. And she would have noticed headlights if a car had driven up the drive. She concluded that the fire had simply made a peculiar noise and turned back to her craft.

She set the brush aside and held the wastebasket in both hands, one underneath and one inside. Turning it away from the harsh light of the floor lamp beside her, she let the fire's glow play against the glistening scene she had created. She nodded. "Snot rags today, the Louvre tomorrow," she said aloud and jumped. Another noise—just as the last syllable had rolled off her tongue. A quiet scrape, like a window being opened or a shoe scuffing against the hardwood floor.

Slowly she lowered the wastebasket to the floor and narrowed her eyes at the entrance to the hall that accessed the rear of the house. It was a dark rectangle in the corner of the room. She unraveled her legs and rose, grimacing at the achiness of her thighs and the pain in her lower back. Out of habit, she silently cursed her ex, the good-for-nothing who'd taken her best years and then moved on just as Cynthia was coming to understand that middle age paused for no amount of wrinkle cream or tummy scrunches. She guessed that he'd come to that conclusion sooner than she had. At least she was getting the house.

She took a step toward the hall. The noise that reached her at that moment was more puzzling than frightening: A light *click, click, click, click, click, click*—quick and growing louder. Whatever was causing the sound was coming down the hall toward the living room.

The telephone behind her rang, and her heart careened against her chest; a mousy yelp escaped her. Frozen, she stared at the dark hallway entrance. Silence . . . which the phone's second ring shattered along with Cynthia's nerves. Keeping a vigil on the doorway, she backed to the end table, groped for the handset, and raised it to her face.

"Hello?" she whispered.

"Cynthia! I didn't see you at church Sunday." The voice was whiny, as if Cynthia's absence had been a personal affront. It was Marcie, a quasifriend who needed constant assurance from her acquaintances that they still thought highly of her, regardless of the time. "I brought you that book that we—"

"I think there's someone in the house."

"What? In your house? Someone's there?"

"I think someone broke in." She pulled her eyes from the hall entrance to scan the room for something that could be used as a weapon.

"Are you sure?"

"I said I think."

"Can you hear them? Are they moving around?"

"I heard . . . I think I heard nails . . . *claws* clicking against the floor."

"A bear!" Marcie lived in town.

"Not a bear, Marcie. A dog, maybe."

"A dog? Oh my heavens!"

Cynthia could imagine Marcie's next five calls: "*Cynthia Loeb thinks a dog broke into her home. And she didn't attend church on Sunday. The poor thing's not well.*"

"Should I call the police?"

The police? She thought about that. She knew widows and divorcees who wanted so much to think someone still cared that they became completely dependent on anyone willing to give them the time of day. The world was full of needy people. That's not the kind of woman she wanted to be.

"No," she whispered, "not yet. But can you hold on for a minute?"

"Why, yes. What are you going to do? You can't just . . ."

Cynthia set the phone on a magazine. Stepping around the wastebasket and over the pallet of unused colors, she edged over to the fireplace, where she lifted a heavy iron poker from its stand. The heat from the fireplace rolled around her legs as she advanced toward the hall. Except for the fire's crackle and Marcie's tinny voice still emanating from the phone, the house was still. Drawing courage from the heft of the poker and, inexplicably, from the knowledge that a benign human waited for her return to the telephone, she stepped into the hall entrance.

Past the kitchen threshold on the left and the wide opening for the dining room on the right, the hall disappeared in shadows. The weak luminance from a bulb in the refrigerator's water dispenser caught the edges of the kitchen doorway and seeped into the hall. The light contracted Cynthia's pupils just enough to make the shadows seem blacker.

Then came the sound of breathing, as though the shadows themselves had come alive. Deep and steady, inhale, exhale.

"Who's there?" she called, disgusted by how weak her voice sounded. She cleared her throat. "Who's there!" Better.

Click, click, click, click, click, click.

An animal appeared out of the shadows, its eyes glowing green. It was a dog . . . or a wolf. Despite the shaggy gray-black fur that covered its body, she saw its strength in the hulking muscles of its shoulders and haunches. Its head was lowered, and its black-rimmed eyes were fixed on her through the softer-hued hairs of its eyebrows. Under a long snout, fangs glimmered. Its lips, hiked up over ebony gums, quivered, and the thing snarled.

"Back!" Cynthia yelled. She jabbed at the air with the poker.

In an instant, the animal bounded twice and leaped at her. She felt the air burst from her lungs as its paws slammed against her chest, knocking her back into the living room toward the front door. Her hip struck a small table where she kept her keys, and she and the animal and the table and the keys crashed to the floor. An odor not unlike a monkey house washed over her, followed by the beast's breath, smelling of rancid meat; nausea cramped her stomach. She covered her throat, knowing that's where the animal would attack. Instead, it backed away. She sat up. Her chin was wet, and she wiped at it. *Not blood,* she thought thankfully as she glanced at her glistening palm. Slobber—hers or the wolf-dog's, she didn't know.

The animal stood between her and the fire, its furry outline radiating white and yellow. When she raised the poker, it quavered like a Richter needle in her trembling hand. The animal simply glared.

Stifling a groan, she got her feet under her and stood. "Go!" she raged.

She heard the clicking again and caught movement out of the corner of her vision. Another wolf-dog broke from the shadowy hall. It was in the air before she could fathom how to respond. Its jaws clamped down on her extended wrist. The poker flipped out of her hand, thudding loudly on the hardwood, banging against the front door.

Pain raced up her arm and turned into a piercing scream when it reached her throat. The weight of the beast wrenched her arm down. Blood appeared to bubble out of its nostrils, and then she realized that it was her blood, gushing out of the deep wound, staining the animal's muzzle, pouring to the floor. She staggered but managed to stay up. Suddenly, her other hand flared in agony. The first animal was chomping on it, trying to gain purchase on her wrist. She tried to flail her arms, to beat away the monsters, but they were too heavy; their mouths gripped her muscles and bones too securely. The effort caused her to stumble into the floor lamp, which toppled. The bulb exploded, leaving the room bathed in the flickering orange of the fire.

Shadows danced everywhere. It took her a moment to grasp that a shadow of one of the wolf-dogs was, in fact, a third animal. It stood, half in the room, half in the hall, watching her futile maneuvers. The other two had stopped tugging and grinding; they seemed content to hold her dripping arms. Dizzy from pain, she moaned at the watching animal and swayed forward, then back again.

She heard her name, dim and distant. She rolled her eyes toward the ceiling, half-expecting to see it melt away under the brilliance of a celestial hand reaching for her. Her name again . . . and reality floated back. The voice was coming from the phone on the end table.

"Marcie!" she cried. "Mar—"

The third dog stepped completely into the room. Directly behind it came a man. He was not tall but was extremely muscular, with broad shoulders made broader by animal pelts draped over them and clasped in front. It was impossible to tell where the pelts ended and the man began. His beard and mustache exploded from his face in great, rusty profusion; his matted hair hung long but was swept back away from his eyes. Wide, handsome eyes, without a hint of emotion. His face was glacial: deeply crevassed, icily stoic. But he wasn't old, simply *worn*. The mouth was a gash, down-turned seemingly not by anger or displeasure, but by fierce determination. A heavy shirt hung beneath the pelts and was cinched at the waist with rough leather. Pants clung to legs bulging with power and vanished into high boots. He was entirely out of place, Cynthia decided—not just in her home, but in her time, in *anyone's* time for countless generations. The realization added to her confusion, to the surrealism of this intrusion.

Her eyes widened when she saw the object clenched in his right fist: a length of wood, smooth and well used, like a narrow bat or club. Then he shifted, and the fire caught a broad plane of metal attached to the club. She was looking at an ax. The man held it almost unknowingly, the way someone else might hold a briefcase or wear a watch. She took some hope from this casual treatment of the weapon.

"What—," she started, but his sudden movement silenced her. He strode toward her, lifting the ax over and behind his head. His left hand rose to grip the other end of the long handle. The wolf-dogs growled with excitement as the blade came back around, slicing through the air like a bolt from the fire it reflected. She hitched in a sharp breath but had no chance to scream before the metal found her neck.

The dogs released their hold, and the man watched the woman's body tremble and fall. On the floor, it rolled to one side, draining crimson. He heard a thin voice and saw the phone off the hook. Still clutching the ax, he stepped to the end table, picked up the phone, and listened.

"Cynthia, what was that? Cynthia? I'm calling the cops! Cynthia!"

In a deep voice, heavily accented, he said, "She is dead, you fool." Then he gently cradled the handset and turned back to the task at hand.

4

Standing in the darkened living room, Brady Moore felt the house around him. Still. Quiet. His nose sensed a curious blend of dust and Pledge. He was less meticulous about cleaning than his wife had been, and he would hate to see the size of the dust bunnies under the furniture. Pretty soon, he'd have to get them licensed and vaccinated for rabies. He smiled. Zach would like that one.

Moonlight glowed against the sheer curtains hanging over the three panels of glass that made up a big bay window. The window's bench seat was cushioned and comfortable, but he never sat there. In this hour before bed, he liked to roam. At first, over a year ago, he'd varied his meandering. Now, it always followed the same course: living room, dining room, kitchen, den . . . then along a hallway, through a small foyer, and back to the living room, where he'd start the next leg of his circuit. One hundred eighty-four steps. Ten leisurely laps. Plenty of time to think.

Following his routine, he prefaced tonight's stroll with a visit to the teak credenza that contributed the majority of the lemony polish smell to the room. Crouching, he opened a door panel and withdrew a crystal decanter of bourbon and the only crystal glass the cabinet contained. He set them on the marble top. He and Karen had seldom imbibed. When they did, their preference was wine, an occasional beer. But this was different. Medicinal, he told himself. A sleep aid. Just two fingers.

As a criminal psychologist, he knew all too well the dangers of seeking respite at the bottom of a bottle. He splashed the amber liquid into the glass with the fatalism of a junkie filling his veins with a narcotic he knew would someday kill him. Okay, four fingers. He didn't have to drink it all. He took a sip and felt the fire burn its way to his stomach. At least he wasn't used to it yet. He had chosen bourbon because it was just so awful, like sucking on the planks of an old barn. He didn't want to enjoy it.

With glass in hand, he breathed deeply and took step number one of the first 184.

THE CLOCK'S shrill alarm cut through the haze in his head, jolting him upright. Eyes closed, he reached for it, but it wasn't there. The noise stopped anyway. This puzzled him for about a millisecond. Before his addled brain could drift back to oblivion, it shrilled again. It was on his chest. No, in his shirt pocket. And it wasn't the alarm clock; it was his cell phone. He frantically dug it out of the pocket and opened his eyes. He was in the living room, sprawled on the sofa. It was still dark outside, but the moonlight, which earlier had given the sheers a silvery radiance, was gone. The house seemed preternaturally dark, an unlit stage awaiting the day's first flip of a switch.

Brady glared at the phone's glowing screen. The words seemed indistinct, the screen's illumination too bright. He closed one eye and brought it closer to his face. He made out the name Alicia Wagner and her cell phone number. He hit a button.

"Hello?" he said, trying to sound as though his tongue hadn't doubled in size and grown hair. Silence. "Hello?"

He looked at the phone. He'd hit the wrong button, cutting off the incoming call. *Figures.* His head rotated on creaking tendons to see the crystal drinking glass, nearly full, perched on one of the sofa's fat leather arms. He wasn't sure what number refill that was, but he felt confident he'd gone past four fingers. He jumped when the phone in his hand rang again. Concentrating, he punched the answer key and repeated his greeting.

"Did you hang up on me?" Alicia's voice battered against his eardrum.

"Whaddaya mean?" He managed to sound more indignant than befuddled.

"I must have hit a dead pocket. Cell phones. Did I wake you? Stupid question. I hope I didn't wake Zach."

She was in one of her excited states, which were always work-induced. Something was happening.

"What time is it?"

"Uhhhh . . . 1:10. My time. Ten after three for you."

Brady moved the phone from his ear and pushed the button that lowered its volume. When he put it back to his ear, she was saying, ". . . believe it? So soon?"

"What's so soon?"

"Brady! Where are you? I just said *he struck again*! It's been only *two days* since the last one. Hold on—"

He heard a horn blare and what may have been tires squealing.

"Alicia . . . ?"

She came back on without a hitch. "The one before that was four days. If this guy's pattern is accelerating . . . I don't want to think about the implications."

"Where are you?"

"On my way to the scene, where you should be! Listen, you have to get out here *now*."

"My ticket—"

"Is no good. You were going to fly into Denver, right? Then drive up to Ft. Collins? Change it to Colorado Springs, and then drive north to the next town. Hold on."

The rustle of paper. Maps, Brady presumed. His mind was clearing. One dose of Alicia had that effect.

"*Two* towns," she said. "Palmer Lake. Wait a minute. When will you get here?"

"If there's a flight, and I leave home in an hour—"

"You're right, you'll get here too late. Seven hours soonest. The locals are waiting for me at the scene, and they're not happy about it. What else is new, right? Anyway, I gotta dive in as soon as I get there. Call me when you land, and I'll guide you in."

"How did you—"

There was an electronic click.

That was Alicia: what else was there to say? He supposed the call could have consisted of a single line: "Get here now, then call me." Good thing she was feeling talkative. In the state he was in, he probably would have chalked up the words to a dream and gone back to sleep. But encountering her for longer than a few moments was like slamming down a triple shot of espresso.

He rubbed his face with both palms. Even the sandpaper scrape of his whiskers sounded loud.

This isn't good, he thought for the umpteenth time. He envisioned himself in ten years: fifty pounds heavier, cheeks and nose mottled with rosacea, hiding the boozing but not its effects, barely getting by at the Bureau on luck and sympathy. Worse, Zach would hate him by then—for all the missed baseball games, the times the boy had to be responsible because his old man wasn't, the lost weekends and years. It would not come to that, but, he reminded himself, it *could.*

He had no intention of throwing away everything else he had because the most precious thing in his life had been stolen from him. But for the first time, he truly understood why tragedies catapulted some people into a watery abyss of bitterness and despair, a Mariana Trench of hopelessness. No one who had not been there could grasp the appeal of that abyss, the way being there seemed to atone for not dying too; the numbness it offered to replace the pain; the feeling that by wallowing there you were shaking a fist, however pathetically, at the cold, uncaring world. Maybe that explained the booze and the decidedly unwholesome turn his vocabulary had taken lately: he was dipping his toe into the abyss, checking it out.

Come on in! The water's fine!

Thank God for Zach. Without him Brady would have plunged in a long time ago. But not before hunting down the scum who'd plowed into his jogging wife, his "I'll just run to the park and be back before breakfast" wife. Not before hunting him down and blowing his brains out . . .

He shook his head vigorously, as if trying to dislodge a parasite that was burrowing into his scalp.

Focusing his thoughts on a cold shower, he lifted himself off the sofa. Then crumpled back onto it. The Alicia Espresso Machine was fine for prying open welded eyelids and jump-starting the synapses, but it was going to take more than that to shake off the lingering ghost of Jim Beam. He remembered a Red Bull energy drink in the fridge. That would be a good start. He hoisted himself up and, teetering only slightly, headed for the kitchen.

———

"ZACHARY?"

Brady gently shook the sleeping boy. Zach tried to roll away, but Brady pulled him back. His eyes fluttered into a squinting gaze, though the only light came in dimly from the hall. He smiled.

"You smell good," he said.

Brady had showered and shaved and spent extra time scrubbing the alcoholic film from his teeth. He had given his body a squirt of Lagerfeld Photo, which Zachary had given him for Christmas two years before.

"Thanks." He brushed the hair back from his son's face. "It's not time to get up yet, but I have to go. Miss Wagner called."

Zach came more fully awake. "Did he do it again? He killed again?"

"Yes, and now's the best chance we have to learn more about him."

"Evidence collected in the first twenty-four hours after a crime can make or break the case," Zach said matter-of-factly.

"That's right."

The boy thought for a moment, then he hardened his face and looked deep into his father's eyes. "Catch him."

Brady nodded. There were dual purposes to that goal: to make the world better by eliminating a worm that was chomping his evil way through it, and to make his parting from Zach worthwhile by accomplishing something good. These two motivations appeared as one, but to a boy and his departing father, they were as distinct as the love for family is from the love for friends.

They kissed and hugged. Then Brady leaned down to the foot of the bed and pushed his face into Coco's fur.

"You take care of Zachary now," he told the dog, who immediately rolled onto his back to get his belly scratched. Brady complied. "You hear me? Got your first-aid kit and cell phone, Coco?"

Zach grinned.

Brady rose. "I'm confident you're in good hands . . . uh, paws. Mrs. Pringle will be here in a few minutes, but with Coco's skills, maybe I should tell her never mind."

"Yeah!"

Brady snapped his attention back to the dog. "What's that?" he said. He leaned in close to hear some whispered doggie secrets. Coco pawed at him for more loving, and Brady nodded. "You don't say?"

To Zach he said, "Coco wants Mrs. Pringle to stay. Says she showers him with tummy rubs and beef chews when you're at school."

Zach gave in. "Okay, she can stay, but only as long as Coco says so."

"Deal." They high-fived, and Brady saluted as he went over the threshold and shut the door.

In the hallway, he leaned heavily against the wall. He'd done his duty; he'd left on the right note. But, man, his head *throbbed*.

In a dark ocean of pines and aspens, the lights pulsed like a lost vessel. Red chased blue and blue chased red along dense walls of bark and needles. The light bar on one of the three patrol cars was canted, which put its rotating beams into a diagonal trajectory that Alicia Wagner found a bit dizzying. She slowed her rental car and took in the scene: a string of cruisers and unmarked cars aligned on the left side of the narrow lane, broken only by the entrance to a long unpaved driveway; one officer standing guard at the drive, his butt half-on, half-off the trunk of the nearest vehicle and a cigarette between his fingers, forgotten as he scowled at her windshield; neighbors from unseen houses milling around fifty yards up the lane, curious and uneasy.

She reversed, then pulled in behind the last car, a beige sedan with federal government plates. As she got out, the loose red dirt under her feet gave way, and she had to jump into a three-foot-deep drainage ditch to keep from falling. At least it was dry. Then she thought about snakes and scrambled up the embankment, grabbing hold of her car's rear bumper. All of it reminded her of the backwoods parties where she had learned to drink and decipher male intentions—except for the strobing colors. Those always came later, closer to dawn.

She pulled a spherical leather case from the trunk and set it on the ground, then hefted out a heavy valise and slung its strap over her shoulder. It dug in and made her blouse pucker and pull. She slammed the trunk lid and, case in hand, headed for the drive entrance and the young man in the gray uniform of an El Paso County deputy.

When he saw her trudging toward him, he slid his buttock off the car and adjusted his utility belt. He took a hard pull at the cigarette. As she drew closer, his lips slowly bent into a crooked smile, smoke drifting from it, as though his mouth had been freshly formed with a laser.

Alicia had been told she was pretty enough times to believe it, though in her experience pretty attracted more demons than angels. Five feet six, with oversized green eyes, full lips, and a small nose that turned up at the tip. Straight blonde hair swept across her forehead and fell to her shoulders. One long-forgotten boyfriend had told her that, except for her coloring, she was Ariel from *The Little Mermaid* come to life. In high school, she had stopped using makeup to lure male attention. Now she applied it sparingly simply to feel more feminine. God knew she had "more boy than girl inside of her," as her father would proclaim at discovering a frog in her socks drawer or a sharply worded letter from a teacher.

She had never *felt* like a boy, as far as she knew. She had played with Barbies and an Easy-Bake Oven; she liked to wear dresses; she teared up at chick flicks and felt a yearning deep inside at the sound of a baby's cry. But she also had kept an army of G.I. Joes to defend her Barbies; she favored distressed bomber jackets when the weather turned bitter; she liked *Terminator 3* and was as gung ho about catching the bad guys as any boxer-shorts-wearing he-man in the Bureau. To her eternal surprise, it was this last characteristic that seemed to irritate the Bureau brass the most. Heaven forbid she should do her job better than Mr. Testosterone did his.

She focused on the gravel driveway that apparently led to the crime scene and didn't slow her pace as she approached the deputy. Without a word, he blocked her path with his arm. She turned toward him and noticed it wasn't her Disney-sculpted face the deputy was appraising, but her chest. To the dismay of her teenage self and the gratitude of her current self, *busty* was a word that no truthful person would ever apply to her. Even so, this jerk was *leering*, almost challenging her to confront him. She centered her gaze on his crotch and said, "Special Agent Alicia Wagner, FBI."

It took him another five seconds to comprehend the object of her attention. He let out a nervous but good-natured laugh, which startled her into raising her eyes to his.

"I'm sorry, ma'am," he said through a strained smile, any hint of lecherousness gone. In the reflected dimness of his flashlight, she detected a rosy blush rising into his face. "If I was staring."

"You were." Though she remained firm, she felt her anger melting. This kid could not be older than twenty-one, the minimum age for most deputy sheriffs, and an age when most men were still knee-deep in the ocean of adolescence. Add to that the cockiness that often came with a gun and badge, and Deputy—she looked at his name tag—Britt was bound to have some womanizing tendencies needing exorcism. By twenty-six, he'd be over it . . . or grounded in it for life. She blinked to break her glare and smiled a half-hearted acceptance of his apology.

Deputy Britt tossed away his cigarette and asked for her ID. She set down the case in her hand, bent to deposit the heavier one on the ground, and fished her FBI credentials out of a hip pocket. After studying her picture, he directed his flashlight beam into her face.

"Nice to see it done right for a change," she said, squinting.

The man produced a clipboard and began transcribing the information. She sighed and craned her neck to see the house. The nearest pines appeared to be jumping forward and falling back as the strobe lights caught and released them. Behind those, more battalions stood in her way. Finally, she picked out a hulking shape, blacker than the dark landscape around it, about a hundred yards away. She saw no lights burning in the windows. That was a good sign.

He finished and handed her the clipboard and pen. "Agent Wagner, ma'am, would you please sign in the space next to your name?"

The form appeared to be more than a mere visitor's log. Text too small to read in the glare filled the top third of the paper. Hers would be the eleventh signature.

"What is this, exactly?"

"It says that you agree to provide any requested exemplars, such as hair, blood, shoe prints, fingerprints—"

"I know what *exemplar* means, Deputy."

"We also ask that you provide a report explaining your involvement in the investigation and your actions while at the scene."

She lowered her head to conceal a smile and signed the paper. Agreeing to provide fingerprints and samples of hair and blood was a given. If the lab techs found unidentified DNA at the scene, they would need to rule out the people authorized to be there. Likewise, if some fool messed up the crime scene or lost evidence, everyone there was expected to explain themselves and what they witnessed. Calling that obligation a "report" and demanding signatures was an attempt to scare away people who had the authority but not the necessity to be there—department heads, assistant district attorneys, politicians if the case was high-profile.

"Just up the drive, ma'am. They're expecting you."

She lifted her case, pulled the valise's strap onto her shoulder, and started toward the house. Remaining at his station, the cop kept the ground before her illuminated until she rounded a small bend; by then she was comfortable that the drive was free of potholes and ruts. She walked farther, then stopped to adjust the strap pressing into her shoulder. For a moment, she was astounded by the stillness of the area: no hum of distant traffic, no whisper of wind through the trees, no animal or insect noises at all. There was only silence. The air was crisp and smelled of pine and moss and dirt. She could almost believe she was standing in the remotest place on earth, a place unspoiled by man. Then she noticed how the moonlight coming through the trees landed on the ground in a classic blood-spatter pattern. She shook her head and got her feet moving.

A few seconds later, she was startled to see the flare of a cigarette as someone drew on it; she cursed the crunching gravel for making it impossible to hear anything else. She discerned a dozen shapes on a concrete pad in front of a garage door. The garage lights were extinguished and the area was out of the direct gaze of the moon, so the people appeared as slivers of gray where reflected moonlight brushed a profile here, a bald pate there. Several dots of undulating orange indicated more than one smoker among the group. Their smoke rose and caught the moonlight streaming over the peaked roof.

One of the men jerked his head around, spit something to the ground, and rushed toward her.

"Agent Wagner?" His voice was more gravelly than the driveway, the calling card of a lifelong two-pack-a-day habit.

"Yes. Agent Nelson?" He appeared to be just south of sixty, heavyset, with a full head of silver hair, lightly streaked with stubborn black strands. He wore a dark suit that had likely come off the rack at Sears, rumpled, but nothing like Columbo's overcoat; a thin, colorless tie; and shoes that must have last held a shine when Clinton was president. He was assigned to the Colorado Springs resident agency, which reported to the Bureau's field office in Denver. Maybe it was because of the smaller-city pace or the relative lack of political or competitive pressures, but she tended to get along better with RA agents than with their FO counterparts. It seemed to her that an agent's aggressiveness and aloofness increased with his proximity to Washington or the size of the office to which he was assigned. Her own office of record was the FBI Academy in Quantico. Case closed.

"Jack," he said. "We spoke on the phone. Let me help." He reached for the strap, and she let the heavy bag slide off her shoulder. It swung into his leg, knocking him off balance. *"Man!"* he said.

"Laser printer," she explained. "Supposedly portable."

He gestured at the other case. "Going bowling?"

She smiled and hoisted the case, which did resemble a bowling ball bag on steroids. "This is why I'm here. The future of crime scene processing."

He gave it another look, his eyebrows crinkling in wonder.

"Hmm. Okay," he said. He brought his hand up to his mouth and popped in several sunflower seeds. Behind closed lips, his teeth started working to de-shell them.

She lowered her voice. "Thank you for being so on top of this."

"Doin' my job."

"Getting locals to wait for us is above and beyond."

She surveyed the people standing in the shadows. They seemed to be watching them but were not particularly interested in their conversation. "How do they feel about our involvement?"

Nelson switched the bag to his other shoulder and leaned closer. "The point is, we're not involved. The County Sheriff's office has a crack investigative unit. One of the highest clearance rates in Colorado—every one of their homicides last year. Fortunately, the Bureau has a great rapport with them, mostly because we know when to stay out of their business. You're here because you asked for a chance to check out your new gadgets, and someone in your department had already done the groundwork at the capitol for lending investigative support on any Pelletier killings in the state. I'm not saying you're not welcome, just that you gotta tread lightly."

She nodded. "That's what I needed to know. Which one's in charge?"

He leaned to one side and spit out the sunflower seed shells. Half a shell flipped over his lip and stuck to his chin. "Detective Dave Lindsey," he said. "My height, balding, mustache."

"Thanks." She stepped around him and waded into the group of detectives, deputies, and technicians. She nodded at their stares as she marched up to a man who was leaning one shoulder against the pillar that separated the garage doors. He had managed to work his expression into one of bored curiosity. "Detective Lindsey, thank you for waiting for me. I'm Special Agent Alicia Wagner." She stuck out her hand.

He paused before taking it. "This better be good," he said, coming off the pillar. "I got half a division twiddling their thumbs and a murder scene I can't process because you have friends in high places."

"Be nice, Dave," Nelson croaked from behind her.

Alicia knew at least a measure of Lindsey's agitation was a show. It told her and his people that he was boss, despite having deigned to grant an outside agency's request to assist. It also helped cover his butt if the delay in processing the scene led to problems. The blame was squarely on her now, and he had witnesses. She wasn't worried about that. The information flow had been uncommonly fast. Because of an advisory she had put out about the possibility of the Pelletier murderer striking again in Colorado very soon, the patrolman who'd investigated the 911 call knew what he'd stumbled onto. Even before dispatching an investigative team, the sheriff's Law Enforcement Bureau chief had called Nelson. Alicia's drive from her hotel room in south Denver had taken forty minutes. Nelson had told her the sheriff's offices were in south Colorado Springs—at least twenty-five minutes from Monument. The delay could not have been longer than fifteen minutes.

But there was something else about the way Lindsey was getting in her face. She guessed that Nelson had not told him the agent coming from Denver was a woman.

"I understand your concern, Detective," she said. "You know the corruption of crime scene evidence is the leading cause of botched investigations and mistrials. Even the suggestion that evidence was mishandled can ruin a prosecutor's case. Think O.J. Usually, it's not the investigation team's fault—the very act of analyzing a crime scene can irreparably taint it."

"Locard's Exchange Principle," the detective interjected, nodding.

"Exactly." She pushed her hair back behind her ear. It was a casual, girlish gesture that she was fully aware made her seem less intimidating. "The best way to preserve the viability of a crime scene is through documentation. What was the exact condition of the premises at the moment the perpetrator left? Were the lights on or off? The doors and windows opened or closed? The carpet pile up or down? You know the drill. So we send in the troops: people to dust, people to photograph, people to sketch and look and bag evidence, people to examine the body."

Lindsey jumped in again. "And all those people leave traces of themselves, of their having been there."

She smiled. "That's where this comes in." She nudged one of her cases with her foot. "This baby will give you lots of documentation—without lots of people." She paused, then said, "If this is a Pelletier killing, there are four other investigations already under way. I've got the equipment that will help your department be the one to bring this guy down."

She stopped there, convinced he'd think about the other investigations. The apprehension of a dangerous felon was always everyone's top priority, regardless of who did the catching or who got the credit. Still, she'd never met a law officer who didn't want to be the one who got the bad guy. Right now, Detective Lindsey was wondering if her equipment really could give him an edge.

He pretended to be looking at the spherical case and the bigger valise Nelson had set beside it, but she knew he was really mulling over her involvement. He could play the jerk and make her time here difficult for everyone, or he could cut her some slack, let her call enough shots to ensure optimal conditions for whatever it was she wanted to do, and maybe she'd leave him with something he could use to get a big feather in his cap. He surveyed his troops, and she saw what he saw: curiosity, enthusiasm, a tentative willingness to harness their horses with hers.

"All right," he said loudly, "whaddaya got?"

6

The interior of the old VW minibus was ripe enough to melt plastic. Perspiration, greasy food wrappers, boxes of putrefying Chinese takeout joined with the lingering ghosts of mystery spills and things burned on the now-broken gas stove to exude an atmosphere of olfactory hell. But because it was a new aroma, all Olaf could smell was blood. It would be that way until the dogs licked themselves clean. He cranked the window open a hand's width and savored the rush of cool night air. He was chugging west on State Highway 24, a meandering roller coaster of asphalt that cut into the heart of the Colorado Rockies. He'd already coaxed the van over Wilkerson Pass, and except for the relatively minor Trout Creek Pass, it was pretty much downhill to Johnson Village, where he'd ride 285 and then 50 into Cañon City. Now that he was in the valley between the two passes, he kept an eye out for a wooded turnoff that would provide a place to clean his weapons and let the animals out.

In the back, one of the dogs growled and snapped, and another yelped. Olaf guessed that the chastened animal had tried to swipe a taste of gore from the other's snout.

"*Góð stelpa!*" he yelled in the language that had been native to his family for thirty generations. Immediately, a furry body scrambled atop the maps and trash that littered the floor next to the driver's seat. It spun in a quick circle where the passenger seat had been before Olaf heaved it onto the side of the road. The dog was Freya, an exceptionally beautiful creature, ·but the smallest of the three and too timid around the others.

"*Afhverju í veröldinni ertu fúl?*"

Recognizing Olaf's teasing tone, the animal leaned back on her haunches and moaned at him.

"Hvao?"

The dog shimmied closer and lowered her head. Olaf scratched the heavy fur between her ears and ran his hand down her neck and back as far as he could reach. Despite her position as runt of the pack, she was a massive animal; ninety pounds at least. Olaf had trained her to take down her prey by hurling herself into their chests. He knew from experience that the blow could break ribs. He felt the bands of muscles under her pelt and shook his head at the power they represented. Breeding wolf-dog hybrids had been a part of his people's culture for as long as the storytellers could remember. They had perfected the genetic composition of the breed: the wolf's strength and hunting instincts mixed with the teachability and loyalty of the German shepherd. To their masters, they were attentive servants and companions; to their masters' enemies, they were as lethal as lions. After a minute of scratching and rubbing, he gave the animal several pats and returned his hand to the wheel.

He approached a junction and saw a break in the trees across the road. He eased off the gas. The van slowed abruptly, as if it were underwater. When he reached for the stick shift, he felt Freya's moist nose. She'd known just where to position herself. Olaf scolded her sharply and shoved her muzzle away. "Not now," he mumbled in his ancient tongue. She scurried into the back, where one of her companions promptly snapped at her.

He pulled off the road, aligning his tires with two deep ruts from previous excursionists: local revelers and hunters, no doubt. Before passing beyond the first copse of aspens and pines, he stopped and switched off the headlamps. Lights from another vehicle headed toward him from a few miles off. Otherwise, he was alone. He allowed the van to drift into the forest, guided as if on rails by the tire tracks. Shortly, he reached a clearing, pulled into an obvious turnaround, and killed the engine.

He swung the door open into the utter stillness of an alpine meadow. When he'd purchased the van two weeks ago, the door hinges screeched like hawks. A few minor adjustments and WD-40 gave them the silence he required. He had also installed a new starter and battery and performed a major tune-up. He liked the harmlessness the aging van exuded, but he couldn't have it stranding him after a killing. Outside, he called to the dogs; they bounded over the driver's seat and out the door. They zigzagged their way through the long grass to the trees at the far end of the meadow, where they sniffed the air and sprayed the foliage to claim their territory.

The moon gave the area a dreamlike luminance. It reminded him of home. The ache in his chest, the pain he tapped to fuel his rage when his tasks necessitated it—this ache deepened and left him short of breath. Around the passenger's side, he opened the sliding door. A stained paper cup and crumpled magazine fell out. He pushed back the trash that had not yet escaped. Another of his modifications was a false floor. The van was old enough and odd enough that most people would not immediately suspect anything wrong with the elevation of the rear compartment; plus, he had covered the plywood not with wall-to-wall shag but with rusty sheet metal and patches of the original carpet. He reached under the van to a small button and pushed it, causing a section of the floor to pop up.

In the compartment were two aluminum cases and a long bin of assorted hand weapons: knives, axes, spearheads. He removed a long pouch from the top of the pile, and from it he pulled a bearded ax—named for the triangular shape of its blade—with an oak handle the length of his arm. Tossing the pouch back into the compartment, he raised the ax to examine the blade. It was smeared with gore: blood and filaments of flesh, a few strands of hair. The handle near the blade, too, was caked with brownish-red globules. He retrieved a canteen and a rag from a plastic crate and walked to the trees ten paces away. Leaves removed most of the offal, then he poured water over the blade and began rubbing.

He heard the car engine before seeing its headlights.

It was coming through the trees slowly, almost to the clearing. He turned quickly to see the dogs huddled together, their long faces pointing toward the intruder. As he watched, their heads—all three at once—came down in a hunting posture. The car was turning into the clearing, its head-lamps making a clockwise sweep across the landscape, seconds from captur-ing the dogs in their glare. No time to call them back, to get them into the place he had designed for them under the false floor.

"Fara!" he yelled, and they faded into the trees before the lights panned past.

Olaf held the ax behind him as the car came around, catching first the van, then him with its blinding white eyes. He donned a toothy smile.

Then the flashing red and blue lights on the car's roof came on.

R obocop."

Someone behind her whispered it, causing a ripple of quiet laughter. If only they knew how unoriginal the observation was. It was also accurate, at least superficially. The helmet alone was an intimidating black dome, extend-ing from shoulders to crown, with a formation of gadgets marching up one side and down the other. The weight of the helmet necessitated a collar not unlike a deep-sea diver's, giving the shoulders a large share of the burden and making them appear unnaturally stout. The faceplate was a convexity of opaque plastic. Special boots, belt, and equipment strapped to each shin and forearm completed the "Robocop" ensemble. The official name of the system was Crime Scene Digitizer—a moniker that managed to be both un-inspired and awesome in a techno-geeky kind of way. Her preference was CSD.

She turned to Detective Lindsey. "I'll go in first."

Transmitted through small speakers in the front and back of the collar, her voice sounded tinny and far away. A microphone also picked up her voice and fed it back to her through an earpiece, which resulted in an echoing feedback only she could hear. She had reported the problem, but until it was fixed anyone using the helmet was doomed to suffer a horrendous headache. Fortunately, the gremlins had fiddled with only the ancillary systems, like the microphone and a few creature-comfort devices. If the core systems malfunctioned, it would jeopardize the crime scene analyses they were conducting, and the Bureau would never get funding to push the project into everyday investigations.

"How about if only you and one technician follow me on the first pass, to help preserve the scene? The CSD will generate a plan of attack for the other technicians afterward."

Appraising the outfit, Lindsey made such a comical expression of disbelief that Alicia was sorry she had not yet switched on the cameras.

"All right," he said tentatively. He managed to pull his jaw closed and turn from her. "Fleiser," he snapped.

A bespectacled man in a long white lab coat nodded and picked up a leather doctor's bag.

Alicia positioned herself at the bottom of a flight of wooden steps in the garage. According to the responding officer, the steps rose to a combination laundry and mudroom. From there a hallway led to bedrooms and another corridor, which accessed the home's front rooms.

"Systems on," she said.

Instantly the staircase became clear and shadowless under the hotwhite light of halogen lamps mounted to her shoulders and shin pads. A display, showing the view of the digital video camera on top of the helmet, flickered to life inside the visor. In her abdominal muscles, against which a black box was strapped, she felt CSD's hard drive whirl up to speed.

"Mapping on." The high-pitched whine of a small motor started. There was a vibration against the top of her skull that radiated to her jaw. Another problem to report. The red beams of a dozen lasers flashed past her field of vision. They would be a thousand times more visible in the area around her not washed by the halogens.

"Whoa!" Lindsey said.

She used a button located on her left forearm to switch to a rear-viewing camera. Lindsey's expression of sheer incredulity had returned.

"They're used to help an optical range finder map the crime scene. CSD will create a detailed, accurate blueprint—furniture, evidence, and all."

"Whatever."

She started up the stairs. "The perp came down this way," she said. She pointed to a three-inch gash in the unpainted drywall, deeper on the downward side. It was crusted brown. "I'll mark it on the map." A red beam shot out from her fingertip. When the dot on the wall touched the gash, she pushed a button. A beep sounded, and the laser disappeared.

"Fleiser," Lindsey said behind her, "wanna tag that?"

She stopped again in the laundry room. "Hold on a sec." The lights dimmed like dying suns; the rotating lasers clicked off. A single laser sliced the dark. It stopped on the floor. "Shoe print," Alicia said. "Big, size twelve or thirteen, coming into the laundry from the hall." The halogens flashed on again; the range-finding lasers restarted their rotation. She was holding her finger toward the spot.

"I don't see—"

"I used infrared. That's why I turned off the lights. Can you get around me and tag that?"

The tech, Fleiser, leaned forward and set down what appeared to be a miniature pylon with a number on it. Alicia instructed CSD to map the print as well.

They stepped over the pylon and invisible print into the hallway. The soles of her boots consisted of half-inch rubber posts at each of the corners and insteps, designed to minimize disturbance of the ground and leave unique tread marks. They also contained sensors that identified the type of surface upon which the wearer trod. When the diagram of the house and crime scene was complete, it would show that this part of the house was floored with hardwood. The hall was narrow and lined with framed photographs chronicling the formation, mitosis, and activity of an average American family: school portraits, weddings, births, vacations in sand and snow and places with giant plaster dinosaurs.

Alicia's throat tightened. Death stole so much more than a person's future. For the victim, the universe ended. All that was and is and will be— gone. For the family, even happy memories were suddenly tinged with the sadness of knowing a principal player was no longer making new memories.

A light housing on her shoulder clipped one of the photographs. Alicia spun and caught it before it hit the floor. She handed it to Lindsey. She stepped through an open doorway on the right. The lasers danced around the room, noting dimensions and the placement of furniture. The room's simplicity and dustiness implied a seldom-used guest room. It contained one window. Behind its raised lower half, a circle of glass was missing, corresponding to where a brass lock would latch when the window was closed.

"Point of entry," she said, stepping nearer. "There appears to be a clump of animal fur stuck on the wood frame. The screen's on the ground outside. Mud on the sill . . . dirt, pine needles, leaves on the carpet inside." She pointed at each with the fingertip laser.

Lindsey and Fleiser swept in behind her.

"Going infrared again," she said, and the lights faded. After a few seconds, the laser, bright in the darkness, touched two spots on either side of the window. The halogens reignited. "Got prints on the window casing, twenty inches from the bottom on the left, nineteen and a half on the right. Looks like a couple of fingers and a palm."

"Well, I don't see a dang-pickin' thing," Lindsey said stupidly.

That's why they're called latent, she almost countered, but checked herself. Instead, she said, "They're there."

"No gloves? That doesn't make sense."

"They found prints at the other crime scenes as well," she informed him. "Maybe the killer simply doesn't care."

She stepped out and moved down the hall. Two more doors, both closed. The first was an office of sorts. A computer monitor on a small desk, the computer itself stashed underneath. A chair, a printer, a smattering of mail and printed pages, a metal filing cabinet. The rest of the room contained teetering columns of stacked plastic wastebaskets.

At the last door she powered down the halogens for an infrared look at the area. Light was spilling from beneath the door. She backed into Lindsey, who had come up behind her. "Light," she whispered. "Did the responding officer—"

"He rushed out of here so fast, he might not have cleared it. Turn those airplane lights back on." He edged around her, his pistol already drawn. Slowly he turned the knob—and burst through, Alicia on his heels. He moved quickly, swinging the weapon around the room. He cleared it, the closet, and a small bathroom in six seconds.

She rotated to face the room. The first thing that struck her was the bed. It was king-size with a fat down comforter and green sheets, purled in ivory lace. On one side, the top half of the comforter and upper sheet were folded back. Two pillows lay fluffed against the headboard. An open paperback formed a miniature tent by the pillows. A ceiling fan rotated lazily overhead. Though the halogens overpowered it, she knew the small lamp on the night-stand was burning.

"Looks like she was in bed when something disturbed her," Lindsey said.

"No, the sheets are too smooth." She hoped the tinny speakers were fil-tering out the melancholy in her voice. "This was her reward. A comfortable bed and a good read at the end of a long day. She prepared it ahead of time, perhaps just after dinner, so it was waiting for her. She didn't want to have to work for it when she was tired. She wanted to simply fall into bed and enjoy."

"How would you know that?"

"Because that's exactly what my mother did. Every day of her life. Sometimes she would . . ." Her voice trailed off. Why should she share her memories with some guy who couldn't possibly give a squat? She'd spoken without thinking and regretted it.

Lindsey eyed the neatly arranged items. "She was probably getting ready for bed when the intruder broke in."

"Sure."

"Will you *look* at this place!"

She followed his roving gaze. Every surface—the nightstand, the dresser, the chest at the foot of the bed, the bookcase shelves—was cluttered with knickknacks. They all seemed to be religious in nature: a ceramic chapel, praying hands, a monstrous nail capped with a red ribbon, a dish ornately painted with the words "Feed my sheep," countless crosses, tracts, angels, and figurines of Jesus Christ. The walls were covered with dozens of paintings, some depicting the Messiah in various poses, others of beautiful landscapes with Scripture passages in calligraphy across them. She turned in a 360-degree circle, watching the video display to capture the valueless treasures.

"Another religious nut—"

"Detective!" She pointed to the video camera and microphone perched like the eye of a baleful god atop the helmet. Video walk-throughs were used in all sorts of ways besides helping investigators reconstruct crimes. They'd been known to settle judicial doubts about the original location or condition of key evidence. And relatives and friends often viewed them either to satisfy themselves about the handling of a crime scene or to help investigators identify items missing or out of place.

He looked stricken. "As I was saying, another religious person gone home too soon. It burns me up."

Fleiser came in, little black bag in hand. "Anything in here?"

"Doesn't look like it," Lindsey said, pushing past him to get to the hallway.

Alicia had not noticed it before, but she suspected there was one place not overrun by trinkets. She looked and smiled. A bare spot on the nightstand, the size and shape of a teacup saucer. Mom relished her chamomile. She wondered what Cynthia Loeb favored.

"Coming?" Lindsey called. "There's still a body to be found!"

Suddenly, Alicia was not so keen on finding it.

8

Just his luck that a cop saw his detour into the woods.

Olaf held his grin as a spotlight came on, spearing the night sky before it dropped and found the minibus. The cruiser had stopped thirty feet back. Its lights illuminated the van's rear and right side, leaving the left side, with its open side door, in darkness. The cop was blind to the raised section of floor and the compartment beneath it. Holding the bearded ax behind him, Olaf sauntered over to the van. The cop would not like that he had moved out of view. Quickly, he tossed the soiled rag on top of the weapons, leaned in, and lowered the floor into place. He slid the ax into his belt above his right buttock, letting the blade catch the rough leather. It would take him three seconds to pull it straight up and swing it forward . . . half that time if he simply snapped the leather.

He stepped back into the light and into the cop's line of vision. He placed his hands on his hips, slightly forward so the cop could see they were empty. The spotlight stopped on him, then clicked off. The strobes died as well; he suspected they had been flashed only to inform him that the newcomer was not a bad guy.

The cop took another minute to run the van's plates.

Fine, thought Olaf. *It's not the van you have to worry about.*

Finally, the door opened and a state trooper emerged. He pushed on a wide-brimmed hat with one hand; the other, Olaf noticed, rested on the butt of his holstered gun. Stepping around the door, he called, "Good evening!"

"Evening, Officer! Don't tell me I'm trespassing!" His tone was friendly; his words carried not the slightest trace of an accent.

The cop crossed in front of the headlights, his shadow jumping at Olaf, dropping away, then jumping again. He stopped before reaching the van. "No, the land's here for the public to use. I saw you pull in and wanted to make sure you were okay. You okay?"

"Peachy." He pushed his lips into a wider smile. He knew his physical appearance was unsettling. Stocky and muscular, hairy as Bigfoot, dressed like a Norseman of old, which in fact he was: heavy knit shirt, long and, unfortunately, filthy; tight sheepskin pants; high leather boots. When he was on a rampage, his visage served to intimidate his victims, stunning them for the briefest of seconds—time enough for Olaf to gain the advantage, to make his move. In a situation like the one he was in now, it served to ensure that cops didn't stand around making small talk, but was sufficiently innocuous to avoid biased persecution or overzealous investigation: he was weird, but not *that* weird. The clothes were comforting to Olaf. His wife, Ingun, had made the shirt; he had skinned and tanned the material for the pants, and Ingun had cut and sewn them. His sons had been with him when he picked up the boots from the leather smith. They had oohed at the craftsmanship and praised his stature when he slipped them on.

The trooper pulled a flashlight from a loop on his belt and switched it on. He stepped up to the rear window and peered through. "California plates," he said, as if Olaf would appreciate the knowledge.

"Yeah, San Luis Obispo."

"That the place with the birds?"

"You're thinking of San Juan Capistrano. I'm five hours northwest."

The cop nodded. He stepped around to Olaf's side of the van. He was in his midthirties, a little younger than Olaf. He had earnest eyes that said he loved his job, and deep frown lines that said maybe he loved his job a bit too much for a healthy family life. Olaf pictured the man volunteering extra hours to train rookies and spending a lot of time at the shooting range. If anybody was going to give him a hard time, it was this guy. He wondered if the man knew about the latest murder. Unlikely. It was less than two hours fresh, and law enforcement agencies weren't that quick about disseminating crime information, especially interagency and when they didn't have a clue about who they were looking for or what type of vehicle he was driving. He was sure nobody had seen him make his way to Palmer Lake from the west, a direction with no thoroughfares and few residents.

The trooper aimed his beam past Olaf into the open door. "Lotta trash."

"I'm a pig when I travel."

"Where you heading?"

"Taos. See a cousin." He anticipated the cop's next question and added, "Came in on I-70 so I could visit friends along the way."

"*Lotta* trash." He was shaking his head, playing the beam over the garbage. His nose crinkled; he grimaced. He had just caught the odor.

Olaf stifled a smile. There was only one reason he, himself, tolerated the stench: to knock people like this trooper off balance. If the cops wanted to search the van, he was reasonably sure it would be a quick search, and the searchers probably would not be at their best. And if they were looking for someone with dogs, they wouldn't detect them with their noses. It was no violation of law to possess a vehicle that smelled like an outhouse. The crimes the outhouse helped conceal were another matter.

The trooper took a step back. "Got your driver's license?"

Olaf reached behind him. "Am I in trouble, Officer?"

"Not at all." The words were amicable, but they fell from scowling lips like an insult.

Olaf produced a tattered nylon wallet; he fished out his ID, which was newly minted but looked a thousand years old.

Something snapped in the trees nearest them. The trooper's head whipped around. His flashlight followed. He was holding it in a bent arm, at shoulder height—a javelin of light. His other hand had sprung back to his gun.

"Anything wrong, Officer?" Before the sound, Olaf had caught a glimpse of one of the dogs. They had circled around the perimeter of the meadow and were now positioned just out of sight.

"Are you alone?" Olaf could tell the cop was kicking himself for not asking the question sooner.

"'Course I am. Why, something out there?"

"Would you please step over there, sir?" He directed Olaf to a spot farther away from him and halfway to the tree line, where he could see both Olaf and the shadowy area from which the sound had issued. He inched closer to the trees, panning the light back and forth.

"Don't think it's a wild animal, do you?"

The cop didn't answer. He dropped to one knee, bending to peer under the branches . . . scanning. Then he cocked his head at Olaf, but he wasn't looking; he was listening. After a minute of silence, he stood and approached Olaf.

"Should I be afraid?" Olaf asked, wide-eyed.

The trooper grunted. "Must have been a deer." He took the driver's license, squinted at it for about three seconds, and returned it. A layer of greasy perspiration coated his forehead, gleaming in the light. He stepped back, flashed the beam into the van, into the woods, at Olaf. He seemed on the edge of some decision. Then he backpedaled toward his cruiser, casting furtive glances at the trees and prattling to justify not exposing his back to the weirdo in the ridiculous clothes. "If you make a campfire, be sure to douse it with water before leaving . . . Put your trash in properly marked receptacles, or keep it in the van if you prefer. Have a good trip."

"Thank you, Officer."

The man navigated past the front of the cruiser, down the side, and around the open door without turning away from Olaf—a home movie played in reverse. Without removing his hat, he tucked his head under the roof and slammed the door. Electronic door locks engaged with a loud *thunk*. The green glow of his communications terminal gave him an eerie presence behind the windshield. The cruiser made a tight circle, found the tire ruts where the path cut through the trees, and became an indistinct white glow—flickering with occasional brilliance, adorned by winking red taillights—that faded with the noise of the engine.

He may come back.

It mostly depended on whether or not he believed Olaf was alone. Clearly, he did not. But if he caught Olaf in a lie, what did it matter? Did it prove a crime was committed? No, all it really did was expose the trooper unnecessarily to potentially dangerous people. Even when he heard of the murder, he would be hard-pressed to make a connection. The killer had dogs—at least one. The sound in the woods could have been made by such an animal, but there were no other signs of it. And what animal owned by man stayed hidden and silent? Then there was Olaf's speech. A description of the killer would include a heavy accent, as heard by the woman on the phone. Most people might try to disguise an accent while committing a crime, but rarely would they invent one. He was a strong believer in an abundance of red herrings.

"Freya! Thor! Eric!"

The dogs crashed through the branches and sat in a semicircle around him.

"Góan dag!" he praised them. "I have something for you. You want something?" He leaned into the van and came back with a burlap pouch. He withdrew a bulging handful of beef jerky and tossed it in front of the first dog, a monster called Thor. The animals looked at the pile, then shifted their gaze back to the master, waiting. He gave the other two similar helpings, then said, "Eat." By the time he'd replaced the pouch, the pile in front of each dog was gone. "Now go play. We leave in five minutes." They tore into the meadow as if their tails were on fire.

Again he lifted the false floor. He pulled the ax from his belt and tossed it into the bin of weapons. Reaching deeper into the compartment, his fingers felt along the side. They found the plastic business-card pocket glued to the wood and worked out a tightly folded piece of paper. He turned, sat on the edge of the opening, and unfolded it. Names, descriptions, addresses. In small, careful hand lettering, the list contained fifty people. He'd counted them, thought about each one, how his life would intersect theirs, ending it. Cynthia Loeb's was the fifth from the top of the first column. A thumbprint of dried blood partially obscured the next name down. Olaf scraped at the smudge with a fingernail until the letters beneath were legible: *Trevor Wilson, age 12.*

A physical description and home address in Cañon City, Colorado, followed.

The corners of his lips pulled into a frown, as if attached by a thread to the growing heaviness in his chest. Of course, he'd known the boy occupied this position on the list. But here he was, the next to die. It made him think of his own sons. His hand rose to trinkets that dangled from braided hemp round his neck. He fingered a wood-carved *Othel*—a diamond shape with legs continuing beyond its bottom point. It was his people's symbol for family. Seven-year-old Jon had spent a month whittling it in secret to present to him upon his departure. The child had kissed him and pushed his face into his breast. His tears had felt like blood trickling through Olaf's chest hair.

His hand moved to a rabbit's foot from his other son, Bjorn's, first kill. It meant the world to the boy, so it had deeply touched Olaf when he had handed it to him. Eleven-year-old Bjorn, thinking himself a man, had held back emotionally and physically. He had hugged his papa and wished him a safe trip, and then quickly stepped away. Bjorn's determination to be strong had meant as much as Jon's tears.

And now this boy, Trevor Wilson. *How his parents will mourn.*

Olaf stiffened his jaw, began refolding the list.

What must be done, must be done.

Turning back to the exposed compartment, stashing the paper, he resolved to grant what mercy he could. He slammed down the false floor and nodded. Yes, he could do at least that. His clan's edict to always face one's enemy, to look him in the eye, granting him the chance—however small—to fight and triumph over his own death, did not apply to children. He would visit the boy late at night, when he was certain to be asleep.

———

NEARLY HALF a world away, a cell phone rang. A man awoke, blinking against the morning sun that filled his hotel suite. He squinted at the infernally chirping device on the nightstand and picked up a jewel-encrusted watch beside it—8:50, which meant 6:50 in his own time zone. He slipped on the watch and picked up the phone.

"What is it?" he said gruffly in his native tongue.

The caller spoke his name. The words were filtered through an electronic voice changer, jarring him fully awake.

"Yes. Who is this?" He realized it was a stupid question.

"Speak English," the caller ordered.

He complied. "How did you get this number?"

"Pippino Farago is ready."

"Pip?" The man sat up. "Ready for what?"

"For you. He has what you want. Be persuasive. Do it now."

"What do you mean? Hello?"

The line was dead. He looked at the phone. The screen informed him that the caller was "unidentified." Of course. But did that matter? If his information was correct, he had just received an extraordinary gift. His heart was racing when he started scrolling through the phone's memory for Pip's number.

9

Alicia's lights panned into the kitchen and almost immediately captured the screaming horror of Cynthia Loeb's severed head. It was perched upright on the edge of the counter, its chin hanging over the edge, in front of a stack of unwashed dishes and an open box of Cheez-Its.

Alicia hitched in a sharp breath, which through her helmet's little speakers sounded like a squawk and reverberated back to her as a piercing crack. Her shoulders came back instinctively, a slight move, exaggerated by the bulky lights mounted to them. Detective Lindsey, who was standing immediately behind her in the hall, caught one of the lights squarely in the forehead.

"Hey!" he yelled painfully. "Watch it now!"

"Sorry," she whispered.

He pushed past her, rubbing his head. Then he saw the thing on the counter and made a sharp choking sound.

The tech, Fleiser, entered next, squeezing by her on the other side. He didn't make a sound, but Alicia felt a hand grip her arm.

"So this *is* a Pelletier killing." Lindsey's voice was flat, like a documentary's narrator. Until now, he'd had to trust the assessment of the responding patrolman who had set everything in motion.

Fleiser cleared his throat. "I heard the name, but why Pelletier?"

Alicia suspected the man would have asked anything that would, however insignificantly, move his thoughts away from the grotesque sight before him.

"Nicolas-Jacques Pelletier," she answered. "In 1792, he was the first victim of the guillotine." This nugget of trivia had popped from the mind of one of the investigators at the first known killing by the assumed perp in Utah. The name had stuck.

The head's strawberry blond hair was matted and sticking up in a pointed swirl. Alicia realized with sick vividness that the killer had carried it by the hair. But there hadn't been a trail of blood. She lowered her view to check again, bringing the lights with her.

"What are you doing? Go back to the head! The head!" demanded Lindsey, sounding panicked over the possibility of Cynthia Loeb's head taking flight in the dark and whispering in his ear.

"Hold on."

The floor was clean, except for a few thin swirls of brown—obviously dried blood. Almost as if the spilled blood had been wiped up. But why? Then her lights caught a mark on the floor, and she stepped closer. Three-quarters of a dog's paw print, made of blood. And it came to her: the animals had licked the floor clean.

"Come on, lady." The detective was really pouring on the charm now. Slowly she turned back to the head.

Cynthia's irises—green, Alicia noticed—had rolled up slightly, as if just becoming aware of how atrocious her hair looked. One eyelid was drooping. Blood filled both nostrils and caked the left temple and cheek. A purple-yellow bruise had blossomed on the other cheek. Dry lips were twisted in a sour grimace . . . a bloated tongue . . . blood . . . pooling, dripping onto the floor.

A ridiculous saying came to Alicia's mind—*I wouldn't be caught dead*—and she realized this was what that meant. *All the times you primped and groomed and applied your makeup just so,* thought Alicia, assuming this woman had shared the cares of her gender. *And you end up like this. No one else to impress. Not even yourself.*

She moved her eyes away, keeping the halogens trained on the gruesome orb for the benefit of the two men. The circle of light was wide enough to catch a mustard-streaked knife, bread crumbs, and a thin strip of clear plastic, the kind you tear off a pouch of cold cuts to get at the meat. An empty bread bag, crumpled and flat like a deflated balloon. She shifted the lights just a little and saw the rest of the meat package, empty. Behind it was the mustard bottle. Her eyes roamed the countertop, stopping at the pool of blood.

"The perp made a sandwich," she announced.

"Huh?" It was Fleiser.

"How do you know the woman didn't make it herself, before she died?" asked Lindsey.

Fleiser snorted. "Thanks for clarifying 'before she died,' Dave."

"You know what I mean."

"There are crumbs on top of the blood." She centered the lights on them.

Fleiser took a step. "Yep. Some of them are still white, unsaturated."

"Judas priest."

Silence, for a time, as each of them imagined the macabre scene. Alicia sensed that even hard-nosed Lindsey was a bit dumbfounded.

Then Fleiser said, "What's that on her forehead?" He edged closer, mindful of the bloody floor.

"It was in the notice I sent out." Alicia instructed the video camera to zoom in on the small mark above the right eyebrow.

"It looks like a burn . . . a brand." The tech was close enough to kiss the unfortunate Ms. Loeb. "It's a sun."

"A sun?" Lindsey repeated.

"About the size of a dime. Little flames radiating out from it."

"The others were branded the same way," Alicia said flatly. "She'll have them on her left palm too. When we find the body."

"Is that some satanic symbol?" Lindsey's tone rose on the word *satanic*. "We got ourselves a devil worshiper?"

"Maybe." After reviewing the case file on the Ft. Collins homicide, Alicia had searched for the sun symbol in the Bureau's database of symbols and signs. Lots of suns were associated with known occult groups, but nothing precisely matched this one. The closest was a *Sonnenrad* or Sun Wheel. Originating in ancient Europe, it was especially prominent in Old Norse and Celtic cultures. It depicted crooked rays emanating from a center point. Nazis often used the symbol in place of the swastika, which centuries ago had derived from the *Sonnenrad*. Neo-Nazis adopted the symbol to circumvent bans on Nazi imagery. In different cultures, the *Sonnenrad* meant different things, sometimes satanic or occult, but not always.

She had learned that many religions still deified the sun or had elements of sun worship tinting their general theology, even Hinduism and Buddhism. Cynthia Loeb obviously had some spiritual leanings. A connection?

"Could mean anything," she said.

"It *is* burned into the skin," the tech said with some wonder.

"We think the perp heats something like a small branding iron with a lighter flame." She bit her lower lip. "Then he applies it."

Fleiser nodded.

Alicia went through the ritual of checking for latents with the infrared and then imbedding the location of each item—head, blood, sandwich supplies, paw print—in the mapping software and evidence databank. After that, she walked back into the hall, stiffly and awkwardly under the cumbersome helmet, vest, arm and leg pads, gloves, and boots.

She found herself in the awful situation of wanting to get away from the head but knowing the next thing she'd find was the body. That dilemma alone, however, could not explain the extent of her discomfort—why her skin felt clammy, why her heart pranced like a racehorse at the gate, why she had to exert so much willpower to keep from hyperventilating. She had examined hundreds of crime scene photographs, had witnessed the aftermath of heinous acts of violence, had examined gunshot wounds, fatal lacerations, bodies crushed in cars—but there was something about a severed head that got to her. Maybe Brady would have some insight into it; she sure didn't.

"Think the murderer left the rest of the body?" Lindsey was right behind her.

"He did at the other killings." She hesitated. Through the opening at the end of the hall, she could see an overturned end table or plant stand. A ring of keys and scrap of paper lay near it on the floor. A crack in the hardwood snaked over from deeper in the room, like a river on a map. Then she understood and swallowed hard. The crack was actually a thick ribbon of blood.

"Well then?" Lindsey called from farther behind. "Get a move on!"

She moved toward the room.

Lindsey grunted. "So that thing's supposed to suggest a sequence for processing this place?"

Alicia knew what he was thinking: Entry through a back bedroom. A head in the kitchen. The place of the attack—obviously—in the front room. The crime scene was expanding, growing in size and complexity by the second. It could quickly get out of hand once the rest of the team plowed into the house.

"We call it a POA—plan of attack. It suggests which techs should enter when and what they should process to preserve as much evidence as possible. I'll also give you most of the information your people will need for their reports."

"Right away?"

"As soon as I plug it into the printer. It'll spit out a blueprint with evidence markings; a master sequential list of steps, designed to minimize damage; and the same list broken down by personnel, so each person knows precisely what to do, without redundancy or omissions."

"Well . . . I'll need to consider them first."

"Of course."

The corpse's feet and legs came into view. As Alicia stepped out of the hall, the halogen beams slid up the body, making painfully evident the violence of the woman's demise: splotches and dots of brownish crimson speckled the top of her beige shorts and the bottom of her chambray shirt, growing in number and size, like a gradated screen, as more of her was revealed. By mid-thorax, the blood obliterated the shirt altogether. A stub of neck protruded from the collar—more neck than Alicia thought possible. It stopped cleanly where the head should have been, making her think of a badly framed photograph.

Using the keyboard strapped to her left forearm and the laser on her fingertip, she entered the body's coordinates. Another key click and the lasers at the top of the helmet, which had been cascading around the room, all swung forward and down. They converged on the body and began flitting over it so fast that they appeared as one growing red luminance engulfing the corpse. A still camera mounted at ear level snapped and hummed: its

35-millimeter film would provide flawless images to the Luddites still resistant to the high-res digital video accumulating on the hard drive.

As soon as this process was finished, she turned away. In front of the fireplace there was a palette with drying clumps of paint. Beside it was an acrylic wastebasket, still glistening with wet paint. She bent to take in the illustration.

"Do the overhead light switch," said Lindsey behind her, "so I can turn it on."

She turned to see him pointing. "Infrared first," she said and began the routine again: lights off, infrareds on, lights on, laser-mark the evidence . . . New location, lights off, infrared on, lights on, laser-mark . . . until she'd covered the entire room. Finally, she checked the light switch and surrounding area for latents. "Clean," she squawked through the helmet's pitiful speakers. He threw the switch. The glare of the halogens prevented her from detecting any change in the ambient lighting.

There was nothing else to look at but the body again. Squatting, she positioned herself to capture the top of the neck—wet, complicated anatomy that was never intended for display. Next, she trained the CSD's various systems on one of Cynthia Loeb's mutilated wrists. Veins and tendons jutted out from a gaping wound like a torn electrical cable. The mess was surprisingly bloodless, as if it had been washed clean. Or—her stomach contracted—*licked* clean. A constellation of tiny punctures fanning out from the wound bore witness to the animals that had somehow assisted in the slaying. A pool of blood had formed in the woman's open palm. On the fleshy orb under the thumb, the small branded sun. The ring finger had been chewed off.

Alicia stood suddenly. The weight of the helmet tried to throw her over. She took a step back to keep from falling, knocking into a piece of furniture behind her. It let out a deep chirp as it slid over the wooden floor. She swore under her breath. In her mind she saw herself stumbling about the room, pulled along by the weight of the helmet, careening against furniture and walls, crushing evidence, tripping over the body . . . Suppressing her curiosity over which piece of furniture she had bumped, she forced herself to stand still. When she felt equilibrium return, she powered down the system, unshackled the helmet from its shoulder-pad moorings, and pulled it off. She stood there, wavering slightly, holding the helmet with both hands. The overhead lights were on all right but seemed inadequate for the room. Her head felt ready to explode.

"Is that thing off?" Lindsey's voice was loud after the relative isolation of the helmet.

Alicia took a deep breath—a mistake, since she managed only to fill her sinuses and lungs with the heavy odor of blood. "It's off."

"Thank God," he said and released a dazzling example of volcanic flatulence.

Just what she needed. Alicia spun on her heels and strode away.

10

Ben-Gurion Airport
Near Tel Aviv, Israel

As usual, the big, black Mercedes limousine was waiting on the tarmac for the Gulfstream IV bearing Fr. Adalberto Randall. He eyed it through a porthole as he waited for the pilot to open the door, lower the steps, and offer a hand. He was old, too old for this. His back was bent and his knees were shot and he no longer possessed the muscle mass that would have compensated for these deficiencies in a younger man. At least he did not have to fly commercial.

The limo's back door opened as he approached. Leaning out, Pippino Farago grazed him with his eyes before disappearing back into the cool darkness of the car's interior.

Climbing in wrenched Randall's back even more.

The passenger compartment was laid out like a living room, with two plush bench seats facing each other—one directly behind the driver's seat and one at the rear. Pip and his boss, Luco Scaramuzzi, lounged in the rear seat, so Randall fell back into the one facing them.

Luco smiled warmly. He leaned forward to extend his hand, and Father Randall shook it.

"Good to see you again, Father," Luco said. He was one of the handsomest men the priest had ever seen, on-screen or off—he could have been George Clooney's Italian brother. He was lithe, muscular, and tall. At forty-two, his thick salt-and-pepper hair had not receded one centimeter off his forehead.

And God had not denied the man any trappings to make the most out of his good looks. If charm were a poker hand, Luco came up with a royal flush every time. Children adored him, men wanted to be him, and women . . . well, whoever coined the phrase "God's gift to women" must have had Luco Scaramuzzi in mind.

Randall smiled inwardly at the gaudiness of his description. You'd think he was the man's press agent instead of his theologian. But he offered no apologies. It was all true; bless him, it was.

Randall supposed Luco required every one of his superior genes to achieve the goals he had set for himself. And that reminded him of another of Luco's qualities: he was a hard worker. He never seemed to sleep. When he wasn't tending to his duties as Ambassador of Italy to Israel, he was planning world domination . . . really. Or toning his muscles in his workout room, scuba diving off the Lipari Islands, skiing on St. Moritz . . . or doing whatever seemed strenuous and fun.

So with all that going for him, it was a shame the man was also the embodiment of pure evil. His history of bad deeds included the deflowering of young girls, sexual affairs for the sole purpose of breaking a husband's heart, robbery, embezzlement, extortion, arson, battery. And murder; don't forget murder.

In fact, it was his assassination of a politician five years ago in the Asia House—the very building from which he now conducted his own politicking—that secured his position as ambassador.

If someone asked Randall what he was doing with such a despicable person, he'd lie. But he had his reasons, and he was able to look at himself in the mirror at night. Most nights.

"Father, you want something to drink?" Luco asked. He pulled a bottle of springwater from the limo's small refrigerator for himself.

"Wine, please."

Luco slid a bottle out enough to read the label.

"Brunello di Montalcino?"

"Splendid."

Luco uncorked the bottle, poured a taste into a Riedel Vinum wineglass, and offered it to Randall.

He held up his hand. "I'm sure it's fine."

Luco poured half a glass and handed it to him.

"Pip?"

Luco's assistant raised his hand to decline. He was staring out the window, lost in some problem. Randall thought he knew what it was.

Luco stretched out his legs, checked the crease in his trousers, sipped his water. At last he said, "You ready, Father?"

Father Randall smiled, his thin lips turning the color of his skin. "I have your bombshell."

"I can't stress enough how important this meeting is."

"I understand."

"Then what are we babbling for?" Luco laughed.

Every six to twelve months, Luco's board of directors—that's how Randall thought of the Council—met with Luco in Jerusalem to review activities and progress, to strategize, and, if warranted, to grant Luco more control over the empire that awaited him. Randall's duty was to continually confirm Luco's status as rightful heir. It was a job like none other in the world, for these meetings and these directors were like none other in the world.

Each meeting was a battle of wits: Luco making every attempt to win over the board, detractors doing their best to knock him down. Today's meeting was particularly crucial. Not only did Luco intend to wrest more power from the board's grasp, but the outcome also would either encourage or dampen the faith of his worldwide followers. Next Sunday night, a select number of these believers—who were not as influential as the Council but nevertheless important to Luco's ascension—would meet in Jerusalem for what Randall thought of as a pep rally. Equal parts mass, reception, and ceremony, the event was officially and enigmatically called the Gathering.

He turned to the window and watched the landscape stream past. They were approaching Sha'ar Hagai, where the corpses of armor-plated vehicles from the War of Independence rusted among the mimosas. The land here was vegetative and green, hemmed in by the Judean hills, which were actually mountains, in their own scruffy way as beautiful as any Italy had to offer. Except the Alps. Nothing compared to them.

Luco watched something approaching on his side of the car. He pushed a button on his armrest. The glass partition that separated the cab from the passenger compartment slid down into the driver's seat back.

"Sir?" the driver said.

"Pull over here, Tullio."

Pip spun to look out his side of the limousine, instantly alert for danger. Seeing nothing but countryside, he fell to his knees and leaned toward Luco's window. "What is it?"

"Children. Down in the meadow."

"The stone throwers? But if we just keep going—"

"Shhhhh." Luco opened the door, letting dust and heat billow in. He stepped out. Just beyond the shoulder, the ground sloped steeply for a dozen feet, then sailed off in a rolling meadow toward the mountains. Bushes and trees cast splotchy shadows, tricking the eye into seeing more than was there, and less. A perfect place to hide—unless you were naive enough to wear white T-shirts. There were six of them, all boys, huddled behind a large shrub fifty yards away. They were talking to one another and glancing up at the vehicles going by on the highway. Probably waiting for a nice, window-lined bus to come around the bend. They were unaware of the stopped limousine. Luco ducked his head under the door frame. "Pip, give me your gun."

"My gun?"

Randall leaned forward. "Luco . . . ?"

Luco snapped his fingers impatiently. Pip pulled his semiautomatic pistol from a shoulder holster, hesitated, and then placed it in Luco's hand.

"Luco!" Randall said sharply. "What are you doing? This is not—"

"Hush!" Luco snapped. He stepped away from the car to the edge of the shoulder.

"Hey!" he yelled.

The little faces turned his way. The youngest about ten, the oldest maybe fourteen. They dropped out of sight behind the bush.

Luco reached inside his jacket for a handkerchief. He wiped the entire pistol, ejected the magazine, and rubbed it down. Randall knew that the gun was untraceable; that was Luco's way.

Luco looked up to see the kids eyeing him again. He waited for a beat-up Peugeot minivan to pass. Then, with no other cars in sight, he held the pistol high above his head, waggling it. He tossed it down the embankment toward the gawking boys.

Randall shook his head. He pulled a battered silver cigarette case from his breast pocket, extracted a hand-rolled cigarette, and pushed it between his lips. He summoned a flame from an old Zippo. He leaned toward the open car door, blew out a stream of smoke, and glanced at Luco—his back to the car, hands on his hips, waiting to see what the children would do. Turning, he saw that Pip was looking the other way, out the window again.

Pip's left leg was shorter than his right, the result of a tragic boyhood accident. The shorter leg was crossed over the other, and Randall squinted at what looked like two paperback books taped to the bottom of his left shoe.

Randall quietly said, "Pip?"

No response.

Randall reached out and touched Pip's shoe.

Still no response.

Randall sighed and sat back. Over the past few months, he and Pip had become friends. Their conversations, however, had turned to Luco's servile treatment of Pip, who had been Luco's "friend" for three decades. Randall had encouraged Pip—as recently as that very morning over the phone—to come out from Luco's shadow. It was clear Pip was struggling with painful memories and difficult decisions.

"Pip?" Luco called from outside.

Pip swung around, avoiding Randall's gaze. "Yes?"

"What was that, a nine?"

"A Llama—9mm, yes."

"Gimme a box."

Pip pulled a box from a cubby under the armrest and handed it to him. Luco tossed it down the embankment. When it hit the ground, bullets scattered everywhere. He pointed at the small treasure he was leaving, nodded at the boys, and climbed back into the limo.

He scowled at Randall's cigarette and said, "Father, *please.*"

Randall pulled deeply on the smoke and then tossed it out the door, into the dirt.

Luco shut the door. To his driver he said, "Let's move it, Tullio." He showed Pip a big grin. "Graduation day for the rock throwers!"

Pip nodded ambivalently. As they rode away, Randall craned to look out the dark glass. The first of the boys was just breaking cover and running toward Luco's gift. The others followed, then the limo arced away between two hills, and the boys disappeared from view.

Luco crossed a leg and began wiping the dust off his shoe with a handkerchief, smiling smugly.

"One of those boys is going to shoot you dead," Randall said.

The smile faded. Luco's eyes caught Randall's, and the old man chuckled dryly.

"No, Luco, that is not a prophecy. Only sarcasm."

"Your jokes aren't funny."

"Nor are yours," he said. "You are destined for bigger things. Why piddle with juvenile pranks?" His tone was fatherly.

Luco shrugged. "Amusement." He turned to Pip. "Maybe we should take the Mevo Modi'in road home." He grinned. "I hear Route 1 just got more dangerous."

He snapped the handkerchief at his clean shoe, then switched legs and started wiping its mate. After a few breaths, he said, "So, Father, how long can you stay this time?"

"I fly out this evening."

Concern flashed across Luco's face. "What about . . . ?"

"I'll return for the Gathering, never fear." Father Randall took a swig of wine. He closed his eyes and put his head back. It was going to be a long week.

11

Two years ago, Brady would have skipped the 6:40 flight out of Dulles to Colorado Springs and taken the next one. The FBI required him to wear his pistol whenever on duty, which included Bureau-related travel. The Federal Aviation Administration understood the need for certain law enforcement officers (LEOs in cop-talk) to carry weapons on board and accommodated that need—provided the LEO completed an FAA class on the subject and adhered to strict guidelines. One of the guidelines prohibited "boarding an aircraft armed within eight hours of consuming alcohol." Best Brady could figure, he'd stopped drinking—the term *passed out* never occurred to him—around midnight. Despite feeling sober and alert, technically he violated a federal law when he boarded at 6:25 a.m. Technically.

He envied Alicia's expediency. She never let something as trivial as the law hinder her pursuit of a felon. If the irony of that ever bothered her, she kept it to herself. Certainly, she wouldn't kill without provocation or steal for her own gain. Stomping on the civil rights of a perp was, however, less problematic. So was conveniently forgetting protocol, the accumulation of which Alicia thought of as weights on her ankles in the race for justice—and of which Brady thought of as a wall that delineated cop from crook.

He had never made a show of following proper procedure or pointed out when others didn't; he'd done his puritanical best silently, believing that acts of virtue were done for oneself or for God, not for others.

Brady had always been the kind of person who paid separately at hotels for in-room movies, though they were always as innocuous as, say, *The Lord of the Rings* or *Remember the Titans*, so they wouldn't be charged to his

Bureau MasterCard. He wondered now why he'd been so fastidious. Since Karen's death, he'd found himself increasingly willing to initiate or overlook lapses in protocol. While he had never believed good behavior should earn him special consideration in the blessings department, he had thought it should count for something when it came time for the Big Guy to pick who got needlessly slaughtered by a drunk driver and whose life would be ripped apart by the event.

The realization that bad things happen to good people did not give him a feeling of being a kindred spirit to fellow sanctimonious saps as much as it got him thinking the opposite was equally true: good things happen to bad people. Not that white lies and small vices made people bad, but he had become aware of how many of his colleagues—mostly hardworking, decent agents with excellent reputations for closing cases—did let the government pick up the tab for their hotel movies and room service, and did stretch truths to secure search warrants, and did apply intimidation tactics to un-cooperative witnesses. Essentially, they breached all sorts of ethical, legal, and moral principles, to varying degrees. Some claimed that in the current climate of "criminal rights," it was the only way to get bad people, truly bad people, off the streets.

And nailing bad guys was something he yearned to do now, even more than before. Aside from time with Zach, helping put bad guys away was the only balm he'd found to soothe his anguished soul. If he had come to view his life as a vandalized, dilapidated house with ripped-apart furnishings and graffitied walls, locking up a perp felt like repairing a smashed figurine and placing it back on a shelf. And if bending a rule or two—or more impor-tant, developing an *attitude* that breaking rules in the name of expediency or tough-mindedness—got the job done, then that was for him.

The passenger on his right, a broad-shouldered business type, attacked the morning's *Wall Street Journal* with aggressive eyes and furiously page-turning hands, as though fully expecting to find personal libels hidden among the text and tables. To facilitate his search, Mr. Business annexed the airspace in front of Brady's face, snapping the paper wide to scan its columns. Brady nudged the hand away. The man mumbled an apology and then a few minutes later snapped the hand back with the turn of a page.

A wisp of an elderly woman occupied the seat to his left. She apparently understood air travel to be a grand opportunity to socialize—if socializing meant telling a complete stranger every imaginable detail of her life. Whatever good his metabolism and four Tylenols were doing to alleviate the symptoms of his foolish minibinge last night, this woman effectively counteracted them.

"Ma'am?" Brady said finally, after the plane had leveled off at thirty-five thousand feet.

Her history droned on unabated.

"Ma'am?" More firmly.

She paused, seeming surprised to find a live person looking at her.

"I'm sorry, but I really have to do some work." He bent to retrieve a three-ring binder and a legal pad from the soft-sided documents case stashed under the seat in front of him.

Her monologue clicked on again, picking up midsentence, precisely where Brady had stopped her. He sighed and decided she wouldn't notice he had moved on to his own affairs, or care if she did notice.

He lowered the drop-down tray in front of him and centered the pad of paper on it. The binder went on top of the paper; he wasn't ready to open it yet. Instead, he sat with his fingers resting lightly on the front cover.

Through the bottom opening of the binder, he could see three yellow dividers. They separated the documents into four sections, one for each of the presumed Pelletier killings, not including last night's. The locals for each case had faxed the paperwork and some of the crime scene photos to the Bureau only yesterday, after some cajoling by John Gilbreath, head of the laboratory and training divisions. Brady had made copies for the trip to Colorado.

Among the reports, interview transcriptions, and crime scene sketches were photocopied death shots—snapshots of the victims in graphic, bloody detail. As part of their training, LEOs, from county sheriff deputies to FBI agents, view dozens if not hundreds of death shots. The exposure is calculated not only to sharpen their investigative skills, to teach them, for instance, how to read the truth in blood splatters and to recognize suicides that aren't suicides, but also to desensitize them to the extreme horror of violent physical trauma. Vomiting officers can wreak havoc on crime scenes, and investigators can hardly reconstruct the events of a death from bodily wreckage when the sight of it makes them nauseated and light-headed. The extent of violence people inflict on others and themselves cannot be exaggerated: faces sheared off by shotgun blasts, leaving hanging gristle and gore-filled sinuses, eye sockets, and throats; eviscerated bodies that are nothing more than hollowed-out husks; dismembered victims bagged and buried.

In light of other mutilations he'd seen, decapitation didn't seem so hideous. Still, the thought of it made his stomach roll. There was something about its finality that rattled his mind. Throughout history, people have survived horrendous assaults. They've recovered from gunshots to every conceivable body part. They've lived through amputations and brutal slashes. Stabbings, impalements, electric shocks, chokings, flayings, poisonings, beatings, burns, bites, falls.

But never decapitation. It left no hope, no chance for survival. Which was probably the reason this killer chose it. Beheading was a more gruesome version of popping two slugs into the skull, the coup de grâce favored by mobsters and despots.

It was Brady's job to bear witness to these crimes, to study their aftermath, and to construct an image of the person who could commit such atrocities. On his best days, he felt like a gallant knight blazing a trail through hell so that others would not have to. When he was down, and the murders were particularly repugnant, he was a voyeur in an alternate world where everything was the opposite of what it should be. Birth, vibrancy, hope, life, love, beauty—he dwelt in the exact converse of these. Most days, his view of his job fell somewhere between.

With a sigh, Brady lifted the binder. It came to him that it was lighter than it ought to be, that somehow it should bear the weight of the lost lives it represented. Drawing it close to his chest, making sure its contents were hidden from the woman (the newspaper was wall enough on the other side), he cracked it open.

12

Under Jerusalem

L uco Scaramuzzi took a deep breath and tried not to visualize the people on the opposite side of the massive conference table as a big pile of corpses. As much as he'd like to facilitate that vision, he needed them. He needed their money, their power. For now.

Bare bulbs over their chairs in the dark room made their faces appear disembodied, hovering above the table's edge like Halloween masks hung from fishing line. It was an altogether eerie sight, which perfectly complemented both the locale and the business at hand.

They occupied an octagonal chamber sixty feet below the streets of the Christian Quarter in Jerusalem's Old City. The room was part of an underground complex that had been appropriated and modified by various occupying governments for three millennia. For the last few hundred years, it had remained sealed off and forgotten by the surface world. Then, twenty-three years ago, workers broke through a wall in the basement of the Latin Seminary and Patriarchate, revealing an ancient water tunnel. This tunnel sloped down into a vast labyrinth of tunnels, catacombs, caverns, and rooms. Situated just inside the Old City wall between Jaffa Gate and New Gate, the discovery was well away from the famous Hasmonean Tunnels, Tsidkiyahu Cave, and Jerusalem's other known subterranean structures. No one suspected its existence, and the quick thinking of a man who was at the time the rector of the school ensured its secrecy. He made some calls, collected a handsome finder's fee, and granted to what he thought of as an *organizzazione oscura*—a shadowy organization— exclusive access to the entrance. The workers were paid off (though one tale had them all murdered). New workmen installed an iron door at the threshold and constructed a separate basement entrance and walls that gave an element of privacy to those who entered and left the regions below.

Like Luco. And the twelve men and women he faced across the table.

Around them, columns dimly caught slivers of light along their fluted lengths; they stood at regular intervals along the perimeter and marked out the room's dimensions. Eighty feet across, it resembled the ancient tomb of a king more than the barracks it had once been. The surface of its stone walls had crumbled, forming a concave ramp of sediment between floor and wall. The columns supported capitals and entablature whose ornate carvings of vines and faces had worn into bumps and grooves more closely approximating scar tissue. Stone beams arched up to meet at the apex of a high domed ceiling, now invisible in the gloom.

The bulbs had been strung from pillar to opposing pillar. They cast a faint illumination on the flawlessly constructed cherrywood table, which seemed as incongruous with its surroundings as a Krugerrand in the hand of a junkie.

Luco was seated in one of twenty matching chairs widely spaced around the table. The eight men and four women seated opposite him constituted the governing body of an organization euphemistically called the Watchers. Its actual name was ancient and heavy on the tongue; few said it, or even knew it, in this age. Most of these directors had followed their fathers or mothers into their current positions, both here and in the wider world. A few had been recruited to combat attrition through barrenness, disloyalty, political or financial misfortune, or premature death leaving children too young to assume the mantle of responsibility. Every director was wealthy and powerful—equals among the world's elite.

Having experienced lifelong privilege and preordained responsibilities, their distinct personalities had been shaped primarily by pedigree and nationality rather than by the average person's complex blending of desires hard-won and desires never to be. When any passion can be easily and immediately satiated, the experiences that stir even the most exhilarating emotions in humankind—love, accomplishment, adventure—soon take their place among common things. Consequently, the emotion that defined each of them was boredom.

Until Luco had entered their lives. He was everything they had dreamed about and hoped for, and like nothing they had ever seen. When he thought about his effect on them, a phrase came to mind, a bit of teenage ego-centricity—*I rock their world!* Corny, yes, but perfect for Luco in regard to these aristocrats whose worlds had not been rocked since the shock of leaving the birth canal.

A man seated directly across from Luco was conferring quietly with his colleagues. This was Koji Arakawa, heir to a real estate fortune, super-intendent of this committee's muscular financial arm, and de facto leader of the Watchers. Even in the chamber's unflattering light, his regal good looks were undeniable, and Luco knew him to be quick-witted and intelligent. It was easy to imagine him receiving subjects and issuing proclamations at his company's Tokyo headquarters, an Asian Solomon with the world at his feet. If Luco could admire any of these people—these scavengers who waited to pick the bones he left on his plate, who pretended to guide him, guard him, grow him, but who kept their talons in what was rightfully his—if any engendered his admiration, it would be Arakawa. Always stoic, he displayed a steely resolve the others could only mimic.

Luco lifted a bottle of Daggio springwater to his lips and drained half of it. When he returned it to the table, Arakawa was looking at him. He possessed a voice as noble as his appearance.

"Luco," he said kindly, "we are unsure of what it is you want."

"Everything," Luco said.

"What do you mean, 'everything'?" asked Niklas Hüber in a sharp Teutonic accent. On *everything*, he slapped the table, as if smashing a bug. He was a German telecommunications magnate and Luco's fiercest detractor. He had fat black caterpillars for eyebrows, an explosion of silver hair, and the grim face of an Edvard Munch painting.

Luco kept a passive demeanor as he studied the stern countenance of his adversary.

If looks could kill . . .

The others too were waiting for a response. All except his countryman Donato Benini. Good ol' Donato. Luco's most ardent supporter, almost a fan. His ever-present grin had dimmed with embarrassment, perhaps shame, over Hüber's ill manner.

Donato sat at one point of the crescent of people on the other side of the table, Niklas at the other point. Through what Luco was sure was an unconscious polarization process, the Watchers had adjusted their seating positions over time, so that moving right from Donato, watcher by watcher, trust in Luco and enthusiasm for his plans gradually waned, culminating with Hüber's utter contempt.

It was Luco's goal to stabilize in his favor this spectrum of opinions, to turn the others' doubt into Donato's fawning conviction.

"Everything," he said again and shrugged. "The bank accounts, real estate holdings, securities; access to the politicians, media barons, investors; control of the technicians, clerics, assassins . . . everything."

"You are mad!" shot Hüber, squashing another bug with his palm.

The lot of them began clamoring in shock and indignation, some at Luco's words, some at Hüber's.

Arakawa alone held his tongue. He met Luco's gaze, and a smile creased his lips. Luco found the man's expression impossible to decipher. It could be saying, "How did we end up in the company of such fools?" Or just as possibly, "You're in trouble now."

After a moment, he quieted the others. To Luco, he said, "You do realize we have a plan for you, a timetable?"

"Your timetable isn't mine."

"Do you have some information that indicates we are moving too slowly?"

"I know it . . . *here*." Luco touched his chest.

A beautiful woman in her forties, wearing a silk sari in shades of purple, held out a hand as if to offer something. "Mr. Scaramuzzi," she said. "We have already given you so much. Your personal income alone—"

"Princess Vajra Kumar," Luco interrupted, bowing his head, "excuse me. I realize I am somewhat wealthy and wield a small measure of political power—"

"You have the Italian prime minister's ear," interjected Hüber. He seemed ready to launch into some tirade, but Luco spoke first.

"As an ambassador, yes. Still, I feel that I am being held back, that the prophecies are being . . . hindered."

Their disturbance showed in their mouths. A few parted in astonishment, but most tightened in anger. Even ultrapoised Arakawa managed a frown.

In most institutional settings, it would be the reference to prophecies that provoked high emotions. But the Watchers was a theocratic organization, immersed in concepts alien to Harvard Business School—though three of the people in attendance held graduate degrees from that esteemed academy.

No, it was in fact the suggestion that they were *impeding* prophecy's fulfillment that stirred them. It was the organization's mandate to recognize, expedite, and exploit certain prophecies. And here was Luco Scaramuzzi, essentially accusing them of dereliction of duty.

Niklas Hüber snapped his attention toward Arakawa. His eyes were bulging; his face had taken on the hue of a spanked bottom. Luco smiled at the thought.

Hüber began, "I do not think—"

Without turning away from Luco, Arakawa stopped him with a raised hand.

"If you can't have *everything*, what specifically are you after?" asked Arakawa.

"I'll start with Italy."

The regal Japanese man held Luco's gaze, then looked at each of the others in turn.

"It's time," Luco added.

For a moment Arakawa appeared to study the empty water glass before him. Then he said, "Luco, would you give us a few minutes to discuss this among ourselves, please?"

Luco nodded. "Of course." He rose and walked away from the table, into the darkness of the chamber. He felt their lingering eyes. With his tailored clothes and the slightest hint of a swagger, he knew he looked great.

Just as he had hired behavioral scientists to figure *them* out, he had contracted image consultants to figure *him* out, or at least to make his appearance as impressionable as his words and actions. They had perfected his
wardrobe, hairstyle, and body language to convey strength and leadership.
Slowly—sometimes too slowly for his liking—he was becoming the man the
world would expect him to be.

At the wall, he turned to survey his board of directors—his inquisitors.
Leaning toward Arakawa's central position, they whispered and gesticulated,
pointing out one another's errant logic. He raised a finger to his ear, as though
to flick out an irritant, and clicked on a nearly invisible earpiece. Instantly
their overlapping whispers came to him.

". . . this is too soon!"

"It has always been our intention, the *sole* intention of this organization,
going back—"

"Nevertheless, I'm still not convinced . . ."

He'd had ultrasensitive minimicrophones wired into the strand of bulbs
above that side of the table. He was able to attribute the voices to their owners either through familiarity or by watching the movements of their lips.
The tenor of the conversation was disappointing, if not surprising. They
would tell him they needed evidence, some sort of sign it was time for him
to reach beyond his present station. Signs were not what they actually
wanted, however. They wanted to know *for sure* that he was who he said he
was, the one they had been awaiting. Their faith in him had brought him
this far, but the next step, the step he had just pushed for, was the event horizon, beyond which there was no turning back.

He had prepared for this. A one-two punch that was certain to quash
their doubts. Maybe not Hüber's—but the others would be so convinced
they would force Hüber to go along. Luco would present the first piece as he
had all the other evidence, laid out before them, vetted by their own experts.
But this one was strong, perhaps the strongest yet. The second piece was his
masterwork, designed for maximum impact. At that very moment, it was in
motion in the United States—thanks to Arjan's tactical brilliance and the
Norseman's homicidal prowess. He would not bring it to the Watchers.
They would uncover it themselves, and therein lay its power to convince.

Prodded by his own impatience, he started for the chamber's arched exit. No door, just a single threshold into a corridor. Guards waited with lamps somewhere out there, but so distant or around so many bends, the corridor may as well have been filled with dense black smoke. Through his earpiece, he heard someone whisper, "Where's he going?" before Arakawa called out, "Luco?" The raised voice, echoing through the electronics as well as the room's air, pulsed into his skull. He reached up and turned off the earbud.

"Luco?"

Without turning, he raised his index finger so they would see it. A moment later, he stepped into the corridor, and the blackness engulfed him.

13

Aside from the killer's MO, nothing readily linked the Pelletier victims. The first, Joseph Johnson, was a forty-six-year-old father of five in Ogden, Utah. An accounting prof at Weber State University. Caucasian. The investigator's notes indicated that Mr. Johnson was in fit health, an avid skier, active in the Mormon Church. Born in Ramstein, Germany, where his father was stationed with the Eighty-sixth Airlift Wing, he'd moved to Utah at the age of eleven. Lived on Hill Air Force Base for three years, then moved off base into the neighboring town of Layton when his father retired. He was a Weber State alum, graduating with a BS twenty-four years ago. Overall, his life had been uneventful. At least it seemed so to an outsider reviewing a hastily compiled biography.

On the pad in front of him, Brady jotted a line of particulars about Joseph Johnson's life. On his right, Mr. Business was still engrossed in the *Journal.* On his left, the elderly woman was still engrossed in herself. He turned to the next section.

Vic number two was William Bell, a twenty-four-year-old plumber's assistant in Moab. Never married. Caucasian. Graduated from Grand Country High School with a low-C average. No college or trade school. Native of the town in which he died. Plenty of citations for public drunkenness and fighting, according to the notes.

Vic number three: Jessica Hampton in Orem. Forty. Housewife. Married to the same man for twenty-two years, a mortgage broker. Son and daughter in high school.

Strike off gender as a victim criterion.

What made the killer choose you? Brady thought, looking at a blowup of Jessica Hampton's driver's license photo. It showed a brunette with floppy curls cut above the shoulders. Toothy grin, smiling eyes. Slightly overweight, if the apple-cheeked motif continued into her body. Nice-looking lady, and not a bad photo for a DMV shot. He knew the next page contained snaps of the woman at the crime scene, death shots. He didn't want to see them, not now, and flipped to the next section.

For the fourth victim, the killer had crossed over into Colorado. Big mistake. Once the lab techs found a definitive link between at least one of the Utah killings with one from Colorado, the FBI's jurisdiction would be established and the Bureau would swoop down en masse. Brady smiled to himself. Contrary to popular belief, the FBI never "takes over" an investigation. Rather, it coordinates the efforts of local investigators and brings in laboratory, surveillance, and investigative assistance no other law enforcement agency in the world can match. Sometimes, locals needed reminding about the Bureau's resources and its jurisdictional right to bring them to bear. Whether this constituted assistance or bullying was a matter of semantics.

Brady liked to think criminals who brought the FBI down upon themselves had screwed up big-time. Truth was, the type of criminal who'd do that usually didn't care. In fact, many relished the idea of drawing federal attention. Who wanted to play a high-risk game with local yokels? Bring in the big guns. "Big guns"—that's how the general public, and its criminal subgroup, perceived the FBI. Credit for that image went to filmmakers, whose scripts required Bureau approval if they wanted Bureau cooperation, and to the staff spin doctors who trumpeted the agency's triumphs and downplayed its failures. And thanks as well, Brady reminded himself, to the organization's own high standards and record of success. Ten thousand agents, 13,000 support staff, $3 billion budget. It was no wonder they caught their man. But the status also intrigued demented individuals with catch-me-if-you-can death wishes.

The vic in Ft. Collins, Colorado, was a thirty-three-year-old man named Daniel Fears. High school phys ed teacher, a coach. Divorced, one daughter. African-American.

Though most serial killers murdered within their own race, that wasn't always the case. Brady wasn't sure they were dealing with a serial killer anyway; his geographic movement and short time between kills pointed to a spree killer—no difference to his victims, major difference in creating a strategy to catch him.

The detective on Fears's case had noted he collected coins, worked out at a gym three times a week, and was an elder at First Baptist Church.

Hmm. Joseph Johnson had been active in his church. Different denominations. There was no mention of Jessica Hampton's beliefs. If William Bell had been a churchgoer, his numerous citations indicated the sermons had not penetrated very deeply.

No, whatever similarity the killer saw in each victim, it wasn't apparent. Their ages were as broadly placed as their geographic locations. So were their positions on the socioeconomic ladder and their levels of education. Not gender. Not race. Ogden was a college town. So was Ft. Collins. He didn't know about Moab or Orem. He made a note on the legal pad to find out.

As disparate as the victims were, the killer's MO had not varied. Decapitation. Each head had been placed away from the body, but otherwise there was no posing—the killer had left the bodies where they had fallen. Fangs had pierced the skin, muscles, and ligatures of the hands, wrists, and forearms of each vic. Jessica Hampton's right hand had been nearly severed. On two bodies—Joseph Johnson's and Daniel Fears's—the coroners had found deep animal bites around the ankles and feet as well. Ogden's lab had determined that fur found at the scene came from a wolf-dog hybrid, at least two different animals. The aggressive animals were now illegal in about thirty states; if the killer was using these creatures to restrain his victims, he must live in a state that still allowed wolf-hybrid ownership. Or else he lived in a remote area. A person couldn't keep these dogs a secret in an urban or suburban setting.

All the victims were killed at home. Had he already known where to find his targets? Did he have their addresses? Or had he been cruising for random targets and spotted them outside, making his choice then and there? Maybe he had selected them someplace else, a grocery store or gas station, perhaps, and followed them home.

Brady jotted another note: "Out earlier in the day? Where?"

He closed the binder and closed his eyes. Had his brain not been pickled when Alicia called, he would have asked her about last night's victim. Awful as it sounded, more victims meant a better chance at identifying a pattern. No matter how obscure or irrational, there was always something the victims of a single killer had in common. This commonality often became the key in predicting the next target or locale and maybe—a *slim* maybe—preventing the next killing.

With the steady drone of the plane's engines in his ears and a few scant hours of alcohol-addled sleep pressing on his consciousness, Brady drifted off.

Surprisingly, what danced in his head were not visions of flying skulls or maniacal ax-wielding fiends. No carved cadavers or disembodied screams in fields of blackness. He dreamed of his wife and son: Zach rolled down a grassy hill as Karen laughingly caressed Brady's cheek with a daisy. A baby inside her made her belly big, and his fingers moved over the tight skin with the same delicateness as the petals on his face. He realized, in that semi-informed way of dreams, that she was pregnant with a child they never had. They looked at each other with something beyond joy. Their laughter mingled and swirled with colors as it rose into the sky.

When the flight attendant gently shook him awake, he could still feel the petal on his cheek. Touching it, he found a tear.

14

When Luco reappeared in the chamber's threshold, the disembodied faces of the Watchers rotated toward him. He stopped and turned back. Father Randall emerged from the corridor's lightlessness into the pale illumination of the chamber's bare bulbs. As he shuffled past, Luco pointed to a chair on the unoccupied side of the table.

"Right there, Father, please."

Randall's attention was on the stone floor three feet in front of him, and Luco wondered if he could see his pointing hand. When the old man angled in the correct direction, Luco again looked back into the corridor.

An echoing *clop . . . clop . . . clop* preceded Pip's appearance. *Clop . . . clop . . . clop.* Getting louder. Finally, the faint image of a cardboard box floated into view, the fingers of two hands gripping its bottom corners. Then the possessor of both the box and the *clop* stepped through the threshold and into the light. Luco smiled. Like his leg, Pip's face had barely grown out of childhood, though he was Luco's age. Only the most callous hearts did not take an instant liking to him, with his smooth skin, big brown eyes, thin eyebrows, and small nose.

Pip's next step was silent, but every time his left foot came down, it made that awful hollow-horseshoe noise, and his body leaned way over in that direction. For years, Luco had offered to pay for a prosthetic foot or elevated orthopedic shoe or surgery . . . whatever it took to make Pip more comfortable. Pip always refused, opting instead for homemade remedies: paperback books, plastic videotape boxes, blocks of wood taped, tied, or glued to the bottom of his shoe.

He was halfway to the table when Luco took the box from him.

"Thank you, Pip," he said.

Pip nodded and took in the stares of the men and women at the table. He brushed his hair off his forehead, seemed about to say something, and then lowered his head and left, his noisy gait trailing behind him like strong cologne.

Luco set the box full of notepaper and photocopied manuscripts on the seat next to Randall and pushed it closer to him. He moved to Randall's other side and sat in his customary chair.

"You all know Father Randall," he said. "He has uncovered something that *should*"—he paused, stressing the suggestion—"alleviate any doubts you may have."

Randall raised his head. "Gentlemen . . . and ladies," he said in a hardy baritone completely at odds with his wispy body. He infused the word *ladies* with a lilt and a nod; for a fraction of a second he could have been a schoolboy asking for his first dance. "Good to see you all again."

The Watchers nodded or mumbled their greetings, but Randall had already turned away to rummage through his papers.

To Luco, the old man seemed as ancient as the papyrus he was endlessly poring over. His skin even resembled the stuff: heavily creased, dry and delicate, stained by time. His lips had narrowed and faded to flesh-tone, rendering his mouth invisible when closed. His nose was too large, his cheeks too hollow, his hair too gone—but the fire in his eyes instantly blinded observers to those imperfections. They were Russian blue and saw everything. They'd been seeing everything, in fact, for a long, long time. Wisdom ran deep in those eyes, as did intrigue and humor and compassion. Something about them made you appreciate the attention, as if they were capable of conferring some great knowledge upon whoever fell within their purview.

Even Luco, impervious to masculine allure despite exuding it so effortlessly himself, found turning from Randall's gaze a painful experience. Mostly, though, he envied its enchantment. His own charm was an amalgam of expressions, wit, and aura. Randall's eyes could captivate, and so manipulate, all by themselves. Luco thought, *The old coot must have been a sexual dynamo in his day, priest or not.*

A bulb above him illuminated Randall's gleaming head, making what little silver hair he had appear even more diaphanous, as though his scalp were smoldering. His clothes—charcoal shirtsleeves, black pants—floated about him, a size too big. The material hung over his bony shoulders like drapery. From the sleeves jutted the thinnest of speckled arms, hairless, but host to magnificently interesting hands. Gaunt, with yellowed nails and brown nicotine stains, they were big hands with long fingers—piano fingers, Luco's aunt would have called them—and they fluttered like doves when he spoke, dancing to the cadence of his words. But Randall wasn't talking, so the hands stayed down, shuffling papers.

He said, "Ahhhh"—drawing it out the way one would after a splash of cold water on a blistering day—and pulled a sheaf of papers from the box.

Luco caught a glimpse of the minuscule handwriting covering the pages from edge to edge. He wondered how Randall hoped to find a note again once it was relegated to the thousands of identical lines he scribbled every day.

Randall fanned the notes out on the table. His head moved back and forth as he read. Suddenly, he laughed robustly. With a look, he invited the Watchers, then Luco to join in his merriment. Their reticence did not diminish the joy in his eyes or his openmouthed smile.

What an odd duck, Luco thought. Passionate and excitable, yet deliberate and reserved. Not so odd, really. Focused. Fervent about things that mattered to him, apathetic about everything else. Luco understood that; he was like that himself. Only *his* passions encompassed a world of pleasures; Randall's were limited to a few choice studies—each of which served Luco quite nicely.

Now that was an understatement. He could only imagine where he'd be without Randall's work. Back in Rome, likely. At *Centro di Psicoterapia Cognitiva,* the loony bin, playing Old Maid with God and Napoleon.

"Now!" Randall proclaimed. "Gregory the Great's *Moralia* . . ."

Luco put a hand on his arm. "One sec, Father." To the other twelve, he said, "Your own scholars have already reviewed this prophecy."

"John Stapleton knows about this?" asked Niklas Hüber, skeptical.

"Oh, yes," answered Father Randall. "I have . . ." He stuck his hand into the box, and this time it immediately returned, clutching several single sheets. "I have his statement right here, concurring with my conclusions.

And one from Dr. Noyce. And Professor Inglehook." He dropped each letter on the table as he announced its writer.

"We should like copies, if you please." This from Tirunih Wodajo, a tall Ethiopian seated beside Hüber.

Randall patted the side of the box. "I have bound copies of my report, supporting documents, and these concurrences."

Several Watchers nodded appreciatively.

See, not so odd at all. Luco felt like hugging the old man. He always came through.

"Now!" Randall proclaimed once more. And starting with an incidental notation made in the margin of a manuscript by Gregory the Great in the year AD 598, he began a detailed accounting of the steps through ancient writings that ultimately brought him to this latest discovery. Pantomiming the retrieving, opening, and scrutiny of great codices, the unrolling of precious scrolls, the sneaking of glimpses at forbidden manuscripts, he described this arduous journey—with side comments about bibliotics and methods of exegesis.

Listening to Randall's impassioned recitation was excruciating. Randall always did it this way, as though a conclusion could not be appreciated without first comprehending the processes that derived it.

At last he fell silent. His eyes darted from one floating face to another, expecting a word of praise or a question or at least a startled expression. When nothing responsive materialized, Koji Arakawa spoke up.

"I'm sorry, Father Randall," he said. "I'm afraid you've spoken over our heads. Could you tell us again, in layman's terms, what the prophecy is?"

Randall lowered his head and closed his eyes. Finally, he leaned back, drew in a deep breath, and said, "As a young boy, the Son of Perdition will murder, rather I should say, *will have murdered*"—he looked at Luco; *a great touch*, Luco thought—"his mother."

That got the response he'd been looking for. Gasps and questions and calls for order. Many of the stares coming across the table fell not on Randall but on Luco. They all knew his history. A dark incident from his boyhood, long buried until the thorough background investigation they had initiated disinterred it, had now become . . . something else, something extraordinary.

Luco could not help but smile. He had them.

With a sharp sound still ringing in her ears, Alicia Wagner woke. Her eyes snapped open, and her face came off the mattress. She was lying on her stomach in the bed she had crawled into at six that morning. The digital clock on the bedside table told her it was 10:27. Four and a half hours of sleep, if you could call the restlessness she had just experienced sleep. A sheet, moist with perspiration, entwined her torso like a boa constrictor. Her skin was clammy. The pillows and heavy hotel covers had fled the arena of her nightmares sometime during the morning. She turned her stiff neck toward the window. Light was stealing through the edges of closed curtains.

Bam! Bam! Bam!

She nearly flipped off the bed. Someone was knocking at the door. Probably had been knocking for some time.

"What?" she tried to say, but her throat was too parched to make more than a raspy noise. She grabbed a quarter-filled glass of water off the table, swallowed painfully, and called out: "What is it!"

Loud mumbling answered her.

"Oh, for heaven's sake." She rolled off the bed, got a foot tangled in the clothes strewn on the floor, and stumbled for the door.

The peephole framed the distorted face of Brady Moore. He had not landed by the time she had finished at the crime scene, loaded up her equipment, and headed for a hotel, so she had left a message on his cell phone, letting him know her hotel and room number. He was looking down the corridor one way, then the other. He squinted at the peephole, wiggled his tie, checked his watch.

"Hold on a sec," she said.

The woman staring out at her from the bathroom mirror was not her, no way. That woman had Alicia's blond hair, but Alicia wore it shoulder-length, styled back away from her face. This other's hair was sticking out in spiky clumps, with one side perfectly flat and rising above her head a good four inches, the other side attacking her face with fingerlike protrusions. Her eyes were big and green, like Alicia's—and not too bloodshot, she noticed. The bluish coloration under them, however, was a fashion Alicia never fancied. Too Goth.

"Ohhh," she moaned and began running her fingers through her hair. She had never been very concerned with appearances, but this was ridiculous. After fifteen frustrating seconds, she realized a brush was right before her on the counter. She reached for it, then stopped. "Oh, forget it." She supposed putting on something other than the panties she'd slept in was the minimum required of her. She yanked the fluffy white hotel robe off the back of the bathroom door, cinched the belt tight around her waist, and pulled open the door.

He looked perfect. Even needing a shave and with a trace of red in his eyes, he could have played an FBI agent in the movies. She instantly regretted not taking more time to spruce up.

He gave her a halfhearted smile. She'd learned that was about the best he was capable of. Except around his son. The boy was the only thing she'd seen in the year they'd worked together that got Brady's happy meter above "okay."

"Good morning, sunshine," he said flatly. He made no attempt to enter the room.

"What took you?" She pulled the robe tighter, making her muscles taut as she did, stretching.

"First flight out was 6:40. How 'bout I meet you in the café downstairs, grab some breakfast?"

She shook her head and looked over her shoulder into the room. The CSD cases were on the floor at the foot of the bed. "I'll order room service. I want to review the CSD data from last night."

"How'd it go?"

Thinking about it—the technology, not the victim—made her smile.

She felt the last vestiges of grogginess fall away. "Good . . . great, really." She shrugged. "Lead Dee's a crotchety coot, didn't like the Bureau stepping in, didn't like my gender, and didn't like me thinking I was going to tell him how to process his crime scene."

"So did you?" Brady asked. He stuck his hands in his pockets, looking casual and comfortable standing in the hotel corridor.

"Oh, yeah. You should have seen him. After going through the scene with him and a tech, I showed him the POA. He was just about stammering with excitement." She laughed. "I spread the floor plan out on the hood of his car and started explaining the symbols—suspicious latents, blood spatter, a couple heel scuffs, what I'm pretty sure was dog hair—and this guy was like 'Ooooh, ahhhh.'"

Brady smiled appreciatively, and she was reminded of the disparity between his relative dapperness and her own dishevelment.

"Look, I gotta make myself presentable. Come back in half an hour."

He took in her robe, her hair. "I think you're going to need more time than that."

"Ha-ha."

"I'm down the hall, in 422." He cocked his head in the direction he meant. "Give me a ring when you're ready."

She shut the door and pressed her back against it. Brady was a handsome man. Not movie-star handsome, but he could hold his own in a room full of former high school studs and the neighborhood hunks, whom housewives clucked about while stitching patches into a quilt or burning cookies for a school bake sale or whatever it was housewives did when they gathered. She wasn't sure if his stoicism added to or detracted from his charm. He could be either mysteriously brooding or depressingly sulky. His usually successful efforts at humor—which Alicia interpreted as his way of either deflecting scrutiny or keeping others from being sucked into his void of depression—made his melancholy appear more like a personality trait than an emotional problem.

There was also something utterly romantic about his sadness. His wife had died, what, a year and a half ago? And still, Alicia got the sense that if it weren't for the sake of his son, Brady would plunge into that eternal darkness after her. In a heartbeat. He must have really loved her. Alicia knew couples who had claimed to have found their life mate but who insisted that if one died the other should try to find love again; each wanted only for the other to be happy. Alicia suspected it was all garbage. In reality, everyone wanted to be irreplaceable. Distill that desire to its core, and you'd behold a subconscious emotional death wish for your spouse; if you died, you wanted your lover's heart to break so completely, nothing could ever grow there again. After all, how deep were all the professions of undying love if they could be shifted to another? What we all yearned for, Alicia decided, was a love so deep it could never reach the surface again.

Unpleasant. Downright selfish. But true. And extremely romantic.

Ironic too. Because someone who could love that deeply was very attractive to someone who desired to be loved that deeply.

Alicia shook her head. What was she thinking? Romance with Brady? She pursed her lips. Okay, she'd thought about it before, once or twice. Female colleagues at the Bureau had described the old Brady to her. They'd used phrases like "full of life" and "spark in his step." That was a cool Brady. Could he be like that again? If he could, would it negate the very romanticism Alicia found so appealing?

Maybe she was different. Could she draw him up from the depths without the very act proving he wasn't so far down to begin with? Then down he would go again, this time weighted with love for *her*.

Aaaahhhhh! her mind screamed. *I must really be tired.* Brady was Brady. Her partner. Good looking but awfully moody. Nice guy but too selfish to understand how much of a bummer he could be. *Besides, I'm not in the market. I'm not! Work is my lover, my spouse. That's the way it has to be for now . . .*

Her hand rose and felt the hair exploding from her head. She laughed out loud, short and humorless. Even if she thought of Brady only as the partner he was, she didn't want him holding in his head an image of her as a disheveled cow. Well, that wasn't true. She knew that if Brady was just some other guy, she wouldn't care less what image of her he possessed. Just get the job done.

She pushed away from the door. *Get your head on straight, Alicia,* she thought. *You got work to do, girl. No time for daydreams, especially about . . . about* that. She padded into the bathroom, thinking she'd keep the shower cold today. Very cold.

16

Outside the Old City walls, in the Hasidic neighborhood of Me'a She'arim, boys played in the streets, their hands continually rising to make sure their *kippots* had not slipped from their heads. Men mingled in small groups or sat on benches reading *saddur* prayer books. Their uniformly long beards could have made them Haight-Ashbury princes or ZZ Top fanatics. They appeared almost regal in crisp black suits—black to symbolize the sect's mourning of the destruction of King Solomon's temple in AD 70—but no neckties, because they believed the garment represented the cross of Christ. Women were dressed more contemporarily but also in dark tones, with long sleeves and scarves that shielded their hair from lustful eyes. Attesting to the busyness of their days, the women scurried from one vendor to the next, procuring fresh ingredients for the evening meal. They spoke only briefly to one another, snapped at children to "play nice," and left their male counterparts alone to ponder God.

Through this idyllic streetscape clopped Pippino Farago, tugging on his left pant leg to move faster. He kept his head low and stayed close to the buildings. He pretended not to notice the frequent inhospitable glares—leveled at him, he knew, not because of his gimp leg, but because he was obviously not Hasidic. The residents here were fiercely protective of the garden of strict Judaic devotion they had managed to cultivate in the center of wild commercialism and tourism. They were like wolves, raising their hackles, growling at the sight of an intruder.

The address he'd been given was in the heart of Me'a She'arim. It was an odd place to meet for non-Hasidics. But perhaps that's what made it perfect for a clandestine meeting. The tranquillity and lack of outside encroachment, along with narrow, winding lanes, made spotting a tail especially easy in this district. Since parking his car in a hospital lot, Pip had taken the usual precautions: doubling back around entire blocks, crossing open spaces, frequently inspecting the area behind him. So far, he'd spotted no one suspicious.

Anywhere else in the city, he would have worried about people he knew sitting at an outdoor table or browsing the markets, looking up to see if the clopping rhythm they recognized was indeed poor ol' Pip. In Me'a She'arim, he knew no one and no one knew him.

Still, he was uneasy. He had no business meeting with the person who'd phoned him earlier in the morning. If Luco found out . . . Pip didn't want to think about the consequences. An image came unbidden to his mind, of Luco in a blind rage bludgeoning a head already so pulped that identification was impossible. He shook his head. Of course, that was no premonition—leave those to the nuts lurking around Luco these days. It was, rather, a memory, wicked and vivid.

Without pausing, he turned into the open doorway of a bakery. Just inside he stopped, waited. The baker was behind a glass counter, busy with the only customer. The yeasty aroma of fresh *hallah* reminded him that he'd missed lunch; his stomach was too upset to eat now anyway. From a breast pocket he pulled a scrap of paper and again read the directions. He nodded to himself and put the scrap away. Figuring he'd given anyone following him enough time to reveal himself, he clopped back onto the sidewalk, boldly facing the way he had come. No one suddenly stopped; no one turned away.

Pip turned and continued on. A few minutes later he was standing at the entrance of Yifhan Street. It was deserted but for an old woman, who sat in a chair on a second-story balcony, chewing on something—probably nothing more than her gums. She was stoically watching Pip. He pulled the paper from his pocket. Yifhan Street. Numbers on a metal plate over a nearby door indicated the address he wanted was on the right side, but he could see no other numbers. He had assumed the address would prove to be a café or some other public meeting place. Yifhan Street appeared completely residential. And all but deserted. He walked on cautiously. With each second step, he gently lowered to the ground the paperback books taped to the bottom of his left shoe.

A door creaked and he stopped. In a narrow alley thirty yards on the right, a shadow stirred, then moved into the sunlight and became a man. He wore black pants and a long-sleeved black shirt. In front, a small white apron fell from his waist, making him look like a waiter from an upscale restaurant. He squinted at Pip.

"Mr. Farago?" the man said.

"Yes?"

"This way, please." He sidestepped away from the mouth of the alley and held an arm toward it, bidding Pip to enter.

Pip hobbled slowly forward. At the mouth of the alley, he stopped. Too dark to see anything. He looked at the waiter, who smiled and nodded once. The man's cologne was subtle and expensive. Something Luco would wear. Pip's stomach twisted painfully. What if this was all a setup? A test of his loyalty? Was Luco waiting in the alley, knife in hand and a stinging indictment on his lips?

As if understanding his mind, the waiter assured him, "Your host is waiting, sir."

Over his shoulder, the old woman gazed impassively from her perch.

Pip moved into the alley and immediately saw an open door on his left. In the room, a faint red light glowed. He stepped through. As his eyes adjusted, his olfactory nerves took in the hearty and somehow comforting aroma of coffee, spices, and tobacco. He could see now that he was in a wood-paneled antechamber. The only light came from three candles in red glass containers on three small tables. The door behind him closed, and the waiter stepped past.

"This way, sir," he said. He led Pip into a long, wide hallway, lined on both sides with heavy wood doors. Wall sconces cast soft light at the copper ceiling.

He stopped at one of these doors and, without knocking, turned the knob and pushed it open. More candles flickered within. Pip could make out the muted walls of a room no larger than a coatroom. High-backed leather chairs faced a small, round table in the center. A teacup and saucer were set on the table. Steam rose from the cup. Just as Pip was beginning to believe the room was empty, a man leaned out of the darker shadows of one of the chairs.

"Come in, Pip," Niklas Hüber said pleasantly. His German accent was heavy and sharp, a linguistic broadsword. "I'm glad you could join me."

17

The phone rang, and Brady looked at his watch. As usual, Alicia was early, this time by three minutes. He answered on the second ring.

"The train's leaving the station," Alicia said.

He heard the other phone clatter in its cradle, then disconnect. He nodded to himself. In a hurry and on the go. She had said they would review the CSD walk-through in her room; that's why she didn't want to meet in the restaurant. Now she sounded eager to split. She must figure they could view the walk-through in the car or at the crime scene.

Alicia was something of a crime scene junkie. As impassioned as she was over the gadgets coming out of their division, and as proficient as she was with them, she never lost sight of their raison d'être: to solve—and possibly prevent—crimes. At heart, she was a trench warrior.

Not a week went by that she didn't appeal to their division chief, John Gilbreath, to combine field testing with field investigations. The result would be Alicia's dream job: helping to develop cutting-edge investigative tools while being on the team charged with actually identifying and capturing the perps. With each appeal came Gilbreath's shaking head, like a stone guardian's refusal to grant admittance without the correct password.

Early on, he had tried to explain his reasoning. If unproven equipment somehow tainted a crime scene or was found inadmissible in court, it could put a killer back out on the streets and cripple the Bureau's relationship with local law enforcement. Eventually, he began stopping her midpitch and telling her to come back when she had work to discuss.

Brady hoisted himself off the bed, retrieved his holstered pistol from the nightstand, and clipped it to his belt. He snatched up the television remote and switched off the news program he wasn't really watching. He pulled his jacket off the back of the room's single chair, slipped into it, and picked up the satchel that contained his case binder. On the way to the door, he grabbed the telescoping handle of the wheeled suitcase he hadn't yet opened. Brady had not been in the room long enough to spread out.

Agents were required to keep their equipment, case files, and luggage in their hotel rooms when they were there and in their rental cars when they weren't. Being called away at a moment's notice—to a new crime scene, a lead, or a new assignment—was as much a part of the job as stale coffee and mountains of paperwork; a delay in responding, whether to retrieve belongings from a hotel room or finish a meal, was unacceptable.

Alicia's door was propped open with a case he recognized as the one for the CSD's helmet, the one the uninitiated mistook for a bowling ball bag. He stopped at the threshold. Alicia was nowhere in sight. Even without the aid of her personal belongings (which she had certainly packed up by now), the room looked as though a hurricane had blown through it. Bedding was strewn everywhere but on the bed. Dresser and nightstand drawers stood open. For a reason known only to Alicia, a pillow was perched on top of a lampshade.

If Brady were forced to make a list of Alicia's virtues, tidiness wouldn't be anywhere on it. Her work area in the Evidence Response Team R&D unit was an eight-foot-long table piled high with reports, memoranda, newspaper clippings, technical journals, and gadgets, along with the typical desk paraphernalia. File boxes under the table caught the overflow. Her chair fronted a clean semicircle on the table. Her bosses and colleagues tolerated the mess only because she gave 200 percent to the job, evidenced not only by long hours but by consistently impressive results; her projects garnered the most ooohs and aaahs in the R&D division and progressed from idea to prototype to assimilation into field investigations faster than anyone else's.

"Hello?" he called.

"Just a sec!" Her voice came from around a corner that blocked a small portion of the room from his view. He heard the *bbbbrrrrriiipppp* of a heavy zipper. When she appeared, charging for the door, two bulky cases

hung from her shoulders, and she was pulling a wheeled suitcase similar
to his own.

"Whoa," he said, taking a step back. "Let me help."

She stopped and let out a long sigh. When she was ready to do something, she wanted to just do it.

He took her in. Dressed in a coffee-colored mock turtleneck and cinna-
mon pantsuit, she made Brady think of a latte. She wore dark brown heel-
less leather shoes. She had once complained about their price but explained
they were as comfortable as sneakers and she wouldn't have to kick them off
to chase down a suspect. So far, the most evasive things she'd chased in those
shoes were her own ambitions. In truth, her ensemble was conservative and
right, considering her penchant for flouting protocol. She'd managed to
tame her hair as well; it now traced the curve of her face, appearing at once
schoolgirlish and mature. If she wore makeup, it was so subtly applied, Brady
couldn't tell.

"Hey," he said, "you fix up real nice."

That seemed to catch her off guard. She paused, maybe searching for a
snappy comeback. In the end, she simply smiled. "Yeah, you too." She nodded toward the bowling ball bag. "Could you get that?"

He secured his satchel on the extended handle of his suitcase and picked
up the other bag, using his foot to keep the door open for her.

As she passed, she said, "Such a gentleman."

In the elevator, neither set down the cases they held. Ignoring the orches-
tral mutilation of a Billy Joel song pouring from an unseen speaker, Brady
said, "Tell me about last night's victim."

"Cynthia Loeb," she said.

Female, he thought and began fitting that fact into the case analysis he'd
started on the plane. *Second female.*

"Age forty-two," Alicia continued. "Caucasian."

Jessica Hampton was forty, also white.

"Was she a mother?" he asked.

"Two sons in college." She turned to him. "What are you thinking?"

"Nothing yet." Mother-hate didn't jibe with the killer's three male
victims.

"She was recently divorced."

He made a quick calculation. One victim had been single, two married, two divorced. Nothing there to latch on to.

With a *ping!* more pleasant than the infernal Muzak, a green floor indicator changed from L to P, and the elevator doors slid open. A young woman holding the hand of a little girl waited to board. Alicia and Brady trudged out, laden with bags. A single entrance and exit portal in a far corner and dim sodium-vapor lamps kept the underground parking garage in twilight. Cement walls and pillars, mottled with water stains, seemed to absorb light while throwing back amplified noise. The slamming of a car door reverberated from deep within the array of vehicles.

"Yours or mine?" asked Brady.

"Mine." She was heading for an aisle nearer than the one in which he'd parked. "You need to view the walk-through before we get to the crime scene."

As they passed into and out of the glow of overhead lights, their dim shadows rotated around them like dual sundials.

"Cynthia Loeb," he said. "What else can you tell me?"

She walked without answering. Then in a low voice, she said, "I'm trying to remember the pictures of her on the hallway wall." She shook her head. "What keeps coming up in my mind is the gruesome head we found on the kitchen counter."

"Take your time."

They stopped behind an aquamarine Taurus, and Alicia produced a key and opened the trunk. The dark compartment appeared to hold her attention, and she stood there, both hands on the raised lid.

"She seemed like someone I would have liked," she said finally. "She painted plastic wastebaskets and sold them on eBay." She laughed as she said this. "One of the techs found invoices and packing slips in this makeshift office with stacks and stacks of trash cans, as high as my head. Wasn't getting rich, but dang if she wasn't trying to make a go of it." Alicia turned her face to Brady. "The place was kinda rustic, cozy. I can just see her sitting in a chair made of raw tree limbs, sheepskin slippers on her feet, sipping a big mug of hot chocolate, maybe spiced a bit with Bailey's, telling a friend who had stopped by how she was going to make it on her own selling waste-baskets or picking up dog poop or peddling cider at mountain festivals—*anything* to prove to her cheating ex that she could make it on her own."

"Her husband had been unfaithful?"

She hoisted her wheeled suitcase and the larger of the two CSD cases into the trunk.

"That's what a few of the neighbors who were milling around last night said. Who knows?"

She moved aside to let him stow his suitcase. The last thing she put in was the bowling ball bag. Then she unzipped it and spread it open. The quantity of components stored in the bag and the sophistication of their organization surprised Brady. The helmet was upside down. In the bowl it created were a laptop computer and two smaller devices. As Alicia pulled these things out, he could tell they had been held firmly in place by some molding in the helmet. Evidently the designers placed as much importance on secure storage and transportation as they did on performance. If only all engineers were so thorough.

Indicating the hardware in her hands, she said, "This is what you need. Let's go."

18

Seeing Hüber seated in the gloom, Pip almost took a step back. Meeting any of the Watchers outside preappointed venues, away from Luco, was stupid . . . taboo . . . imprudent. Meeting this particular director was treasonous.

Turn and go, he thought. *Just walk away.*

Instead, he came fully into the room and selected the chair opposite Hüber. He heard a click and saw the door was closed, the waiter gone. He observed the other man's cordial expression and felt the muscles in his jaw tighten.

"You told me to meet you here . . . or else."

Hüber shrugged. "I'm sorry for the melodramatics, Pip. I was only trying to stress the importance of this meeting. I'm sure you understand."

What he understood were people like Hüber. To them, anything they thought was important must be important to everyone else. They were masters at cajoling, threatening, and manipulating people into seeing things their way. Luco had long been such a master. And Pip had been the guinea pig upon whom Luco had perfected his craft.

He realized he was poised on the edge of the seat, betraying his fear. He slid back, letting the chair engulf him. At five feet eight and 130 pounds, he was a small man, made seemingly smaller by his handicap and baby face. Not helping matters was his subservient demeanor, a source of constant internal struggle. He crossed his shorter leg over the other and nervously fingered the edge of the gaffer's tape that held the books to the bottom of his shoe. He raised his gaze.

Hüber was staring at him with calculating eyes, sizing him up. The older man's lips creased into a tight smile, suggesting satisfaction. It was as though he believed he had won a battle that had not yet begun; it only had to unfold the way he knew it would.

Pip wanted to say something witty and stunning, something that would smack that smile right off the man's face and inform him that he had underestimated Pippino Farago. But nothing came to mind. Before he could ask what it was Hüber wanted, two sharp raps came from the door. If it had been kicked open by a SWAT team, Pip would not have jumped higher.

Hüber's smile broadened. "Come," he called.

The waiter entered with a tray, set it on the table, and left. On the tray were the components of a nargila, a water pipe for smoking a mixture of tobacco and dried fruit. Luco had owned one, but he called it a bong and had used it to smoke substances more potent than cherry tobacco. That was before his current health kick.

Hüber leaned forward and began assembling the pipe. He poured springwater into its amber glass base, then sealed it with a brass manifold. Protruding from the manifold was a gummi pipe, which ended in a flexible cloth-covered tube and plastic mouthpiece. Most people associated smoking tubes like this with the opium dens of the Orient.

"I think we can help each other, Pip." Hüber didn't look up from his work. He placed what looked like a brass sink strainer on top of the manifold, and a ceramic cup on top of that. "I know you think you and I are on opposing sides. I can assure you that is not the case."

He leaned back to push a hand into a front pocket of his pants. It reappeared, clenching a leather pouch. He opened it and shook a portion of its contents into the ceramic cup. The tang of tobacco with a hint of apples reached Pip's nostrils.

Hüber looked at Pip. "Your boss is a cruel man."

"He's my friend."

"Yes, yes, you say that. But, Pip . . ." He lowered his eyes to Pip's fidgeting fingers, which had worked the edge of the gaffer's tape into an inch-long flap. "Was it not Luco Scaramuzzi who made you a cripple?"

Pip's stomach cramped.

How could he know that?

He felt perspiration form on his scalp, making it itch. He raised his hand to scratch, thought better of it, and returned his fingers to the flap of tape, flicking it, flicking it.

Hüber let the question hang in the air. He picked up a square of aluminum foil, withdrew a pen from a breast pocket, and used it to punch holes in the foil. He shaped the foil over the ceramic cup, forming a small bowl out of the foil.

Pip's eyes were aimed at this activity, but what he saw was a thirty-year-old memory.

Four boys, playing hooky from their fifth-grade class in tiny Raddusa, Sicily. Skinny-dipping in the cobalt water of Lake di Ogliastro. The sun hot on their skin. The rope Enzo lashed to a branch over the surface giving them hours of fun, sailing out, flying off, flipping through the air. Who can make the biggest splash? Who can go the farthest? Who can somersault in the air the most times? The lake is rimmed by a rising and falling ribbon of pine-topped cliffs.

Luco, growing bored, points to one of the nearby bluffs. "Let's jump from up there!" he says.

The other boys look, laugh, shake their heads.

Luco disappears into the trees, reappears through a gap a quarter of the way to the top. "Come on!" he calls. "Babies!"

"We'll watch!" Enzo replies.

"Yeah, we'll watch you break your neck, Luco! Go on!" says Raffi.

"Pip, come here!"

Pip shakes his head. "I like the rope!"

"Pip, come here! Now!"

Pip's heart sinks. Luco has just started to be nice to him, and the boys who picked on him for being small and not athletic have noticed; they have even allowed him to hang out with them, smoking behind Saint Giuseppe's, shoplifting from Papa Uzo's market, harassing smaller boys. Six months ago, he would have been looking at their empty seats in class, wishing he had the guts to cut school and wishing he had the kind of friends who did. Now he does, thanks to Luco. He isn't going to let him down.

But why does he always want to do the most dangerous, scariest thing?

"*Coming!*" *Pip yells. He hopes the false bravado rings true to the other boys'*
ears. "Babies," he calls them for good measure.

When Pip catches up at the top, Luco is leaning over the edge, holding on
to a branch.

"No problem," Luco says. "Look."

Pip edges forward, realizing how much greater the height appears from up
here. It's dizzying. But there's water below, so how awful could a plunge be?

Luco moves out of his way.

Pip grabs the branch and leans. Immediately, he sees there is a boulder a
meter under the surface, directly below them.

"Luco," he says, "there's a—"

He feels the blow to his lower back, a sharp kick. He's falling and spinning,
thinking he can grab hold of the branch once again, but he's miles from it now.
Luco's face is leaning out over the edge, smiling, receding. There's a millisecond of
wet coolness, then searing white-hot pain, and then nothing.

He wakes in a hospital bed. His leg is hoisted two feet off the mattress in a
sling attached to wires, pulleys, a metal stanchion. A plaster cast extends from his
toes to his groin. Metal pins as thick as his finger protrude from a dozen places.
The pain is so great, he can't tell where it's coming from: the leg, his hips, his
internal organs—they all hurt unbearably.

The room's walls are stone with sloppily applied grout, like many of the
buildings in the one-thousand-year-old town. A coat of whitewash tries vainly to
give the room a semblance of sterility and modernity. Pale sunlight pushes
through a grungy window set high in one wall. Beeping and clicking monitors
watch him from stainless-steel carts. A fat fly buzzes over to greet him. It circles
his face. A hand snatches it. Pip jerks his head and sees Luco standing there, hold-
ing the fly in his fist, looking squarely at him. He's bearing the same grin Pip saw
as he fell, and Pip believes it has never left his face.

"You're awake," Luco says. "About time."

"You pushed me," Pip says. His words come out weak and dry, as if filtered
through sand. They hurt his throat.

A fierce hardness, fiery anger, flashes across Luco's face, instantly replaced
by jovial patience, the kind reserved for a retarded brother.

"You jumped, silly," he says. "Enzo and Raffi saw you. Bravest thing they

*ever saw. You're a hero at school. Swan dive from space." He raises his palm and
slowly brings it down, illustrating a graceful aerial maneuver.*

"You—"

"Yes, I saw it too. It was spectacular."

*The hardness comes back to his expression. He extends his fist to Pip's face,
squeezing until the knuckles turn white. He opens his hand onto Pip's chest
and wipes the fly across his hospital gown.*

He whispers, "You're a hero," and walks out.

*So that's what happened—he jumped and became a minor hero for a time.
When the other kids inspect the site of his gallantry and ask, "Why didn't you
look first?" he says, "Where's the adventure in that?" Just as Luco instructed him.
And instead of appearing stupid, he is praised as being braver still.*

*The upper growth plates of his tibia and fibula are shattered. As his right
leg's growth outpaces that of his left, he increases the height of the spacer on the
bottom of his left foot. He adjusts, and he never wanders far from Luco's side.*

"Pip!"

He is startled to see Niklas Hüber eyeing him curiously. No one in
Raddusa had known the truth of his accident. Except Enzo and Raffi, and
they had never hinted at anything other than the official story of his heroic
leap, even when they were alone together. Pip figured Luco had warned
them, as he had warned Pip, probably with a punctuation more substantial
than a smashed fly. It didn't surprise him that this nemesis of Luco's had
dispatched investigators to dig up every detail of Luco's life, but his
unearthing that private truth was genuinely unnerving. What else had he
turned up?

"Are you with us?" Hüber said with a smile. A piece of charcoal was
smoldering on top of the perforated foil on the nargila. He drew on the
mouthpiece as though kissing a snake. He held in the smoke for a few seconds, then let it drift out of his nostrils and a slit between his lips.

Pip watched. Quietly, he said, "Just thinking."

"Think about this: Scaramuzzi is defrauding the wrong people this
time. I know about the petty scams in Italy and Greece, bilking widows out
of their grocery money. And the bogus arms deal with . . . who was it, Syria?"

Perspiration formed on Pip's upper lip and forehead. He wiped it away.

He said, "Luco's past doesn't have any bearing—"

"You know it does. But now he's not deceiving housewives or some Podunk cult in Gelnhausen or Stroud or Toledo . . ." Hüber's voice had grown louder. He took a deep breath, and then a toke on the water pipe. He continued to speak without releasing the smoke he had inhaled, so his words, while calmer, appeared to steam out of his mouth. "*Collegium Regium Custodum et Vigilum Pro Domino Summo Curantium* is a global power with infinite resources: wealth, politicians, business leaders . . . assassins."

He whispered this last word, emphasizing it, then paused only briefly.

"As you know, we take our mandate very seriously. Everything we have ever done has been in service to it. When Scaramuzzi is exposed as the fraud he is, we won't run him out of town or have him imprisoned; we will slaughter him. We will wipe away every vestige of his existence: his family, his associates, his . . . friends. Six months after his grip on my less-discriminating colleagues loosens, the name Scaramuzzi will be gone from the world. There will be no record of it; no tongue will speak it. Do you believe me?"

Pip tried to swallow. His mouth and throat were as dry as scorched concrete. He had already bet on Scaramuzzi to win the terrible game he was playing, so he did not have to scramble to make a decision. All he needed now was courage. It was in him, somewhere. He found a little and said, "I believe you have the power to do what you say. I do *not* believe Luco will ever be exposed as anything other than who he says he is. Why do you doubt him?"

"More importantly," Hüber said, "why do you believe him . . . if you do?" He leaned forward. Candlelight illuminated his piercing blue eyes. "Why do *you*, Pip, believe Luco Scaramuzzi is the Antichrist?"

19

Brady was situated in the passenger seat, the computer open on his lap. Cables snaked from its left side down into the foot well and the components Alicia had taken from the helmet case. Brady didn't know squat about digital video rendering, but the images on the screen were stunning. About a dozen men were standing around an open residential garage looking at the camera. He could see the complexion of each face, right down to the whiskers and blemishes. The entire frame was uniformly clear, without the washed-out areas and deep shadows indicative of bright lighting.

Craning to look out the back window, Alicia squealed out of the parking space.

Brady closed his eyes and told himself to just relax. If his doctor could witness Alicia's driving, he'd prescribe a diuretic and a beta-blocker to keep Brady's blood pressure from spiking into the coronary zone. Or more likely, order him to take a cab.

On the screen, Alicia moved onto a staircase. Here and there, smudges marred the walls, down low, where dark soles had grazed them. Brady could make out a thin film of dust on the upward-marching baseboard. Tapping the laptop's space bar, Brady paused the playback. He turned to Alicia just as she steered the car onto the exit ramp. Sunlight flooded through the windshield, lighting up her face. For the briefest moment it appeared to Brady that the illumination came not from the sun, but from Alicia. It took his breath away, but the next second he let out a single chuckle. The games the mind can play.

"What's funny?" she asked, dropping the visor and reaching for sunglasses stashed in a center console cubby.

"Uh, it's just . . ." No way he'd attempt to explain *that* illusion: His inner voice took on an Italian accent. *I saw you glowing like the Madonna, mi amore!* Yeah, right. He went back to his reason for pausing the playback. "You did it," he said. "You solved our biggest hurdle."

When Brady had joined the Evidence Response Team's R&D unit a year ago, Alicia had already logged ten months on the CSD project. The first demonstration he'd seen was less than impressive. The image had been shaky, grainy, and alternately underexposed and overexposed. Without better resolution, he hadn't seen how the device would benefit either profilers or prosecutors. Brady's job was to help CSD programmers understand what information profilers needed from it, to prepare a manual that would guide users in getting that information, and to field-test progressive iterations, always with Alicia. This was the first time the image had been nearly as clear as the human eye, an objective the entire team agreed was necessary but many believed was unattainable.

He continued. "This image is worlds beyond the last field test, just . . . what? Six weeks ago."

She grinned. "Well, I'm only the person who rags on the technicians until they produce what I want," she said humbly. Then, with exaggerated pride, "I'm *really* good at *that*."

"Whoever or however, it got done. I had my doubts." He hit the space bar again and watched Alicia ascend the staircase. "How is it so smooth?"

"The cameras are mounted in gyroscopic housings that act like mini-stabilizers," she said. She punched the gas and cut through the narrow space between two cars to reach the third lane over. Horns blared, but she was oblivious. "Like the Steadicams they use to make movies, but a hundred times smaller. Even with them, the raw footage still shakes and vibrates enough to give you a major brain crunch after a few minutes. So one of the things the VAC does is use software to further calm the image. We can do that because we're filming in high-def digital, which is nothing more than computer language itself."

Speaking of brain crunch, Brady was getting one, whether from Alicia's techno-jargon or her driving, he didn't know. Viewing the crime scene walk-through wasn't going to help, but he had to do it. He started the video again. Low mumbling reminded him the volume was turned down. Sometimes comments by professionals touring a crime scene helped eliminate ambiguity about things on the video. He pushed the volume-increase key. From the tinny speakers, Alicia's voice said, "Hold on a sec . . . shoe print."

"Oh, hey, try these," she said next to him. She reached into the backseat, groped blindly, and then took her eyes off the road to look. The rear end of a semi was coming up fast. She handed him a set of gold headphones, braked sharply, and changed lanes seconds before hitting the truck.

"They're noise canceling," she said, "which is really a misnomer. You can still hear ambient sounds, but they help quiet everything around you and make whatever it is you're listening to really crisp."

He jacked them into the computer and turned them on. Immediately the engine and road noise dimmed to a low roar, like shutting a window on a beach house.

Video-Alicia said, "I used infrared. That's why I turned off the lights. Can you get around me and tag that?" Loud and clear. By the time the walk-through reached the laundry room at the top of the stairs, he was totally immersed. He was there.

20

Hüber's question was the reason Pip was restricted from meeting with a Watcher alone. He was not prepared for a direct assault. Holding up under a grilling was not in his nature. Ask him to fly down to Palermo to pass out bribes or retrieve documents from locked government offices in the black of night or review files with a destructive eye toward anything that did not support a particular cause—these things he could do; at these things he excelled. But pointed questions about issues that truly mattered flustered him. Even telling the truth was difficult when the questioner's agenda was counter to his own, when the stakes were high. He always thought he'd be the type who confesses to a crime he didn't commit because he couldn't take the pressure of a police interrogation.

Hüber was waiting for his answer, holding the nargila's mouthpiece, smoke leaking from it.

Why did Pip think Luco was the Antichrist?

He didn't think *Why not?* was the answer Hüber wanted to hear. It was, however, closer to the truth than anything else Pip could think of. Eight years ago, Luco had explained he'd stumbled upon a man who claimed to have knowledge of an organization that was waiting for the Antichrist. Luco had found that many prophesied aspects of the Antichrist's life uncannily matched his own. Those that didn't, Luco had explained, could be reinterpreted, retrofitted, or manufactured. He had a plan, one that involved more than two years of study and "sowing"—that was the word he used. He would then make sure the right people noticed him, not people within the Watchers' organization, but people who knew people who knew people.

"Are you in or are you out?" he had asked Pip. If Pip had not actually said, "Why not?" what he *had* said meant the same thing. The scheme had sounded far-fetched and risky, but so had every one of Luco's scams. And those scams had earned the two—charming, irresistible Luco and hard-working, behind-the-scenes Pip—lifestyles far exceeding those of their criminal friends back in Raddusa.

They had heard that the Watchers had a bequest to give the Antichrist when he appeared, but neither had any idea of the vast wealth and power that awaited the Beast of Revelation. By the time they realized the enormity of what they'd gotten themselves into, it was too late to back out. Pip suspected Luco would not have agreed to quietly disappear, even if they could. The scheme was too challenging, the rewards too tempting.

Hüber already knew about the prophecies credited to Luco. If he had not bought into them by now, Pip wasn't going to convince him. With little enthusiasm, Pip said, "There are world conditions that prove this is the time."

"Yes, yes. For the first time in twenty-six hundred years, there is an independent Jewish state. The Christian Church is in upheaval, bickering amongst itself. People are fed up and confused, running from one spiritual experience to another. They are teetering on the brink of apostasy, if they are not already swimming in it. Secular society too is in crisis, economically, politically, in every way a good anarchist could hope for. I agree, the world is primed for Antichrist's arrival. That thrills me, of course. To be the generation that receives him! After two thousand years, to be among the few who will welcome him with an empire of more accumulated wealth and power than has ever been wielded by one man. But one man *will* possess it; one man will use it to achieve the greatness prophesied for him."

Hüber leaned forward, staring past the smoking nargila into Pip's eyes. "Luco Scaramuzzi is not that man."

"Okay," Pip said. "Forget about world conditions; forget about his general background and personality. Luco has fulfilled specific prophecies. He . . . he . . ."

Hüber raised his hand and closed his eyes. "Don't bother, Pip. I know which prophecies he claims to have fulfilled. I also know certain of them

ROBERT LIPARULO

could have been—*were*—bent and tweaked and twisted to force an alignment with Scaramuzzi's life. How convenient that he has Father Randall and his team of theologians to explain and correct the Watchers' interpretations and those of our own theologians."

Pip sighed and leaned back into the chair's supple leather. "If you are this suspicious and doubtful," he said with resignation, "even of the wisest theologians we could find and in the face of empirical evidence, how do you expect to ever find him—the *right* one, according to you?"

Hüber smiled, but his smile was cold and without a trace of humor or joy. "I know in my blood. Right now, it tells me Scaramuzzi is not that man. It tells me you know it as well. I only wish my colleagues knew it. But they will, Pip. Don't imagine they can be fooled forever."

He held Pip's gaze a moment, then leaned forward to check the smoldering charcoal. Apparently satisfied, he said, "This has all happened before, you know?"

He nodded at Pip's surprised expression. "My predecessors were no more discerning than my colleagues, apparently. Hitler, Napoleon, Justinian, Nero. Each manipulated prophecy to suit his own circumstances. With the help of the Council or its predecessors, each rose to great prominence. And each drenched the earth in blood."

That smile again.

"You don't have to be the real Antichrist to butcher millions. You just need someone who believes in you."

Pip's head was starting to feel like a buoy on high seas. He said, "What are you saying? That Luco will try to conquer the world and slaughter millions of people in the process?"

"Of course. He is pretending to be Antichrist, isn't he? The Antichrist conquers ten nations, according to Revelation. He unites them into a single empire, then declares war on the rest of the world. Through no small measure of charm, intelligence, ruthlessness, ambition, and coincidence, Scaramuzzi has—for now—the backing of the Watchers, an organization of immense wealth and power. With our resources, there is nothing he cannot do."

"And what he wants to do is fulfill Antichrist prophecies," Pip added.

"Right down to Armageddon."

Pip considered this. He said, "If it's so awful, why do the Watchers want to help?"

"First, let me clarify. The Bible is clear there are many antichrists, destructive beings who hate God and seem . . . hell-bent, you might say, on causing harm to His creatures. Those pretenders I mentioned—Hitler, Nero—most certainly were antichrists. As is your boss, probably. But the term *antichrist* can be applied to them only in the way good children are called 'little angels': they are no closer to being angels than cows are, but their good behavior is what we think of as angel-like. Would-be despots *act like* Antichrist, but they are not he, and the Watchers are not interested in them. Our desire is to assist only the real Antichrist. The philosopher and Dominican friar Tommaso Campanella called him *l'Antichristo's Massimo*, the Super-Antichrist. Both Daniel and the apostle John dreamed about this man. He has a manifest destiny that we aim to help him achieve."

"But *why?*"

Hüber gave him a sly look. "We know Antichrist will array all the countries of the world under him. He will possess absolute power. He will decide who lives and who dies, who will scrub toilets and who will own houses in Anguilla with servants and harems. His advisers and confidants will influence his thoughts in these matters. They will be the beneficiaries of his reign."

Pip shook his head. "Don't you already have enough?"

"There are things money cannot buy," said Hüber "You know Lord Winston, of course."

The Watcher with the estate outside London. Pip nodded.

"The poor man is confused. He has a . . . hmm . . . *fondness* for little boys. Only a few months ago, the parents of one of his young houseguests made accusations. Had some kind of medical tests to support their claims. If I told you the amount of money and influence we brought to bear on the situation, Pip, you'd fall over dead of a heart attack. Even so, Lord Winston's proclivities almost became public knowledge. It was *that* close." He showed Pip his thumb and forefinger, like pinching salt. "The public would have forced an investigation, which would have uncovered who knows what other indiscretions. Eventually, no amount of wealth or clout would have kept him out of prison, assuming he hadn't slit his wrists by then."

He looked at the nargila as though he'd forgotten about it, stuck the mouthpiece between his lips, and pulled smoke into his lungs. He blew it out, watching it swirl and rise.

"Thing is, Pip, we all have penchants that could land us behind bars or in a back alley, beaten to death. The wealthy, especially. We have tasted as much freedom as this puritanical world will allow us. We want to taste the rest, without the threat of losing everything. When we make the rules and have all the money, morality and public opinion will be"—he took another quick draw and exhaled—"as insubstantial as smoke."

Pip felt sick. Could all of this be about the unrestrained pursuit of forbidden desires? Was sin's pull really that strong? Pride, greed, envy, anger, gluttony, sloth, lust. Dante had it wrong: the seven deadly sins were fatal not to the ones practicing them, but to anyone who got in their way.

"All of your efforts," he said, unable to keep the disgust he felt out of his voice, "all of the Watchers' efforts for fifty generations—so you can pursue perverted desires?"

"So we can experience *everything*. The ultimate life has no bonds, no restraints of any kind."

"But Antichrist's reign is prophesied to last only a few years." Pip could not get his mind around what seemed to him a foolish investment of time, money, and devotion.

"Seven years," Hüber said. "That's not carved in stone."

"Not carved . . . ? You hope to change prophecy?"

"Satan knows God better than anyone, and he obviously thinks he can come out of Armageddon victorious, despite the Bible saying he suffers defeat. Otherwise, why would he try? He's probably defeated God's will, God's predictions, many times. Maybe prophecy is nothing more than God's rousing motivational speech. 'We're going to win this one, by golly!'"

"You can't believe that."

"I do, actually. An unfettered life of pleasure: people have killed and have died for one such day. Imagine, seven years! Now what if—because we know his downfall, his missteps, and we can prevent them—what if we get ten years, thirty years? What if we create a whole new empire that never ends? You would not scoff then, would you?"

Pip blinked. How could he answer such a question?

Hüber adopted a conciliatory tone. "I want to avoid the mistakes of our past, Pip. The needless drain on our resources, the voluminous bloodshed."

Pip wondered which concerned him more. "How do you plan to do that?"

"By ensuring there are no pretenders to the throne on my watch."

"Why don't you just kill him?"

"I have been vocal in my opposition. If Scaramuzzi were to die now, even by an apparent heart attack or in an accident, I and the few of my colleagues who think as I do would be immediately purged in retaliation and to be sure opposition never goes that far again. We are a democratic organization. Majority rules. He must be discredited first."

"But . . ." Pip sorted through his thoughts. He did not want to suggest a course of action against Luco, but curiosity nagged at him. Besides, Hüber and the other Watchers undoubtedly had pondered this and had instituted a policy regarding it. "But wouldn't premature death prove he wasn't Antichrist?"

Hüber chuckled, cold and dry like ice in an empty glass. "I wish it were that easy. We could simply blast away at anyone who caught our eye as a candidate. If he successfully defends himself or the gun jams or he's wounded and recovers—coincidence or supernatural protection? We'd have to try again, and we still couldn't be sure. I suppose if the man dies and pops back up or the bullets bounce off him, we'd have a definitive answer. But if he dies and stays dead, does it mean he was not Antichrist? Or did we thwart prophecy? Or did we merely postpone the inevitable: will he come again in a new body, a generation later, the soul of Antichrist refusing to rest until prophecy is fulfilled? No one knows, but the consensus is that attempting to murder candidates is imprudent. At least until he is no longer a candidate."

"Sounds like you're in a jam."

"That's where you come in, Pip. You and Scaramuzzi were childhood friends. You've been closer than brothers for thirty years. I believe you know without a doubt that he is not who he claims to be, and you know something—you have some evidence, maybe—that could prove it definitively."

He watched Pip's face, perhaps looking for telltale signs of the accuracy of his words. Pip tried to show nothing.

"I said, 'closer than brothers,'" Hüber went on, "but Scaramuzzi has been cruel, has he not? He treats you like a dog."

Pip's jaw hardened. "He's been good to me."

"The way a master is good to his slave. You serve a purpose."

Hüber unscrewed a cap on the side of the nargila's gummi pipe, next to the smoking tube. He picked up an unused tube from the tray on the table and began screwing it over the hole.

"Instead of living like his hound until the jig is up, and he and you and the rest of his camp are wiped out—come work for me. Give me what I need to expose him. I'll give you a comfortable position in my organization with a fat salary and, what's more, guaranteed existence."

Hüber held up the smoking tube he had just attached, offering it to Pip. In his other hand, he held his own mouthpiece. By adding the second tube, he had made a communal pipe . . . a peace pipe. Accepting it meant accepting his offer to betray Luco.

Pip stared at the tendered mouthpiece. Smoke drifted from it, visible, then not, as the candle flickered on the table under it. He knew whether or not he reached for it, his life would change. Men like Hüber did not take rejection well. Luco already knew of Hüber's doubt and desire to bring him down, so Pip could not harm Hüber by divulging the context of this meeting. But once Hüber realized he could not use Pip to get at Luco, he would likely kill Pip, hoping to pull a leg out from under Luco's operation. If he aided Hüber—for he did indeed have what the German sought—he would require asylum until Luco was dead. Then on to a life he'd never have as Luco's lackey—*if* Hüber kept his word. A big *if*.

The smoke drifted, undulated, wafted into the gloom—*much,* Pip thought, *like my future.*

A licia knew the video walk-through Brady was watching had reached the discovery of the severed head when he drew a sharp breath and absently covered his mouth with two fingers. She would have allowed a moment of self-congratulation over the CSD's ability to pull people in, had the circumstance not been so terrible. Eight minutes later he tore off the headphones as though they had suddenly produced an ear-shattering screech. He was breathing faster than usual. He looked at her.

"I thought I was ready," he said.

She nodded. "You should have been there."

"I feel like I was. I could almost smell the blood."

That's on my wish list—only tact kept her from saying it.

He punched a key. "I'll take it more slowly this time. Be more analytical."

"Too late," she said. "We're here."

She pulled the Taurus to the side of the dirt road in what seemed like the exact spot she had parked last night. Six other vehicles crowded around Cynthia Loeb's taped-off drive: two police cruisers, two sedans that screamed "department issue," a white full-size van she suspected had brought more crime scene technicians, and a fire-engine-red Corvette convertible.

She craned to view the house through the trees. "I don't see anyone. They must all be inside."

She ducked under the yellow crime scene tape strung between two trees at the head of the drive.

"Beautiful," Brady said.

Last night she hadn't considered the aesthetics of the scene, but now she saw that the long curving driveway was a pinkish terra cotta. With the green pines, the azure sky, the hundreds of shades of brown, from bark to fallen needles to clumps of earth, the setting was almost breathtaking in its peacefulness.

The drive arced toward the house and ended at a concrete pad in front of a double-wide garage door. The land on either side of the garage sloped up acutely, as if the house had been built on a hill and dug out on one side to accommodate a basement garage. The front of the house faced the drive. Wood stairs marched in a wide crescent from the driveway slab to the front porch.

As Alicia and Brady approached the house, the front door opened and Detective Lindsey stepped out. He stretched and yawned. No doubt he had been here since last night. He spotted them, and Alicia gave him a little wave. Even from thirty yards away, she could see his frown deepen. Her heart suddenly doubled in weight. If the investigative strategy the CSD had devised for him had proved faulty, it would set the program back months, if not longer.

The detective started down the steps. They reached the concrete slab at the same time, and instead of throwing accusations and insults at her, he locked eyes with Brady and marched up to him.

"Who are you?" Lindsey demanded.

"Detective Lindsey," she said, "this is my partner, Special Agent Brady Moore."

"Detective," Brady said and held out a hand.

Lindsey ignored his hand and planted his fists on his hips. "Partner? Where were you last night?"

"Agent Moore just arrived from Quantico."

Lindsey finally turned toward her, flashing a wicked grin. "Quantico? So you *boys* do *think* this is yours to solve." He nodded back over his shoulder at the house.

"Detective, I don't understand," she said. "I thought I contributed something worthwhile to your investigation."

His demeanor softened minutely. "Agent Wagner, you did. The CD . . . CRD thing is an amazing piece of work. I'd love to have one myself. Like I said last night, thank you for your assistance. Now good-bye."

Couldn't be much clearer than that.

"Detective," Brady said pleasantly, "I'm not an advance man for the FBI. You need not be threatened by my presence."

Lindsey inched closer to Brady. "Do I look threatened to you?"

"No, it's just that—"

"What exactly is it you do, Agent Moore? Are you a Robocop too?"

"Have you ever used the Bureau's criminal investigative analyses?"

"Profiles? You a profiler?" Lindsey rolled his eyes. "Oh, yeah, I've used 'em. Besides making me fill out a twenty-page questionnaire, you guys want a fax of every scrap of paper on the case, 'cept maybe the t.p. the investigators use in the john. Autopsy reports, interview notes, ballistic results, maps, theories, photographs. And I gotta beg the local liaison for the privilege of putting all that together before I can even talk to an almighty profiler. Should I genuflect now?"

"Maybe later," Brady said. "The reason we need so much is you never know what's going to be the one thing that brings it all together, like the key word in a cipher. Does the perp play chess, checkers, or Dungeons & Dragons? Does he drink milk or beer? Is he a ladies' man or does he wear ladies' clothing? And while we don't give a rat's butt what t.p. your investigators use, we may be able to tell you what kind your offender uses."

Without taking his eyes off Lindsey, he pointed to Alicia.

"The Crime Scene Digitizer—that's C-S-D, by the way—that Agent Wagner *developed* can make at least half of that truckload of paperwork you mentioned go away. What's the turnaround for Bureau profiles these days, a week, if we get to yours at all? That's an eternity when a little kid is missing or a killer keeps killing and the press and the public and your bosses are all over your back. The CSD can cut turnaround in half and free up manpower for cases we wouldn't have had time to blow our noses on before.

"Now, I don't know if Agent Wagner offended you in some way, other than being female and superb at her job. You said the work she did last night helped you out, and I'd be willing to bet it helped you out *a lot*. I understand territorial rivalry, but that's not what this is about. Believe it or not, we're here to help you, and the last thing we need is to get slapped down for something we haven't done."

Brady had leaned forward while he spoke until the two men's noses were inches apart. Lindsey took a step back, pretending to adjust his waistband. He looked from Brady to Alicia and smiled.

"You two are a pair. I think I've just been told off, but I'm not sure."

"Did your parents have this much trouble getting through to you?"

Lindsey stared uncertainly at Brady.

Brady's smile came slow as a tide.

"Ah . . . !" Lindsey laughed. "You're funny. I hear you, but I can't let you keep sniffing around my crime scene. You screw something up, I'm the one—"

A man's voice bellowing from the house stopped him. Something about showings and escrow.

"Hold on." Lindsey held up a finger and trotted up the steps toward the front door. Alicia and Brady heard the door open—the bellowing rose a decibel—and then slam shut.

"Nice speech," she said.

He made a face. "I thought it would work."

"Don't worry about it. He's got a bug up his—"

Lindsey came down the stairs again, followed by a uniformed cop who was escorting a balding man in his forties.

"Now, just a minute, just a minute . . . ," the man was saying.

Lindsey reached the slab and gestured for them to give the man and the cop some room.

As they passed, heading down the drive toward the road, the man was saying, "I have a camera in the car. Just let me snap a few shots."

Lindsey said, "Sorry. Talk about abrasive personalities."

"Who is he?" Alicia asked.

"Jeffery Loeb. Victim's husband."

"Husband? I was under the impression they were divorced."

"Separated. Divorce hadn't gone through yet. We made the mistake of asking him to look at the house, see if anything obvious is missing or out of place."

Alicia nodded. Standard procedure.

"Did he spot anything?"

"Just a house he'd like to sell. You could almost see it dawning on him as he walked around: *We're not divorced yet. This is mine, all mine.* He wanted to get a Realtor out here today. Didn't like the idea of our seizing it as evidence for a week or two."

Brady said, "Detective, I'd like to talk to him." He took a step toward the two men receding down the drive.

Lindsey touched his arm to stop him. "I don't think so."

"Why not?"

"For one thing, we don't want to spook him."

"What do you mean, spook him?"

"Right now, he's our primary suspect."

"You're kidding. Based on what?"

Lindsey leaned his head back to look at Brady down the bridge of his nose. "Well, I guess you'll have to excuse me for treading in your territory, but there's evidence the killer made a sandwich."

"Uh-huh." That was on the CSD walk-through. Bread crumbs on top of the blood on the counter.

"Correct me if I'm wrong, but doesn't that usually point to an assailant who knew the victim, who was comfortable in the house?" He raised his eyebrows.

"Usually, but—"

"And aren't most violent acts perpetrated by a relative, a so-called loved one?"

"Often, but everything points to this crime being linked to at least four other murders in two states. Did Cynthia Loeb's husband commit them all?"

"I suppose you never heard of copycats?"

Brady just stared at Lindsey. Alicia was equally stunned. Surely Lindsey knew that only scant information about each of the previous Pelletier killings had been released to the press. In every case, major details had been withheld, including the best evidence linking the crimes: that dogs participated in the murders. How would a copycat, one, know that; and two, mimic it? Did he just happen to own dogs trained to restrain victims?

"I'd still like to speak with him." Brady said. "You can't stop me from talking to a witness."

"I can while he's on my crime scene."

As if on cue, a big engine roared to life on the road.

"That'd be his midlife-crisis-mobile," Alicia said flatly.

Sure enough, a flash of red identified the rumbling, revving sound as belonging to the 'Vette. Gravel sprayed out from under tires moving entirely too fast.

Brady turned to Lindsey, disgusted. "Did you at least interview him?"

"No. I invited him to my wife's Tupperware party."

"Could we get a transcript e-mailed to us?" He was trying hard to be nice.

"I'll see what I can do. What's the address?"

Brady produced a card from his jacket's inside pocket. "I'd appreciate it."

"Least I can do."

"Detective," Alicia said, "Agent Moore really needs to look around. It's the reason he got up at three this morning to fly here."

Lindsey's expression reminded her that he'd been up all night and that he cared as much for Brady's sleep schedule or the Bureau's budget as he did whether Pavarotti ever sang opera again. But he surprised her again by asking, "What is it you want to do?"

Brady spoke up quickly. "My job is to make sure the CSD recorded everything a profiler would need to make an accurate analysis of the crime scene. I've studied the recording Agent Wagner made last night. What I need to do is tour the crime scene as though you asked for a profile and the case warranted my coming out. I'll be looking for anything that may be important that Agent Wagner didn't capture on the CSD. That's it. Very straightforward."

Lindsey skewed his face and looked up at the sky. You'd have thought he was contemplating bungee jumping for the first time.

A tech in a white lab coat appeared partway down on the stairs leading from the front door. "Detective," he called. "We need you."

Lindsey pointed his voice at the officer coming up the drive, having safely escorted Prime Suspect Number One off the property. "Vasquez!"

"Yeah!"

"Got another tour for you!"

Vasquez held up his thumb: no problem.

Lindsey headed up the stairs.

"Thank you," Alicia called.

"Be outta here in forty, okay?" He climbed out of sight.

Brady turned to her. "What are you smiling about?"

"I can't wait for the Bureau to establish jurisdiction."

"Can't mix field testing and field investigations, you know. You ready to leave the case?"

"It would almost be worth it to see his face when we take over." She thought about it a moment. "Almost."

22

Back in the Taurus, Brady began fleshing out the notes he'd made during their tour of Cynthia Loeb's house.

Alicia nosed into the property's drive and backed onto the road. They had seen evidence in the dirt of the Corvette's spinning one-eighty. Brady asked her not to attempt the same stunt.

Now she glanced at his hand, drawing quick lines from one observation to another. She said, "Forty minutes isn't long to study a crime scene."

"I think I got what I needed."

"So . . . how'd I do?"

He didn't say anything for a few minutes but flipped forward and backward through his note pad, making connections, scribbling new ideas. Occasionally he would lift the digital camera to check the pictures he had asked her to shoot during the tour. Finally, he nodded.

"You did well. Only a few suggestions."

"I'm listening."

She had driven them out of Palmer Lake and through the town of Monument. Now she pulled onto the ramp for northbound I-25. They had agreed to visit the crime scene in Ft. Collins, where three days ago Daniel Fears, the high school coach, had become victim number four. When Alicia had come to Colorado yesterday, it was to make a CSD recording of the Fears crime scene and be ready to record a fresh scene, should the UNSUB—unknown subject—strike again soon in Colorado. The night she arrived, before she'd had a chance to get to Ft. Collins, he murdered Cynthia Loeb. Brady and Alicia were hoping to find some references to repeated patterns there. The more clues they had, the more detailed the picture of the killer would become. It was like creating a mosaic: the first few pieces revealed nothing; clarity came from studying many fragments.

"Tool markings at the point of entry," he said. "There were scrapes where it appeared the UNSUB used a tool to remove the screen. Close-ups of them would be nice, both on the window frame and the screen outside." He consulted his notes. "Speaking of outside, next time follow the officer who tracks them. Vasquez said they were unable to trail back farther than a hundred yards or so, but if they had found where the UNSUB had parked or waited, that would be invaluable."

"For tire impressions?"

"That, and if the assailant waited, it would show a high degree of planning. What was he waiting for? Other people to leave? Darkness? A time that means something to him? What did he do while he waited? Smoke? Carve something in a tree? Stand there with the patience of a Beefeater? If you find where he parked, the location might tell us something about who he is. If it's a long way from the crime, for example, we'd know the guy is pretty good at finding his way through the woods, that he's healthy enough to trudge that far. If it's someplace only a four-wheel drive can get to . . ."

She was nodding.

He continued. "You did a decent job capturing the oddness of her bedroom, all those religious trinkets. It would have been nice to get each of those things individually recorded from several angles. Don't touch them; just move around them."

"That's a tall order."

"I know it would take time, and with the cops there, you may not be able to do it on the first run-through. Any reason you couldn't go back?"

"Locals are pretty anxious to get what the CSD has for them and get me out of there. Lindsey's attitude isn't unusual. I could *insist.*" She smiled.

"If we found a similar trinket or image at another crime scene or interviewed an UNSUB who worked where one was sold or made—something like that could break the case. One more thing. You panned around the rooms, but try to dedicate some time and focus on lifestyle groupings.

That is, the bookcases, the furniture arrangements, any wall hangings, photographs, artwork."

"I thought the sweep would pick up all that."

"Not with enough detail. If there's an open magazine on an end table, zoom in so we can see the publication name, issue date, and page number. Better too much information than not enough."

"So, missed three?" she asked.

"That's not bad."

She shrugged. "I suspect the CSD will be a continual work in progress, even after I've moved on. Different people will want different things from it, rules of evidence will change, new forensic methods will become vogue."

"Does that bother you," he asked, "working on a project that will never be completed?"

"Nah, not really. Name of the game these days. Imagine being a computer or software designer, knowing the product you're working on every day till midnight will be obsolete a month after you've signed off on it. The CSD's technology-based, so constant upgrades will be the norm. I just want to see it credited with locking up some really bad guy. Maybe watch it become the way crime scenes are approached."

"Something little like that." He smiled at her.

They crested Monument Hill, and a long stretch of highway opened up before them. The Taurus rocketed for the horizon. Brady wondered if Alicia measured driving success by the number of cars she passed. He retrieved the laptop from the foot well. He still had to give the CSD recording of the Loeb crime scene a more thorough inspection.

"Any thoughts about the killer?" she asked.

"Still assessing, but we may not be dealing with a serial killer at all. More and more, he's looking like a spree killer."

"The short downtimes and the way he's traveling?"

"And the apparent lack of common denominators among the victims," Brady answered. "Although I'm not ready yet to say that linkage doesn't exist. Sometimes it only becomes clear after he's caught and explains himself, if he ever does."

"What does the frequency of the killings tell you, the short time between each one?"

Brady considered his answer, then shook his head. "Ambition . . . correlation to some other events . . . a developing taste for blood. At this point, we just don't know."

She said, "Lindsey mentioned something I was curious about."

He looked at her.

"The eating," she said. "He was right about that being suggestive of someone who knew the victim or was somehow comfortable in the house?"

"Suggestive, sure. But the human mind is infinitely complex, which makes every person and every motive different."

"So what *does* making a sandwich next to a severed head tell you about this one?"

"One thing, he's probably a sociopath. He has no sense of morality, no concept of right and wrong."

"What's *wrong* with cutting someone's head off, huh?"

"Exactly. They know society thinks it's wrong; that's why they take steps to elude capture."

"Think this guy grabbed a snack at the other crime scenes?"

"I didn't notice that . . . Hold on." He hooked an arm around his seat back and fished in the satchel on the rear floor for his binder. Using the closed computer as a desk, he flipped open the binder and read. After a minute, he said, "The first vic. Joseph Johnson in Ogden. They lifted two latents on the inside handle of the refrigerator, as though the perp had opened it." He was turning pages more quickly now. "Here," he said. "William Bell was killed in the parking lot of his apartment building in Moab. They place the time of death at about 12:05 a.m. from the coroner's report, and that's when a resident said she heard noises in the parking lot. She thought someone was trying to break up a dogfight. But she didn't see anything when she looked out her window, and the noises had stopped. Now get this. Ten minutes earlier, Bell bought a cheeseburger, fries, and a chocolate shake from a late-night burger joint." He looked up from the page. "He got them to go. The shake was found splattered on the ground near the body. But they never found the burger and fries . . . or their wrappers."

"So Bell ate in the car and tossed the trash out the window." She didn't believe it, but detective work was about playing devil's advocate until every possibility had been considered.

"Not likely," said Brady, reading. "First, the cab of his truck was full of empty beer cans and other trash, including old fast-food bags and wrappers. They examined them, looking for evidence. They were all crusty-old. They did find a hash pipe and a dime bag of weed. Why would he risk getting pulled over for littering when he's got contraband in the truck, especially since he's driving a trash can anyway? Second, he had stopped at a video store before the burger place. The tapes he rented were near the body. Sounds like he'd planned on dinner in front of the tube. The house that Swanson built."

She thought a moment while Brady continued scanning the reports. "You're saying the killer is taking their food?"

Brady nodded. "I'd bet on it."

"That's the *motive*?" She was incredulous.

"No, something else. Maybe it gives him a feeling of power. Or in some way it's a symbolic transference of their life force to him, a delusion many psychopathic killers share. He took their lives and he took one of the requirements of life, food."

"Or maybe he was just hungry?"

Brady raised his eyebrows. "Maybe so."

There were a lot of maybes at this point in the investigation. Or rather, investigations. Each murder was being handled by a local authority, at least until the Bureau stepped in to help compare notes and unify efforts.

The car shot north, not slowing when the speed limit dropped from seventy-five to sixty-five to cut through the town of Castle Rock. Brady looked up from the binder that had diverted his attention from the video walk-through for the past ten miles. He studied the rook-shaped mountain from which the town derived its name. Radio and cell phone masts spired above its plateau. He could just make out the outline of a big star on its side, probably an illuminated, outsized Christmas decoration. What captured his attention most were the layers of strata making up the top quarter of the mountain, stark evidence of the sea that had once filled the Great Plains. Its shores had lapped at the Rocky Mountains and—as it receded—at this jutting plateau. Everything that was then, gone now. As everything now would be gone someday.

23

Leaving Castle Rock, the car picked up even more speed. As it caught the wind and roared over minor road imperfections, it rose and fell gently like a leaf on a rolling sea. Brady pushed the binder back into the satchel behind his seat and opened the laptop.

Alicia pulled a crumpled pack of Camels from her blazer pocket. She smoked whenever she was impatient, which meant she had a pack-a-day habit, by his calculations. She saw him watching her.

"You mind?" she asked, sincerely, not as a challenge.

He shook his head. She lit up and cracked her window. Instantly the smoke whipped away like a soul who'd found a way out of hell.

"Why don't you give me one?"

She eyed him suspiciously. "You don't smoke."

"I'm trying to start."

She kept the pack in her hand. "It's a nasty habit."

"Nastier the better."

She laughed. "Since when?"

Since I realized nasty things fare no worse and sometimes better than healthy, good things, he thought. *Since I decided it doesn't matter.*

He shrugged.

She handed over the pack. "You worry me sometimes, Brady. You really do."

As they approached Denver, traffic slowed and she had no choice but to fall in line.

"We need to get gas pretty soon. Ft. Collins is another hour after we get out of this mess," she said, firing up another cigarette.

One had been enough for Brady. He went back to the CSD walk-through. He would play a bit, stop, replay, move ahead. In this way, he had advanced to the baubles in Cynthia Loeb's bedroom when Alicia spoke again.

"You remember Muniz?" she asked.

A tight smile pushed at the corners of Brady's mouth. He nodded. "The hero," he said. Special agent Rudolph Muniz had been part of an investigative team that had earned a white feather—Bureau-speak for solving a particularly important case. Feathers were especially heady when victory rose out of hopelessness. The case Muniz and his partner, Jack Barrymore, were working looked particularly bleak: the disappearance of an eleven-year-old girl. She'd been missing two weeks already when the locals called in the FBI.

Brady and Alicia had heard the details about two months ago, the day following the bust. They were waiting for the Evidence Response Team's debriefing to begin when Bull Jordans—a former LSU linebacker and New Orleans beat cop, with all the charm and sensitivity you'd expect from someone with that background—regaled them with the Bureau's latest and greatest bust.

"They're making the rounds, right?" Bull said to the dozen faces turned his way. "Reinterviewing everyone. It's grunt work, 'cause they figure the kid's a graveyard steak by now anyway. But they go to the crib of the kid's piano teacher."

Brady winced at the word "crib" coming out of the mouth of a forty-year-old white guy. "Graveyard steak" was more in line with Bull's personality.

"What's this guy going to give 'em, they're thinking," Bull continued. "Thirties, married, no sheet. Normal guy, by all accounts. So they ring the bell, and a minute later the curtains over the front window move. Next thing, the garage door's rolling up and a car's in there revving and revving. Muniz and Barrymore run for the garage. Piano Man's at the wheel of a '68 Charger. Big engine, fast car." Bull flashes an appreciative grin. "As soon as he sees 'em, he pops the clutch and burns rubber outta there.

"Muniz and Barrymore are yelling, 'Stop! FBI! Stop!' They got their gats out, but they don't wanna shoot case this is their guy and he has the kid stashed somewhere. So Muniz drops his piece and—get this—he jumps on the hood. I mean, this thing is screaming out of the driveway and Muniz is holding on for dear life, sliding this way and that. Barrymore is, like, awestruck. He just stands there watching. Says the Charger ripped down the street like some street-racing movie played in fast-forward. Ya know those kick-butt movie cops: when they do that, they got these determined expressions."

Everyone nods.

"Not Muniz. He's got this look like he just woke up on this speeding vehicle and hasn't got a clue how he got there. His face is like this—" Bull perfectly mimics the expression of someone who sees a train rushing toward him. "Muniz is screaming. Not 'Stop the car!' But 'Aaaaahhhhhhhhhhh!!!!!' All the way down the blasted street."

Roars of laughter.

"Barrymore, that idiot, starts chasing after it, yelling, 'Rudy! Rudy! Rudy!' Finally, he gets his wits and runs back to their steed. He gets close enough to see the Charger go round a corner and Muniz fly off. I mean, he *flies*—like forty feet. Rolling and tumbling another fifty feet before landing in some old lady's hedges. Piano Man loses control and pegs a tree. When Barrymore gets to him, he's blabbering, 'I'm sorry, I'm sorry.' 'Where's the little girl?' Barrymore says." Bull shook his head and looked around as if to say, *Some guys have all the luck.* "Piano Man says, 'In my basement! Oh, I'm so sorry! I'm sorry!' Muniz is limping over, holding his arm, but obviously he'll live, so Barrymore drives back to the house and there she is, in the basement, good as new. Ka-ching!"

Over the next few days, more details trickled in. Turns out the little girl wasn't as good as new, but she would recover. Physically, anyway.

"Jumping on the hood of that car," Alicia said now, jarring Brady out of the memory.

He nodded.

"Everyone made fun of him. 'Aaaaahhhhhhhhhhh!'" She showed Brady the face Bull had made. "Thing is . . ." She hesitated. "I want to do that."

She looked at him, apparently expecting surprise or humor or something else less than encouraging. When he nodded again, his face impassive, she put her eyes back on the road and continued. "I want to jump on the hood of a speeding car or run across some field with people firing at me or leap from a helicopter onto a semitruck." She glanced at him again. "You know?"

"All in the name of rescuing a civilian or stopping an archcriminal from causing greater harm."

"Yeah. Not for fun." She paused. "But I think it would be fun too."

Brady cleared his throat. "Jung called that a 'hero complex.'"

"Oh, great. I have a complex."

"We all do. Most of us have several. But *complex* is just a word. It's a convenient way to categorize inclinations in thought and behavior."

"So is a hero complex good or bad?" She suddenly swerved onto a passing exit ramp, apparently having spotted a gas station she liked.

Brady grabbed a handgrip on the door. Alicia approached a red light, braking hard.

When the car stopped, Brady said, "Could be positive or negative. It's good if it gives you initiative and makes you adventurous. It's bad if it leads to foolhardiness and bravado." He watched her think about this. "You might have something altogether different," he added.

"What do you mean?"

"Could be your desire to perform heroic acts stems from your passion for the job. You love being a special agent, and you want to experience it in every possible way. And, sure, you want to save people in the process. That's one of the reasons you joined the Bureau, right?"

Alicia didn't respond. A horn honked. She saw the light was green and accelerated. Finally, she said, "I think I got into law enforcement because I wanted to kick butt."

Brady smiled. "If the butts belong to bad guys, you're a hero. Congratulations."

"You don't feel the same?"

It was his turn to think. More than anything else, he was a desk jockey. He studied case descriptions and crime photographs and tried to turn them into a profile of the perp. Alicia liked the down-and-dirty stuff. She spent her off-hours on the shooting range; his idea of training was a few hours with *The Diagnostic and Statistical Manual of Mental Disorders.* While he had been working on his doctoral dissertation, she'd been in the trenches, learning hero moves.

He said, "Not to that degree, no."

"I bet Muniz pats himself on the back every day for jumping on that hood, despite the razzing he got for it."

"Broke his arm too."

"Oh, pish," she said. "I broke my arm when I was fourteen. Didn't even cry."

"Were you beating up the neighborhood bully?"

Alicia punched the gas to get through a yellow light. It turned red before they reached the intersection. They zoomed through, then braked hard to pull into a Diamond Shamrock. "I was on my bicycle and hit a mailbox," she said matter-of-factly.

"Now *that* I believe."

24

The Middle Eastern sun bathed the city in orange fire that flared off the windows and metallic surfaces of Tel Aviv's modern skyline. A moist breeze coming off the Mediterranean made the air feel warmer than the 68 degrees reported by the large digital thermometer outside Bank Hapoalim's Romanesque headquarters on Rothchild Boulevard. Day-trippers lingered on Gordon Beach, savoring a final plunge into the surf or one last sandy-toed stroll before heading inland to their homes. The office workers who had gone home to shower and change would soon reemerge to fill the many nightclubs on Hayarkon Street. Tel Avivians often surprised visiting Westerners with their cosmopolitan lifestyle and insatiable passion for merri-ment. They believed the day was for hard work, the night for cutting loose and taking it easy.

Except for Luco Scaramuzzi.

Ensconced in his private workout room in the Italian Embassy, he pushed at the limits of his strength and endurance. Rivulets of sweat tracked the sharp contours of his muscles like winter runoff—slicking over straining biceps, quadriceps, pectorals. They poured off his face and ran, glistening, through the fine black hair that swirled over his chest and stom-ach, soaking the waistband of his cotton gym shorts. Each heft of the fifty-pound dumbbells in his fists brought forth more sweat and tight-lipped groans of exertion. Shifting his gaze from a glass wall and the city beyond to a mirror-fronted column, his lids fluttered over stinging eyes. But he liked what he saw, the way his body responded to his daily workouts. He was sitting on a padded bench, the soles of his Pradas flat against the floor, his back straight, and still he saw no folds at his stomach, no fat edging over his shorts. His body tapered nicely from shoulders to waist. He pushed the iron over his head, watching what bulged, what quivered. He was after muscle mass and tone more than strength, so the weights were relatively light and he did lots of reps.

He realized he had lost count and decided to keep raising and lowering the weights until the current track blaring through the iPod earbuds ended. It was "Murder (in Four Parts)" from the movie *Road to Perdition*—brooding and atmospheric, the sound he preferred for furious workouts. This evening his mind was troubled, so he had attacked the equipment with more intensity than usual—first with leg presses, then shoulder rolls, wrist curls, bench presses, a circuit of Nautilus stations, and now the dumbbells. His aching muscles were threatening to shut down. Each push up and draw down became exponentially harder—he lowered the weights with excruciating slowness, the way his trainer had taught him. His eyes squeezed shut. The weights were not merely quivering now, they were wobbling. But he got them up. His arms were on a glass-through-the-veins journey downward when he felt the air pressure in the room suddenly relax: someone had opened the door. With a savage grunt, he pushed the weights up, holding them steady, brought them down, then up again.

See? he told himself. *Mind over matter. There's always more power where you think there's none. You just have to look for it, conjure it.*

He opened his eyes, this time ignoring the sting of sweat. Pippino Farago came into view, looking nervous and intimidated, as if he expected Luco to ask him to bench some free weights. But Luco knew his old friend had other reasons to be anxious.

The dumbbells came down . . . slow, steady. Luco closed his eyes again. Up went the weights . . . then down . . . The song had reached its deafening crescendo, and Luco thought, *Up . . . one . . . more . . . time.* The track stopped. Luco lowered his arms and let them hang with the weights below the bench seat. Perspiration streamed over his skin as he caught his breath. Finally, he lowered one dumbbell to the floor, then the other. The next song in his custom playlist had started—"Elk Hunt" from *The Last of the Mohicans.* It was such a stirring orchestration, he was tempted to let it play

to the end. Business was at hand, however, so he reached to the iPod clipped
to his waistband and turned it off. He pulled the earbuds out and draped
the cords over his shoulders.

"Arjan said you wanted to see me." Pip shifted his weight to his shorter leg.

"Have a seat." He indicated a workout bench across from his own. He
leaned sideways to snag a towel off a hook affixed to the mirrored column
and began wiping his face.

"Get everything taken care of in Jerusalem?" Luco asked. After Luco's
meeting with the Watchers, Pip had not returned to Tel Aviv with him, saying he had errands to run. He'd arrived hours later with one of the security
guards.

Pip seemed to take a sudden interest in Luco's sneakers and mumbled
some response.

Dabbing the towel over his arms, Luco said, "How do I look?"

"Uhh . . ."

"Michelangelo arms, don't you think?"

Pip nodded. "You've always been fit."

"Better now than ever." He ran the towel across his chest and dropped
it in his lap. He leaned over, planting his forearms on his thighs. Pinning Pip
with his eyes, he said, "We have a problem."

Pip winced and recovered quickly. "What's that?"

"I'm aware of your meeting today. With Hüber. Did you think I would
not find out?"

Again, the smaller man diverted his eyes. They darted back to Luco,
then fled away once more. A smile too quivered into place, then vanished.

Luco knew Pip could not bear the weight of direct confrontation, especially when it was Luco applying the pressure. When Arjan had reported
the call Pip received from Hüber, he had shrugged it off. No way would Pip
meet with a Watcher behind his back. Then the meeting took place, and
Luco considered waiting to see how it all played out. Would Pip's better
judgment force him to confess his misstep, or would he surprise Luco by
pursuing motives Luco could not fathom? What could Hüber promise that
Luco had not already given? Then he realized he could not risk Pip's

betrayal, not now, not with the power plays he had set in motion at the Watchers meeting and in the United States. Better to meet Pip's rebellion head-on, find out what was going on, and stop it quickly.

He said, "I understand Hüber moving in on you. He has never masked his disdain for me. But *you* . . . my right-hand man . . . my friend. What possessed you?"

Observing his hands squeezed together in his lap, Pip said, "Funny you should use that term."

"What? Possessed?" He laughed, the sound as cold as old bones.

Pip nodded slightly. "You've . . . changed. You . . ."

"I can't hear you."

Pip's gaze came up. "You've changed. When we started this scam, you were bold but careful. You were—"

"Scam!" Luco came off the bench and stood like a boxer, ready to raise his fists in battle. "Is that how you think of my destiny? Is that why you've become weak?"

Pip remained seated. Good for him. Luco would just knock him down if he stood up. Nerves made Pip's forehead and upper lip wet.

Pip hesitated, then said, "Scam is what *you* called it, Luco. Eight years ago, when—"

Luco stepped in and struck Pip on the head, hard, knocking him off the bench. Pip scrambled up, pressing a palm to the side of his face. He stumbled backward awkwardly.

"Eight years ago!" he said, his voice raised. "You told me about the Watchers and what they were looking for. You said you could be that person. You said it would be the biggest scam ever played. The biggest *scam,* Luco!"

Luco felt his pulse quicken, his shoulders rise and fall with each angry breath. Through tight jaws, he said, *"You don't believe."*

"Believe what, Luco? Believe what? That you can pull this off? Yes, I do. That you are Antichrist?" His shoulders dropped. "No, that I don't believe."

Luco's muscles, already pumped, tightened further, until they were rock hard under taut skin. He scanned his surroundings, saw the dumbbells, and hefted one into his fist. He turned to Pip, who backed away, hands raised pleadingly.

"Is that what you discussed with Hüber? Is this what it comes down to?"

"No! Wait a minute . . . let me talk . . ."

"I've heard everything I need to." Luco stepped toward Pip. "Christ had Judas. I have you."

"Hüber asked me to help him, but I didn't tell him anything. I—"

"How can I trust you now? You went to him." He moved closer.

"Wait!" Near panic now. He took another step back. "You've pushed me around our entire lives . . . but I'm not stupid, Luco. I have . . . insurance."

Luco halted. "What are you talking about? What insurance?"

"The Raddusa case file. I have it."

Luco felt the power drain from his wrath, as though Pip had delivered a physical blow to his gut.

"It's destroyed," Luco said. "Gone."

Months ago, Father Randall had approached him about a prophecy indicating that while in his childhood Antichrist would murder his mother. Randall explained that he had yet to corroborate and vet the prophecy. Still, it was precisely the boost Luco needed to solidify the Watchers' support.

Everyone knew he had killed his mother when he was eleven years old. To the police, he had explained that she was abusive and that she was beating him when he grabbed a butcher knife and thrust it into her chest. He showed them the bruises she had inflicted on him. He cried and babbled his way to credibility, assisted by his forlorn father, who testified that his wife often beat the boy, despite his protests.

"She was a troubled woman, my Maria," he'd said mournfully.

Luco's friends heard a different story: that she had found his stash of forbidden magazines and a little grass an older boy had given him. She threatened to tell Papa, who would have beaten him mercilessly. So he had killed her and gotten away with it. The Watchers knew the story; the prophecy— once it was confirmed by their own theologians, which Randall would make sure happened—would cement their faith in him.

Problem was, he had *not* killed his mother. His father had stabbed her in a drunken rage. At the time, Luco was fifty miles away with his father's sister in Letojanni, Sicily. His father called him home, beat him for effect, and coerced him into taking the blame. "They're not going to do nothing to a kid," he'd said.

One investigator suspected the truth. He had gathered evidence, such as Luco's train ticket from Letojanni to Raddusa, the testimony of a neighbor who heard a fight and screams hours before the supposed time of death, and skin scraped from under Maria Scaramuzzi's fingernails. But with father and son sticking to their story and anonymous threats leveled at the investigator's family, the case was closed. Luco knew, however, that the prophecy would prompt the Watchers to investigate more thoroughly. Especially his detractors, Hüber and his cohorts. The file, with its circumstantial evidence along with the skin samples—which meant little thirty-one years ago but whose DNA would now definitively rule out Luco as the donor—would expose the lie.

The truth of his mother's death was inconsequential—until it became linked to Antichrist's identity.

Luco knew from the start that he had to fulfill all vetted prophecies, particularly those his own theologians uncovered and he approved. One failed prophecy would be a death sentence. Since he knew himself to be the one, Luco suspected that Randall had made a mistake and in his enthusiasm had misinterpreted corroborative evidence. *We tend to find what we seek,* Luco thought. But the Watchers would never accept an error this major; they would believe that both he and Randall were frauds, even if they were not.

Soon after Randall came to him with the matricide prophecy, Luco dispatched Pip to Raddusa. His task: to find the case file and to destroy it. The plan was to burn the entire storage facility to obscure their intentions. Even suspicion of Luco's involvement was far better than leaving the file for the Watchers to find.

Pip had completed his assignment without a hitch. Or so Luco had thought.

"I kept the file," Pip said. "I saw what was happening to you. I needed something to keep you from turning on me as you have so many people who trusted you. I started keeping a journal, but that was just my word. This is *proof.*"

"I don't believe you."

"You were in Letojanni when your father killed your mother. They preserved evidence in a vial. It's marked 'Skin from beneath right-hand fingernails.'"

Luco had once confided the truth to Pip, but he had never given details or spoken of any evidence. Pip had opened and read the file; that much was clear. But had he kept it? Luco believed he had. He did not think, however, that Pip had arranged for it to fall into an enemy's hands upon his demise. That was too risky and too elaborate. If he killed Pip now, he was certain to find the file among his belongings, or he'd find a key or note that would lead him to it.

Abruptly, Luco made his face soften into an expression of resignation. He turned away from Pip and walked to the workout bench.

"You're right, Pip. You got me. But what's more important is that we're friends." He lowered the weight to the floor. "We can't let something like this . . ." He returned his attention to Pip, who had backed to the room's door. "Pip?"

Wide-eyed, visibly trembling, Pip shook his head. He spun and crashed out the door.

25

He should have seen it coming. *Madness!*

Pip moved quickly away from the workout room toward the elevator. He looked back to see the door shut; in the few seconds he watched, it did not burst open again, it did not give way to Luco's wrath, surging to find him, to engulf him, to consume him. An armed guard standing just beyond the door watched him impassively. Pip's eyes flashed to the man's gun, to the walkie-talkie clipped to his belt.

He was at the elevator doors. He pushed the down button. It lit up, but he pushed it again. And again, watching the indicator lights above the doors.

It really happened; Luco had gone over the edge. When? How could he have been so blind? Like Luco, had he been so caught up in the power and money, in the delusion, that he failed to see the transition from actor to madman? Or was insanity so cunning that it invaded slowly, with the stealth of cancer?

He bolted away from the elevator, down the hall to the stairs. Erratic behavior alone would not alarm the building guards; Luco was forever ordering his people to rush here and hurry there. One call from Luco, however, and the guards would strike, like claws on Luco's fingers. Pip pushed through the stairwell door and, grabbing the handrail, descended three, four steps at a time, ignoring the stiletto jabs in his left knee as his gimp leg tried to keep up.

Increasingly over the past year, Luco had spoken more like a man fulfilling a grand destiny and less like one *pretending* to be the subject of that destiny. Privately with Pip, he spoke less of strategy, of how to *convince*, and more of how to *do*. The tone of their conversations had shifted from "What can I do next to impress the Watchers?" to "What should I do now to further my ascension, my reign, my kingdom?"

Pip had thought he was merely witnessing Luco's brilliant acting—method acting à la Brando, à la Pacino. Stay in the role, embrace the role. How could Pip have known the role would embrace Luco, grip him and absorb him? Luco had not become the role; the role had become him.

Three flights down, on the landing of the floor on which he had his office, Pip stopped. His breathing and heartbeat were too loud in his ears to let in any other noises that might be echoing in the stairwell. He looked up through the opening between flights of stairs. He saw no one peering down, rushing to catch him.

Up there was a man who had gone mad. He had tried for so long and so hard to convince others that he was someone he was not, that in his mind, he had become that other person. Pip had heard that Bela Lugosi, the actor who played Dracula in the 1931 movie, came to believe he really was that undead vampire. He had not gone around biting necks, but he always wore the black cape with the red lining and slept only during the day. Toward the end he had refused to acknowledge his given name and answered only to "Dracula" or "Count." And Lugosi had it easy: he needed only to convince the camera eight hours a day for a twenty-day shooting schedule. Luco was under pressure to be the Antichrist constantly and forever. No wonder he had cracked.

Cracked? Pip thought. *The man has shattered. A million pieces on the floor, every one razor sharp and deadly.*

He reached for the door handle and then froze. Was that a sound from overhead? A door clicking shut, more quietly than if it had been allowed to swing shut? He moved back to the center opening. Nothing. He looked at the door.

What's in the office I need? What good is anything if I'm dead?

He continued down, toward the parking garage.

Maybe Luco's madness came and went; maybe the persona of Antichrist only occasionally drifted into his consciousness before plunging away again, like a watery beast that comes up for a sip of air. Maybe. But even if that were so, Pip embraced no hope for himself. Despite their longtime friendship, Pip knew Luco would eliminate him. Luco the Pretender and Luco the Antichrist both had reason to distrust him.

To Luco, *the* Luco, Pip knew too much. Knew of the planning and plotting and preparation they'd done before Luco had arranged for the Watchers to discover him. Knew of the scheming and evidence planting—*prophecy* planting—they'd committed since he had become the Watchers' darling, their best hope.

To Antichrist, Pip was—as he had shown in the workout room—a dissenter, whose doubt was corrosive, made more so by his credibility as Luco's lifelong companion. Indeed, the relationship that should have assured Pip of his safety was the reason he had to die. Ambition bears no tolerance for sentiment, no use for matters of the heart, like friendship, compassion, mercy. And Luco—as well as Antichrist, Pip was sure—was nothing if not ambitious.

Then there was the file. Evidence of the farce, of the lies and deceit. Luco would never tolerate its existence.

Pip's knee was throbbing now, pulsing in pain. The paperback book taped to his shoe had caught several times on edges of stairs, fraying badly. It was starting to look like a grayish pom-pom, puffing out in curling strips.

Like a clown, Pip thought. *I'm a clown in Cirque du Scaramuzzi. But the crowd is not laughing anymore, and the clown must go.*

A door at the bottom of all the stairs, marked with a foot-high letter "P." Unlike the other floors, which had door handles, this one, essential for escape in the event of a fire, opened at the push of a bar that ran its width. Pip slammed into the bar and was in the underground parking garage. A hand seized him by the arm, jarring him to a halt.

A deep voice said, "Hey!"

Pip spun, pulling free of the grip. The guard who had grabbed him took a step back, one hand dropping to the butt of a pistol at his side. His face was hard, all business. Pip wanted to scream . . . to tackle this brute . . . to vanish as a sorcerer might; he wanted to do anything but stand there and let Luco's long arm manipulate this puppet-guard into shooting him. Then the guard smiled.

"Mr. Farago," he said. "You gave me a start, coming through the door like that. What's the hurry?"

Pip's lips were stuck together, his mouth dry. All the moisture must have risen to his forehead, for a bead of it ran into his eye. He wiped it away and realized his face was as wet and slick as a trout's. He meant to chuckle, but it came out a croak.

"You know the routine," he said, friendly, casual. "Everything needs to be done yesterday."

The guard shook his head. "Never ends."

On the way to his car, Pip looked back. The guard had returned to his post by the stairs door, with his back to the wall. He was watching Pip and gave him a nod.

Pip reached his red Fiat sedan and lifted the key to the door lock. His hands were shaking so terribly, he scratched the paint and took a good ten seconds to get the key into the slot. As he climbed in, the paperback book caught on the doorsill, tore away, and fell to the garage floor, leaving hanging strips of duct tape on his shoe. His left foot was his braking foot. He'd have to lean in on that side to brake the car, but he didn't plan on doing much slowing down until he reached Haifa. If he pushed the speed limit and drove all night, he could probably reach Beirut.

He started the car. Its small engine revved and whined like a chain saw. He backed out, pulled forward, saw the light of day just past the guard shack.

Am I going to make it? Really, am I going to get out of here alive?

As he cruised slowly toward the exit—blocked by a wooden arm painted red and white and by metal teeth protruding from the pavement—he saw the guard glance up at him, then back at something lower than the window, most likely a book.

Keep reading, he thought—no, he *willed* it, with all his concentration. *That's not the walkie-talkie you hear. Not an order to stop the perspiring man in the red Fiat.*

The guard didn't look up again until Pip brought the car to a stop directly in front of him. The Fiat's grille wasn't four feet from the barrier arm and spikes. From the shack's window, the guard grinned down at Pip.

"Mr. Farago," he said. But he didn't punch whatever buttons were required to raise the barrier arm and lower the teeth. He just looked at Pip.

Was this it? Had Luco already called the guard? Instead of issuing the simple order, "Kill him," had he said, "Keep him from leaving. I'll be right down"? No reason to handle Pip's murder discreetly.

Luco had instructed Arjan to recruit all his bodyguards and the building's security guards from Palermo. They all knew Luco and Pip from the old days. Remove the two months of training they received at the Paladin Academy of Advanced Executive Protection in Munich—an elite facility Luco had charmed the Italian Foreign Service into springing for—and these men were mere thugs, mafioso with manners. They were loyal and trained to kill—could the Antichrist have better buddies?

Pip looked over his shoulder, through the back window. He half-expected to see Luco standing there, washed red in the brake lights, shotgun pointed at Pip's head. But there was no one. To the guard, he said, "Well?"

"Your pass card?" he said, sounding as though he wanted to add, *Idiot!*

Which is what Pip felt like. He was so used to already having his ID in hand when leaving, he'd completely forgotten it.

He fished his ID out of his jacket pocket and handed it to the guard, who swiped it through a card reader inside the shack and handed it back. The barrier arm began swinging up. Pip assumed the metal teeth were also retracting. He felt his heart slow a bit and inch down out of his throat.

But why would Luco let him go? Pip had seen the look in his eyes when it dawned on him that Pip could do him true harm. He had seen the fury, the mad hate. He'd seen it before, and it had always meant destruction to the person at which it was leveled. Why not this time? Had Pip misread the situation? Misread Luco?

Movement at the corner of his vision made him turn. The guard had raised a finger to his ear. A skin-colored cord snaked from it and disappeared under his collar. Pip stepped on the accelerator. The engine revved; the car went nowhere. He had dropped the manual shifter into neutral when he'd gone for his pass card. His eyes caught sight of the guard's handgun rising from below the window and turning toward him. He shoved the shifter forward with his palm and popped the clutch.

The gun roared in his ear. A searing pain flared around his skull. A tremendous force knocked his head to the right; his body followed. A spray of blood hit the windshield and streaked over the dash and center console as he went down.

The car leaped forward. Pip kept his foot on the gas.

The gun roared again, shattering the window behind the driver's door. Glass rained down like diamonds on Pip and bounded off every surface. The majority of his brain frantically screamed at his body to do something, *anything*—lash out, hit, kick, pull, tug, run, flip, duck, leap, scrunch down, flail out, jump back . . .

However, some small area of cognizance was casually processing the events around him. It told him that he should have heard the tinkling of all that glass flying and bouncing around him. It told him he could not hear it because the first gunshot had made him temporarily deaf in his left ear and largely deaf in his right. It told him that the bump the car had just bounded over was the lowered metal teeth. And when the front end dropped down, then suddenly leveled, it had gone past the sidewalk. Pip cranked the steering wheel sharply. Metal crunched, then screeched as the car pushed itself along the side of another vehicle.

The back window shattered. A bullet hole appeared like magic in the windshield.

He adjusted the wheel and the metal-on-metal scraping ended with a *clang!* The car sprang forward as though shot from a catapult, only to crash to a dead stop. Centrifugal force wrenched him against the stick shift, slamming his head into the glove box. The pain was so excruciating, consciousness flirted with leaving him. He held on to it, he had to. He pushed himself up, knowing he was groaning but hearing nothing but a sustained deep tone. The Fiat had plowed into a BMW parked at the curb. He shoved the shifter into reverse and looked back.

The guard was out of his shack, standing on the parking garage exit ramp. Behind him, the barrier arm was lowering again. The guard held his pistol with two hands, pointing it at Pip through the shattered back window. Pip dropped down. He heard nothing, felt nothing, but when he popped up again a moment later, another hole had appeared in the windshield in front of him. Tires squealing, he backed away fast from the BMW, adjusted the wheel just so . . . and slammed into the guard. The man shot off the rear bumper, blasted through the barrier arm, and slammed into the guard shack. His body dropped limply to the ground.

Deep in the shadows of the garage, muzzle flashes ignited like paparazzi cameras. Sparks sprang up from the trunk lid as a bullet nicked its surface. Two . . . three guards appeared out of the gloom, sprinting toward the Fiat.

Pip found first gear and shot down the street, fishtailing, then straightening. Another bullet tore through the windshield, taking with it a chunk of glass the size of a loaf of bread. Pip ducked, but the movement lowered his head only millimeters; he was already driving hunched over. His face was almost touching the wheel. He realized he could see only out of his right eye. He imagined his left eye punctured and hanging out on his cheek like a dead jellyfish on a beach. If indeed his eye lay like that, he couldn't do anything about it. His left arm rested limply in his lap, refusing to budge when his mind sent it orders.

Three blocks and he turned, bounding up onto the sidewalk to navigate past cars waiting for the light. Pedestrians scattered.

His pursuers would be in vehicles by now, not far behind. He tried to gauge how much of a lead he had, but his thought processes seemed as mangled as his car. He knew the guards would have had to retreat back into the garage for their Hummers, which were large vehicles and less maneuverable on these tight, crowded streets. A minute, maybe two, he guessed.

Again he swerved onto the sidewalk and slammed on the brakes inches before a startled family. When they scrambled into a shop, he surged on, then veered onto the street again. The blast of a horn widened his eye. The grille of an SUV rushed at him. He was in the wrong lane. Jerking the wheel, the Fiat crumpled the front quarter panel of some other vehicle, whose horn sounded like an infant's wail. Everything was dim, gray. Getting dimmer, grayer. He had to push on. They were close, close.

When consciousness finally shook free and fled, Pip sagged right, cranking the wheel that way. Against the hardness of Jerusalem's iron lampposts, the Fiat was no match.

26

Daniel Fears's home was a brick trilevel. From the front porch, you could spit and hit one of the neighboring houses. A uniformed officer met them on the porch, cut the yellow crime scene tape on the door, and let them in. Since the Ft. Collins crime lab had already dusted, scraped, taken photographs, removed the body—*in other words, done all the damage they could do,* Brady thought—recording a CSD walk-through would be only for practice and the Bureau's reference.

Alicia decided to don the suit on a little patch of linoleum inside the front door to avoid drawing a crowd.

"Need help?" Brady asked.

"No thanks. One of those things you gotta do alone."

"I'm going to wander."

"Have fun."

Brady wrote the date, location, and vic's name at the top of a legal pad and began walking the perimeter of the living room. Formal furniture. No clutter. Obviously not used much. He made a few notes. A half-flight of stairs rose from the living room to a hallway with five doors. The first on the right opened into a bathroom. Brady examined the contents of the medicine cabinet and the cupboard under the sink. He noted a pewter cross hanging on a nail.

The next door on the right was the master bedroom. He looked in the dresser drawers and the bed stand.

He examined another bathroom and two bedrooms, one decorated for a little girl.

Alicia was coming up the stairs as he was heading down. He didn't speak, just slipped past her quickly. He didn't like seeing himself on the walk-throughs.

"Check out the painting in the den," she said through the CSD's tinny speaker.

It was over a plaid sofa, which bore the bloodstains of Mr. Fears's untidy end. Brady recognized the print immediately. He'd taken a college course in European art of the fifteenth and sixteenth centuries, and this artist was one of its stars. Hieronymus Bosch. This was a lithograph of the *Haywain* triptych, which depicted paradise, earth, and this one, from the right wing— hell. Dark and depressing, it showed the ruins of burning buildings and animalistic demons impaling, skinning, and groping naked humans. Why anyone would display it so prominently in his home was a puzzle to Brady. But it did create a common denominator between Fears and Loeb.

On one wall of the den was a brick fireplace, flanked by bookshelves. He was still studying the spines when Alicia came up behind him. She was wearing the CSD, but she had turned off its lasers, lights, and doohickeys.

She said, "You want to point out important things I may have missed?"

"These books," he said, his head craned down to his shoulder to read the titles.

"Got 'em."

"Wall hangings, photographs, knickknacks."

"That's the same speech you gave me in Palmer Lake."

"Nothing's changed."

"Then I got everything. Find any linkages?"

"Maybe. Get out of that thing and we'll talk."

"You're as bad as the locals."

Five minutes later, she returned sans the Robocop outfit.

She said, "Did you notice that the painting is similar to the images Cynthia Loeb had painted on her trash cans?"

"Hell."

"In all its fiery horror. And this guy has some crosses here and there. Nothing like Loeb's bedroom, but do people tend to have a lot of religious symbols around the house? Is this normal?"

"Karen kept a few. A cross-stitched Bible verse—'As for me and my house, we will serve the Lord.' A few crosses. A painting of Jesus praying. One of George Washington praying at Valley Forge."

"So what stands out?"

"The images of hell. By definition, they're religious, but it's not the sort of thing religious people dwell on."

"Sounds promising."

"Don't get your hopes up. We have three other vics to check out, and we're nowhere near them, so we'll have to rely on the photos and reports."

"What are we waiting for? Let's get back to the hotel."

21

Luco Scaramuzzi's security force came upon the wreckage from two directions. Their Hummers roared up to the crumpled, smoking Fiat and stopped within a foot of each rear corner. With the lamppost pushing into its engine compartment, there was no way the thing could pull a surprise maneuver and get away. The Hummer doors flew open, and men hopped out.

From one of the Hummers emerged Arjan Vos. He was a man of average stature, five feet ten and thin. But the cords of muscles under his skin bulged and flexed like cables. He appeared densely packed, ready to spring. Even in his face, muscles rippled, carving angular features both hawkish and leonine. Unlike the blue uniform of his underlings, he wore the tan fatigues of a desert soldier. A tan beret covered the top of his bald head; where berets made weak men seem weaker, they made strong ones like Arjan more menacing, as though the beret were a cap on a bottle of destruction.

Arjan surveyed the area. Only curious stares. No police sirens yet, but that would change soon. In the few seconds he'd spent assessing the surroundings, his men had encircled the Fiat. Arms ending with pistols radiated inward from the circle of men. Arjan drew a Desert Eagle .357 magnum from its holster and strode up to the Fiat's closed driver's door.

The car was empty. Lots of blood, no body.

His head snapped up. The onlookers gaped with innocent expressions. Windows and doorways were impenetrably dark in the gloom of early evening. Squinting at the ground, Arjan saw no blood trails, no drops, no sign whatsoever of Pip's escape. He raised his voice to address the crowd.

"Who has seen the man from this car? He is hurt. We are here to help."

A boy of about six watched stone-faced from a nearby curb.

Even he knows we are not here to help, Arjan thought. Still, by making the claim, anyone who ratted out the wounded man could pretend to have believed in the soldiers' benevolence.

"Boy?" Arjan addressed the child. "Where has this man gone?"

The child didn't say a word. A woman came from the shadows of an arched alleyway, grabbed the boy by the shoulders, and hustled him away.

In the fashion of the finest town crier, Arjan turned in a slow circle as he called, "Italy offers a reward for this man. He is dangerous. He will hurt you. Take your reward and free yourself of his burden."

One old man turned and shuffled away. A young woman did the same. Soon the crowd had dispersed, uninterested in Arjan's offers. They knew who he was. They had heard stories of—or had had firsthand experience with—the strong-arm tactics employed by the Italian Embassy to keep the streets around its compound free of enemies and riffraff. He wanted to seize a few of them, take them back to his chambers, and discover what they knew of Pippino Farago. He considered conducting a quick house-by-house, store-by-store search, but that would be severely overstepping his authority, and the Jerusalem police would arrive soon. The telltale warble of their sirens had just now reached his ears. He could enlist their assistance in finding Pip, but once he was found, Jerusalem might hold him while jurisdiction was sorted out, and who knew what tales he would tell? Better to handle this in-house.

"Let's roll," he barked to his men. Pistols found their holsters, doors slammed.

When the first Jerusalem police car arrived, no evidence remained of anyone's particular interest in this traffic mishap. The only curiosity was the disappearance of the car's driver.

28

Cañon City, Colorado

O ver the jump!" Trevor Wilson yelled to his buddy Josiah, pedaling behind him. Even ten feet ahead, Trevor could hear his friend huffing for breath. He didn't feel superior because he was fitter, and he didn't give Josiah a hard time for being fat. He only wished his friend could keep up better so he didn't have to wait for him when they were hiking the rough terrain out past the new construction. Worse was not going on certain adventures at all—like crossing Temple Canyon River into the BLM lands beyond—because Josiah would have died trying.

Where the curb yielded to a driveway, Trevor swerved off the street onto the sidewalk and aimed his bike at a plywood skateboard jump some teenagers had set up. He heard Josiah's bike rattle as it jolted onto the sidewalk behind him. *He's doing too good a job keeping up,* Trevor thought. If Trevor wiped out on the jump, Josiah would plow into him for sure. He pumped his legs harder, wanting to hit the ramp fast and as far ahead of Josiah as possible. Crashing would be bad enough—Mom had warned him about not ruining another Boy Scout uniform—but Josiah and his bike landing on top of him was a nightmare he didn't want to think about.

Ten feet to the ramp. Five. Trevor held his breath and pulled up on the handlebars just as the front tire made contact. A hollow rumble, then silence—he was flying. He looked straight down to see the concrete a good four feet below his sneakers. He hoped the older kids who'd built the ramp were watching from somewhere. Catching air like this might score him some points. Then he remembered his helmet and prayed the teens were nowhere near. Helmets were definitely uncool. Shifting his gaze to the point

of impact, he braced himself and tried to keep the front wheel from
wobbling. He hit and experienced a moment of panic as his bike wanted to
bounce and tumble out from under him, but he held on and kept it under
control. Immediately he veered into a yard and slid sideways to a stop.

He looked back in time to see Josiah take the ramp hard, not lifting on
the handlebars to help the bike over. He was leaning forward instead of back
as he took flight. And he should have been moving faster. The front wheel
plummeted down against the sidewalk, suddenly becoming much slower
than the rear of the bike, which careened upward, sending Josiah over the
handlebars. The boy's death grip kept him from sailing ahead of his bicycle.
Instead, for a few amazing seconds, fat Josiah Millard performed a handstand on the handlebars, as graceful and balanced as a circus bear. Then he
came down—fortunately onto the seat and not in the other direction. But
the acrobatics and the force of their conclusion proved too much for Josiah
and his bike: the two shook violently and went their separate ways. Josiah
landed on the sidewalk, skidded, rolled, tumbled, and came up standing,
just to repeat the skid-roll-tumble once more before halting in a heap.

Trevor leaped from his bike.

"Dude! That was awesome!"

Josiah moaned.

"Are you all right?" Trevor leaned over, appraising his friend's face. His
eyes were open; that was a good sign. A square of skin was scraped off one
cheek. He was holding his elbow.

"Lemme see," Trevor said.

Josiah's hand came away bloody. A gouged-out hole the size of a pebble
oozed goopy crimson.

Trevor scrutinized the wound from several angles and declared, "You'll
be fine."

Josiah smiled faintly. Trevor knew his friend, like the kids at school,
assumed the weeks he'd spent in the hospital after his accident had made
him prematurely wise about medical matters. He did nothing to discourage
that opinion. Why shouldn't something good come out of that awful time?

Of course, being in St. Thomas More ICU had not really boosted his
medical IQ, except in the areas that had directly affected him. He now knew

that in the United States an average of twelve people a day died of drowning. Of that number, ten were male. He knew that "cyanosis" was when skin turned blue from lack of oxygen in the blood supply, and that CPR, even when administered correctly, can cause broken ribs. He knew that broken ribs ached with every breath.

The hospital stay had also taught him that he wanted to do for others what his doctors had done for him. He didn't think it was a coincidence that he'd come out of the coma knowing he had to do something right with his life. He had to do *good*.

He'd started seeing people, especially children, as majestic beings cloaked in eggshell bodies. He'd wondered how many children had died throughout history who would have given the world something wonderful had they lived. He wanted to help them live to achieve their destinies.

Deep thoughts for the ten-year-old he was at the time of the accident. But Trevor had aged beyond the days he was comatose. Except for his brief babbling upon returning to consciousness, his family never addressed this change or the reason for it, sensing the pain, the fright that lay behind it. He wouldn't discuss it even with himself, pushing it away when it threatened to emerge from the recesses of his memory.

Trevor looked at Josiah again, and his eyes grew wide.

"What?" his friend said, scared again.

"Your helmet." Trevor whispered the words. He unsnapped his friend's chin strap and gently pulled the helmet off his head. He half-expected brains and gore to spill out, but there was only messy hair and sweat. He turned it in his hands to show Josiah: A deep crack ran horizontally across the entire front. Broken Styrofoam showed through the cracked plastic.

"That could've been your head."

Josiah rubbed his forehead. "I have a *little* headache, but . . ." He shook his head.

Trevor reached up to his own helmet. It had just become a lot more acceptable.

"Come on. Can you get up?"

Trevor reached out a hand to pull his friend up.

"Hey, look," Josiah said when he was standing, leaning heavily on

Trevor. He was squinting up at the rock cliffs that marked the end of their subdivision and the start of the vast Royal Gorge Park.

Trevor followed his gaze. Boulders and scraggly pines lined the top ridge, pale blue sky beyond.

"I don't—," he started, but then he did; he saw the figure standing way up there, rock solid. Man or woman, he couldn't tell. They watched for a good thirty seconds, but the person didn't move. "Freaky," Trevor said. "Let's get your bike."

It lay in the street, front wheel mangled, spokes jutting out like spindly ribs. Josiah sat on the curb while Trevor tried to make the damaged bike rollable. First the spokes kept getting hung up on the fork. Then the tire peeled off and wrapped around the hub.

"Dude, I think you made out better than your bike," Trevor said. He retrieved his own bike from the grass and told Josiah to walk it home. He lifted the other bike's front end and pulled it down the street on its back wheel.

Josiah was favoring his right leg, but not dramatically, and Trevor could tell he was relying on the bike to keep himself from falling. He came alongside.

"You need to get your mom to take you to a doctor," he said.

Josiah's head swung back and forth. "I'm all right."

They walked silently for a time. When Trevor let loose with a tight giggle, trying to restrain himself, Josiah turned.

"What?"

Trevor smiled. "Man, you should have seen yourself. You did a *handstand* on the handlebars!"

"I did?" Josiah grinned.

"Straight up." Trevor laughed. "I mean, your body was straight up in the air, even your legs."

"I thought you'd like that."

"Oh, like it was on purpose!"

They both cracked up, and Josiah walked a little steadier. At Trevor's house, they wheeled the bikes up to the drive, and Trevor punched a code into a keypad that got the garage door rumbling up.

"He's still there," Josiah said. The figure on the ridge.

Trevor went into the garage and came out with binoculars. After a moment of searching, then focusing, he saw the man—definitely a man, with wild hair and a long, bushy beard. He was looking back at Trevor with his own set of binoculars.

"He's got binoculars too," he said. "I think he's looking right at us."

"Probably a pervert," Josiah said. He cupped his hands like a megaphone and yelled at the man, "This what you want, perv?" He turned around and shook his considerable backside.

Trevor backhanded him. "Knock it off!"

"Ow! Watch the elbow, dude!"

Trevor pressed his eyes against the rubber eyecups. "Hey," he said, "there's a dog sitting next to him. Looks like a Husky."

"Let me see!" Josiah pulled the binocs out of his hands.

"Probably just some construction worker." Trevor sounded doubtful.

Josiah rotated the focusing knob. "Whoa," he said. "Creepy."

Trevor went into the garage. He didn't like creepy things. Not since the accident, he didn't.

29

The boy disappeared into the garage. He was small for his age, and of course there had been no driver's license photo for Olaf to study, but he knew he had found Trevor Wilson. He fit the description: four and a half feet tall, ninety pounds, strawberry blond hair. And he had opened the garage door at the address listed.

The larger boy was still watching him through field glasses. Tomorrow, he'd tell police about the strange man on the cliff. They'd come up here and find where he'd stood, find some dog hairs. Nothing new. But if they snooped far enough, they'd find tire tracks. He'd have to do something about that. He didn't mind leaving fingerprints at the crime scenes, because he'd never been printed and he didn't plan on being caught. At least not alive. The tires were another matter. If the treads were unique enough, police could identify the van as a suspect vehicle while he was away from it, hunting or purchasing supplies, perhaps. They would then have the advantage of surprise, and that was something he wanted to keep for himself.

The big kid had lowered the glasses and was talking into the garage. The other boy, Trevor, leaned out, grabbed his friend by the arm, and pulled him inside, glancing quickly up at the ridge. *He didn't like being watched,* Olaf thought. *Smart kid.*

He panned his binoculars to the back of the house. Then farther, to the greenbelt that conveniently ran like an alley behind the backyards the length of the block. Every yard was framed by a six-foot-high cedar fence, each with a gate opening onto the greenbelt.

His eyes followed the footpath across two streets to where the houses stopped and a small, sodded park filled the gap between the neighborhood and the cliffs upon which he stood. The park consisted of a wooden play set, a row of teeter-totters, and a smattering of trees. A gravel parking lot demarcated its southern border to Olaf's right. A trail appeared to snake west, into the foothills. Most likely, it eventually passed near Olaf's current position, though he hadn't crossed a trail on his way here.

He swung his vision back to the Trevor kid's house. The garage door was closed, the bikes gone.

A sour thought occurred to him: what if the big kid stayed the night? His own boys cherished overnights with friends. Olaf's desire to kill the boy in his sleep meant using more stealth than he had before. That would make it difficult enough without the complication of another child in the room. He lowered the binoculars, taking in the grid of houses from his eagle's perch, and sighed. His mission was paramount. He'd get the job done—neatly or not.

He scanned his surroundings. He needed to be as sure as possible that he wouldn't encounter any surprises when he returned later that night. The trail that began at the park below was somewhere north of him. He turned and headed off in search of it, bounding over boulders and deadfalls far more nimbly than his bulk suggested he could. The dog hung at his side until it was sure of his direction. Then it leaped ahead, sniffing, watching. Together they moved silently and, once in the trees, invisibly.

30

Crime scene photos covered every horizontal surface of Alicia's hotel room. Brady moved from one to the next with a magnifying glass and notepad. Alicia sat at the room's desk, watching her crime scene walk-throughs from Palmer Lake and Ft. Collins in slow motion on her PowerBook. Occasionally she'd freeze a frame and click a button to print out a high-resolution photograph. Whenever he heard the printer, Brady would drift over, take the printout, and drift back to wherever he'd been before the printer beckoned.

Once, he asked if Alicia had access to the Internet. She rolled her eyes, and he said he needed to surf for a bit. She strolled down to a soft-drink machine, and when she returned with a pop for each of them, he was back at the piles of photos. Twenty minutes later, he said, "Okay, ready?"

She watched another few frames of Daniel Fears's house click by before closing the laptop's screen. "Shoot," she said.

He pointed to a pile of photos on the bed. "Vic number one. Joseph Johnson. Ogden, Utah. No images of hell, as far as I can see from the crime scene photos and reports. But check out these books: *Embraced by the Light* by Betty Eadie and Curtis Taylor, *Immortal Remains: The Evidence for Life after Death* by Stephen E. Braude, and *Hell to Pay* by Duncan McAfee."

"What are those?" Alicia asked.

"According to Amazon.com, they all have to do with near-death experiences—NDEs."

"Okay," she said, unsure.

"You know, someone's heart stops, they're clinically dead, and then they get resuscitated—CPR or whatever. While they were 'dead,' their spirits . . . experienced things."

"Things?"

"Maybe they float above their corpse or—what these books all address—they head for heaven."

"Weird."

"A lot of people believe in the reality of near-death experiences." He glanced around at the papers and photos that represented the Pelletier victims. "Apparently, these people did."

He recited each victim's NDE-related books. Even William Bell—the plumber's assistant whose entire library consisted of five books, including *A Decade of Sports Illustrated Swimsuit Photography*—owned *The Complete Idiot's Guide to Near-Death Experiences* by P. M. H. Atwater and *Only Visiting: Glimpses of the Afterlife* by Duncan McAfee.

"That guy keeps popping up," she noted.

"Duncan McAfee. He's the only author owned by at least four vics."

"I think we have a connection."

He let out a big breath. "Now I want to know why these people were interested in NDEs."

"That's what phones are for," she said. "You take three murder books and give me two. We'll call relatives, and I'll also track down Duncan McAfee. I'll use my cell phone so you can use the hotel line."

———

ALICIA WAS on the Internet when Brady hung up from his final call. It had taken a little more than two hours.

He said, "I'm starving."

She scooped up the desk phone. "How about room service? What do you want?"

After she ordered for both of them, she said, "Well, Cynthia Loeb's wonderful ex said her heart stopped during a hysterectomy four years ago. First she said it was horrible. Then she stopped talking about it, but she got obsessed with all things afterlife—heaven, hell, angels, demons. He insisted they'd still be together if she hadn't gone loony tunes on him, his words."

She flipped a page. "I couldn't track down any of William Bell's relatives. His boss said he had some kind of accident a few years ago. Crashed an ATV or JetSki, he couldn't remember. He was in the hospital for a month, but he never talked about it. In fact, he went from being gregarious before the accident to almost reclusive afterward." She shrugged. "Oh, and I found out Duncan McAfee is a Catholic priest in Manhattan."

"A priest?"

"Yep. I got his number too."

"All right. I had two busts. Daniel Fears's ex hung up on me when I asked about his medical history. His mother said he had a 'bad experience' last year when his appendix burst, then *she* hung up on me. Ditto when I spoke to three of Joseph Johnson's relatives. You'd think I was a reporter for the *National Enquirer* asking about their late loved one's transvestite tendencies. Jessica Hampton's husband said she definitely had a near-death experience when her heart stopped during a complicated childbirth. When she first was revived, she was terrified, screaming about demons and hell. In recovery, she told him she'd been taken to hell by demons, who tried to hold on to her when she was getting pulled back to her body. The next day she said she didn't want to talk about it, and she never again did, even though he was supportive and encouraged her to open up. She became very religious and attended Presbyterian services three times a week and a Bible study twice a week."

He had been sitting cross-legged on the bed. Now he stretched his arms and legs and clambered off.

"I'm going to go wash up and then call Zach before room service comes," he said. He left, promising to return in fifteen minutes. Alicia flipped open her cell phone and dialed Father McAfee's number.

On the eighth ring a man's voice said, "Hello?"

Either she'd awakened him or he had been drinking.

"Fr. Duncan McAfee?"

"Yes, who is this?"

"I'm Special Agent Alicia Wagner with the Federal Bureau of Investigation."

"FBI? About my files?"

"Uh . . . what files, sir?"

"You're not calling about my files? What do you want, then?"

"What happened to your files?"

"They were stolen!" he yelled.

Alicia moved the handset away from her ear. "When was this?"

"Three weeks ago! I filed a report!"

"What were these files?"

"My life's work. All my work."

"I'm sorry. Maybe there's something I can—"

"Oh, stop jerking my chain! You people aren't going to do anything. The police aren't doing anything."

"Did your files have to do with your books, your near-death experience books?"

"What else would they have to do with?"

"Sir, I'm calling because we found your books at the scenes of several crimes. I wanted to ask—"

"Am I a suspect now? For crying out loud!"

"No, it's just that—"

"Then stop bothering me!"

Click.

"Hello? Father McAfee?"

Whoa.

FATHER MCAFEE cradled the phone and closed his eyes.

What now, dear Lord? Father Randall's visit three weeks ago had begun a time of restless nights and torment. The old man had not stirred old guilt or fears; McAfee knew how to handle psychological demons. For fifty-nine of his sixty-eight years, prayer alone had driven them from his mind. No, another sort of demon—perhaps even a manifest one, McAfee grudgingly conceded—had haunted the church grounds. Unexplainable shadows, echoing footsteps in empty halls, hideous laughter in the rectory, lasting just long enough to wake him up and let him know it was real, not dream sounds—that's how it started.

A week ago, the harassment had escalated. He'd come into the chapel to find the statues of the saints knocked over, beheaded and delimbed, defiled with what McAfee had thought was blood but turned out to be red paint. Bad enough. Frightening enough. The police had essentially shrugged. Kids, they said. But McAfee knew better. The culprit, he was sure, was whoever, whatever was haunting him and his church—left, seemingly, by Father Randall.

He heard the scuff of shoes on the stone floor behind him and spun. A shadow drifted by on the wall in the hall outside the open door of his office.

"Who is it?" he called. He felt foolish, like someone in denial.

The shadow was gone, but the now-familiar laugh—a cackle, really—floated back to him. As it died, something crashed; glass shattered.

"Go away!" McAfee yelled. "Be gone from here in the name of Jesus Christ!" He crossed himself.

He received no reply, but a few moments later the shadow slid into view again, and stayed. Whoever was casting it must have been just out of sight in the hall. McAfee's heart thumped faster. He closed his eyes, mumbling a prayer. When he opened them again, the shadow was gone.

———

ALICIA ANSWERED Brady's knock with her cell phone wedged between her cheek and shoulder. She waved him in.

"John, listen to me," she said into the phone. "No, it's not perfect, but almost."

She listened.

He went to the table where the room service food was laid out and found his cheeseburger on a plate under a metal cover. He started eating it standing up.

"We've already made headway. We've discovered the linkage . . ."

She sat heavily on the edge of the bed. "Yeah, okay. Thanks . . ." She flipped the phone closed and added, "For nothing."

Around a mouthful of burger, he asked, "Gilbreath?"

She nodded. "They got positive matches on fingerprints and animal hairs from Ogden and Ft. Collins. Same dogs, same perp, different states . . . the Bureau's got jurisdiction."

He nodded and took another big bite.

"The investigative team is flying in tomorrow," she said. "And we're flying out."

She stood, tossed the phone onto the bed, and found her Reuben sandwich. She popped a French fry into her mouth. "These fries are awful."

He reached down and grabbed a handful.

She picked up the Reuben and set it down again. "Don't you want to stay? Don't you want to help close this case?"

He shook his head and swallowed. "I'm cool with what we do, Alicia. I don't like being away from home for long stretches. We contribute. That's fine with me."

She made an exasperated sound. "Always being on the outside is driving me crazy. I want to be in the thick of things. I want to bust bad guys."

"The work you're doing will help put away more bad guys than you could in a lifetime of field investigations."

"Yeah, yeah, yeah."

"What if Edmond Locard had felt that way? Can you imagine crime investigation without the benefit of fingerprints?"

She lifted the sandwich, took a bite. "I spoke to McAfee," she said.

"And?"

"And something's there. His files were stolen *three weeks ago*."

"His NDE files? This is going to be open-and-shut."

"See? But can *we* close it? No, we have to go home and tinker with gadgets."

She rattled on, alternately taking bites and bemoaning her lot at the Bureau.

He watched her and smiled. She had no idea how cute she was.

31

Pain. Excruciating pain, both sharp and throbbing.

It was Pip's first sensation as he drifted up from dark, swirling dreams that instantly evaporated from his memory like morning mist. His face and ribs ached. His head felt crushed, pinned by an unbearable weight. His eyes fluttered open, then closed. The darkness again, the mist. He forced his eyes open. He was in a bedroom, decorated with touches of pink and white lace, white-painted furniture, dolls on top of a dresser. The only illumination was a soft glow coming from a lamp he could not see, off to his right.

On tendons like barbed wire, he rotated his head and wanted to scream in agony. He drew in an audible breath. A woman sat in a wooden chair beside the bed. She looked up from a book.

Where am I? he tried to say, but only a groan came out.

The woman stood and leaned over him. She was in her fifties, sporting short gray hair and compassionate eyes.

"Shhh," she said, and continued speaking in Hebrew. Pip did not understand a word, but his head refused to signal incomprehension. He began moving his lips.

She held up a hand and tried again, this time in passable English. "Do not speak. You were in a bad accident."

He managed a word: "How . . . ?"

"When you crashed, my husband ran to help. You pleaded for him to hide you. You said men were after you. A few neighbors pulled you out and into the building just before soldiers arrived." She made a disagreeable face. "Not Israeli soldiers."

"No," he agreed.

"We don't know what you have done, but we will not turn you over to them."

"I have . . ." He grimaced and reached up to his head. Bandages covered his scalp. "I have to . . ."

"You cannot move right now," she said kindly but firmly. "Whatever you have to do, do it in bed."

"No . . . I must . . . get something. I need to get . . ."

He raised himself off the pillow, watched the room fade to gray, and fell back down. He tried once more. He made it no farther. He looked at the woman pleadingly. "Important," he said.

"You cannot—" Something in his eyes made her stop. She studied his face for a long time. Gently, she patted the bedding that covered his chest. "Maybe my husband can help." She rose and left the room.

Pip thought about how he could convince her husband to help. Just go to the train station . . . to a locker there . . .

Darkness crowded his thoughts and the mist drifted up to claim him again.

"YOU SHOT him?" Luco asked again.

Arjan stood statue-straight, his face grim. "Baducci did, yes."

"In the head?"

"Yes."

Luco shook his head. "I don't understand."

"It happens. A bullet hits the head just so, and the skull acts like a helmet, deflecting it."

"And he drove away, wrecked his car, and disappeared?"

"We found blood but no body."

"Unbelievable."

Now what? Luco thought. Pip would try to get to the case file, then either bargain with it for his life or attempt to get it to Hüber. He had to get to one of them—Pip or the file—before that happened. He eyed Arjan, erect and proper. He made an instant decision: he did not want Arjan or any of his men recovering the file. One mistake was enough.

"Watch his apartment and office, but don't search them."

Arjan flicked his eyes at Luco, puzzled.

"I will do that myself," Luco said. "Understand?"

"Yes."

"Tell your men to kill him on sight, regardless of where he is. Bring the body to me."

"I understand."

Luco doubted he did. But he knew Arjan was a professional, the consummate soldier. The man did not question orders; he only fulfilled them. He squeezed Arjan's shoulder. "I know I can count on you, my friend."

32

As far as Olaf could tell, Trevor Wilson's house had darkened completely at about ten thirty, just over two hours ago. Crouched on the ridge above the community's small park, he could not see the windows on the rear or far side of the house. But it was Thursday, which meant school in the morning for the boy and work for his parents. Likely, they retired early, before midnight at least. His approach from the rear would bring the obstructed windows into view. If he saw a lamp burning or the blue flicker of a television, he could retreat and wait awhile longer. But not forever. His schedule required his arriving in Santa Fe by tomorrow evening.

As much as he disliked the task of killing a child, murdering people just because they were witnesses or tried to prevent him from fulfilling his duties was worse. A name on his list was as good as word from Odin, the god of gods: it was their time, and Olaf was the instrument of fate. Peripheral causalities, on the other hand, were tragic. Not that he would ever hesitate in bringing that tragedy about, should his mission be threatened. In fact, his training and the state of mind he worked himself into before sweeping in for a kill guaranteed a quick blade across the throat of any and all who stepped into his path.

He rocked forward on the balls of his feet, using the bearded ax as a prop to prevent himself from pitching into the darkness beyond the cliff. He'd occupied this spot under the limbs of a massive cottonwood for hours, watching as the comings and goings of residents below dwindled to stagnancy and their world shut down, window by window.

At first, knowing he had time, he had allowed his mind to wander, leaping to memories and storing new facts as images entered his sphere of consciousness. A Mercedes Benz traversing the streets below got him thinking about industry and progress, then materialism and greed. He'd watched as children came home alone to empty houses, and hours later first one parent arrived, then the other—when there was another. He'd seen the plastic bags of food transferred from car to home, where the families would eat what they had not grown and had not killed. Often, one or two or all the members of a household would leave again, returning hours later, the children sweaty and tired from having participated in some unknown recreation, the parents chatty from an infusion of social stimuli. It was as though the company of their kin were not enough; the warmth of hearth, the caress of one another's hands, the verbal sharing of the day's adventures were all insufficient to fill their hearts.

He'd concluded, not for the first time, that his own way of life, the way of his clan, was far superior. He found happiness in family and survival and duty, in knowing the gods were pleased with his devotion. He trained hard and studied hard, truly content to spend his life preparing for a duty that may have never become his to bear.

But it *had* come to him, like a fiery vision that scalds the eyes because it is too beautiful to turn away from. After centuries, the waiting was over. Now his skills, which had been passed on and honed by his father and *his* father before him, were fully needed. Joining his ancestors in Valhalla could not bring him more delight than stepping into this long-awaited role in Odin's service. It was for this duty that he had parted from his family. It was for this that he crouched here in the dark, with the tang of pines and the musk of loamy earth in his nose, his hunting ground sprawled before him.

As the sky dimmed and darkened and the moon climbed, every spark of brain activity began illuminating a single thought: the kill. Slowly, a ferocity toward humankind welled in him. Images of human cruelty, displayed in grotesque photographs and vividly rendered by tribe storytellers, fueled his hatred. Apostasy, immorality, war. What treason *hadn't* the race of man committed?

Five years ago, the remnants who fought for a return to the old ways, for a reversal of apostasy, had announced the arrival of the one who would tear down the temples of self-centeredness and false gods and unite the world as a single virtuous tribe. The forces against him, however, were numerous, cunning and powerful, having strategized and fortified for millennia. Some were malevolent warriors, others—like the boy he would visit tonight, Olaf presumed—unwitting cogs in a machine designed to crush the coming usurpation.

Olaf did not need to know in what way a twelve-year-old child threatened the future perfect world. He trusted others to see the big picture and determine appropriate actions. He was a hand wielding a sword—or more accurately, an ax. Did hands guide themselves or question why they gripped this or struck that?

And so his burning ferocity, his acidic hatred, narrowed its focus from all of humankind to one young boy. He pictured Trevor Wilson: blue eyes, hair the color of wheat tinged by the setting sun, a smattering of freckles, almost effeminate lips. He did not make the boy into a monster. In his mind, no horns sprouted from Trevor's head, no vile curses spewed from his mouth. Destruction came in all forms, some more innocent looking than others. Trevor was a cute kid. If Olaf got to know him, no doubt he'd see in him aspects of his own sons. Compassion, curiosity, big-eyed wonder at the world, love. Yet the brain in this body of which he, Olaf, was only a hand had identified the child as dangerous. His continued existence imperiled man's very redemption. He hated the boy for that, for halting redemption, whether intentionally or not.

The only dispensation he could grant for the child's age and seeming innocence was this late-night approach without the dogs. An adult enemy was always attacked when he (*or she*, he thought, though he was unaccustomed to this new inclusion of female prey) was awake. It allowed a final confirmation that the death was the will of the gods, or for the gods' granting of a last-moment reprieve. If, despite Olaf's training, power, weaponry, and dogs, the enemy found a way to live—through fight or flight or the successful interference of others—then the prey had garnered favor from the Holy Powers. Olaf would accept defeat as divine providence . . . temporarily. Until the order was rescinded, he would strike again and again. The gods could stay his ax continually or eventually let it find its mark.

A child, on the other hand, fell under the authority and protection of his parents. If the gods deemed the killing untimely, they would inspire parental interference. Olaf saw no reason to terrify the boy, nor to simply give him an opportunity to change his fate, when that responsibility was his parents'.

So tonight the dogs stayed in the van. He felt incomplete without them, his comrades in battle. But it would go well, as it always did. He pressed one hand to the shirt Ingun had knitted for him, soft against his calloused finger-tips. He touched each of the lockets his sons had given him, the *Othel* and the rabbit's foot. His wife and boys were his comrades tonight. He felt them with him. He felt their readiness for the hunt.

Olaf's muscles tightened. His nerves became hypersensitive, his senses hyperaware. A faint breeze sifted through the hair on his arms, coming from the east. Good. He would be upwind from his prey. Below in the hunting ground, a door slammed, a dog barked. He quickly assessed their level of threat and dismissed them from his mind. His breathing became rhythmic, as training and instinct brought him to a mental and physical state perfect for killing.

He pulled the ax toward him, its blade scraping on rock, like a violin playing a harsh *sul ponticello* note. The overture to his performance. He slid his hand down the smooth wooden handle. Inches from the blade his grip tightened, and he rose. His eyes traced the route he'd take once he emerged from the wild into the park.

Boy on his mind, ax in hand, he spun and darted toward the trail that would unite the two.

33

Trevor lifted his face off the pillow and looked at the digital clock on his nightstand—12:43—before realizing it was a sound that had jarred him from sleep. He rolled over and sat up in bed. Having relinquished his Power Rangers night-light almost a year ago, he looked around a room as dark as a tomb—okay for falling asleep, really lousy for times like this. Even the moonlight had been kept out with vertical blinds, its rays poking through cord holes and gleaming round the edges. The door was ajar, as he liked it, but the hall beyond was dark as well.

"Mom?" he said softly. "Dad?"

Silence.

He cocked his head, held his breath.

Nothing.

What had woken him? He realized he had to pee. Maybe it was that and not a noise. Tossing back the covers, he swung his legs off the bed.

Clonk. Outside the window, almost too quiet to hear.

Trevor stared, half-expecting some ferocious beast to crash through, glass and vertical blinds flying everywhere. When that didn't happen, he shook his head.

Too many movies, he thought.

Clonk.

Trevor gasped, then instantly rebuked himself for doing such a sissy thing, even if the nastiest monster ever to crawl out of Stephen King's head *were* trying to get him. Stephen King was pretty creepy. Trevor didn't like creepy.

"Oh, it's nothing," he whispered and walked to the window. He noticed how a faint thread of light ran the length of each slat. He thought about bending a slat with his finger and peering out. Then he imagined an eye peering back at him from the other side. That would be creepier than pulling up the whole set of blinds and facing whatever was out there. He reached up and grabbed the plastic tassel at the end of the strings that controlled the raising and lowering of the blinds. He didn't open them right away, however. He knew any second, his courage would realize he was awake and return to him.

A flagstone path ran diagonally through the backyard, past his window. Something was sliding across the stones, making a soft shuffling sound: *sshhhooo . . . sshhhooo . . . sshhhooo . . .*

Trevor snatched his hand away from the cord. His heart pounded in his chest like a bird determined to escape its cage.

Daaaaad!!!! he screamed in his head, but only fast, ragged breaths came from his mouth. He squeezed his eyes closed, gritted his teeth.

It's nothing, he repeated to himself. *Nothing.* He slowed his breathing and felt the bird in his chest calm a bit. Before he could stop himself, he reached up and yanked down on the cord, running the blinds up with a plastic clatter. His eyes snapped open.

The backyard, washed in moonlight. Nothing else.

Sshhhooo . . . sshhhooo . . . Closer to the house.

He looked and let out the breath he was holding. A raccoon, fat and furry, tugged with its teeth on a paper grocery bag whose opening had been rolled closed. With each tug, it took a step backward and the bag moved across the stone path six inches—*sshhhooo.*

Trevor leaned his forehead against the glass, partly to see the raccoon better, but mostly in relief.

"You . . . rascal," he said.

As if it had heard him, the raccoon released the bag and craned to look up at the window. It lifted its front half, resting on its haunches, and sniffed the air. Then it dropped down and waddled past the bag toward the back gate. Halfway there it stopped at what was apparently another treasure it had tried to steal. A family-size soup can. Trevor remembered the chicken noodle they'd had at dinner the night before last. The raccoon lifted it with its paws, tilted it as though taking a swig, then let it fall—*clonk.*

Trevor smiled. "Come back and get your bag, fella," he said quietly. "Trashman comes, it'll be too late."

A shadow fell over him. He looked up to see clouds obscuring the moon, drifting lazily by. His eyes lowered to the raccoon, rocking back and forth as it moved slowly toward the gate, empty-pawed.

"See ya," he whispered. Deciding to leave the blinds open for light, he turned from the window. A faint shadow stretched out from his feet on the carpeted floor. He followed it out of the room, where it disappeared altogether. He found the bathroom in the dark.

34

Olaf had found the trail and was only a dozen long strides down it when he stopped. Holding perfectly still, he listened. After a moment the sound he thought he had heard came again: a bark. Muffled and far off. Not from the neighborhood dog that had barked earlier. Not from just any dog. This one carried a combination of pitch and treble he knew well. It lasted longer than a normal bark but stopped before becoming a howl.

Freya. Something was disturbing her.

Without hesitation, he ran back up the trail. He bounded off it and in thirty seconds passed the spot where he'd crouched for so long, like a gargoyle watching for evil spirits.

Freya sounded her cry again.

She wasn't fighting or trying to defend the van. She was telling him something required his attention, and the others were letting her. Not a matter of life or death . . . yet. As he ran, ducking under branches, leaping over plants, he considered the possibilities: A hiker had strolled past. Teenagers from town were approaching, cautiously because they were up to no good. A vehicle had pulled near, perhaps a police cruiser.

Olaf crested the hill that rose behind the ridge overlooking the town. He plunged down the other side, moving faster now.

He'd parked the van between two trees and hidden it behind cut branches. Odd that it would be spotted so quickly, especially at night. But Freya—

She barked again, clear in his ears now that he was closer.

Freya would not risk detection had she not already been detected.

Two hundred yards from the van, he slowed his pace. He would not simply plunge into a situation about which he knew nothing. If the police had spotted his van and somehow connected it to Olaf's handiwork, they might be lying in wait for him. Perhaps they believed he was in the van, asleep or preparing to fend them off with an arsenal of firearms. Freya would not distinguish an ambush from curious passersby, unless they stormed the van or bathed it in blinding halogen lights, neither of which had apparently happened.

He moved from tree to tree, sniffing for a hint of the danger: cigarette smoke, gun oil, body odor. As he drew close, he crouched lower, making his silhouette less human-shaped. When the branches that camouflaged the van came into sight, he lowered his body onto the ground, fluidly, as if melting into the undergrowth. Looking sideways, forcing images onto the more light-sensitive rods on his retinas, rather than the cones directly behind the pupils, he surveyed the darkened forest. He moved quietly on knees and elbows in a move-stop-scan sequence. He circled the van's hiding spot until he'd examined the complete area.

Nothing. Yet Freya continued her rhythmic barking, once every five seconds or so.

He crawled right up to the jumbled branches that obscured the van and slowly moved aside three of them. He pushed his head and shoulders into the gap he'd created. No one hid under the van. None of the shocks sagged with the uneven excess weight of a man hiding inside—a possibility Olaf thought as unlikely as the dogs sprouting wings and flying away. It would have required recording Freya's bark, killing or otherwise incapacitating all three animals, and then playing back the steady bark on nearly perfect speakers. He rolled onto his back to examine the branches high over the van. No hunter's tree stand. No clinging snipers.

What, then?

He raised his arms and knocked down the wall of foliage. When he stood, all three dogs were staring out at him. Freya whined. He circled around to the other side and slid open the door. The dogs edged up to the opening.

Remaining outside, he studied their faces curiously and whispered, *"Hva vík hóra?"* Then he caught the amber oil light blinking on the dash. He nodded. He had not trained her to draw his attention to it if it activated, but he was pleased that she somehow knew it was important.

"Góo stelpa. Good girl." He said it with enthusiasm so she'd understand how much she had impressed him. He rubbed her muzzle, then her head, neck, and throat. Thor and Erik watched impassively. They were older than Freya and more secure in the place they occupied in his heart. Still, he scratched their heads and told them, "Good boy," before nudging all three into the far back.

He brushed aside an assortment of litter on the floor. He reached under the van, found the hidden compartment's release button, and pushed it. The floor panel popped up. He lifted it and propped it open.

Gently he removed the twin aluminum cases, setting them on the ground. He dropped the floor back over the compartment and unfolded a camper's chair in front of the door. He positioned the cases side by side in the van before him, punched numbers into keypads, and popped their locks. He raised their lids and sat facing a communications station as sophisticated and formidable as that of any army's command post. The flashing oil light had nothing to do with the level of oil in the crankcase or the condition of the engine. He had wired it to signal an urgent communiqué from his controllers. Essentially, it acted as a clandestine pager, and he had just been summoned.

THE POUNDING on Brady's hotel room door was nonstop. He set the murder book he was studying on the nightstand, pulled on his pants, and ran to the door.

Alicia was bubbling, bouncing on her toes, stretching her lips into a huge grin.

"Brady!" she said. "I just spoke to Gilbreath again. He agreed to let us go to New York to investigate the Father McAfee lead."

He saw she was fully dressed and looked back at the clock. "He called you at this hour?"

"Well . . . I called him." She shrugged one shoulder. "I woke him up, but once he heard me out—"

"We *have* to go?"

"Nooo . . . ," she said, dragging out the word. "But don't you want to?"

"No."

"We both need collars, Brady. It's the only way to advance."

"Have fun." He grinned and swung the door closed.

35

With the two aluminum cases open before him, Olaf prepared to phone home.

The right case contained a Motorola SATCOM Crypto Transceiver with an internal power supply and a headset. The left case contained an Apple PowerBook computer. He linked the two pieces of equipment with a ribbon cable and hinged open the PowerBook's display. Next, he pulled a collapsible satellite dish from the rear of the SCT, snaked it up to the roof of the van, and pushed its suction-cup base onto the metal. Looking up, he saw stars watching him through the branches of the trees. He believed the dish had a clear shot at the communication satellite sailing invisibly overhead, a false star that received more appreciation these days than real ones. To Olaf, it was a metaphor of the times: technology had replaced the heavens; people worshiped that which gave them cell phones and HBO, instead of the gods who gave them life.

Given a choice, the furthest Olaf would venture into technology was his 1974 VW minibus, and only then on assignment. He was not so ignorant that he didn't see the advantages of instant communication, of using a network of computers to access more information faster than ever, of storing libraries on a disc the size of a wafer. He just wasn't convinced technology was worth losing the things it killed: knowledge from experience rather than keystrokes, embracing friends after days of journeying to them, oral history through storytelling. Maybe it was those who did not comprehend technology's price who were the truly ignorant ones.

However, as it was explained to him when he grumbled about learning to use the SCT and other electronics, the enemy was vast; they were few. Using every available means to secure an advantage was prudent and expedient.

"They will get you home sooner," explained the man who had come bearing gadgets and Olaf's assignment, along with tasks for the other warriors of his tribe as well. The man—a thin Albanian named Arjan, with intense eyes and bulging veins—had been holding what looked like a toy gun. He had called it a Taser, which "incapacitates without killing."

"I have something for that already," Olaf said, holding up his cantaloupe-sized fist. His compatriots laughed in hearty agreement.

"Perhaps you'd like a demonstration?" Arjan asked.

Olaf rose from the gym floor.

More laughter and boisterous encouragement.

Arjan flipped a switch on the Taser, which emitted a whine that rose in pitch until it surpassed the range of human hearing.

Even with no knowledge of the thing's capabilities, Olaf found the sound disquieting. Still, he stepped up to this challenger. He was only a few inches taller than Arjan, but where Arjan had a sinewy physique, Olaf had flanks of powerful muscles.

Arjan met Olaf's gaze, then eyed him up and down.

"The Taser will work even through your heavy clothes," he said. "Why don't you step away a little. Its range is twenty-one feet."

Olaf turned but didn't take a step. Instead, he spun in a complete circle, using the movement to build speed. His fist came up and crashed into the side of Arjan's face. The sound was like two rocks rapped together. As Arjan's upper half pivoted down, his legs came up. He seemed to levitate in a prone position for a moment before dropping with a thud to the hardwood floor. The Taser clattered away.

Olaf stared down at the unmoving body. "If its range is so far," he said, smiling at his friends, "why did he let me get so close?"

After that, Arjan had agreed to limit his intrusion into their way of life to essential communications and transportation. "Just make sure you get the job done," he had said, glaring at Olaf.

Olaf smiled at the memory and dropped back into his chair. Visibly, the SCT consisted of plugs, switches, dials, a numeric keypad, and a wild assortment of colored lights—all arrayed across four black boxes. Olaf powered it up, set the frequency, the prearranged satellite channel, the primary encryption code, the secondary encryption code—both also prearranged for this date—and his call sign. He punched the button that would send the information streaming to the low-orbiting satellite, which would, in turn, send it to another, then another, until it found the one passing 780 kilometers above the SCT that was transmitting corresponding data. It took about five seconds.

Through the headphone, a clear voice spoke: *"Hvar er salernið?"*

He frowned. Who'd thought up these pass codes? *Where is the toilet?* He understood the necessity for verbal verification, but must they be so adolescent? In Icelandic, he responded, "Why do you want to know?"

"You must be joking!"

"The toilet is in Colorado."

The man on the other end laughed. "I don't think I'm going to make it. It's good to hear your voice."

"And yours, Ottar." He smiled and leaned closer to the SCT. "Have you seen Ingun? Tell me she is well."

"She has been a pest. She insists on speaking to you."

His smile widened. "And my sons?"

"Jon is a newborn calf: find his mama, find him. Bjorn is all the time looking for trouble."

Those were his boys, summed up well. He wanted to wean Jon from dependence on his mother and help Bjorn focus his curiosity and lack of fear into bravery. He ached to be with them, but at the same time, sacrificing the embrace of his family made his victories here sweeter. Perhaps this was the nature of sacrifice, that the love required to make it wasn't only yours, but belonged also to everyone you loved and who loved you. Sacrifice by its nature is love, and love is always shared.

"Olaf . . . you there . . . ?"

He shook his head. He had been trained since boyhood to be a warrior.

Weaponry, stealth, survival, target acquisition, escape. Why had they not prepared him better to leave his home?

"Go ahead," he said.

"Arjan sends word. You have a new assignment."

With that, Arjan returned Olaf's stunning blow. His assignment had been to kill every person on the list of fifty, quickly and without interruption. Arjan had stressed the task's importance to the rise of a new order—or a restored order, in Olaf's opinion.

"I don't understand," he said. He leaned past the aluminum cases to retrieve the sheet of names and biographical data.

"Priority one reassignment," came Ottar's matter-of-fact words.

Olaf unfolded the list. Only six names crossed off.

"Was it . . . *me*?" He did not want to broach the subject of failure, but he had to know. "Ottar, was it something I did?"

"No, no, no. Arjan said, tell Olaf, 'Good job. Wonderful. Everything went as planned.'"

As planned? His confusion grew. He had been given fifty names. Forty-four yet remained.

"What about the others? The other names on my list?"

"Forget them. That's what Arjan said: 'Forget them.'"

Olaf touched the letters of Trevor Wilson's name as though touching the boy himself. He thought, *You have been pardoned, Master Trevor. Live well.*

When Ottar said, "I didn't catch that," he realized he had spoken out loud.

"Nothing. What is the new assignment?"

"I'll send it through."

"Do it, Ottar. I'll sign off now."

"Wait, Olaf. Arjan said to tell you that these next two targets are on the move. If they leave from their location, which is near you, we will notify you and arrange for transportation."

"I understand." Transportation meant a private jet. Sixteen days before, a Gulfstream had deposited him in Utah. How else was he to travel, the way he looked and with the dogs?

"Gods be with you, Olaf."

He peeled off the headset to save his ears from the screeching damnation of data transference. Two color photographs, positioned side by side, began materializing on the laptop's wide screen. Horizontal lines of pixels zipped from left to right, then from the top down. On the left, a woman. Feline features. Upturned nose, green almond-shaped eyes. Attractive, if you liked them that way. Olaf preferred women with more meat on their bones. More *oomph*. The man on the right had dark hair, brooding eyes, green or hazel.

He leaned back in the chair. The photographs had finished rendering. Now, information about each person filled the space underneath. The fourth line, under their names and physical descriptions, caused his eyebrows to rise. This was where their occupation was entered—the same occupation for each—and Olaf nodded in appreciation.

It read: *Special agent, Federal Bureau of Investigation.*

PART ii

VIRGINIA
AND
NEW YORK

Man's mind is so formed that it is far more
susceptible to falsehood than to truth.
                    —*Desiderius Erasmus*

Because I could not stop for Death
He kindly stopped for me.
                    —*Emily Dickinson*

36

If it weren't for Mrs. Pringle, Brady would sneak into his house like a shadow.

Since Zach was three or four, whenever Brady came home from a trip, a game of hide-and-seek would start even before his Florsheims hit the front porch. He'd tell Zach when he was scheduled to touch down at Ronald Reagan National, and that was it. He didn't know if Zach started hiding right at that time, if he calculated his ETA from the airport, or if he watched for him from a window. (He had once asked Karen, who lowered her eyes coyly and said, "I ain't telling.") But whenever Brady arrived home, Zach was hiding. And the kid was good. He'd slip his little body into the tightest nook or cranny and wouldn't make a sound until Brady either spotted him or gave up, which he usually did after forty-five minutes of serious seeking.

The prize for not being found was dinner out at the restaurant of Zach's choice. When the game started, that had meant McDonald's. Lately, it was Olive Garden. If Brady found Zach, they would go for a round of putt-putt golf, which Brady enjoyed more than Zach did. Brady didn't get to do much putt-putting anymore.

Three years ago Brady went to Los Angeles to consult on a case. When he returned, he searched from the attic rafters to the basement drains. Prodded by Karen, he searched for two hours. Finally, he gave up.

Karen led him to the basement, where she slid away a false wall to reveal a small hidden room—and Zach. Their close friend Kurt Oakley had wanted to build a hideaway and playroom for Zach for a long time—he had made one for his three boys and they loved it. When he had heard about the game, he insisted on building the room while Brady was away.

Brady protested that he didn't spend enough time in the basement to know its precise layout. Besides, the wall was perfectly camouflaged, with a rowboat wall hanging and empty boxes of laundry soap and bottles of cleaner attached to the sliding wall, low to the ground. The effect was brilliant in its ordinariness. Finally, Brady had admitted defeat and taken everyone—including Kurt, his wife, Kari, and the boys—out to Red Lobster, a very special treat indeed.

Zach used the hideaway frequently to play, spend quiet time, and hide from uninformed friends, but he never hid from Brady there again. Still, Brady always scoped it out, because he knew the day he stopped checking was the day Zach would be there.

The first time Mrs. Pringle was at the house when Brady showed up for the hunt (this was six months after Karen's death), she had spotted him—to her fading eyes, a mere shadow—creeping up the stairs. She had screamed to wake the neighborhood and clutched her chest. He had thought that was the end of her—if not her life, then certainly her baby-sitting for him. She had recovered remarkably well, however, and made him promise to inform her of his arrival in the future.

So now, after using his key to unlock the front door and after removing his shoes in the hardwood foyer, he found Mrs. Pringle watching *Entertainment Tonight* in the den and cleared his throat for her. She started slightly, gave him a maternal look, and nodded.

A half hour later, Mrs. Pringle was ready to go home, and he had not found Zach.

"Ollie ollie in come free!" he called from the foyer. After a minute: "Zach! Mrs. Pringle wants to go home. Ollie ollie in come free!"

He looked helplessly at Mrs. Pringle, who gave him *that* look and nodded to something behind him.

He turned and there was Zach in the hall leading to the kitchen, the sweetest smile on his face.

"Where were you this time?" Brady asked.

"I ain't telling." Sounding just like his mother.

Brady held open his arms, and Zach ran into them. "I think I'll try the macaroni and cheese this evening," Zach informed him.

"Olive Garden?"

"Of course."

AFTER DROPPING off Mrs. Pringle, but before descending upon Zach's idea of culinary perfection, father and son went to visit wife and mother. Karen's grave site at Mt. Olivet was one of those quaint hilltop plots every person thinks he or she'll occupy one day; the more likely scenario for most people is that their bodies will spend eternity in a flat space the size of a football field, plot number C-10 in a matrix of a thousand graves. Karen had a modest life insurance policy. Most of it went to purchase two adjoining plots in an undeveloped section of the cemetery, under a hundred-year-old oak that the management company agreed in writing to maintain and never remove. Brady had written a check for $60,000, nearly twice the cost of other grave sites.

Each time they visited, Brady considered the money well spent. Away from the milling mourners, from the assembly-line death holes down in the older and current "communities"—as the manager called the various areas of his necropolis, as if he were building neighborhoods of growing families; perhaps philosophically, he was. Away from all that, Zach could spend time with his mother. He could talk and sing and weep and lie still on her grave. On a typical visit, he would do all these. When Brady visited alone, he did too.

Tonight, Zach sat before the headstone, a dusty rose–colored marble with a large heart protruding from one side of the rectangle that spanned the width of two plots. The heart was on the left side, Karen's side. On the right, under which Brady would eventually rest, was an exaggerated Roman vase with a hole in its top for flowers. Brady thought Karen would have liked it.

Zach sat there, running an open hand over the words:

BELOVED WIFE AND MOTHER, DAUGHTER AND SISTER.
KAREN ANNE MOORE

The dates of Karen's birth and death came next. Both Brady and Zach avoided reading them. There was something too blunt, too final about that brief stretch of time; the dates made them too aware of their being carried forward in the river of time, while their loved one stayed behind, growing smaller in the distance, no matter how hard they strained to keep her in sight. Below the dates was Karen's favorite Bible verse:

REJOICE IN THE LORD ALWAYS. I WILL SAY IT AGAIN: REJOICE!
— PHILIPPIANS 4:4

"That seems like an odd choice for a headstone," he had said when she told him once what she would want as an epitaph.

"No, it's not! The Lord is good, and when I finally meet Him, you can bet I'll be rejoicing. I hope you will be too."

"When I go or when you go?"

"Both, but I was thinking when I go."

"Fat chance I'll rejoice, unless I go first."

"Look how much God wants us to rejoice. It's repeated. 'I will say it again.'"

"Can we talk about something else?"

Giving the headstone engraver those words to etch forever on her marker was one of the hardest things he had ever done. Back then, as now, there was little rejoicing.

From his position ten paces back, he could hear Zach quietly talking, telling his mom about his studies and the cool book he was reading and the kid who was picking on him at soccer practice, whom he had stood up to. Brady knew Karen would be hugging him right now, running her fingers through his hair, telling him, "How interesting!" and "I'm so proud of you!" And who knew? Maybe that was what she was doing at this very moment.

He put his hands on his hips and touched the cell phone clipped to his belt. He'd forgotten about it. He unclipped it and punched buttons until he'd set the ringer mode to vibrate. Nothing spoiled quiet moments worse than a ringing cell phone.

He gave the boy a few more minutes alone, then sat beside him. Zach touched his index finger to the *B* in BELOVED. Brady put his finger on top of his son's. Together, they traced the words all the way through Philippians 4:4. As usual, they skipped over the dates.

31

Following directions she had downloaded from a map web site, Alicia drove her rented Dodge Stratus from LaGuardia to a litter-strewn parking lot next to St. Anthony of Egypt on Thirty-fifth Avenue. Her limited experience with both New York City and houses of God had led her to expect a massive, ornate structure of chiseled statuary, rose windows, and heavy wooden doors resembling the rear flank of a Spanish galleon. But this was no St. Patrick's Cathedral. St. Anthony's was puny by comparison, a stone building of traditional church shape: steps leading up to double doors only slightly larger than a residence's, a spired roof with a bell tower. Set into each side wall was a row of narrow stained-glass windows.

Forty feet to the west of the church sat a two-story brick building with dingy windows and no apparent means of ingress. Between this building and the church, set back from the street, was a high wall, whose stones mimicked the church construction but appeared much newer. Dead grass filled the space between sidewalk and wall. Flagstones cut an arching path from the base of the church steps to a wood-and-iron gate set in the center of the wall. Alicia went through the gate into another world.

The courtyard she stepped into could have been the set of a vampire movie, the kind Hammer Films made in the seventies with overcast skies, creepy forests, and creatures howling in the distance. Denuded willow branches hung over the area like a trap ready to spring. In here, twilight became night, the air cooler by several degrees. Three metal chairs huddled around a table, an inch of grime and leaves covering them all. Alicia rubbed her arms. The brick building she'd seen from the street plus two others made up three sides of the court. Set into the side of the building to the left of the courtyard entrance, directly behind the church, was a door and a carved wooden plaque:

RECTORY
FR. DUNCAN MCAFEE

She mounted the concrete slab in front of the door and pushed a lighted doorbell button. A chime sounded deep inside. Moments later, a porch light came on. A wicket door, set in the larger door at face height, opened. Alicia could see nothing behind it, just darkness.

"Hello?" she said.

Somewhere inside, a door closed and a light came on, dimly revealing a sitting area beyond the door. She leaned nearer. A face suddenly appeared. Only wide, darting eyes and a sharp nose were visible through the opening.

"What is it?" said an irritated voice.

"Father McAfee?"

He paused before answering. "Did you open this door? Wasn't it latched?"

"It opened after I rang. But I didn't see anyone until you came." As she spoke, his faced moved back. She could tell he was looking around. He was starting to spook her. "Is something wrong, Father?"

His face reappeared. "He's watching us. You must go."

"Who's watching? Do you need help?"

"Of course not. Who are you? What do you want?"

She held up her FBI credentials. "I'm with the FBI. Special Agent Alicia Wagner. We spoke over the phone last night."

"About the NDEs?" His silver brows furled. "I told you I can't help you."

She stepped closer. "The robbery you mentioned, when did it happen?"

"The robbery? You wanted to know about near-death experiences, some case you were investigating."

"Your robbery and my case may be related."

"Related? How?"

"May I come in?"

He looked around again. Without a word, he shut the wicket door. A long moment of silence passed. Alicia wondered if she had seen all she would tonight of Father McAfee. She sighed. He must realize he could not hide from her forever. Certainly the church was open during the day. She would return in the morning and question him whether he liked it or not. She was turning away when she heard the dead bolt disengage; then the door opened.

Father McAfee's appearance surprised her. He looked like an aging movie star: The crisp blue eyes she'd seen through the wicket door were set in a tanned face. He had a muscular jaw and dimpled chin that complemented deep, long dimples on either side of his mouth. Crow's-feet at the corners of his eyes added a sophistication his face probably lacked when it was younger. Although he was at least sixty, his hair was more black than gray, and it was full, almost luxurious. Gray whiskers studded his cheeks and chin. Shadows filled his eye sockets and the hollows of his cheeks. He was tall, six feet three, she guessed. He didn't look like someone who would scare easily. He wore black slacks and a black button-down, short-sleeved shirt. No clerical collar.

He stepped aside to let her in.

"Thank you," she said. The only light came from a hallway off the sitting room she'd seen through the wicket door.

"I don't know what you expect to gain from this visit," he said, shutting and bolting the door.

"If you could start by telling me—"

He stopped her with a harsh "Shhh!" and put an index finger to his lips. Without a word or gesture, he walked into the lighted hallway. She followed him, out of the hall, through a darkened room that appeared to be a library, into another hall. Constantly his head swiveled, as though searching for a small child. He led her through a door into an office. Dark wood furniture arranged on dark hardwood flooring. Somewhere, incense burned, mulberry or some other sweet plant. It did not quite mask an unpleasant odor Alicia couldn't place.

The priest moved behind a desk and dropped into a chair with cracked burgundy leather. An amber-shaded attorney's lamp was lit on the desk. On a dingy white wall behind the desk was a clean spot three feet square, where a painting or picture was missing.

She surveyed the rest of the room. Two ancient-looking lamps on end tables at each side of a burgundy leather sofa added their light to the room, making it bright but also cozy. On the wall above the sofa was a huge painting of a bearded old man in a brown robe and cap, holding up a staff to repel a hideous flying creature that was part man, part dragon. Red eyes like apples bulged from its long-snouted face, fangs dripped with saliva, clawed hands raised over the staff as if feeling its power. Despite the creature's obvious intent to destroy the man, the man's face was peaceful, almost sublime.

"St. Anthony of Egypt," Father McAfee said. "A hermit. They say demons attacked him frequently. The word of God dispatched them back to hell."

"His face . . ."

"Like a man sunning on a beach, not fending off monsters. Faith in God grants peace in chaotic times." His tone was flat, detached.

She turned to him. "It sounds like you don't buy that."

"Oh, I do. I have no doubt." He looked at his fingernails. He said, "It's a level of faith few of us possess."

He glanced up at the painting, something like resentment making his face hard. After a moment, he asked, "What is it you think I can help you with?"

Alicia sat on a fat arm of the sofa, pulled a small spiral notepad and pen from a blazer pocket, and flipped to a page of questions.

"Father, on the phone you said the church offices were broken into and your files stolen about three weeks ago. Do you remember the exact date?"

"April 20."

"You reported the break-in?"

"I told you I did. And no one wanted to hear about it."

"Who took the report?"

"NYPD, of course."

"And they didn't investigate? Didn't they look for points of ingress and egress, dust for—"

"They did *nothing*!" he snapped. He planted his elbows on the desktop, parting his hands in a gesture of frustration. "You are a very dense young woman!"

Their eyes locked on each other's. As hard as he glared, she refused to look away. After a good thirty seconds, a muscle on the right side of his face twitched. It moved like a parasite under his skin from below his eye to his bottom lip. She realized he was on the verge of weeping.

He dropped his face into his palms and said, "I'm sorry. I'm not usually like this, this ornery. I haven't slept more than two hours straight in weeks. I'm not eating. I'm . . . I'm . . ."

Alicia dropped the notepad and pen on the sofa, went to the desk, and reached out to him. When her fingers touched his temple, he jumped, but his face stayed buried.

"What's happened, Father?" She hesitated. "I'm a friend right now, not a cop, and I'm a pretty good listener."

He raised his face. This close, she saw just how worn he really was. Blue folds of skin hung under his eyes like drapery. Electric currents of reddened blood vessels in his eyes fanned from the corners to the pupils. His flesh was as pale and dry as onionskin.

He let out a heavy breath, and his whole body seemed to deflate. He shook his head.

"I know who broke in," he said. "At least, who ordered it."

"Someone *ordered* the break-in?" She gripped his shoulder, sharp bones under his shirt.

"A Vatican priest, Father Randall, Adalberto Randall." He could not hide the disdain in his voice.

"I don't understand."

"Join the club," he said with a dry laugh. "He came in, claiming to represent the Secret Archives of the Vatican."

"It's actually *called* 'secret'?"

"Yes—*L'Archivio Segreto Vaticano*. Secret, not because nobody knows about it, but because it is closed to journalists and all but a few privileged researchers. Its *contents* are secret."

"What did Father Randall want?"

"He congratulated me, said my files had been deemed *Magnipensa*

Scripta Conservanda. The phrase applies to documents and writings important to the Church: the epistles of St. Francis of Assisi, the Handbook of Creeds, these sorts of things. And now the Holy See wants to include *my* files in this esteemed catalog, to preserve them and make them available to serious religious scholars? Something was rotten in Denmark—or rather, in Rome—and I told Father Randall so."

"What kind of files?"

"Ahh—" He rose, reclaiming a measure of dignity with straight shoulders and an erect spine. Unconsciously flattening his shirt over his stomach, pushing the folds into his waistband, he walked slowly to a door to the right of the sofa and end table. He opened it and switched on an overhead light in a room about ten feet square, lined with old wood filing cabinets, each as tall as Father McAfee. He yanked open a drawer. It rattled on rails, then thunked to a stop. Empty. He pulled out another drawer, from a different cabinet, at a different height. Empty. He held out his palms, helpless.

"My life's work," he said.

She stepped in, opening a drawer on the other side of the room. A lone paper clip resided within.

"What was in here?"

"Newspaper articles, interview notes, hospital records, EKG and EEG graphs, death certificates, journals, drawings, diagrams, photographs, manuscript drafts . . . everything."

"For your books?"

"For my life's work," he said again. "All of it, gone."

"Did you have copies, backups?"

He laughed and shook his head. "I started my research long before personal computers. I trust paper, something I can hold. I like to pore through my research, a sea of paper on my office floor, and write my manuscripts longhand. My books have sold fairly well, so my publisher allows me that indulgence. As for making photocopies . . . well, I simply never thought of it."

He looked forlornly at the file drawers, the way a patriarch might look at the crypts of his prematurely lost family.

"So everything stolen pertained to near-death experiences?" Alicia asked.

"Forty years of research, yes."

"What was in the files that didn't make it into your books?"

"Oh, tons of stuff. Interviews with people who claimed to have endured an NDE but whose stories I couldn't corroborate. Lots of those."

She leaned back against a cabinet. "How do you corroborate a near-death experience?"

"The physiological facts are easy. Were there witnesses to the accident or coronary that caused the heart to stop? Medical records? Was CPR performed? By whom? How long was the heart stopped? Was rapid ischemic damage noted? The metaphysical experience is less definitive, of course. I look for signs that the subject was outside of his body, such as did he revive with knowledge he shouldn't possess?"

"For instance?"

"Knowing something about the activity going on around him when he or she was clinically dead. Ideally, it will be something a living person could not have received through the senses, so knowledge of the conversation taking place around him isn't good evidence. Knowing that a nurse tied her shoelaces or missed the trash can when she tossed refuse at it *is* good evidence. Sometimes, people come back knowing an ancient language or something else uncanny, but that's rare. Most times, they have no gained knowledge that can be corroborated at all. The best evidence is the person's state of mind upon reviving."

"State of mind?" She wished she hadn't left her notepad on the sofa. "What do you look for?"

McAfee raised an eyebrow. "Terror," he said.

Alicia squinted in puzzlement. "But I thought . . . you know, a brilliant light, beautiful music, a feeling of peace . . ."

"You haven't read my books. Most writers—'researcher' doesn't describe their pitiful lack of investigation—most writers do focus on the so-called positive NDEs. I suspect the majority of the stories are pure horsepucky." He smiled. "You see, my dear, I specialize in finding people who have died and gone to hell."

38

The woman was pretty. He'd seen that when she was on the porch, with the light in her face. She had stared directly at him through the wicket door, though he knew she could not discern him in the darkness. After she and the priest had moved down the hall, shutting themselves in the office, he listened at the door. By her questions, he realized she was the one they had told him to watch for. He heard them enter the file room, and he slipped into the office. The priest was listing the items that had been taken from him: ". . . newspaper articles, interview notes, hospital records . . ."

The man smiled, delighted by the grief of loss he detected in the priest's tone. His upper lip cracked. His tongue flicked out to taste the blood. He let his eyes light on the painting of the monk and the demon. A fiction. In reality, the demon would consume the monk with one snap of its jaws.

He back-stepped into the corridor and skittered into the darkness, remembering every turn, every piece of furniture. This was his domain now. The priest was too afraid to venture far from the few rooms he needed, the office, bedroom, bathroom, and kitchen. Soon he'd be sleeping in the office, forgetting food altogether, and voiding his bladder and bowels into the trash can.

When he finally killed the old man, staging a suicide, he would write something clever on the painting. It would be in the priest's handwriting and it would close the book on whether he'd gone over the edge. Something like, "My God, my God, why have You forsaken me?"

He laughed, the sound ragged and animal-like, as though the teeth, filed sharp, had sliced it into nasty expulsions of noisy breath.

He opened a door, stepped into a storage closet, and then pushed past long-forgotten water-damaged boxes to the rear wall. A square of plywood leaned against it. He shifted it aside and felt a light breeze rush out of a hole in the wall. When he had first entered the rectory to find where the priest stored his files, he found the closet and loose board in the back. Curious, he'd shone a flashlight into the hole and found stairs leading down to servants' quarters. A calendar on the wall was dated 1974.

The discovery had given him an inspiration. From this basement sanctuary, he could venture into the rectory and church, terrorizing the old priest. He could strike—say, vandalize the property or cast his shadow where it would be merely glimpsed—and then retreat to the old servants' quarters, where no one would find him. In this way, he would be able to execute a slow, grueling campaign of terror. When he became bored of the game, as he surely would, he would slaughter the priest and vanish into the shadows of the city. It was a perfect plan.

Besides, he had been instructed to watch for this investigator—anyone asking about the files and near-death experiences, taking more interest than the theft of old papers warranted. Why not have some fun while he waited?

He descended the flight of narrow stairs. A candle burned on the floor in front of a scattering of blankets and dirty clothes. He sat on the pile and pulled a tattered duffel bag into his lap. From a side pocket, he withdrew a sleek new cell phone and flipped it open. He punched a number, twelve digits long. He listened and then punched in another four digits.

A deep voice answered, speaking briskly in a foreign tongue.

The man in the rectory basement said, "She's here." He listened, his grin widening, splitting his lips in three places.

39

F r. Duncan McAfee motioned for Alicia to step out of the file room and back into his office. She did and dropped onto the sofa, reclaiming her notepad and pen.

Father McAfee turned off the file room's light and shut the door. He was about to sit down at the other end of the sofa when something caught his eye, and he walked to the door they had used to enter the office from the hallway.

"Did I leave this door open?" he asked, pointing at a six-inch gap between door and jamb.

Alicia shook her head. "I don't know."

He stepped into the dark hallway, looked one way, then the other. Back in the office, he shut the door, holding the handle until the latch clicked. He took his position on the sofa, sighed, and ran his fingers through his hair.

"My endears . . . ," he said thoughtfully.

"I'm sorry?"

He looked at her as though surprised he had spoken aloud. "Endears, that's what I call people who have had a near-death experience. 'NDE-ers' is too awkward for my old tongue, and it's too clinical sounding. Besides, they are very endearing people, passionate for life because it was snatched away for a brief time." He smiled warmly.

Alicia found herself sufficiently charmed. "You said these people, your . . . *endears* . . . went to *hell*?"

"Naturally, they didn't stay there," he said. "They came back, scared out of their minds. And you have to get to them quickly, else they tend to repress the memories. It's that terrible. But talk to them within a day or two of their finding out just which direction their souls are heading, and you can tap a reservoir of vivid images and feelings. Few people actually believe they are heading for hell, and those who suspect it have no clue how truly hideous it is. Afterward, many find God and worship Him. Others try to make amends by feeding the poor, doing good deeds. The change in behavior and attitude is usually quite startling. You could say they literally got the hell scared out of them."

Alicia thought for a moment. "Do any become obsessed with religion?" she asked.

"Wouldn't you? You have just discovered not only that hell exists, but you've earned a ticket to it. But if there's a hell, there's a heaven, right? So that becomes your new goal: to make it to heaven. To hell with hell. You visualize it, read about it, keep reminders of it around—you do all the things someone serious about attaining a goal does. To answer your question, yes, many people who've glimpsed hell go a little overboard with their efforts to reach the other side. They attend every service or mass their church offers. They wear crosses and T-shirts with religious messages. They collect Bibles, and some actually read them."

Alicia thought of Cynthia Loeb's bedroom. "What about angels? Could someone become obsessed with angels?"

"Residents of heaven, sure," he said. "They represent the place an endear desperately desires to go. He wants them to be his friends and neighbors. And another thing: I've interviewed several endears who've expressed a strong belief that God's angels pulled their souls out of hell and put them back in their bodies. These angels, they believe, wanted them to have another chance. So they develop a fierce gratefulness to angels. One way of acknowledging this debt is by collecting angel paraphernalia—books, illustrations, statuettes."

Cynthia Loeb to a tee. But then, the panels she painted on plastic trash cans were fiery and hellish. Like the Bosch print in Daniel Fears's den.

"With endears," she said, "can a fascination with heaven coexist with an interest in hell?"

He didn't answer right away but turned his head to look at her from the corner of his eye, as if sizing her up, wondering if she knew more than she was letting on. Finally, he said, "This case you're working . . . I would love to know more."

"I can't say anything at the moment, Father, but I'll remember you when I can. Please, my questions are important."

He thought about that, nodded. "More often than not, an endear's initial enthusiasm for religion subsides into a gentle awareness of his soul," he said. "His passion becomes . . . if not altogether subconscious, then at least subtle. Where once he hummed Beatles tunes, now he's humming hymns. His doodles might start leaning toward religious themes. When the experience of going to hell seeps into the subconscious, endears may be as inclined toward hellish images or symbols as heavenly ones."

"Are you familiar with the works of the painter Hieronymus Bosch?"

He laughed, two loud hacks that could have been to clear his throat if it weren't for the merriment on his face. "Oh, Agent Wagner, I am going to hold you to your promise to open up to me about this case when you can. Bosch is a favorite among endears. No matter that his depictions of hell and of demons devouring and torturing sinners are dark and vile; they hold a strange, almost hypnotic wonder over them, who seem to be at once repelled by the artwork and attracted to it."

Alicia looked down at her notepad. In the Pitman shorthand the academy had taught her, she scribbled reminder words: *endear, hell, religious obsession* → *subconsciously*—what word had he used?—*inclined! toward heaven/hell imagery, Bosch favorite* . . .

She looked up to see him watching her write. "Any idea why Bosch is an endear favorite?" she asked.

"Endears themselves don't know. I've asked. By the time they stumble upon his work, their minds have repressed much of the horror they witnessed. But still, he resonates with them. My guess is Bosch was an endear. He'd witnessed the demons and hellish landscapes he depicted in his paintings. His work captivates endears because they've seen them too."

"Hieronymus Bosch painted what he saw during a near-death experience?"

"That's what I believe, but there is no historical evidence to prove it. His life is a complete mystery. He seemed to have intentionally shielded himself from the world. Even his name is a pseudonym. His real name was Jerome van Aken. Let me show you something."

He pulled himself up off the sofa. Alicia could hear his joints popping. He opened a desk drawer, withdrew a heavy coffee-table book, and returned to the sofa. Seated again, he placed the book between them on the cushions, facing her. It was called *Heaven and Hell in Art*. Under the title was an apparent Bosch painting, demons committing all sorts of atrocities to humans. He opened the book to a marked page, a double spread of a painting showing some kind of religious ritual in what looked like the ruins of a cathedral. There was a monk in a blue robe, a priest with a high hat and gold garb, a monkey holding a skull on a tray, and a finely dressed woman with the face of a mole. Around them, a city burned and wicked-looking creatures rode deformed fish, fowl, and rodents. Alicia felt a tinge of nausea.

"This is the center panel of Bosch's *The Temptation of St. Anthony*," Father McAfee said.

She glanced at him, a question in her eyes.

He nodded. "My St. Anthony. That's him in the blue robe. It's a Black Mass, meant to ridicule Catholic Mass. Participants worshiped Satan. They used urine instead of wine. The services were often conducted by defrocked priests, who recited Scripture backwards and spat on the cross. On the altar they put animal corpses and severed human heads. Medieval practitioners believed that just as Holy Mass invoked the miracle of the transubstantiation—that is, the transforming of wine and bread into Christ's blood and body—Black Mass put evil into the dead flesh. They would later deliver the infected corpses and heads to their enemies, hoping to curse them."

She moved her eyes away. Here was a vileness obvious even to non-religious people, the kind of *wrongness* that kept atheists fighting on the side of a generic "good."

Father McAfee pointed to the spot on the wall where a painting was missing. "For ten years, I kept a framed print of this panel right there."

"Why would you want such a disgusting thing *here*?"

"For the same reason I think Bosch painted it. For inspiration, and to honor those whose faith endures through onslaughts of temptation." He planted a finger on the Black Mass in the book. "This ritual represents temporal distractions: carnal pleasures, rejection of institutions, our own will versus God's. But see? St. Anthony is holding strong. He's not participating. See how he's on his knees in prayer, looking out at the viewer as if to say, 'My strength comes from outside my world, and it is greater than the pressure to give in'?"

Alicia thought that, like most interpretations, Father McAfee's favored his own beliefs. He saw what he wanted to see.

"An endear I interviewed years ago found the print and sent it to me. If nothing else, it was a great conversation piece."

"I see how it would be. Where is it now?"

"The Vatican, I imagine."

"A print?"

"I doubt the *Museu Nacional de Arte Antiga* in Lisbon will give up the original, but my print disappeared along with all my files."

"The files Father Randall wanted?"

"For the Vatican archives, he said. The Holy See maintains one of the largest archival libraries in the world. It owns documents that chronicle how every major and many minor world events affected the faith, the Church, the human race: alliances, treaties, prophecies, visitations, exorcisms, as well as the mundane—births, baptisms, marriages, annulments, deaths. Since the time of Christ and before. It's an amazing collection of knowledge and attitudes throughout history. Randall wanted to pull my work into this erudition, make a new collection out of it. He said he would send over a truck and people to box it up the very next morning."

"But you didn't give it to him?"

"Of course not! Every time I published a book, some journalist would contact the Vatican for the Church's 'official position,' and every time I was made out to appear a little unhinged. Not enough to warrant removal or sanction, but the message was clear: Father McAfee has his own agenda, his own hobby; leave the Church out of it, thank you very much. I told him I'd be happy to bequeath my work to the Church, but short of my death, my files weren't going anywhere."

"How did Randall take your refusal?"

"First he acted dumbfounded that I would defy his authority. He stammered about taking the matter to his boss, a cardinal with immense power and respect within the Church. In fact, he was once favored for the papal seat. Now he's too old. I told Randall, 'Well, have him call me so I can tell him what I'm telling you.' He grew insistent, and naturally I became a brick wall for him to pound his head against. Veins were bulging in his head. He said, 'We will see what your archbishop says,' and I said, 'You do that.' I showed him out, and that was that."

"But it wasn't."

"No. I worked late that night and came in early the next morning. The place was trashed, my files were gone. How's that for coincidence?"

"You didn't hear anything?"

"I sleep on the second floor, right above us. My housekeeper's room is just down the hall. Neither of us was disturbed. There must have been several of them, all working very quietly. I wish I'd caught those . . ." He tightened his lips on the word he had in mind.

Alicia felt her mind drop down into a low gear the way a four-wheel drive does to trudge through mud and over trenches. If this break-in had anything to do with the Pelletier killings—and for all of its strangeness, she thought it did, somehow—Father McAfee and his housekeeper would never know how lucky they were not to have awakened that night.

"Why didn't they take the file cabinets, any idea?"

He thought for a moment. "They're heavy as statues. Maybe their transport to the airport or to Italy couldn't accommodate the weight."

Sounded reasonable. She wasn't ready to accept the Vatican's involvement, but if it wasn't, he was right about its being an extraordinary coincidence.

"What did you do?"

"I called the police! Two detectives showed up, scribbled on a clipboard, and told me to take it up with my diocese."

Alicia nodded. "It does sound like an internal dispute over Church property."

"They were my private papers!"

"Did you contact your diocese?"

"Of course. They said they'd look into it. After a week, they said no one at the Vatican had requested my files."

"And Father Randall?"

"A researcher in the Archives, but he told the diocese he'd never heard of me, let alone gotten into it with me over files he certainly had no use for. I tried contacting him myself. Always unavailable. I tried Cardinal Ambrosi, the prefect of the Archives. He won't take my calls or return them. Even more disturbing . . ." He trailed off. His eyes roamed to the hallway door.

"Yes? Father, what is it?"

Whatever distraction from his worries her visit had provided left him. His eyes became distant, his complexion paler. "I know Father Randall's purposes are evil because of what came into this sanctuary with him, because of what he left behind."

"I'm sorry?"

"Someone . . . some*thing* has"—he swiveled his head back and forth, looking for a word—"*haunted* this place since that night. A shadow, always watching me from dark corners. It vandalizes the rooms. Smell that lovely odor, just under the jasmine?"

Her nose had grown used to the smell she had sensed when she first entered the room. She sniffed, caught an unpleasant hint of it. She nodded.

"Rotten eggs, thrown on the floor and in my desk drawers. I think it's urinating on the carpets, or at least oozing a stench." He paused, thinking, looking as weary as a beaten dog. "This thing, it howls and laughs. At night, it screams in my bedroom, but when I turn on the light, nothing is there. Maria, my housekeeper, couldn't take it anymore; she left a week ago."

"What about the police?" Alicia asked, thinking she knew the answer.

"They suggested setting up a video camera. They wanted proof I'm not mad."

"Did you?"

"The *thing* keeps stealing the tapes. Whether it's demonic or human, Father Randall brought it here."

"Demonic?"

He turned disheartened eyes to her, unwilling to go there with an obvious unbeliever.

She looked down at her notes, made a few more.

"Father, in your books do you identify endears by name?"

"They'd have my head if I did, most of them. They want their privacy, and I promise to honor that."

"No way at all to identify them?"

"I change their doctors' names, the names of hospitals, employers, street names—anything that can give them away. The average endear, especially one who's gone to hell, is more cautious than a homosexual these days. There's no one standing up for them, telling the public that having a supernatural experience does not make you a freak. And going to hell? Well, that does tend to cast aspersions on one's reputation."

"But they talk to you."

"It helps that I wear a collar. And as I said, I get to them quickly, before they've fortified their defenses."

"How do you become aware of a possible NDE?"

"I give lectures at hospitals, speak frequently on radio programs and at conventions for people who appreciate this kind of thing."

"What kind of thing?"

"Supernatural, paranormal. I fit right in with the UFO and poltergeist crowds. Point is, I get the word out. A lot of people know what I do and how to contact me. Even skeptical physicians . . . when they come face-to-face with a resuscitated patient screaming about fire burning their flesh and creatures snapping at them, they suddenly believe or have enough questions that they pick up the phone and call me."

"You drop everything and go?"

"Until recently, NDEs were fairly rare. Now that we have more ways of reviving people whose hearts have stopped, I'm getting more calls. Now I 'drop everything and go' only when the experience seems particularly vivid."

"So you have the names, addresses, details of, what, hundreds of hellish endears?"

"Thousands . . . or, I used to."

"They were in your files, all the information about these endears?" This was it, the heart of the matter.

"I kept the door locked." He pointed over his shoulder at a heavy dead bolt on the file room door. "They must have picked it."

She scribbled a note about that. Then she flipped back a few pages, found the sheet she wanted, and ripped it out. She held it out to him.

"Do you recognize any of these names?"

He squinted at the list, mouthing each name, shaking his head. Then his eyebrows shot up.

"William Bell," he said. "I interviewed him. Initially, he interested me because he was young, twenty if I remember. This was three, four years ago. He was living in Utah."

"Moab," Alicia confirmed. Bell's bio placed him in Moab his entire life.

"He had been jet-skiing, hotdogging it, cut a turn too sharply and flew off. Hit his head on the handlebar and went under. Friends of his pulled him out, gave him CPR. Resuscitated him after twelve minutes, give or take. Woke up screaming for help, clawing at the air. Said, 'They got me! Oh God, make them let me go! Please!' Something like that. One of the EMTs who responded to the call knew of my work and contacted me."

"You said you were *initially* interested in him because of his age. Was there something else later?"

"In about 10 percent of the cases I investigate, instead of the NDE making the endear resolve to get to heaven, it just depresses them," he said. "They go into what we used to call a blue funk. Nothing can get them out of it, and they go through life in dead-end jobs and dead-end relationships, as if they're determined to start their sentence in hell early. He was like that."

"No hope?"

"People like William believe either they're fated to hell and they just happen to find out before their time, or getting from hell to heaven seems too overwhelming, because it's too much work or they aren't privy to some secret pass phrase that grants entrée into God's kingdom. A shame, really."

He stared at the list.

"Cynthia Loeb . . . maybe . . ." He pushed the paper toward her. "Ah, my memory's not what it used to be. And a lot of names go onto my Incident Report and right into the files without much thought, especially if nothing about the event stands out. I'm sorry."

She surveyed the list. Everyone on it had been brutally murdered, decapitated. Why? Father McAfee's information was enough to convince her that all the victims were endears, probably believing they had visited hell. She thought it was all a load of bull, but the important thing was that someone believed it. McAfee did and recorded their names. She felt sure the killer did as well, and had used McAfee's records to identify targets.

Conducting a major investigation was like organizing a room: it got messier before it got cleaner. Now that she understood what linked the victims, even more puzzling questions assailed her: Why would someone want to murder people who claimed to have seen hell during a near-death experience? How did the Vatican—or at least this Fr. Adalberto Randall—fit into the plot? Why would they have wanted Father McAfee's files enough to have stolen them, if they did? To assist a killer? Why, why, why? All she could do was continue to fish.

"Father, do you have any idea why someone would want an endear dead, specifically *because* he is an endear?"

"Dead? No, I . . . All of these people—" He pointed at the sheet in her hand. "Murdered? But my heavens . . . *why?*" His eyes roamed as thoughts swirled behind them. "My files. But there are so many!"

He had said there were thousands, but for the first time (it was something about the way he said "so many"), the implications of that struck her. Thousands. Could the five victims they knew about be the first of thousands? It was incomprehensible. But the sudden frequency of the killings hinted at ambition. Brady had said so.

Father McAfee said dourly, "Ms. Wagner, I must ask: Were any of the victims children?"

"No, but . . . have children had near-death experiences?"

"Oh, yes, many."

"Where they've gone to *hell?*"

"Unfortunately, yes. Whether children can go to hell is an eternal debate among Christians. My studies have convinced me that they can and do. Which opens up new debates. Calvinists will say it proves the doctrine of election, that God chose before time whom He will save. Catholics believe christening—that is, baptism—saves children from hell until they are old enough to choose for themselves to embrace or reject Christ's love. However, I have interviewed baptized children who had vivid and corroborative visions of hell while clinically dead. It is hard to understand how a loving God could relegate little ones to eternal torment."

She nodded solemnly. "What do you believe?"

He smiled. "That God is indeed loving, and His ways are higher than our ways."

She hesitated, then said quietly, "There were children in your files."

"Yes. A few dozen, at least."

She had an instant vision of the CSD's lasers flittering over the de-capitated head of a child. Abruptly, she stood up, shaking her head to dis-lodge the thought. "Father, I . . ."

She felt the need to do something, but she didn't know what. She wanted to get her thoughts into her computer where she could organize them, shuffle them around, attempt to make connections that were too tenu-ous to make mentally, with a million facts and possibilities and images col-liding into one another. She wanted to talk to Brady. A rekindled sense of urgency was pushing at her. She needed answers, needed them now.

Why was someone killing endears? Were a thousand names on his list?

Father McAfee stood, put a hand on her arm. "Agent Wagner, would you like some tea? You look as startled as I feel."

"No, thank you. I need to gather my thoughts. You've been extremely helpful."

She started for the door and saw that it was cracked open again. In a flash, she had her pistol out of its holster. She dropped the notepad and pen into a blazer pocket.

"I don't think—," Father McAfee began.

She silenced him with a raised palm. She used her foot to pull open the door. The hallway beyond was dark. She pressed herself against the jamb and squinted into the hall in one direction. Too dark to see anything. An ancient photograph of smiling priests in an ornate frame hung on the wall opposite the door. If other frames marched down the hall, she could not see them. She rolled around the doorjamb and stepped into the hall, her gun held out in both hands. She could almost feel the depth of the blackness where the hall opened up into the library, the way spelunkers know they've reached a cavern, even in utter lightlessness.

"FBI!" she yelled. "Step into the light! Now!"

She had not seen or heard anything, but the ruse was worth a try.

She snapped a glance over her shoulder. The corridor behind her was like black cotton.

She sidestepped back into the office and shut the door. She pressed her ear to the crack, held her breath. After twenty seconds, she turned to Father McAfee.

He whispered, "Did you see . . . ?"

She shook her head. "Nothing. Father, would you like me to stay? I could search the rectory and the church, sleep in your housekeeper's room . . . tonight, at least."

"Thank you, but your visit has reminded me that there are worse things than scary shadows and sounds. There are things out there that bite and kill."

"Whatever is tormenting you may have those things in mind."

"God will protect me."

Yeah, He will, she wanted to say, *like He protected Cynthia Loeb and Daniel Fears and William Bell . . .*

Instead, she said, "I'll find my way out."

She opened the door and jumped when he said, "Wait!"

He pulled a book off a shelf and handed it to her. *Hell to Pay* by Duncan McAfee.

She nodded her thanks. "Take care, Father," she said and slipped into the darkness.

40

Brady inserted *Scooby-Doo's Alien Invasion* into the DVD player. He heard the microwave ding in the kitchen. A minute later, Zach came in, dressed in pajamas and holding a big bowl of popcorn.

"Double butter," he announced, displaying the bowl like a trophy.

"Bring it on," Brady said. He dropped onto the sofa and patted the cushion beside him.

Zach ran over and hurled his rump at the spot. Popcorn flew everywhere.

Brady caught a sharp correction before it left his mouth. He was determined to give Zach the fun time he had promised. He wondered if his son was testing him, seeing if he'd resort to his typical grumpiness at the slightest provocation. As much as the boy wanted back the fun-loving dad he'd had before Karen died, Brady understood it had to be genuine to count. He laughed and picked popcorn off his lap. "Remind me not to ask for a drink," he said.

"Oh, I forgot," Zach said, plopping the bowl in Brady's lap and hopping up. "Don't start it without me." He darted toward the kitchen.

Brady's laughter felt good. He was here with his son, making his son happy. That was something. He held a mental hatch cover closed over the dark thing that could too easily unfurl and suffocate any joy he was feeling. He had loosed it many times, turning potentially joyous moments into pity parties. Any time it was easy to envision Karen's presence, when it was clear her being there would make it better, more lively, the specter of her absence wanted to invade Brady's consciousness. For Zach's sake, he'd learned to hold it back. It was a skill he hated having to learn, but it was that or lose Zach one way or another.

Zach yelled something from the kitchen.

"What?" called Brady.

"Pepsi, Sprite, or root beer?"

"Mountain Dew."

"No Mountain Dew. Pepsi, Sprite, or root beer."

"Dr Pepper."

Zach returned with two cans. "Here's your Dr Pepper," he said, handing Brady a Pepsi.

"Oh, thank you; my favorite."

Zach opened a Sprite for himself, set it on the coffee table, and took the bowl of popcorn from Brady. "On with the show!" he commanded.

Brady raised the remote, and the menu screen changed to an FBI piracy warning.

Zach leaned against his arm, nodded at the screen. "Do you do that?" he asked. A handful of popcorn disappeared into his mouth.

"No, someone else goes after those evil movie copiers. They're way too scary for me." He grabbed his own handful of popcorn.

"I bet they get all kinds of free movies, those guys who go after them."

"Probably, but then they have to arrest themselves."

Coco trotted in, his tags jangling merrily. Standing on the area rug in front of the TV, he turned his buggy-eyed, lolling-tongued face to Brady and Zach, hoping for a kernel or two. Zach tossed a few over the table to him. The dog's bushy tail vibrated as he licked them up. When he realized nothing more was forthcoming, he turned in a circle and lay down.

The goofiness of the cartoon had Brady laughing with Zach within five minutes. Zach kept nuzzling closer to him until he was pressed against his side, a hand resting on Brady's forearm. The popcorn bowl, still half full, was safe in the crook of Zach's legs. Brady started to reach for it, realized the movement would break the position they had settled into, and decided he'd rather not ever taste popcorn again than do that.

Brady stopped in midlaugh when he realized he'd heard something that had not come from the TV. A thud, like something falling over outside. Zach continued chuckling at Shaggy's clumsy antics, and Brady almost let the noise go until he heard a scraping sound, and Coco raised his head, ears perked.

"Don't go in there!" Zach yelled at the television. "Why do they always go into the darkest, scariest places?"

Coco hopped up. He was staring at the darkened hallway that led to the kitchen. The dog's low growl reached Brady's ears over the show's laugh track. Coco took a step back, looked quickly at Brady, then back down the hallway.

"Dad?" Zach was looking up at him. "What's wrong?"

"Shhh." He gently pushed Zach off him and stood. Zach reached for the remote control, probably to mute the television's sound, but Brady grabbed his arm. "Wait a sec," he whispered. He couldn't hear anything over the television, but instinctively he thought it best to keep the sound going.

He thought of his pistols—one in his bedroom, the other in the kitchen. Both were in safes that had fingerprint locks; a touch of his hand quickly opened them. But neither was near.

Coco was whining now, continually looking to him for assurance while trying to keep watch on the hallway as well. Finally, he'd had enough and bolted for the laundry room, where a doggie door would release him from the house.

Brady felt it too. Something was coming.

Without taking his eyes off the darkness, he reached down, moved the popcorn bowl out of Zach's lap, and hooked the boy under the arm. "Come on," he whispered. He pulled his son close to him and walked him around the coffee table. The laundry room also had an exterior door for humans. They tiptoed toward it. Brady reached for his cell phone clipped to his belt, so small these days he often forgot it. Using a single hand, he flipped it open and pushed 911 with his thumb.

"911 operator. What is your emergency?"

Brady whispered, "There's an intruder in my home. Come quick." He gave the address.

"Sir, can you—?"

He flipped the phone shut and dropped it into his pocket. They were near the door. A long wail, ending abruptly, reached them from just outside the door. They froze. It clearly had been Coco.

Zach lunged for the door. "Co—," he began.

Brady slapped a palm over the boy's mouth and yanked him closer.

The pungent odor of animals hit Brady like a strong wind. And he *knew.* He snapped his head around, expecting to see the wolf-dogs bounding from the hall. Nothing . . . then a stirring of shadows . . .

Brady bolted past the laundry room door to the only other exit at that end of the room, the stairs to the basement. Pushing Zach down the first few steps, holding his arm to keep him from falling, Brady pulled the door closed. Quietly. Quickly.

"Go, go, go," he whispered sharply and let Zach loose. The boy shot down the stairs, sure-footed and surprisingly silent.

The basement door had a dead bolt, keyed on the outside to prevent Zach from opening it when he had been a toddler. On the other side, it was operated by a lever to prevent someone from being locked in. Brady engaged the dead bolt and descended the stairs. He moved more slowly than Zach had but just as quietly. In the seconds it took for him to hit the basement's concrete floor, Zach had his hideaway door opened. The boy stepped in and turned, eyes wide and wet.

Brady stopped halfway to the small alcove.

No good, he thought. The dogs would sniff them out. What . . . what to do? His eyes darted around the room. A washer and dryer, a water heater, metal shelves with cans of paint, cleaning products and . . . He spotted a tub of grease he'd used to lube his SUV's universal joints. Could they strip and cover themselves in grease—would that mask their scent? He remembered a class he'd taken at the academy to acquaint agents with the use of canines in tracking and defense. The instructor said a dog's sense of smell was a million times more acute than a human's. "Even if the target was completely submerged in water," she'd said, "a dog could pick up his scent from a bubble of breath that breaks the surface."

Claws began scraping against the door at the top of the stairs.

"Dad, get in," Zach hissed, pleading.

Brady's eyes took in his son and then darted to the stairs. He could make a break for the gun in the kitchen . . . just burst through the door and run for the safe . . . and be torn apart.

Would that end the hunt? Would the dogs and the killer leave Zach alone? As much as his heart ached at the thought of Zach losing him now, it would be better than the boy dying. So far, the killer had never taken two victims at once.

Sweat stung his eye. He wiped it away.

"Daddy," Zach pleaded behind him.

But this was different. The killer had left his geographical killing region to come for one of the investigators of his crimes. Was this attack intended to be a warning to back off? Vengeance for assessing blame on the killer by seeking him? Whatever else this was, it was something new.

But will the killer be satisfied with my death alone? Brady thought, getting back to the only thing that mattered.

The noises of *Scooby-Doo* on the television upstairs abruptly stopped. Someone had switched it off. Next, he would break open the door at which his dogs were scratching.

Brady moved to the base of the stairs.

"Daddy?" Zach still whispered, but desperation made his voice harsh.

Brady grabbed the broom, stepped on the handle near the bristles and snapped it upward. He held up the three-foot stake. The break was sharp and pointed. If he reached the top of the stairs before the door opened, he might be able to surprise the killer, jab the broom handle through his neck. Brady knew he stood no chance with the dogs. They'd surely kill him. But without a master, they would at most scratch and stiff at the hideaway's entrance until they got bored or help arrived. Zach would live.

He turned to tell Zach to close himself in the hideaway and not come out no matter what he heard. And his eyes fell on a bottle that he must have inadvertently placed on top of one of the fake boxes attached to the hideaway door. It was a chance, though so slim he shouldn't take it. If it failed, Zach would die.

A tear broke from Zach's eye and streaked down his cheek. Brady decided his next actions before the drop hit the floor.

He grabbed the bottle of bleach, relieved to feel the weight of a near-full container. He unscrewed the cap and poured the liquid on the floor, making sure to cover the area around the hideaway first, then out to the base of the stairs. He began splashing the rest of the floor so the area nearest the hideaway would not look as though it had received special attention.

He pointed at the shelf of cleaning products and whispered, "Zach, the ammonia."

Zach ran to the bottle.

"Pour it on the bleach," Brady said. "Hold your breath."

The basement door rattled.

"Hurry," he said.

Seconds later, Zach said, "Done."

Brady's eyes immediately started stinging. The back of his throat felt raw. Bleach and ammonia formed nitrogen trichloride, a toxic gas. Brady had read that the mixture killed a couple dozen uninformed housewives a year. The fumes should be a million times more offensive to dogs. He hoped that it would keep them from entering the basement, even when their master found the hideaway, as he inevitably would, and Brady sprang out with the stake. It would be an uneven battle, ax against stick, but with the dogs out of the way, Brady thought he stood a chance. Perhaps, if luck favored the Moore men tonight, the killer would retreat at the prospect of a face-off without his combat hounds. Not likely . . .

"Okay, okay." He pushed Zach into the alcove, stepped in beside him, and quietly pulled the door closed. He stooped to look out the peephole. The fumes must have filled the entire basement in the thirty seconds since they mixed the chemicals, for it seeped though the hole, causing his eye to water. He wiped it and stared at the base of the stairs.

The basement door crashed open. Claws clicked rapidly on the wooden steps. Two dogs—for the life of him, they looked like wolves—shot to the bottom step and froze. One howled and jumped back, disappearing up the stairs. The other whined. It tried to sniff the floor but jerked its head back violently. Still, it brought its paw forward to step down, whined again, then slowly backed up the stairs.

A voice boomed from out of sight. Brady couldn't tell if the words were jumbled by the wall between them or if they were spoken in a foreign tongue.

Another wolf-dog, this one smaller but equally ferocious looking, came into view. It approached the basement cautiously, looking back frequently to someone who issued sharp but still illegible words. Like the last dog, its head snapped back suddenly from a whiff of the fumes. It turned to go up, then circled around for another attempt to enter the basement. It made a choking-coughing sound, turned again, and was gone. The voice came like staccato drumbeats, angry.

Brady pulled his eye away, wiped it. It felt like someone had rubbed a pencil eraser over it. Zach was gripping him from behind, his hands trembling. Brady reached back to rub his arm. He put his other eye to the peephole.

He almost jumped back when he saw a man standing in the basement. He had come down quickly . . . and completely silently. Brady's first thought was that he was in costume. Long, tangled hair flowed to his shoulders. A red beard bushed out from his face and down over a knitted shirt. He wore tight pants that appeared to be tanned leather and boots that rose to mid-calf. A shaft of wood extended down from his right hand, culminating inches from the floor in a broad blade. He was stocky and muscular. Brady wondered if his broom-handle stake, stuck anywhere in that tree-trunk body, would bring him down or just tick him off.

The man was squinting at the wet floor. The rise and fall of his chest indicated he was taking short, shallow breaths. Smart. He stepped close to the washer and dryer, barely visible to Brady's left. In a move that made Brady's stomach fold in on itself, the man hefted the ax over his head, ready-ing it for quick service. He leaned out of view. Brady heard the washer lid bang open, then the dryer door.

Didn't he know the appliances' small capacities? Brady thought, a chill finding his spine. Or could he be looking for Zach specifically?

The man stepped into the center of the basement, halfway between the stairs and where Brady and Zach hid. Starting at the steps, he scanned the room, slowly rotating like a sprocket in a machine. He was taking his time, hunting for clues to his prey.

That's when Brady's cell phone rang.

41

Jumping back from the peephole vision of the killer in his basement, Brady felt the cell phone spasm silently at the bottom of his front pants pocket.

Thank God they had visited Karen's grave before heading to the video store and then home for cartoons and popcorn. The cell phone's ring was still set to vibrate. However, after three vibrating rings, it would automatically switch to a loud chirping. It was on its second vibrating ring as he shoved his hand into his pocket. He got his fingers around it and pulled. His fist, gripping the phone, refused to leave the pocket. Ring number three. Frantic, he blindly pushed several buttons with his thumb, hoping one of them would be the disconnect key, which silenced the ringer until the call was lost. His heart lodged in his throat . . . The fourth ring didn't come. He let out the breath he had been holding and leaned to the peephole.

The killer had not heard. His eyes were red and watering. He was continuing his slow rotation in the center of the room, scrutinizing every possible hiding place, every crack in the wall. The house had been built before the fire code that required basement windows. The bleach and ammonia were wet. The dogs had identified the door upstairs through which they had fled. The killer knew his prey was down here, somewhere.

He turned and faced the hideaway door. He stared directly at Brady, but Brady knew the rowboat wall hanging made the peephole and his eye invisible, even to close inspection. The killer scanned the top edge of the "wall," then squinted down at the fake boxes attached to it at floor level.

Just boxes, Brady thought, willing the words into the killer's head.

The man stepped toward Brady. And kicked the boxes. They made a hollow thud and held firm. He immediately raised his ax to strike the hide-away door.

Brady reared back. He pushed Zach against the far wall, held up the broken broomstick, and braced himself.

That ax will tear through like a knife through bread, he thought.

But nothing tore through. After only a moment, Brady ventured a peek. The killer was there, ax poised high, both hands gripping the handle. He was squinting at the exposed main-floor joists that composed the basement's ceiling, as if deep in thought. Then Brady heard the distant but increasing warble of a police siren.

Yes! he thought. *Go! Run, you scum!*

Instead, the killer dropped his gaze to the wall and swung the ax.

Brady jumped away, a half-second ahead of the blade as it ripped through the wall. It tore a jagged line down the drywall from head-height to waist-height. Crumpled gypsum and dust exploded over Brady.

Zach screamed, a startled yelp. He must have pushed against the light switch, because the single bare bulb above them came on.

Seeing the power of the ax, Brady realized their only hope lay not in the broom handle but in stalling their demise until the cops arrived; the sirens were near. Brady dropped the stake and did the first thing that came to mind: he grabbed the ax blade. He felt the flesh of his left palm split under the metal's sharpness. The killer yanked on the ax. The blade slid partially away from Brady's grasp. Blood made it slippery. Brady tightened his grip. He felt certain the blade was touching bone; he could squeeze no more. The killer tugged again, but Brady held on. He opened his mouth to scream an obscenity at this beast who'd invaded his home, but what came out was a guttural roar.

A booted foot burst through the wall, striking Brady's knee. At the same time, the blade pulled from his grip and vanished through the wall. He fell back, smashing Zach against the rear wall. His legs folded and he sat down hard. Zach collapsed next to him. Through the rent in the wall, Brady saw the killer staring at him.

The man's bearded face was tight in anger. His dogs were barking and howling at the top of the stairs. He cocked the ax into position for another blow at the wall. He hesitated, then spun away, out of Brady's view. Brady heard footsteps pounding up the stairs. The dogs dropped into silence. A door overhead banged—either open or closed, Brady couldn't tell. And then . . . nothing.

The house was suddenly and eerily still. It was as though a tornado had screamed through and departed.

The chemical fumes roiled around them; he had barely noticed before. His eyes stung, his throat was aching, his lungs felt compressed. Zach pulled in a ragged breath. The boy looked as though he'd been crying for a week.

"It's all right, son," he said. He reached a hand to him. Blood poured from it, and he lowered it.

Zach rose to his knees and embraced his dad. He hitched in a breath and let it out in a slow, low moan.

Brady pressed his uninjured hand to the back of the boy's head. "It's all right."

A tinny voice reached Brady's ears. He assumed it was coming from a police radio but soon realized it was nearer. "Brady!" it said. "Brady!" He released Zach, easing him back to sit on the floor. He fished the cell phone out of his pocket. He must have punched the answer key when he had tried to keep it from chirping. He held it up to his face.

"Brady!" It was Alicia.

"I'm here," he said. His voice was raspy. If they did not leave the basement quickly, the chemical would do the killer's job for him. Holding the phone to his ear, he rose and reached down to help Zach up.

"What's going on? What were those noises, that crashing sound? Are you all right?"

"The Pelletier killer, he came after us, he almost . . ." He was starting to realize the enormity of what happened, of what could have happened. "We're okay. Zach and I, we're okay."

Alicia was silent.

He used his damaged hand to slide the false wall away. It moved reluctantly, wanting to snag its broken and bent frame on the floor and fixed wall. He put his arm around Zach and led him to the stairs. His racing thoughts took a turn down What If Lane. What if Kurt had not made

Zach this hideaway? What if the police had not come or had not used their sirens?

"Brady?" Alicia's voice was thoughtful, measured. "Listen. Don't go to the cops. Not the locals, not the Bureau."

As if on cue, someone pounded mightily on the front door upstairs.

"That's them now," Brady said. One step at a time, he and Zach climbed toward the kitchen. "What are you talking about? Why—"

"Something's not right," she said. "Just . . . listen to me. Get yourself somewhere safe, but don't go to the cops. Trust me on this."

He knew she was right. The Pelletier killer . . . *here*? Something very messed up was going on.

The pounding on the front door continued.

"They're here, though," he said. There were too many thoughts in his head. "We called 911."

"Tell them it was a mistake."

Pause.

"Go tell them, Brady. You don't want them sweeping in, or our guys. They'll pin you down, make you an easy target." She hesitated. "Zach too."

Brady squeezed his eyes shut. "All right, for now. I'll call you back."

"For *now*?"

He disconnected.

Standing, he touched his son's face. "Everything will be okay."

More pounding. The cops would break in any moment.

"We need to make up a story. I'll explain later." In a few seconds, he told Zach what to say. Then he went to answer the door.

42

The phone clicked and Alicia was listening to that more-than-silent void of a disconnected line. Brady had hung up on her. She cradled the phone and sat on the hotel room bed. He said he wouldn't bring in the cops, so she knew he wouldn't. At least not until he spoke to her again, gave her a chance to voice her concerns.

Her concerns? She wasn't even sure what they were. Only that nothing added up. A serial or spree killer attacking a federal agent, unprovoked, was strange enough. Flying across the country to do it was beyond strange. It was creepy and suspicious and . . . and . . . She couldn't think of the adjective that could describe the icy-footed creature that had scampered up her spine when she'd heard Brady say he'd been attacked. It was now squirming around her brain, gnawing at her sense of reality. This wasn't right. It wasn't *real*.

She realized her mouth was dry from nervous tension. Absently, she stood and walked to the room's low dresser. Inside the ice bucket was a folded clear plastic bag, because God knew what people did with ice buckets besides put ice in them, and you certainly couldn't trust room service to make them clean again. She pulled out the bag and dropped it onto the desk. She grabbed the bucket, made sure the room's key card was in her pocket, and went out the door, pulling it tight behind her.

She padded barefooted down the hall past the elevators to a T-junction. She followed a sign to an alcove crammed with pop and candy vending machines and an ice maker. In the time it took her to put ice in the bucket, she had decided to get to Virginia as quickly as possible.

She started back toward her room, absently shaking the bucket, making the ice rattle.

Brady would be dancing on the edge of hysteria, not because of the threat on his own life, she knew, but because Zach had been there. She couldn't blame him for freaking out, but he needed someone with a calmer head to help him think through the situation and course of action. It was under a four-hour drive, if you didn't pay attention to speed limits . . . and who did? When he called back, she'd tell him to get someplace safe, if he hadn't already, and she'd be there shortly.

This was scream-out-loud scary, but she didn't deny the thrill it gave her. To the top of Everest without oxygen—dangerous, stupid, unnecessary. But people did it, and she knew how they felt.

She paused at a door marked Housekeeping. It was on the other side of the hall from her room and about thirty yards away. She'd made a mental note of it as she walked to her room upon checking in. She'd even gone back to check the handle. It had been locked. Hotels and motels were notorious venues of crime; her frequent stays in them had made her habitually watchful.

Now the door was ajar. Standing to one side, she pushed it inward. The light was off. She propped the door open with her foot, reached in, and flipped the switch. Shelves and shelves of folded bed linens and towels. A cart full of cleaning supplies, tissue boxes, and tiny bottles of shampoo. Stocked and clean, ready for battle in the morning. A Dumpster-size hamper sat empty next to a laundry chute. No lurking bad guys with criminal intent.

She switched off the light and pulled the door shut. It locked automatically.

Paranoid and overcautious. *Nah,* she thought. *Just good at what I do.*

Back in her room, she glanced at the phone to make sure the message light wasn't blinking. Her cell phone was next to the hotel phone on the nightstand. If someone had left a message on her cell line, the phone would beep every thirty seconds.

Should have taken it with me, she thought, walking into the bathroom. But she didn't expect Brady to call back so soon. He had the 911 cops to deal

220 ROBERT LIPARULO

with first. She set the ice bucket on the counter, popped a crescent-shaped piece of ice into her mouth. Crunching on it, she flipped a protective cardboard cap off a water glass, dropped in a handful of ice, and filled it with tap water.

She swallowed the pulverized ice and brought the glass to her lips, then froze.

Her gun. She had set it next to the cell phone on the nightstand. She had a sudden and clear image of the nightstand when she came back from the ice machine: hotel phone, cell phone, her collapsible travel alarm clock, a TV remote. The pistol and holster were gone.

The shower curtain vibrated almost imperceptibly. She caught the movement in the mirror, over her shoulder. Before she could react, before she could *think* about reacting, a hand appeared and the curtain peeled back, its metal hangers clanging together and rattling on the rod like a long strip of Velcro. Arms behind her flew up, then down, bringing something over her head. She started lifting her hand, the one gripping the water glass. She wanted to reach back over her shoulder, to grab the attacker by the hair and yank him around. Something knocked her arm inward. The glass in her hand slammed painfully against her cheekbone, slid up along her face, out of her fingers, and was gone. It flipped in the air, wetting her hair and face, arched over her head, and began its descent.

She could not move that arm. It was pinned to her face.

A garrote! she thought. She felt its wire slice into her forearm. In the mirror, her eyes were wide with panic. Blood jutted from the wound, sprayed the mirror, and poured down her arm, off her elbow. She shook back and forth. The person behind her held firm. He had not lassoed her neck as he had intended—from his hiding place in the tub, he could not have known she had raised a glass when he made his move. But he was determined to fell his quarry. He tightened the wire with what must have been all his strength. The wire cut to her radius; it slid upward along the bone, toward her hand, essentially filleting the muscle and tissue from her arm. The wire pressed against the back of her neck. Her arm kept it from cutting into the soft areas in front and on the sides, where the carotid arteries and jugular vein ran to and from her brain.

Most people supposed garrotes were designed to strangle. When wire was used, however, the killer intended to all but sever the head from the body. All that prevented decapitation was the spine. A few years ago, Alicia had seen crime scene photos of a garroted mob boss. The wire had sliced through muscles and ligaments, veins and arteries, the thyroid cartilage and trachea. It had embedded itself in the fourth vertebra so deeply, the perpetrator had been unable to pull it free (serrations within the cut had indicated an attempt to dislodge it). Alicia thought of none of this except in the nanosecond flashes of memories and images that fueled her terror. She knew without thinking what she would look like when they found her. Her head impossibly pivoted around, fulcrumed at the spine. The inner workings of her neck exposed, but too much congealed blood for its parts to be identified—except for the spine, around which a piano wire would be looped and stuck forever.

All the killer had to do was yank her arm around back so the wire could reach the front and sides of her neck. She knew that. She was sure he did as well.

She flailed back with her left hand, but the killer easily dodged away. She could not lean forward to level a powerful kick backward at her attacker's groin, but she could lift her foot and thrust it back. When she did, her heel struck something that gave way to the pressure of her foot. Her attacker fell backward, without loosening his grip at all. Pulled backward, she tumbled into the tub. She could no longer see the mirror, thank God—who would want her last image on earth to be of her own brutal murder? She landed heavily on a body that felt sharp and hard, all bones. Her legs were draped over the edge of the tub. Her pinned arm was now over her face. Blood poured onto her cheek, into her mouth. She spat, gagged, roared with anger and fright. Her assailant struggled under her, tugging tighter on the garrote.

When she reached back this time, he could not duck away. Her fingers found an ear. She twisted and pulled, trying for the life of her to tear the thing right off his head. She had never let her fingernails grow long, but whatever nails she had she pushed into the soft flesh in her grip.

He screamed, pain making the sound high-pitched and effeminate. She kept twisting and pulling, feeling now the warmth and slipperiness of blood.

Something—probably the assailant's forehead—slammed into the back of her head. Her vision swam, dimmed.

His hands were at the base of her neck, where the ends of the wire came together, she presumed, in two handles. He shoved up with amazing strength, propelling her off of him. Dazed, she was passively compliant. He jerked her up, down, sideways.

He's trying to saw the wire through my arm! Then she realized the fierce shaking was merely a by-product of his jostling to get his feet under him, which he soon did, for he suddenly rose, pulling her with him.

The mirror again. Alicia's image startled her. She already looked dead, limp and gray, her eyes half-closed, mouth slack, blood everywhere.

This is not right.

It was her turn to head-butt. She gritted her teeth and threw back her head. The movement made the wire bite deeper; pain exploded up her arm, pierced her mind in white-hot starbursts. It was worth it: she heard a loud crunch and knew she'd smashed his nose.

He grunted wetly but refused to relinquish the advantage of having her arm pinned and her throat so near the slicing wire. Perhaps fearing a series of maneuvers of which the nose-breaking head-butt was only the first and weakest, he thrust forward. They went down again, this time outside the tub. She hit the counter hard and continued falling. Her head smacked against the toilet seat.

The garrote sprang loose. He groped for the free handle. She extended her arm; the handle, hanging from a wire cutting through her arm, followed, and it was out of the assailant's reach. It was a wooden dowel, about six inches long, an inch round. It was well used, shiny and smooth, darkened by dirty hands and blood. He yanked on the other handle, pulling the wire through the meat of her forearm. She screamed. The loose end slid up to her arm and stopped. Knowing what was coming, she hooked her arm around the base of the toilet. He tugged his end of the garrote. She felt the wire grate against her bone. The handle jerked against her arm but did not pull free. He tugged again. She might as well have had the loose end gripped in her hand instead of imbedded in her arm, her purchase on it was so sure.

The wire was a taut red line in front of her face. She expected him to wrap it around her head, despite his not having hold of both ends. It would slice into her cheek and eye and nose. What would she do then?

But he had other plans. She felt him push against her back to rise. She swung her hand to grab at him. He caught it and twisted. She was lying on her side on the cold floor tile—white tile, streaked red with her blood. He had one of her arms wrenched up and back; she tightened her damaged arm around the toilet. She caught a glimpse of her wound, a long U-shaped gash. It looked like a fish's mouth, drooling crimson.

Turning, she found a demon standing over her. The grimacing face was a mask of hate. Dark irises in bloodshot eyes. Blood trickled down his jaw-line from his left ear. Four parallel gouges raked his cheek; blood streamed from his nostrils: she had done some damage. From his scalp, black hair sprang in gnarled profusion, spilling over bony shoulders like the mane of a dying lion. Whiskers grew in splotches on the upper lip, chin, and hollow cheeks. Tight lips pulled back, revealing rows of pointed teeth. What issued from between them was something between a growl and a hiss. Spittle sprayed out and landed in warm droplets on Alicia's face.

This man-demon-thing had hold of her wrist and was wresting it around, forcing her to twist on the floor. She realized she would wind up facedown. Not a position she wanted to be in with him standing over her. Then again, he had one foot on either side of her, and that was definitely not a position an assailant should assume. She pulled her leg up until her knee was almost touching her chest and shot her heel into his crotch. Eyes bulging, air escaping his lungs in a great *hhhhooooo!* he flew up and away, right out the open bathroom door.

Alicia rose on her arm. Her breath hissed through clenched teeth. The arm gave out, and she collapsed again. She rolled over, pushed up with the other arm, sore from the twisting he'd given it, but usable. Grabbing the toilet, the counter, she rose, expecting a blow to crash down on her, return-ing her to the floor, where she'd stay until the medical examiner began prob-ing her to establish time of death. A door behind her banged. She spun. The room door had hit the wall and was rebounding shut. She sprang for it, caught the handle before it latched, and was about to yank it open when she was shoved from behind into the door.

43

Brady held his bloody palm up to the cop standing in his foyer. His partner, a short woman packed into a blue uniform a size too small, had stepped past Brady and was surveying the living room, her hand resting on the butt of her gun. Her holster was unsnapped. At the door, he had displayed his FBI identification. They were unimpressed. This was a town in which one in thirty residents was an active duty G-man or retired from the Bureau. And since, hard as they tried, agents were human first, feds second, they tended to have as many run-ins with the law as civilians. Consequently, the mystique and prestige of being with the Bureau had long faded from the consideration of local cops.

The cop talking to him was tall and lanky with close-cropped gray hair. His eyes were startlingly blue: they didn't so much look at Brady as they did *search* him.

"An electric knife?" the cop said, repeating the story Brady had given him. His name badge identified him as Anderson.

"Pretty stupid, huh?" Brady said, sounding calm despite a slight tremor in his hand. What was he doing? He wanted to dance for these cops, do the Victim Freak-out, in which disbelief, indignation, and relief, fueled by adrenaline, caused uncontrollable shaking and flapping arms as the victim repeatedly pointed to pertinent aspects of the assault, coupled by a pattern of silent reflection and nervous banter along the lines of "What are you going to do about this?" and "In my own home! My own home!"

He wanted to say, "A serial killer attacked me and my boy! He took off when he heard your siren! He can't be far off! Let's go!"

What he did say was, "You'd think I'd know better than to hold the ham when I'm cutting it."

"You'd think," Anderson said dryly.

"Where's your son now, sir?" the female cop asked, eyeing him suspiciously.

He hesitated. "He's, uh, getting ready for bed, I think." He wondered how that sounded. He knew the cops were trained in neurolinguistic programming, a branch of behavioral science that identified telltale signs of truthfulness or falsehood. When lying, people tended to shift their eyes up and to the right; people searching their memories looked to the left. Liars frequently covered their mouths. And they volunteered too many details, incorrectly believing minutiae equaled truthfulness. In fact, the ability to fabricate details seemed to be wired into the human DNA and was certainly much easier to do than to remember the details of a harrowing event. Most truth-tellers conveyed only pertinent information. But knowing the tics that gave liars away didn't mean one could avoid doing them. Brady touched his lips, then quickly dropped his hand.

"We'd like to speak with him, if you don't mind," she said.

Brady held on to his smile, one he was sure cinched these cops' opinion of him as a simpleton. The whole time, he had been holding up his injured hand as though begging for change; all he got was a palmful of blood still oozing from his wound.

"Could you call him, sir?"

"Sure, yeah." He called for Zach, waited five seconds, and called again.

"What about your wife, sir?"

"She passed away. Eighteen months ago."

"I'm sorry. Girlfriend?"

Brady shook his head. "There's no one."

Footfalls sounded on an uncarpeted floor, coming across the kitchen. A moment later, the boy's shadow rose up on the hallway wall, followed by Zach himself.

"Yeah, Dad?"

In pajamas, Zach was the poster child of wide-eyed innocence. Except that his hair was a mess and dust from the shattered wallboard gave him a thick white streak where a part should have been. Brady would have stepped over and casually brushed it out, but the lady cop stepped between them.

"You're Zachary?" she asked.

He nodded.

"Who else is in the house?"

Zach looked startled. "Just me and Dad."

"Did you call 911?"

Zach lowered his head. "Yes, ma'am."

Good boy, Brady thought.

Anderson said, "You're not in trouble, son. But can you tell us why you made the call?"

Zach looked at the cop, at Brady, down to Brady's hand. In a small, contrite voice, he said, "Dad hurt himself. I heard him yell and ran into the kitchen. His hand was all bloody and . . ." He looked at Brady, then lowered his head once more, silent.

Brady said, "It's okay, Zach." He suddenly realized that he'd committed the same mistake that criminals did with amazing predictability, one that belonged in the same category as providing too many details. He'd fabricated an unnecessarily elaborate cover-up. Why hadn't he just admitted to making the call and claimed he had been mistaken? Why had he pulled Zach into it? The attack had shaken him up, sure, but that was no excuse. He felt foolish and unworthy of Zach's trust.

"Well . . . Dad was saying bad words, real bad words." He met Brady's eyes. Tears were pooling on Zach's bottom lids. Then, in a whisper: "He never talks like that. I knew it had to be terrible for him to say those things. I just . . . grabbed the phone."

The lady cop smiled at her partner. Then she asked Zach, "You told dispatch there was an intruder?" He nodded.

"Why?"

"Dad always tells me that's the best way to get help fast, that you guys don't respond so fast to other calls."

That was true, but Brady had forgotten that he'd mentioned an intruder. He was surprised Zach was able to reason so clearly and quickly under the gaze of these cops.

The two police officers looked at Brady. He smiled sheepishly.

Eyes locked on Brady, the woman said, "Why did you whisper when you called?"

It was Brady's turn to look startled. Was she really calling them on the lie, using the question to tell Brady she knew he'd made the call? Before he could respond—he had no idea what was going to come out of his mouth—she turned away and said, "Zach?"

"Dad . . . I didn't want him to get mad, but I knew he was hurt bad and needed help. When he showed me the cut, it wasn't so bad that I should have called . . . you guys." He pressed his lips together. "I'm sorry."

Anderson chuckled, and tension left the room like air in a pressurized chamber suddenly unsealed. He said, "Well, better safe than sorry, huh." If the cop had been standing nearer Zach, Brady was sure he would have ruffled the boy's hair.

Zach smiled weakly. A tear dribbled down his cheek.

The woman's hand came off the gun, and she squeezed Zach's shoulder. "You did the right thing," she said.

Brady watched his son accepting this reassurance. A vague sense of concern stirred like a slumbering dog in his mind. The boy had lied well. He hadn't expected deception to come so easily. His own naïveté was another reason to feel foolish. He'd be wearing a hat with bells by midnight at this rate.

". . . looked at."

He turned to Anderson.

"I'm sorry?"

"Said you better get that hand looked at." He stepped out the door, and his partner followed.

At this point in the movies, Brady thought, *one of the cops would spot something—an ax buried in the door, a disemboweled animal on the porch—and say, "Now, wait a minute, what's this?" And the killer would spring out from the bushes and slaughter them all.*

But this wasn't the movies. The cops nodded, smiled.

"Thank you, officers," Brady said and shut the door. He turned to Zach. "You were great! You are such a terrific act—"

Instead of the big smile he'd expected, his son's face was wrenched into a mask of sorrow and fear. His lips quivered, and tears now gushed from his eyes. The boy hitched in a deep breath. His arms flew open and he ran to his father. Brady dropped to his knees. Zach's arms clamped around his neck. Zach's face pushed against Brady's chest, as if the boy wanted to take refuge *within* his father, to get away from the world into the harbor of his father's very being. Brady wrapped his arms tightly around his son, coming as close to encasing him as possible. He was aware the blood from his hand had ruined the pajama top, and he didn't care. He rubbed his face into Zach's hair, smelling shampoo and drywall dust.

He whispered Zach's name over and over. "You're okay. We're okay. I'm not going to let anything happen to you." It dawned on him what the boy's fear was, and he said, "I'm not going to let anything happen to *me*." For long minutes, he squeezed and reassured.

When Zach's weeping softened and he was leaning into Brady, breathing deeply, Brady pulled back so they could see each other's faces. He said, "I'm going to take you to Uncle Kurt and Aunt Kari's."

Zach shook his head. "No," he said and started to cry again. Kurt and Kari Oakley had moved four years ago to Wilmington, Delaware, two and a half hours northeast of Garrisonville. Brady trusted them implicitly. Zach would enjoy it there, and he would be safe. The chances of anyone— even anyone inside the Bureau—knowing about them was minuscule at best.

"Zach, I need to go take care of this. I have to make sure the person who attacked us can never come after us again. Do you understand?"

Zach's face brightened. "Let's both go to Uncle Kurt's. We can stay there. No one will find us." He sniffed.

"I wish we could, son. But some monsters in this world don't go away just because you avoid them. You have to find them and face them."

"Like David did with Goliath." Zach said it, but Brady knew from the smallness of his voice he didn't want his father to be David. He wanted his father with him.

"Like that, yes."

They soaked in each other's face, each other's presence. There was nothing more to say. They hugged again, long and hard.

"Now go throw some clothes and your toothbrush in a gym bag," Brady said. His tone said, *Let's do this; let's do it now*.

Zach seemed more himself. He started up the stairs, stopped, and started back down in a hurry. Brady caught him. "What? Where you going?"

"Coco!" Zach said, nearly screaming.

"Zach! Get your things. I'll look for Coco."

Brady retrieved his pistol from the gun safe in the kitchen and turned on the backyard lights. He remembered the dog's wail and how it had ended abruptly. He stepped out of the French doors by the breakfast table and onto a flagstone patio. Each of the properties in this neighborhood boasted a large lot, with most of the land allocated to the backyard. Perfect for kids. It was the reason Karen had settled on this home and why they had overextended themselves to get it. He looked toward the far fence, which was obscured by darkness and trees. He hoped he wouldn't have to venture into that blackness, not without backup. Staying oriented toward the far darkness, he sidestepped along the rear of the house, softly calling to Coco. He had walked to the side fence and was about to backtrack over to the other side of the patio when something caught his eye, an unnatural glimmer. Something dark and wet, there, on the leaves of a boxwood bush. He touched the wetness and held his fingers up to the light. Red . . . blood. With more apprehension than he'd felt since coming home to face Zach after sheriff's deputies had pried his arms from around Karen's body on the side of the road, he lowered himself onto all fours.

"Coco?" he whispered.

He dipped his head. His breath stopped. It was dark, but he could see the Shih Tzu's beige fur just under the branches. It wasn't rising and falling as it did when the animal slept at the foot of Zach's bed. He reached out his uninjured hand, touched the fur, pushing gently as if to wake him. No response. He curved his hand around to pull Coco out and hooked his fingers into a mess of warmth and wetness. The sound it made was like stepping in mud. He yanked his hand back, saw it covered in blood. Dirt and leaves clung to it. His breath came out in a *whoosh*. Before he realized it, he was dragging his hand across the grass, wiping and wiping. He looked at the lump of fur again.

"I'm sorry, big guy," he whispered.

He leaned back to see the second-floor window directly above him. Zach's room. The blinds were closed. He thought for only a second before deciding to lie and say he could not find Coco. Zach would not want to leave without the dog, but Brady would convince him Coco would be safe; he would tell Zach the Garners next door would search for him and take him in for a few days.

Soon after Karen's death, Brady had sat on the living room couch, glass of bourbon in hand, and felt fragile, like a china doll with stress cracks. He knew he couldn't take another emotional hit, not for a long while. He had no clue what would happen if he did, have a heart attack maybe or commit suicide or go mad . . . something. He realized now time had not diminished that sense of brittleness. This assault on him and Zach made him feel shaky, ready to break. At the same time, Zach's involvement gave him the will to be strong, to see this through. He could break later, probably would, after Zach was in the clear, after he was safe.

Despite the boy's apparent resilience, Brady did not completely trust that Zach was as strong as he seemed. Somewhere inside, his son had to have stress cracks like Brady's, had to.

He did not want to test this theory tonight. He would not drop Coco's corpse on Zach's spirit and see if it shattered.

He heaved himself up, absently wiping his palm against his slacks. Feeling about a hundred pounds heavier than he had when he stepped outside, he trudged back in. His mind fixed on two pressing needs: to scrub his hands and to get out of Dodge fast.

FROM INSIDE his van parked at the curb two blocks away, Olaf watched the two police officers leave the Moore house. He let out an audible sigh and heard rustling noises behind him—the dogs lifting their heads off clumps of trash to aim curious stares at their master. No amount of adjusting the binoculars' focus wheel could bring the cops or their cruiser or even the house into precise definition. The trouble lay not with his equipment, but with his eyes; the chemical fumes his target had used to hinder the attack had taken their toll. The cops stepped off the porch, and the front door closed. Olaf lowered the binoculars. He rubbed his sleeves over his eyes. He'd have to pick up a bottle of eye drops . . . lozenges too; his throat felt raw and abused.

More rustling, then Freya's snout nudged against his hip. He scratched her head, rubbed her ears.

"What do you think, girl?" he said. "Pretty smart the way he kept you at bay, huh?" He smiled. "*Really* smart."

He raised the binoculars again. The house appeared calm. That was odd. He'd expected an onslaught of law enforcement personnel. He wondered if it were a trap, if scores of armed men had sneaked in the back while he was watching the front; now in there waiting for his return.

The gods had spared Brady Moore and his son—at least for now. But the death warrant had not been rescinded, so he must strike at them again. He must honor the warrant. Discerning between Odin's will and his own mistakes was not always easy. The god of gods always worked things out, set things straight, but Olaf had some serious thinking to do: What had he done wrong? Why had his mission failed? Obviously, he had been too loud approaching the residence. It had given the targets time to set up a defense. He would have to work on his stealth skills. What else? Judgment. He felt now that he had retreated too soon. The prey—they were in sight, but the sirens had driven him away. Thirty seconds longer. He should have stayed thirty seconds longer.

He squeezed his eyes closed. Tears soaked his lashes and soothed the fire that flitted on his corneas. He reached down and pulled the lever that dropped the seat back into a reclining position.

What would you do, Odin? he thought. *When would you make your move?*

He pictured himself prone before the halls of Valhalla. He was nothing in this high place, a flea to be squashed. But he sought guidance, so he humbled himself further: dirt on Odin's sandal, not even alive, that's what he was. Lower still . . . he brought himself down . . . lower . . .

Then he felt it: a breeze on his face, a rumbling in the air that vibrated his bones. The door had opened. Odin was favoring him with his presence.

His mind dimmed toward utter blackness as Odin pulled him into the Sacred Hall.

Now incapable of physical speech, he issued deafening words where his mind soared. Feverishly, he began to pray.

44

Alicia's cheek and forehead hit the edge of the door, slamming it shut. She was dazed. Her attacker slipped his arm around her neck, still intent on strangling her. He had feigned an escape only to ambush her again when she started to pursue. She felt the arm tighten like a noose. Instantly she needed to cough and couldn't. The choke hold was cutting off all breath, all sound from her throat. She screamed into the auditorium of her mind. In there, it was shrill and loud. She clawed at the arm, then gripped the wrist in both her hands. She pulled and pulled; no amount of exertion relieved the pressure on her neck.

The arm tightened further. She imagined her larynx crushing under the pressure. If that happened, even if she could free herself, she'd strangle from a pinched windpipe—*Look, Ma, no hands!*

Trusting that her attacker had braced himself for a struggle, she forced her feet up and began walking up the door. Often, the best moves in hand-to-hand combat were counterintuitive: When an attacker or a captive struck out or twisted one of his victim's body parts, most people fought the action by stiffening up or applying force in the opposite direction. That gave the movement striking or twisting power. Most times the better response was to go with the movement, giving it nothing to act upon. "Like trying to push a rope," her close-quarters combat instructor at the academy had explained.

If her attacker had known this, he would have backed up at the moment her bare feet began ascending the door. She would have lost her leverage, and her feet would have dropped to the floor again. Instead, he acted like most dense bullies do: he became determined not to let her move him. Her bare feet rose over her head and she pushed off the door, flipping over the attacker. The power of the flip and the strength of her neck and upper body wrenched her free of his choke hold. He fell backward as she swung her legs down. Her feet hit the carpet just as his head did—precisely between her feet. She knew she should heave herself up and bring a knee down on his chest, but she just didn't have the energy. Her lungs cried for air. Her tortured throat protested, then relented. Shards of glass seemed to scrape down her throat.

The attacker reached up to grab her, puncturing her thigh with sharp nails. She dropped straight down, twisting to land her knee directly on his neck. He saw it coming and rolled to one side. Her knee caught his shoulder, slipped off, hit the carpeted floor hard. She sprang up, turning toward the bedroom.

Where was her gun? Had he hidden it or taken it? No time to look, but there were other things in the bedroom she could use to defend herself.

As she took a step, he grabbed her ankle. She went down. Her hand snagged her blazer, which she had tossed on the end of the bed. She hit the floor; the blazer settled over her head. She felt, more than heard, a thump: the object she had earlier unclipped from her belt and dropped onto the jacket. Flipping the blazer away, she spotted a leather pouch within reach. She grabbed it and unsnapped it with her thumb.

The attacker began crawling up her legs, gripping her with one hand, then the other.

From the pouch she pulled a metal cylinder, similar in size to the spool that holds a roll of toilet paper, but much heavier. She twisted around and slammed the cylinder on the hand—the talon—that had seized her right side. The hand opened. The attacker hissed in pain, exposing twin rows of fangs and a black maw beyond. His other hand was gripping her left thigh. She smashed the metal into that hand as well.

The hiss became a howl. She kicked at his face and shoulder, sliding backward to get out from under him. They rose at the same time, opponents squaring off for another round.

He eyed the cylinder in her hand and laughed. "Go ahead," he said in a voice at once high-pitched and grating.

Alicia thought of a hyena. Yes, this thing before her reminded her of a hyena.

"Pepper spray does not bother me."

She said, "Then I'm glad I didn't bring any to the party." She flicked her wrist. With the suddenness of magic and the sound of a blade coming out of its scabbard, the metal dowel telescoped into a three-foot black metal police baton. If it had turned into a pigeon, her attacker could not have registered more surprise. Without pulling her arm back for more power, a move that would have also projected her intentions, Alicia snapped her hand forward. The baton cracked into the side of her attacker's head. He did not so much fall as *fly* down to the bed. His body bounced up and crumpled into a ball on the floor.

The impact sent a new bolt of fire up her forearm, reminding her that it had been sliced to the bone by the garrote. The baton spun out of her weakened hand. It hit the floor, and before it stopped moving, she snatched it up. She pulled it back behind her head, ready for another swing. He did not spring up as she expected, so she waited.

She stepped back with her left leg and shifted her hips back over it, freeing her forward leg to kick out or lead her body in a defensive turn. It was the standard Tae Kwon Do stance called *fugal sogi*. She realized several of the evasive moves she'd made since the attack started had been from her martial arts training, but she had not consciously evoked them. Instructors at the academy harped ad nauseum on the importance of reacting instinctually and correctly in the heat of battle. Consequently, they made students practice the same moves over and over and over until they became second nature. She had never fully appreciated the result of all that repetition until now.

When the hyena didn't move, she edged forward, kicked his shin. He didn't budge. She pointed the baton at his body like a rapier. She jabbed him in the ribs. Nothing. She shifted the baton to her left hand. Cautiously, she bent over the body and pushed her right hand into the folds of shoulder and head and coat until she touched his neck. A pulse pushed rhythmically against her fingers. He was out but not dead. Too bad. She stood and used her foot to push him over. The part of his head she'd struck came into view. A four-inch gash rode the crest of a welt as prominent as his sharp cheekbones. Blood oozed into the surrounding hair.

Restrain him first, she thought, spotting her purse, where she kept a set of handcuffs. *Then find your gun and bandage your arm.*

As she did these things, she considered how to deal with Hyena. What came to mind was brilliant—and absolutely, utterly insane. She loved it.

45

The Anacostia Freeway running north out of Garrisonville was like an electrocardiograph on the pulsing heart of human pluralism. Farms and woods represented the downbeats, the rests. Everything seemed at peace. A burning porch light in the distance marked the occasional home where all other lights had been extinguished early, its occupants now deep in slumber. Then the heart would beat again and a city emerged, its sodium-vapor radiance revealing the bustle of activity. Bump-BUMP, bump-BUMP. Farm-city, wilderness-town.

Brady chased his vehicle's headlights along that ECG line. Through urban upbeats, he tried to hold his speed to eight over the posted limit; most cops went after the ten-and-over crowd. Brady opened it up through rural downbeats, figuring these stretches didn't provide enough pickings to attract round-the-clock watchdogs.

He glanced at Zach in the passenger's seat, fast asleep. It was not yet nine o'clock, but Brady knew from experience that extreme stress was exhausting. The boy was leaning against the door, his head on his balled-up blankie. His legs were pulled up close to his body. His breathing was slow and deep.

The Toyota Highlander was comfortable; the drive was easy. But it gave him plenty of time to think, and that was hard. He'd already worked through the reasons the Pelletier killer might want him dead. He hadn't thought he and Alicia had discovered enough to threaten him. Maybe they were closer than they knew. Even if they were, how would the killer know? Was it possible the killer had latched onto him simply because he was an authority figure? Or did he possess some trait the killer was looking for in his victims, something the others had also possessed? The most disturbing possibility was the one that had spooked Alicia: that someone was controlling the killer, and this person knew intimate details of Brady's life and activities. That brought him back around to his original question: why would someone want him dead? The circle of questions was maddening.

He reached over and popped open the glove box. He pulled out a metal object about the size of a paperback book and shut the compartment door. He held it up to the light rushing through the back window from the car behind him. A chrome flask. Etched into the front were his initials—BDM—in old English script. It had been an anniversary present from Karen. She thought it was perfect because it was both personal and impractical—he had such little use for it. Back then he occasionally liked to spike his coffee, just a little splash. She'd had no idea it would become an item of daily use. He used his thumb to spin its lock-down collar and flip up the hinged stopper. He brought it to his nose and winced. Jim Beam.

Zach's presence beside him tugged at his conscience the way heavenly bodies drew smaller objects into their gravitational field. He did not look again at the sleeping boy, but his awareness of Zach had not been greater since leaving the house. The flask held so much more than whiskey; it was an acid that could dissolve his family—his *remaining* family—his career, his son's future.

At least I'm not in denial, he thought and took a swig, a small one. *An aspirin, that's all a sip is, liquid aspirin.*

He was thinking about taking one more nip—take two and call me in the morning—when his cell phone began vibrating. It was protruding from the unused ashtray. The few coins in the bottom of the tray rattled metallically with the phone. He picked it up and looked at the screen: UNKNOWN CALLER. He thumbed the answer button.

"Hello?" he said quietly.

"It's me." Alicia's voice.

"I'll call you back from a land line."

She recited the hotel's phone number. "I'm in 522, but make it quick; I'm changing rooms."

Ignoring his curiosity, he said, "Give me five," and disconnected. If someone within the Bureau had sicced the killer on him, God knew what lengths he or she would go to to finish the job. Tracking the communications from a specific cell phone was as routine for the FBI as business lunches for civilian companies. And pinpointing the precise location of a cell phone was even easier than paranoid novelists claimed. With relay towers littering the landscape, every call was picked up by multiple towers. Typically the tower nearest the phone received the strongest signal and it would appropriate the call. By measuring the signal strength in all receiving transponders—with programs already heavily used by the government's alphabet soup agencies—the phone could be triangulated to within a foot of its location, even while it was in motion.

He passed a highway sign listing a variety of amenities available off the next exit. Anything would do. He exited and found a gas station with a phone in the lot. He owned a calling card but didn't want to use it. Before leaving home, he'd taken a handful of quarters out of a big mayonnaise jar full of coins on his dresser. He pushed eight or ten coins into the slot and dialed. When the hotel operator answered, he asked for room 522.

"What is the name of the guest?" the female operator asked.

"Wagner."

The line clicked and rang once.

"Yes?"

Definitely her, but Brady asked anyway, "Alicia?"

"Can't you tell?"

"Shouldn't we have a code word? How about 'perplexed'?"

"Not funny. Let's use 'Morgan.' Say, 'Is Morgan there?'"

He realized she was serious. "'Morgan'?"

"Yeah, proper names make good pass codes. If everything's okay, we'll reply, 'This is Morgan.' But if something's wrong, like you can't talk freely or you think the line is bugged or someone's coercing you, use the word *wrong*. Like 'You must have dialed the wrong number.' Okay?"

"Are you sure this is really necessary?"

"You were attacked tonight."

"I just thought—"

"And so was I."

Silence. Finally, Brady said, "What are you talking about?"

"Some*one*—" Her voice broke on the second syllable. She was playing tough, but whatever happened had really shaken her. She tried again. "Someone broke into my room. He tried to kill me."

"Alicia . . ." He didn't know what to say. His heart felt squeezed and his stomach had somehow become untethered and was floating and flopping loosely inside. It was the same sensation he experienced whenever he thought of the jeopardy Zach had barely escaped tonight. He leaned his shoulder against the booth. "Are you all right?"

"I'll survive," she said. "Look, I was going to come down there, but now I've got some things to handle here. Can you come to New York?"

"I'm on my way. Really. I'm less than three hours away."

"Don't say anything else. Don't come to my room. Go to the third-floor stairwell landing. I'll leave something there for you."

He felt like Dorothy whipping around in a cyclone; any second it would deposit him in a world so foreign anything could happen.

"Brady?" Alicia whispered.

"I'm here."

"Be careful," she said and hung up.

———

ALICIA SAT on the bed in room 522, her back resting on pillows piled against the headboard. In the corner of the room, sprawled on the floor and handcuffed to the stout leg of a climate control unit, her attacker was still unconscious. *Well, not still,* she corrected herself. He was unconscious *again.* Ten minutes ago, he'd stirred and groaned. She wasn't ready for him yet, so she'd given him another taste of the baton. She eyed the travel clock on the nightstand. She had called an old acquaintance thirty minutes ago. He had said to give him an hour. She thought the hyena would be good for the remaining half hour.

Prior to talking with Brady, she'd been making calls to other rooms in the hotel. On the bed between her raised knees was a legal pad with a list of numbers. The Marriott Times Square towered to a height of fifty-two floors. Each floor contained between twenty and forty guest rooms, depending on whether it also accommodated specialty areas like meeting rooms, lounges, workout space, and large suites. The first one or two digits of each room number designated the floor on which it was located. Her room was on the fifth floor. Twenty floors above her, she presumed, was room 2522. A call to the front desk—pretending to be a hick tourist awed by the majesty of such a grand hotel—had revealed that there were 1,528 rooms in all. And her cousin who was flying in later in the evening and who had failed to make reservations—"I swear the woman would forget her head if it wasn't screwed on!"—could rest easy: this was a slow time of year and the Marriott had plenty of vacant rooms available.

She knew that most hotels tried to keep occupied rooms clustered together, which often resulted in whole floors void of guests.

Consulting her notes to see where she'd left off, she picked up the phone and dialed 3314. She listened to it ring. At nearly nine in the evening, it was not the best time to hunt for empty rooms. An unanswered call could mean the guests were at dinner, catching a Broadway show, or doing any of the ten thousand things New York City offered tourists at night. She depressed the disconnect button, released it, and dialed 3316.

A gruff voice answered: "Yeah?"

"Sorry, wrong number." On her note pad she wrote "3314/3316." She drew a line through "3316." Taking a deep breath she dialed 3414. No answer, so she dialed 3416. No answer, so she tried 3412. A breathy woman picked up, sounding like she was expecting a call. But not from Alicia.

Twelve minutes and fifteen floors later, she found her empty corridor. No one answered calls to any room from 4910 through 4929. She was willing to bet dollars to doughnuts these rooms were empty not because everyone checked into them was out sampling the Big Apple, but because the hotel had avoided putting guests into them.

"Your room is ready, Mr. Hyena," she said in a syrupy voice. The man on the floor didn't so much as twitch.

Gingerly, she ran her fingers over the hand towel she had wrapped around her injured forearm. Warm stickiness. Her fingers came away with spots of blood on the tips. Soaked through again. Third time. Her eyes found the clock. Her friend would be able to do something to stop the bleeding. Apollo was, after all, a physician, though he had not practiced medicine in a long while. His other trade—the one she had called him about—was much more lucrative and, according to him, more enjoyable. Watching the way the light played on her glistening fingertips, she regretted not telling him about her injury. At the time, she had been more concerned about Hyena and what she was going to do with him. Thinking about it now, she smiled, despite the knots in her stomach.

46

E n route to the Oakleys' place in Wilmington, Brady detoured off the freeway system several times. Though he hated to lose time deviating from a straight course, he had to be sure they weren't being followed. Nothing was better for doing that than long, narrow country lanes. Once, he pulled over, got out, and surveyed the skies. No helicopters. Two hours into the two-and-a-half-hour commute, he cursed at himself and took the next exit. In the darkened bay of a self-serve car wash, he took a flashlight from the glove compartment and crawled under the SUV. He checked all the typical places for a tracking device and found none. Then he made a random search and again came up clear. He didn't have the sweeping equipment that would tell him definitively of the presence or absence of a tracker, but when he climbed back into the driver's seat, he felt sure he'd have found it if one was there to find.

He started the vehicle, and Zach stirred. Brady watched as the boy rubbed his face, stretched, and blinked away sleep. When he saw Brady, he smiled. That warmed Brady, knowing his son was comforted by his presence. He wanted to live up to that trust.

Zach looked out at the car wash walls and the closed strip mall across the street. "Where are we?" he asked.

"'Bout a half hour from Uncle Kurt's."

"Is this a *car wash*?"

"Yeah, I thought I'd hose down the car, make it pretty. But the thing's broken."

Zach looked at him, not believing a word.

"Hungry?" Brady asked. There was a tube of Pringles in the backseat.

Zach shook his head, smacked his lips. "Thirsty."

Brady reached back, found the Nalgene bottle of tap water he'd put there with the chips, and handed it to Zach.

"Need a bathroom break?"

Zach had to think about it. "Yeah."

"All right, we'll find a place. Then on to Uncle Kurt and Aunt Kari's." *And New York and God knows what,* he added to himself.

"Do they know we're coming?" Zach asked.

"I called them from a pay phone. They're excited to have you. The boys started whooping in the background when Uncle Kurt told them."

Zach smiled.

Brady hesitated, then said, "Look, Zach. I didn't tell them about the man who attacked us tonight. I don't want to scare them."

The boy nodded. "Our secret."

Relieved, Brady explained the rest of his plan. "Let's just say I have to go out of town for work, and our regular baby-sitter wasn't available, so we thought this would be a good time for you to visit." In fact, this was the story Brady had already told Kurt.

Zach lowered his eyes, pursing his lips.

"Son, I know you don't like to lie. That's a great quality about you. But this is an unusual situation. I'm afraid if they know what's really going on, they'll try to help in some way. Maybe they'll call the police or try to reach me at the Bureau. Then maybe the bad guys will know where you are." Brady paused. He hated himself for what he was about to say, for rekindling fear in Zach's heart.

"Zach, they may come for you again. And they may get you next time." A tear spilled out of Brady's eye. He hadn't known it was there, hadn't even realized his emotions were churning. He supposed feelings of loss and despair had been just below the surface for so long, he'd become inured to them. He smiled and wiped it away.

Zach did not smile. His big, dark eyes traced the path of Brady's tear. Brady thought the boy might reach out and touch his cheek. Instead, Zach moved his eyes to Brady's. He said, "Are you afraid they'll hurt Uncle Kurt, Aunt Kari, and everyone?"

"I'm afraid . . ." Brady swallowed. "I'm afraid they'll hurt *you.*"

"Were you afraid for Mom? Before she died?"

He thought about it. "No, not really. In a vague way, maybe. I worried about car accidents and bad people, but I don't think I ever understood that wonderful things can be taken away from you. Just like that, they can be gone." He looked out the windshield. All the shapes—of the street signs, trees, the strip mall—were in shades of blue-gray. He could imagine a world that was like that everywhere, always. Just gradients of grays, hints of blue. He turned back to his son. "I don't want you to be gone too."

Zach leaned over the center console, trying to get his arms around his father. Brady leaned in and they hugged. Zach said, "I don't want you to be gone either." He released Brady and pushed back to see him. His eyes were dry: Brady's words had not made him weepy; they had made him determined.

In a strong tone, Zach said, "So neither of us will do anything to get gone, okay? I won't tell Uncle Kurt and Aunt Kari about that guy and his dogs. And you . . . and you won't let that guy and his dogs get you. Okay?"

Brady shook his head. "You never cease to amaze me."

"Deal?" Zach held out his hand, insistent. Brady shook it.

"Deal."

Brady dropped the transmission into drive and pulled out of the car wash, on the lookout for an all-night convenience store.

———

FORTY MINUTES later, they stepped into the Oakleys' living room. More lights were burning than was necessary, and Brady knew Kari had turned them on to make the house feel inviting. Taylor, born the same week as Zach, had stayed up past his bedtime to greet his friend. He had all kinds of ideas for things they could do, involving everything from s'mores to AirSoft guns. Taylor scrunched his face to break the news that his parents would make them do some things with his younger brothers, ". . . but if they become pains in the butt—"

"Taylor!" his mother reprimanded.

Brady wasn't sure if it was the language or the threat that riled her.

"Why don't you show Zach your tent?" she suggested, laughing.

Taylor took the bait. "Wanna see my tent? We can sleep in it!"

"Uhhh . . ." Zach turned his eyes to Brady.

"Go ahead. I'll come say good-bye."

Zach said okay and followed Taylor. To Brady's surprise, instead of running out the back door, they charged up to the second floor.

Kari smiled, seeing his expression. "He put the tent up in his room."

"It's pretty cool, actually." Kurt laughed.

Both Kurt and Kari laughed easily—sometimes at things that were lost on Brady. But they were great people. He and Karen had arranged for them to have custody of Zach in the event of both of their deaths—an ethereal improbability at the time; now not so far-fetched. Brady still felt this would be the best place for his son. Perhaps he'd learn to laugh a lot. Brady could think of worse things you could teach a kid.

"Brady!" Kari exclaimed. "What did you do?" She lifted his hand and examined the bandages. "You're still bleeding."

"Oh, I was cutting some ham," Brady said weakly. "It looks worse than it is."

"I have some gauze," she said, heading toward the rear of the house.

"No, really," he said. "It's fine. Just needs some time to heal."

She eyed him skeptically.

Kurt peered out the front window at the SUV. "Coco out there?"

"We couldn't find him when it was time to go."

Kari made an exasperated sound. "You did not leave that dog at home!"

"He went out and—"

"*Out?* You left him *outside?*"

"He's been slipping out of the yard lately. When we're not home and he's done terrorizing the neighborhood, he goes to the house next door. He'll be fine."

No wonder so many people lie, he thought. *It's easy.*

Kari shook her head good-naturedly and invited him into the den for coffee.

"I can't," Brady said, sincerely disappointed. It'd been almost a year since they'd gotten together, and he wondered why. Perhaps it had something to do with the difficulty of wallowing in grief around people who cared tremendously for you.

Kurt asked what was going on, and Brady told them there were some work issues he needed to settle. He said they were highly sensitive and it would be better if they didn't try to reach him. When he added, "Under any circumstance," their concern turned to anxiety.

Kurt's brow furrowed, and he stepped in to put a hand on Brady's shoulder. "What are you saying, Brady? What if something happens . . . ?"

"Under any circumstance," Brady repeated. "Don't try to reach me through the Bureau. Don't leave messages at home or on my cell. I'm sorry, I can't tell you any more. But I will . . . when I get back."

"Which will be when?"

"I don't know. A few days, a week. And please don't press Zach for information."

"Of course we won't!" Kari sounded offended.

Brady felt a tinge of shame; he knew them better than that.

"I'll call when I can. Every day, at least." He'd figure out a way to do it without jeopardizing Zach's location.

"Does Coco going missing have anything to do with this?" Kurt asked. He glanced with new suspicion at Brady's bloody hand.

Brady hesitated. He was asking if his mysterious errand was personal. Brady didn't know how to answer that. The Pelletier killer had made it personal. And Alicia had made him promise not to throw it right back into the Bureau's court.

"No," he said simply and asked if he could get a thermos of coffee, black.

Kari marched off to the kitchen, and Kurt tried to apologize for seeming nosy by talking about nothing and asking innocuous questions: Taylor wanted to join Cub Scouts, and how did Zach like it? Was it okay if Zach rode their ATV? How about them Orioles?

When Kari returned with a dinged-up metal cylinder, Brady went upstairs to find Zach. They hugged and kissed, and Zach said, "Remember our deal."

"You too."

Zach nodded. He followed his father outside. Brady reversed out of the drive, Zach standing next to Kurt and Kari on the porch, waving solemnly. Brady honked and drove away.

47

Midnight. He had made good time and now stood on the third-floor landing in the Marriott Times Square stairwell. The entire chamber—walls, floor, stairs—was made of concrete and coated with a sealant that made the surfaces appear wet. Bulbs in metal cages cast just enough light to dissuade people who took tumbles down the flights from claiming they could not see.

What Brady could not see was the message Alicia said she would leave here, informing him of her location. She'd said she was changing rooms and not to go to 522.

Okay, Alicia. Then where are you?

He scanned the floor, the door, the ceiling. Nothing. A fire extinguisher hung on the wall beside the door. He tugged it off its hook, gave it a cursory glance, and . . . there it was, written along the length of the red cylinder in what looked like a black Sharpie:

$$\frac{me + you - show + Z}{arm}$$

Great. One thing Brady was not was a cryptographer. He even avoided the rebus word games on the funny pages. What is meant by this: 2000washlbs? Answer: Washington. Get it? Wash-in-ton, 2,000 pounds being a ton. Ha-ha. But Alicia would know that, wouldn't she? They'd spent a lot of time together, but he couldn't remember if they'd ever broached the topic of word games or cryptography. He suspected she would keep it easy but make it something only he could break.

He thought about the first word, *Me*. She was leading him to her room, so the code must translate to a number. He thought: *"Me" is Alicia. What numbers are associated with her? Height: about five-six. That's sixty-six inches. Weight: Uh, 120? Age: thirty-one.*

Age was the only one that was definitive, at least to the extent of his knowledge. Well . . . what about the number of letters in *Alicia*? Outsiders could figure that out easier than her age. He decided to go with her age. Thirty-one.

"You" is me. Thirty-three. Show . . . Show . . . Show what? Show off. Show up. Show me yours, I'll show you mine. Show me the money. Show business.

Neither she nor Brady was an outspoken fan of live performances, though he and Karen had attended a few concerts. Bruce Springsteen, Shawn Mullins, Jars of Clay. This line of thought wasn't going anywhere. Here they were, near Broadway, the epitome of the word *show*. He tried to remember if there was a show with a number in it. He realized he couldn't name three current shows, with numbers or not. She would not expect him to be up on Broadway shows or to get a newspaper. Another kind of "show" . . .

Television show!

Of course. They shared a favorite: *24*. Kiefer Sutherland played an agent with a government counterterrorism organization. The gimmick was that each season depicted exactly one day, and each weekly episode showed one hour of that day. Somehow the writers kept it exciting and believable, despite there being no way so many things could happen to one person in a single day.

Z. Capitalized. It took all of three seconds: Zach. He was nine, so:

$$31 + 33 - 24 + 9 = 49$$

He decided the next line was intended to be worked out on its own, not to be added to or subtracted from or divided by 49.

Arm. The length of an arm? Too iffy. Five fingers? No, she would have written "hand." Different kind of arm? Firearm?

Revolvers held six rounds. Semiautomatics anywhere from six to sixteen. His, a Glock semiautomatic with an extra-capacity magazine, held 23. She would not want him guessing, knocking on doors looking for her. It had to be something more precise.

Alicia, would it have hurt to have simply written the room number? Who would find it here?

He stepped down two stairs and sat on the landing. He scrutinized the puzzle on the fire extinguisher, turning it sideways and rotating it, as if the answer would appear if the ink was viewed from a different angle.

Arm . . . arm . . . arms race . . . arm in arm . . . something about an arm . . . recently . . .

Then he got it. Yesterday, on the way up to the Ft. Collins crime scene, they had talked about Rudy Muniz jumping on the hood of the kidnappers' speeding Charger. Alicia had said she'd broken her arm. When? At what age? Brady had visualized her at that age . . . fourteen. 4914. He opened the stairwell's fire door and entered the plush hall of the third floor. A sign pointed to the elevators, and he went that way, trying not to run.

SHE CRACKED the door after his second series of raps. An eye, peering past the security bolt. Brady noticed a cut on her brow, blood crusting in the fine hairs, smeared across her forehead. As soon as she saw him, the door closed, then immediately opened wide.

"Hurry," she said, stepping aside. She was holding a washcloth to her right forearm. He was ready to ask about it when movement deeper within the room caught his eye. A tall black man dressed all in charcoal-colored clothes turned from something Brady could not see. The man eyed Brady suspiciously. A deep frown tugged at heavy jowls. His countenance resembled the tragedy mask in the Dionysus symbols of theater. His skin was so black and wrinkled, it seemed to be made of the same material as his. He was a specter of darkness in the lighted room.

Without a word, the man turned back to his hidden interest. Brady made a face at Alicia.

"Easy," she whispered, closing the door and bolting it. "That's Apollo. I asked him to come."

Brady watched as the man stepped sideways, revealing the object he was attending to. Brady's breath caught in his throat; he took an involuntary step back. Tied to a straight-back chair was a man. He was staring straight ahead, showing Brady only his profile. He looked frail, with skin as white as Apollo's was black. A great profusion of wispy black hair flowed from his head. His chest and stomach rose and fell rapidly. The man strained at leather straps binding his wrists and ankles to the chair. He uncoiled his fists, splaying long bony fingers ending in pointed, dark-painted nails. As if sensing Brady's scrutiny, he snapped his face around and let out a sustained hiss.

Brady reversed another step, bumping into Alicia.

The man's irises were chips of obsidian. They darted around the room before locking onto him, making Brady think of a panicked animal. His upper lip, right cheek, and ear were smeared with blood. Blackish-blue folds hung like drapery under each eye. His teeth had been filed into stubby fangs. He continued to hiss until Apollo, standing behind him now, slapped him on the back of the head.

"Stop that!" the black man ordered. His voice was deep and smooth, a submarine gliding at maximum depth.

The man snapped and growled at the hand it could neither see nor reach.

"What in the name of—," Brady started.

Alicia touched his arm and urged him closer to the thing in the chair. "This is the man who attacked me. He won't tell us his name; I call him Hyena."

Hyena opened his mouth to growl or hiss, but before he could utter a sound, Apollo seized a handful of hair and yanked his head back sharply. He leaned low and said, "Do you want me to tape your mouth again?"

Hyena's eyes flicked left, right, left, as if trying to comprehend the source of the voice. Then he spasmed, and Brady realized he was shaking his head *no*.

"Then shut up." Apollo released him and gently patted the top of his head: *Good boy.*

Brady turned away. On one side of the expansive room were two double beds. A nightstand stood between them, cluttered with a clock radio and a smattering of Alicia's things. Above it was a wall-mounted lamp with two lights, each on its own articulated arm. One of these lights was on, barely radiating through its small shade. Evidently it was designed for reading in bed. Between the second bed and the wall farthest from the door, a floor lamp beside the desk glowed brightly. The other side of the room, behind Apollo, contained a compact sitting arrangement: love seat, chair, coffee table. Shadows reigned in his half of the room. On the love seat, Brady could see several open Halliburton cases, the expensive, brushed-aluminum kind. Scattered about were wires and bandages and various medical instruments. He wondered if it was Apollo's preference to work in the dark.

The entire wall opposite the door was glass, from just above a room-length climate control unit to the ceiling. Heavy drapes were bunched in the corners like columns. A billion lights twinkled and flashed far below. The way the lights radiated out and eventually dissipated in the distance made Brady think of a phosphorous atomic bomb; and here he was hovering over ground zero.

He faced Alicia and saw that what he had mistaken for a washcloth on Alicia's forearm was a thick padding of gauze taped there. Blood oozed through. She was touching it gingerly. She noticed his scrutiny and pulled back a section near her wrist. Her skin had been ripped in two long furrows about three inches apart. The gashes disappeared beneath the gauze, which extended nearly to her elbow. The edges of skin were red and inflamed. Between the crusty lines, deep bruising marbled the flesh. Black stitches closed the wound at half-inch intervals. Brady could not imagine the cause of such a hideous wound.

Alicia pushed the gauze back into place. Nodding toward Hyena, she said, "He tried to garrote me. Caught my arm instead."

It hit him how awful it would be to lose her, not because she was a fellow agent or his partner, but because she was . . . *Alicia.* He didn't know what other word to use. Beneath her gruffness, her unapologetic ambition, her elastic ethics—maybe because of these things, he didn't know—she was a better human being than 90 percent of the people he'd ever met or even heard about. She was irreplaceable.

He touched his fingers to her throat, as if to make sure it had suffered no damage. The gesture was unexpectedly sensual. A single butterfly flitted in his stomach. If he raised his eyes to hers, he knew it would validate the touch as more than a caring comrade's inspection. This feeling for her was so unanticipated, he was not sure he wanted to take it any further. He saw something and bent around to look. Toward the back of her neck was a scabbed-over string-thin line, no more than an inch long. The garrote had reached her neck; it had been that close.

He spun around and smashed his fist into Hyena's jaw.

"Whoa, whoa, man," Apollo said, holding up his hand.

Brady rubbed his knuckles and stared into Hyena's emotionless eyes. He fought the urge to punch him again. Hyena flexed his jaw back and forth but made no other indication that the blow bothered him. Brady felt Alicia's hand press against his back. He shifted his gaze to Apollo's impassive expression, then down to see what the black man was doing. Three intravenous bags hung from a stainless-steel stand. From the bottom of two of the bags, tubes ran to needles that had been inserted into the crook of Hyena's arm. As he watched, Apollo followed the tube from the third bag to its terminating needle. He leaned around and deftly plunged it into a vein in Hyena's other arm.

Hyena squinted at the needle and appeared to smile.

Brady looked at Alicia, at Apollo, back to Alicia. "What's going on?" he asked.

"Apollo's a medical doctor," Alicia said. "Used to work exclusively for the government as an interrogation specialist."

Brady said, "Interro—"

She cut him off. "He went freelance, what, three years ago?"

Apollo nodded and looked up at Brady. He said, "I am assisting you because of what this fellow did to my Alicia."

It was the kind of line that usually came with a grin. Not this time.

Apollo delivered it stone-faced (if that could be said of someone with jowls as fleshy as Apollo's). His diction was perfect, as though he had studied English as a second language and had worked hard to get it right.

"Wait a minute," Brady said. He looked squarely at Alicia and pointed at Apollo. "How do you know this guy?"

Alicia sat on the bed directly in front of Hyena. "We met a few years ago when the Bureau was tracking down terrorist leads in New York. This was right after 9/11. I was field-testing new surveillance gadgets, but with the pressure the Bureau was under at the time to make some big arrests, my involvement became more operative."

He remembered the panicky atmosphere at Quantico, where he was part of a team attempting to develop a profile of the typical terrorist. It was an impossible task. Still, no one let up. He and other members of the team interviewed convicted terrorists at maximum security prisons. A few unmarried volunteers took off for Afghanistan to interview the terrorist hunters there. In addition, they cataloged everything there was to know about every suspected or convicted anarchist for the past five decades: from gender to favorite color . . . no aspect of their lives was left unexamined. Patterns, always looking for patterns. In every division, agents and administrative employees burned with high-octane energy for months. A lot of protocol went out the window, replaced by a singular mandate: to get results in the form of arrests.

Alicia continued. "Everyone believed more terrorist strikes were imminent. We needed intelligence—immediate and actionable intelligence."

He nodded.

"Nowadays, interrogators threaten and negotiate to get the information they need, even if the life of a kidnapped child hangs in the balance. Most times, perps realize anything they say puts them closer to a jail cell, so they clam up. Investigators are left with no choice but to hit the streets, praying for that one clue that will break the case. You know all this."

"So tell me something I don't."

She smiled, then absently touched her wounded arm and winced. "Before World War II, we—the U.S. government, law enforcement, whoever—were more open-minded about doing what it took to get information from suspects, especially when lives were at stake. Physical torture wasn't uncommon. Most police agencies kept red pepper on hand to rub into suspects' eyes during interrogations. Pliers, blowtorches—"

Brady held up his hand to stop her. He looked nervously at Apollo, who was now fiddling with a thick rope of what Brady recognized as wires for either an ECG for monitoring heart stress or an EEG for monitoring brain waves. "You're not thinking of—"

"Brady, let me finish. After the Nazis showed the world how grotesquely far torture could go, most governments backed away from using it. There were already laws against it on the books, but after the war they passed the word through cloak-and-dagger agencies: 'We mean it this time—no torture.' No big deal, really, because a new method for extracting information had been gaining favor anyway."

Brady saw what the man who didn't look like any "medical doctor" he knew was now doing and understood. "Truth serum," he said.

Apollo laughed but did not turn away from the syringe he had pushed into one of the IV bags. Inside the clear plastic bag, red liquid dripped from the syringe into clear fluid—probably saline solution, Brady guessed. The bag's contents turned darker and darker pink with each drop.

"You can call it that," Alicia said. "In reality, there's no such thing. It's not serum, never has been. And the term makes it sound easy: give a shot, get the truth. It's much more complicated than that."

Watching Apollo, he had figured out that much.

"The trick," Apollo said, continuing his preparations, "is to break down inhibitions, primarily the inhibition of divulging secrets. The best way to do that is to bring the subject right to the line between consciousness and unconsciousness. We call it the twilight zone. It's like being groggy and drunk. Defenses are down, mind and body relax."

He peeled off the backing of an electrode, realized he was not ready to position it on Hyena, and held it out for Brady to hold. He grabbed the collar of Hyena's T-shirt with both hands and ripped it down the center. Hyena snapped at him. The skin beneath was hairless and nearly translucent, revealing a network of blue veins.

"What's this now?" Apollo said. He held open one of the flaps of the

T-shirt. Above the left nipple was a brown inverted pentangle, the five-pointed star often associated with the occult. It was the size of a fist.

Alicia rose from the bed, squinting at the mark. "Is that a tattoo?"

Apollo ran a finger over it. "This was burned into the skin. It's a brand."

"Take his shirt off," Brady said, excited. "All of it."

Apollo ripped away the arms, then tugged the material off the emaciated body. Alicia pulled the floor lamp closer, pointing it like a wizard's staff. Shadows leaped up on the walls behind Hyena and Apollo and danced to the rhythm of Alicia's unsteady hand.

Hyena's torso was covered in symbols: a crescent moon and star, a swastika, the double lightning bolts used by the *Schutzstaffel* in Nazi Germany, the Star of David in a circle, a cross with a fishhook on the bottom—Brady thought this was an upside-down question mark with a crossbar. It had something to do with the questioning of God's deity. Satanism and occultism were popular topics among criminal psychology students.

"Not here," Alicia whispered.

"What's not?" Apollo asked.

"Are there any more?" Brady asked.

"Here." Apollo pointed at Hyena's back.

The light didn't reach that far. Alicia yanked the cord out of its socket. The room dimmed to a murky glow from the underpowered lamp between the beds.

Brady was leaning in close. He said, "I think . . ."

She found a new outlet and plugged in the lamp. Light washed over Hyena's back.

There, burnt into the skin over his left shoulder blade, was a sun with curving flames and filled with vertical lines: the same symbol burned into the foreheads and palms of every Pelletier victim. This one was many times larger.

There were other symbols on Hyena's back. On the right shoulder blade was the letter *A* in a circle. Brady recognized it as Anarchy. It symbolized a saying in Latin that translated to "Do what thou wilt"—the law of Satanists. Lower on the spine were a *Udjat*, or "Eye of Satan," and three sixes marching in a circle, their upper stems pointing inward.

Brady's eyes couldn't stray from the sun for more than a few seconds.

"Brady?" Alicia said.

"Yeah, that's it."

"What's it?" Apollo asked.

"That sun," Alicia answered. "Very uncommon. Not cataloged in any of our databases."

"But you've seen it before?"

Alicia nodded. "On some dead bodies."

Hyena suddenly threw his head back, then forward with so much force the chair rocked. He was grunting and jerking back and forth, left and right, putting everything he had into breaking his bonds. The chair legs pounded against the carpeted floor, thumping like an erratic heartbeat.

Brady stepped back, then stepped forward again—he had to do something before the man broke free, shattered the chair, or caused enough noise to draw attention. Before he could decide on an angle of attack, Apollo turned a thumbscrew under one of the IV bags. Clobbering him over the head could not have rendered him unconscious any faster. He was a tsunami of fury one second and *nothing* the next.

"Fast acting," Apollo said with a smile, the first Brady had seen.

48

Alicia once thought Apollo had assumed the moniker because of *The Iliad*'s portrayal of the son of Zeus as a healer, as the creator and reliever of plagues. One of her colleagues had disagreed. "It's because the mythologi-cal Apollo was all-seeing, all-knowing," he'd said. "And with that tool kit of chemicals of his, believe me, *this* Apollo can see everything people don't want him to."

When she asked him, Apollo simply grinned, the folds of his face pushing out like a bulldog's with a mouthful of kibbles, and said it was because the Greek god was so pretty.

She watched him now, his bulldog face tight with concentration as he readied his equipment.

Hyena was out cold. His head hung limply, chin to chest. A gossamer thread of saliva trailed from his lip to his thigh. His white skin, branded with symbols of hate, stretched over discernible ribs.

Apollo clipped a wire to one of nine electrode patches he'd stuck to various parts of the Satanist's torso. He was reaching for another wire when Hyena groaned and bobbed his head. For the hundredth time in ten minutes, Apollo sent him back into the immunity of sleep with a quick turn of the knob on an IV bag. Apparently, the drug wore off nearly as quickly as it worked.

Alicia had already photographed the symbols with a digital camera. Brady had moved the lamp back to its original position, which illuminated Hyena from the front. Now he stood a few feet from her, his hands crossed over his chest, glaring at the unconscious attacker. Brady's reaction to her

attack had surprised and delighted her. She wondered if he would have gotten so worked up if Hyena had attacked a male partner. Certainly, he would
not have touched a male partner the way he had touched her throat. His
fingers had been charged with electricity.

He turned toward her and she looked away, instinctively masking the
movement by smoothing her eyebrow.

He stepped closer. "This room, is it in your name?" he asked.

She shook her head. "The other one is, 522. Not this one. I think this
entire floor is unoccupied."

"How'd you get in?"

The current generation of electronic door locks were notoriously difficult to pick.

She nodded toward Hyena. "Same way he got into my room." She
walked around the first bed, reached under a blazer, and withdrew a small
object. She came back and handed it to him. It was an electronic gadget the
size of a pack of cigarettes. A thin plastic card protruded from the top.

Brady flipped a small button, and a liquid crystal readout lit up.

"Takes about five seconds," she informed him.

He cocked his head skeptically at the attacker. "*He* had *this*?"

"Looks like a homeless junkie, doesn't he?"

Brady turned the device over in his hands. No markings of any kind,
and it was free of dirt, smudges, foreign matter. "Someone supplied it to
him."

"Someone's giving him orders."

"There," Apollo said, standing. "Ready when you are."

Brady clicked off the device and tossed it onto the bed.

"What's going to happen here?" he asked.

"I'll let this creature rise into consciousness, but just barely," Apollo
explained. "I'll hold him in the twilight zone with this." He pointed to the
IV he'd been using to keep Hyena under. "Barbiturates. My own recipe."
His eyes flashed. "Sodium amobarbital, pentothal sodium, and seconal.
Small doses, smaller than the ones I've given him so far. In the twilight
zone, the mind can't think fast enough to fabricate a lie. She doesn't even
realize that lying is what she should do."

"She?"

Apollo looked surprised. "The mind." He moved his open hand in an arc several inches over Hyena's head. "It is beautiful, simple and complicated, spiteful and forgiving, truthful and deceitful. Female, definitely." The folds of his jowls rose into a broad grin.

He continued: "Holding someone in that state of near-unconsciousness is tricky. Too much sedative and they go under. Too little and they are aware enough to avoid the truth. And everyone is different. Some require lots of truth juice, others only a little. Some respond quickly, others not at all. Some get happy, others sad." He thought for a moment. "Or agitated, as though the subconscious knows the conscious is saying things she shouldn't."

Brady indicated the other IV bags. "Barbiturates in one. What are these other two?"

Apollo touched one. "Scopolamine, mostly. The original 'truth serum.' I've found a squirt of this helps if my recipe doesn't take the subject all the way. A psychotropic drug. It can cause hallucinations and extreme panic. That's why it was abandoned. I've added other hallucinogens, very fast-acting ones, like the barbiturates. Confusion helps break down defenses."

He touched the third bag.

"Stimulants. Benzedrine and Methadrine. The barbiturates relax the mind's inhibitions. The stimulants get her talking. Yap, yap, yap, yap, yap." He used his hand to mimic a talking mouth. "No good having a mind willing to spill the beans if she is too groggy to talk."

Simultaneous narcotics and stimulants. Alicia wondered how many of Apollo's subjects suffered coronaries or strokes. She hoped the EKG machine helped Apollo prevent such incidents.

Hyena began to groan again.

"Ready?" Apollo asked.

Brady looked at her, concern etching his face like age lines.

She nodded. "Let's do it."

49

The EKG was on a coffee table near Apollo. He flicked a switch and the machine's pens began recording Hyena's heart rhythms. The sound was like fingernails moving back and forth on a desktop. Apollo crouched behind the attacker's chair, his head barely visible.

Pay no attention to the man behind the curtain, Alicia thought.

His hands moved rapidly from one IV flow knob to another. "The drugs must be constantly adjusted," he explained. "I'll ask a few questions to make sure our subject is in the proper state of mind. Then you can have a go."

Alicia felt her stomach tighten. She'd seen several of these, what the Bureau called Amytal interviews. But she had never conducted any herself. She knew the questions had to be worded precisely or the answer could come from anywhere, including the subject's memories of childhood. So a question like, "Did you attack that man?" might yield an affirmative response, but what the subject was admitting to could be throwing an eraser at his fifth-grade teacher.

She reached for a small digital voice recorder on the bed and pushed a button. Hyena's head rolled up on its neck, then down again. As if startled, he snapped his head up. His lids were at half-mast.

"Uhhhhh . . . ," he said.

Apollo's voice boomed from behind the chair. "Listen to me! What is your name?"

"Uhhhh . . ."

Apollo's hands jumped to a knob, then another.

"What is your name?"

The man's eyes flicked open. He stared directly at Alicia. The skin on her arms and at the nape of her neck tightened as the hairs bristled. She realized he was looking past her, at something only he could see.

His lips formed a silent word. Another.

"What is your name?" repeated Apollo.

The man's face revealed an *aha* moment. He said, *"Me`nya za`vout Malik."* His voice was girlish and gravelly at once. A chain-smoking Girl Scout, Alicia decided. Coming out of that evil-looking body, it severely creeped her out.

Brady whispered, "Is that Russian?"

Alicia shrugged.

"Speak English," Apollo demanded.

"Ang`liskam?"

"Da," Apollo answered.

"Hara`sho. Uh . . ." Long pause. "English, yes." Accented and slurred.

"What is your given name?"

"Malik."

Malik, Alicia thought. She wanted to think of him by that name. Somehow, it made him less frightening, more human.

"What is your complete name?"

He groaned in confusion or possibly distress.

"Malik, what is your whole name?"

"Malik . . . Ivanov." His accent stretched out the first part of each word before clipping it off with the last syllable.

Apollo leaned around the chair, signaled with his head for her to approach. She knelt beside him.

"I've interrogated Russian subjects before," he whispered in her ear. "Ivanov is Russia's most common surname. Like Smith in America. I can't tell if that's his real name or one he's making up. Malik is less common, so it's probably right."

She nodded, rose, and stepped back next to Brady.

Apollo asked, "How old are you?"

"Twenty-eight."

He appeared ten years older.

"Where are you now?"

Malik appeared confused by the question. He looked around the room, fixing on Alicia and Brady for several seconds each. Slowly, the lids closed.

"Are you in your home?" Apollo clarified.

"Hotel," said Malik, without opening his eyes.

"Did someone tell you to come here?"

Both Alicia and Brady stiffened.

"Yes."

Apollo nodded at Alicia. Her turn.

She looked at Brady. He gave her an encouraging smile.

"Who told you to come to the hotel?"

Malik frowned, grimaced.

"Who?"

The scratching of the EKG pens became higher pitched—moving faster. Malik's breathing became labored, as though he were trying to draw wind through a towel. He whispered, "Scary movie."

"I may have lost him," Apollo said. "Just a sec." He adjusted each IV knob. It made Alicia think of fine-tuning into a channel on an old television.

"Scary movie!" Malik yelled.

"Try a different line of questioning," Apollo suggested.

Alicia's shoulders slumped. Who had sent him was what she wanted to know. She tried to think of something else to ask.

Brady said, "What do you know about the man with the dogs? The killer with the dogs?"

"Nice doggie." Malik's hands moved in a gesturing motion. "Here, doggie." Suddenly his face twisted into a savage beast's. His hands formed fists that he pumped up and down as much as his restraints would allow. He laughed, a chilling stutter of short breaths.

"I think in his mind, he's bludgeoning an animal," Brady whispered.

Malik's fists stopped. His head stretched forward, his tongue came out, and he began licking the air. With each upward stroke, his tongue slid into his mouth, his lips closed, and he slurped.

"He's . . . ," Brady said, but he did not finish. His face registered his disgust.

Alicia's hand covered her mouth. Malik was lapping the blood of some remembered kill.

"What do you know about Father McAfee?" she asked quickly.

The licking halted. The tongue ran greedily over the top lip, then the bottom. "Mac-Aff-eeeeeeee?" he questioned in a singsong tone.

"Yes. What do you know about Father McAfee?"

"A pig. He is a pig. He thinks he can hide. He hides behind his God. *God . . . is . . . nothing.*" He sneered, scrunching his nose wolfishly.

"Malik, have you been frightening Father McAfee?"

The laugh again. "Ohhhhh. Malik makes Mac-Aff-eeeeeeee understand."

"Understand what?"

"His God is nothing. No protection, does not care."

Apollo held up a hand, wanting to interject. "That's good, Malik. Yes, Father McAfee's God is nothing."

"Nothing," Malik repeated.

She knew Apollo had felt an infusion of sympathy was in order. He provided it as he would have a shot of morphine.

"What are your plans for Father McAfee, bad Father McAfee?" Apollo nodded, giving her control.

The noise Malik made was of a starving man set before a banquet. "Oooooohhhhhh. Bad Mac-Aff-eeeeeeee." He leaned his head back as if scanning the ceiling, but his eyes remained closed. "So high, the sanctuary. *Sanctuary.*" Sheer disdain. "Mac-Aff-eeeeeeee will hang from its chandelier." A lecherous grin twisted his lips. "By his bowels he will hang."

Ice water dripped down Alicia's spine. She shut her eyes, swallowed. Her arm throbbed. She had no doubt this was indeed what Malik planned for Father McAfee, that dear old man. When she opened her eyes again, the room seemed dimmer. She turned to check the floor and wall lamps. Both were burning.

She asked her next question with her eyes fixed on Apollo; she could not bring herself to look at the creature in the chair. "Malik, did you steal Father McAfee's papers?"

His head lolled lazily.

"Hold on." Apollo fiddled with the IV knobs, all the while watching the EKG. Satisfied, he gave her a nod to continue.

"Did you steal Father McAfee's papers?"

Malik's head snapped up. "Of course! Who said Malik did not? 'Get the files, Malik. Bring them all to me.' Who said Malik did not?"

"No one said Malik did not. Malik did well. Who told you . . . who told Malik to get the files?"

"The priest."

She eased her breath out. "Yes, the priest, but who—"

Brady touched her arm.

"Malik," he said. "The priest told you to steal the files. Yes?"

"Yes."

"What is the priest's name?"

"Randall."

Adalberto Randall, the priest who had claimed to represent the Vatican archives. She glanced at Brady and nodded.

"Where is Father Randall now?"

"Home."

"Where is home?"

"Not here. Home."

"Malik, where is Father Randall's home?"

Nothing.

Brady: "Where is *your* home?"

Pause. More ragged breathing. When he spoke, his voice was an octave lower. The gravel in his throat became stones. "The pit is Malik's home. Black . . . dark . . . so *hot!*"

Alicia glanced at the voice recorder. Someone listening to the recording might not realize the voice was Malik's.

"Why hot?" Brady asked.

"Fire. Burning. Blood." He began rocking at the waist. He opened his mouth in a wide grin. His gums were black, studded with those awful teeth.

He let out a long, airy hiss. His breath hit her, rank and putrid. Hamburger gone bad.

She took a step back. The backs of her legs hit the bed, and she sat.

"Blood!" he called as if ordering a beer. "Let the child's blood flow! Cut it! Cut it now!"

"Malik!" Apollo's voice reverberated against the walls. His face reflected the same distress Alicia felt.

Malik jerk his head around. "Master? Master, is that you?"

Alicia leaned forward. "Who is your mast—"

"Master! We have the children! More children for you!"

His hands began flexing. His head rolled in a circle.

"He's in a trance," Brady whispered, bewilderment straining his voice.

"Our bodies are yours. Our minds are yours. Our children are yours. We are naked for you, Master! We bare all. Take all!"

They were losing him.

Alicia came off the bed to crouch beside the chair. She gripped Malik's straining forearm, searched his face for answers.

"Malik," she said, pleading, "where is Father Randall's home? Who does he work for? Who is your master?"

"Scary . . ." He worked his mouth, snapping and stretching. "Movie." A cackle pealed from his gaping mouth.

Brady scowled and stepped back, repelled by the sound.

Apollo hunkered lower behind the chair. The puppet master wanted nothing to do with the behavior of his puppet. Only obligation kept him wiggling the strings, as his hands fluttered from one IV bag to another.

Malik froze, as if listening to words only he could hear. Suddenly, he cried, "I do! I eat their flesh. See? See?" His head shot out, and his teeth clicked. He chewed, flashed his tongue, chewed. "I eat their flesh!" The cackle, more wicked than ever.

His feet kicked out. Bound at the ankles, the movement was nevertheless enough to tip the chair back. It would have crashed to the floor had it not hit Apollo first. Apollo heaved it back with his shoulder.

Too late, Alicia saw Malik catch the IV bag with his teeth. His jaw twisted and his neck strained as he jerked the bag from its hook and shook it furiously, the way a shark rips at its food. Liquid sprayed everywhere.

It splashed into Alicia's face. Droplets scalded her eyes. She tasted something bitter. A citrus-alcohol tang assaulted her nostrils, her sinuses. She shot up, staggered back, and fell to her knees beside the bed.

50

The chemical in the IV bag Malik had torn open stung her eyes and burned her tongue.

Blinking in pain, she forced herself to orient on Malik—if more danger was coming, it would come from him. He was staring at the ceiling, slack-jawed. Then she saw it: a black coil of smoke rising from his mouth. It formed a swirling cloud above him, enlarging as she watched. Tendrils of the oily smoke lashed out from it like striking snakes, then pulled back into the churning mass. Heat vapors radiated from it, rippling the ambient light, toasting her skin. It sucked in her breath, leaving her heaving for air.

This isn't real, she told herself, but her heart leaped at the thought that it was.

She rubbed her eyes, feeling a sandy grittiness move under her lids.

"Slice the children!" Malik called. "Eat them up!"

Alicia gasped.

She saw children! Their faces were pushing out of the swirling cloud as though from inside a balloon. Small heads; frightened, innocent faces.

She clamped her eyes closed, but the children followed her. They formed from the shadows in her mind—boys and girls, toddlers to prepubescents. They took perfect shape and perfect color. They turned and floated across her mental landscape like a movie montage. Their expressions were twisted in distress, as if caught in the grip of unseen hands. In unison, all the young faces started to scream.

Alicia snapped her eyes open. Brady rushed toward her, calling to her, asking if she was all right.

She looked past him, saw no faces trying to escape the gathering storm hovering over Malik.

Brady reached for her. She reared back. His hands were blackish-purple with reptilian scales and claws. Light fingers touched her face. Not reptilian. She realized that the scaly hands she saw must be from something behind Brady, something reaching around him for her.

Brady blew away, as if by a heavy wind, and she was gazing at Malik in the chair. Although the room lamps cast light on his surroundings, he was in shadow; the edges of his silhouette were indistinct, hazy, as though he were becoming the substance of the smoky cloud. She saw that this in fact was true. His face was elongating, blending into the funnel that rose from his mouth to the gathering storm above him.

Yet somehow he found his voice.

"See! See!" he said. "He is here!"

Bile rose in Alicia's throat. "Make him stop!" she yelled, thinking someone . . . someone was here with her, someone who could help. Who? Who was she calling to?

"Open yourself to him!" Malik ordered.

His shadow-form was stretching into something else. He was slipping his bonds because they had bound human limbs and he was no longer human.

"Take me, Master!"

Every word he issued increased the thickness of the rising funnel, added to the breadth of the cloud. Their utterance sliced at her mind, crimped her heart. She did not believe they were mere words anymore. They had become tangible tools of chaos, and she understood: he was speaking destruction into existence, creating evil from breath and sound. Something—not children—was in the cloud after all, taking shape. What might have been an elbow protruded, moved, and pulled in again. Then something larger—a knee, a head—appeared and was gone. She was witnessing a hideous imitation of fetal movement beneath the taut belly of a pregnant woman.

She tried to rise, but moist pressure held her down, pushing on her face. Brady . . . back with a cloth, wiping at her. She pushed him away.

"No!" she screamed. "Can't you hear him? Can't you see it?"

"Yes, Master! I have the blood! I saved it for you!"

A chorus of voices spoke the words. Blackness continued to pour from between Malik's lips and rise to the cloud. The room was getting darker, the lamps powerless against the vortex of evil. A stench hit her, and she snapped her head away. For an instant she remembered the putrid odor that had billowed out of a black trash bag when investigators had cut it open to reveal the decomposing corpse of a woman who had been kidnapped three weeks earlier. And in that instant she was sure, absolutely sure, the corpse from that bag was in this room, stashed under the bed or behind the love seat, stirring with malevolent animation. She wanted to bolt from the room, to run and run and run.

But she couldn't. The movement of her muscles was sluggish, constrained by air as thick as water.

What . . . ? she thought. *What . . . ?* Nothing more of her question came to mind. The word was enough, however, to convey her confusion and horror. She wanted to scream it—and did.

"WHAT?"

A bead of sweat trickled off her forehead, snaked over her cheek. She wiped at it. Her face was soaked in perspiration—or *something*, she had a vague recollection of being splashed, by what she had no clue.

Blood, she thought. *The blood of children.*

She held her hand up and saw it drenched in dripping crimson. Then the color faded, leaving only clear fluid on her open hand.

What is happening?

Her heart raced as possibilities—none of them good—flashed against her psyche: Malik was a warlock or a demon . . . she was already dead . . . she was stuck in the most vivid nightmare of her life . . .

But all of this was *real*—she knew it!

A change in the room drew her attention. Reluctantly, she turned to the roiling cloud. A taloned hand was pushing out from it, straining to tear through a veined membrane. She trembled at the conviction that when it did, everyone in the room would perish . . . then everyone in the hotel . . . in the city . . .

She had to do something . . . had to . . . She turned and saw it resting on the nightstand: her pistol. She had retrieved it from Malik's waistband after she subdued him in room 522.

Was that today? Was that me or someone else?

Without another thought, she dived for it, landing flat on the bed and scurrying up to lunge again. She vaguely realized her sluggishness was gone now that she had decided to fight and not flee. In one swift motion, she gripped the gun, slid off the bed, and rose with the weapon extended out from her face in two hands. She took aim at the shadowy Malik form, transmogrifying in the chair.

A creature rose from behind him. Like the thing in the cloud, it was all black and humanoid. It challenged her.

"Alicia," came its voice. It was familiar. She shifted her aim to center on this new creature's head.

"Where's Apollo?" she asked. "What have you done to him?"

"I'm right here," the creature said slowly. "The Scopolamine . . . you . . ."

"No!" She shook the gun at the creature, emphasizing its presence. The cloud was growing; soon it would be above her and most of the room. The taloned hand was still pressing out, joined now by another, both reaching toward her.

Sudden exhaustion fell on her like a blanket. She felt dizzy and took a step to steady herself. The edges of her vision dimmed. She shook her head. She could not pass out with these creatures . . . these *demons* in the room with her. But she knew she could not hold on to consciousness much longer. Only thing to do: be the last one standing before she collapsed. Bracing for the recoil, she tightened her finger over the trigger.

A flash of movement—coming at her from the side, from over the bed. An impact on her arms sent the gun flying.

Brady! He's with them!

He was grabbing her, turning her, wrapping his arms around her from behind, squeezing her close.

"No!"

She thrashed, trying to free her arms . . . bite him . . . anything.

He had her in a tight bear hug. They fell backward onto the bed. She kicked and twisted and slammed her head back, each time making contact with only the bed.

The dark creature behind Malik rushed forward and seized her legs.

"Hold on to her," it ordered, "until she comes down."

51

I t all seemed so real," Alicia said, shaking her head.

She was leaning back against the bathroom counter, touching a towel to her hair. Apollo had insisted she take a long, hot shower. It seemed to Brady that both the shower and the passage of time—thirty minutes since he released her from the full-body hug—had done her a world of good. Her eyes were bloodshot, but considering the mind trip she'd endured, she looked remarkably composed.

Then she raised a drinking glass, and he saw how rattled she was: her hand shook so violently, water sloshed out of the glass and she could not quite align it with her mouth. He took it from her and held it to her lips. She gulped. When he lowered the glass, she smiled, a weak smile that reflected embarrassment at needing help. He knew she would make a superhuman effort to regain her independence, her strength, to be the old Alicia.

She had changed her clothes and was wearing a pantsuit nearly identical to what she'd worn before, but the colors were switched. The mock turtleneck was beige, the blazer—waiting for her on a door hook—and pants were coffee, no cream or sugar.

She had rebandaged her arm; he saw that blood had already soaked through. He touched the gauze on his hand. It was sticky with blood, the wound beneath it tender.

"Apollo said you probably got the equivalent of several hits of acid."

She closed her eyes and pinched the bridge of her nose. "Remind me never to do drugs."

"I don't think I'll have to."

Her jaw tightened. *Working it out,* he thought, amazed by her fortitude. When her eyes opened, they were focused and determined. She nudged her head toward the door.

"So what do we do with this guy?" she asked.

Brady tugged up on his pant leg and rested his foot on the edge of the tub. The air was still heavy with steam. It helped relieve a tightness that had developed in his chest. The door was shut, but they could hear Apollo packing up and warning Malik to stop his squirming and mumbling. He had stuffed gauze in the assailant's mouth and sealed it shut with duct tape.

"Leave him," he said. "After we've put some distance between him and us, we'll phone the New York field office. Let 'em know where he is and that he's connected to Pelletier."

She shook her head. "There's nothing to connect him. The symbol alone means nothing."

"Can you burn a CD of the audio? That ought to give them something they can use."

"Yeah. Me going out of my mind." She looked at him hard. "We held him against his will, drugged him up. We're the ones who'll get indicted."

"Any better ideas?"

She thought about it, then shook her head. "We can't hang around. There are still people who want us dead. For *whatever* reason."

Her last remark jarred him hard. They were no closer to knowing *why* people were after them. They had a few clues for tracking down those responsible, primarily a name: Fr. Adalberto Randall. But the motive was still mysterious, which somehow made the unfairness of being targeted exponentially worse. They could not plead their innocence or bargain for a settlement or change anything to appease their pursuer. They simply did not know what he or she hoped to accomplish by killing them. "Frustration" did not come close to describing their feelings.

"All right," he said, glad to wash his hands of the revolting creature in the other room. "What's our next move?"

She brightened, always ready to take the next step. "We find this Father Randall. Maybe see what we can do about finding the leak within the

Bureau. We do our jobs. We follow leads and take one step at a time until we come to the end."

The investigation's end or our end?

He didn't say it. He was being pessimistic, and he was getting as tired of it as he was sure she was. Something was stirring in him that he had never felt before. It paced and growled. It wanted to protect the people he cared for and to rend revenge from those responsible for putting them in danger, for hurting them and frightening them. He wasn't sure what the emotion was, exactly, but it felt powerful and wrathful and freeing. It was a tiger on a leash. He didn't want to tug it back into its cage, but he was equally afraid to untether it.

Alicia touched the tips of her index fingers together, indicating what she thought their first step should be. "Let's get on the phone and find out—"

From the bedroom came a crash and a deep-throated cry of pain. Alicia threw open the door and charged out. Brady was right on her heels, reaching for his pistol. The room was in near-darkness. The floor lamp had fallen over, shattering its bulb. Only the bedside lamp cast a tepid glow over the scene. Malik was standing. One wrist was lashed to the arm of the chair, which he swung around without any evident difficulty. Something glinted in his free hand. Brady quickly assessed it was a knife or razor, the way he held it out toward them. He stood in the center of the room, closer to the wall of windows than to Brady and Alicia. At his feet lay Apollo, propped up on one elbow, the other arm curved defensively over his head. His forehead and left side of his face glistened. Brady could not see its color in the room's twilight, but it didn't take a teenage Xbox freak to recognize blood.

"I thought he was still unconscious!" Apollo yelled. "He . . . he waited for me to—"

"Aaaagggghhh!" Malik howled through gauze and tape. He slashed down at Apollo. The arm of his shirt split open. Apollo pulled in a sharp breath and fell back on the carpet. Lying at Malik's feet, he must have felt completely vulnerable, but rising on an arm put him in easy striking distance of the blade. Brady saw him make the decision to stay down.

Brady aimed his pistol at Malik.

"Put the blade down now!" he yelled. "Now!"

Malik glowered. He was breathing hard and fast, his bony shoulders rising and falling like bellows.

Beside him, Alicia whispered, "Where's my gun?"

"I've got him covered," Brady said.

"Shoot!" Apollo shouted.

Malik bent at the knees, sliced down, and opened up the skin on the back of Apollo's hand.

"Stop! Stop! Stop!" Brady ordered, but Malik had already done the damage he was going to do and was standing again.

"Brady?" Alicia whispered. "Can you do this?"

"Shhhh."

"Why didn't you shoot?"

If he did, it would have to be a kill shot, through the heart or the head. Anything less would give Malik an opportunity to fatally wound Apollo; it wouldn't take much: a slice across the throat, a stab to his chest or into his eye or temple. And yet, he did not trust himself to make the perfect shot. He had never fired his weapon in the line of duty. Should he turn over his gun to Alicia? That would mean re-caging the beast inside, and that was something he did not want to do.

Malik clawed at the tape over his mouth. One side of it fell away. It hung off his right cheek, a clump of wet gauze clinging to it. He raised his eyes, his arms, and his voice. "Master, help your servant now!"

Apollo—*the idiot,* Brady thought in a flash—raised one of his big hands. Brady saw it coming, wanted to shout, "No! Wait!" But it all happened too fast.

Apollo seized Malik's crotch. He squeezed, and the veins in his hands bulged out. His big white teeth flashed as he gritted them with effort.

Malik screamed, for a moment in too much agony to perceive its source or plan a way to alleviate it.

"Now!" Apollo boomed. "Shoot now."

"Do it, Brady!" Alicia. "Shoot! Shoot!"

His finger slipped from outside the trigger guard to the trigger. Four pounds of pressure. That's all it would take. He hesitated. How could he take this man's life when another life was not immediately at stake? What if the pain of Apollo's grip were enough to make him drop the blade?

But it wasn't. Malik's tortured expression turned malevolent. He lowered his head and swung the blade down in a wide arc. It sank deep into Apollo's forearm. Apollo screamed but refused to let go. Malik yanked the blade out—Brady saw that is was a scalpel. It rose again, trailing a thread of blood. If Malik stooped on the next thrust, he'd be within reach of Apollo's head.

The gun roared. Smoke burst into existence in front of Brady. Through it, he witnessed Malik take the hit in his shoulder. The slug passed through and knocked an eye-sized hole in the window behind him. A fissure broke from the hole and ran up the window; another ran down to the sill. Sounding like ice breaking underfoot, a fractal pattern of infinitesimal cracks radiated from all points of the hole. The force of the impact spun Malik around. Brady would never know if what happened next came from the assailant's presence of mind or from the hands of chaos and chance. As he spun, Malik's arms flailed up. The chair tethered to his wrist rose and crashed through the weakened glass. Cold wind rushed in. Malik tumbled out, chair first.

Apollo, stubbornly gripping the man's groin, hit the climate control unit, which slanted like a ramp toward the window. As Malik disappeared, Apollo slid up toward the night sky. His head and hips smacked against the window frame's metal uprights.

"Let go!" Alicia screamed, dashing forward.

"He's got my wrist!" Apollo said. Fear squeezed his voice an octave higher.

Alicia tried to lean over Apollo. "Can't see," she said and clambered right on top of him. Kneeling on his body, she braced her hands against the frame and leaned out to look down.

Brady clenched his fingers into the material between her shoulder blades and leaned back to counterbalance her recklessness. Flailing, Apollo kicked him sharply in the ribs.

Alicia said something, her voice lost in the buffeting wind.

"What?" Brady yelled.

She looked over her shoulder. "He's got his claws dug into Apollo's wrist! Give me your gun!"

He immediately saw the insanity of that.

"You can't let go!" he yelled.

"He's not letting go either! He's not trying to climb in. He's pushing his feet against the side, trying to take Apollo with him!" Her right hand released the frame and opened to him.

He slapped the pistol into her palm. Her arm whipped out of sight.

"Get him off me!" Apollo bellowed. He squirmed under Alicia, who rocked farther out the window.

"Hey!" Brady screamed. "Stop moving or all three of you will fall!"

Apollo squirmed harder, frantically trying to roll off the climate control unit and onto the floor. Malik wasn't giving him an inch.

Alicia cursed.

"What?"

"Your gun! It fell!"

Apollo gave himself a mighty shove away from the window frame. At that moment, Malik must have tugged, for Apollo buckled and half-slid, half-rolled out the window, jostling Alicia. She rose, trying to get her feet under her, backpedaling on him, as though balancing on a log. Her legs flew up and she went down. She hit the sill with her rump and tumbled forward.

Brady saw her turtleneck rip away from his fingers, saw her spin to grab something, saw her face twist in sheer terror, saw her drop away from the window.

Then he saw her no more.

52

Fingers—two sets of four, gripping the sill.

Brady rushed for them, blindly reached over to grip the wrists. He looked down.

Alicia's face was two feet below the edge. Wide-eyed panic.

Apollo was gone, probably still falling toward the huge marquee that announced the Marriott's presence in Times Square. The thought of Apollo plunging to his death ruptured a bubble of disbelief in Brady's mind: This was happening, and where Apollo went, Alicia could follow.

No, she won't! he thought. *No, she won't!*

Her mouth moved, but the wind tore her voice away. He read her lips. She was crying out to him.

"I got you!" he screamed. She could not hear him, but he hoped she understood.

Below her, Malik dangled, one hand in a death grip on her ankle. His other hand hung down, attached to the straight-back chair. The chair swung in the wind, battering his legs.

And below Malik, far below Malik, the multicolored flashing gaudiness of Times Square. As huge as the signs were, they were too far away for Brady to recognize any of them. Spots of lights, like iridescent ants, marked the vehicles trying to push through the intersection. The sound of car horns, as constant as the press of people, could not climb this high; only the wind's voice found Brady's ears.

He pulled. And pulled. Alicia didn't budge. His hand began to throb. He ignored the pain and tightened his grip.

He hooked his foot under the climate control unit and tried again. He leaned his body back, taking advantage of his weight to leverage her up. She rose an inch and scrambled for another purchase, this one on the front edge of the climate control unit. Her head was above the sill. He quickly repositioned his hands to her biceps.

Lean and *puuuulllll* . . .

Her stomach rose onto the sill. He gripped her under the arms. *Puuuulllll* . . .

She was in. And clenching her teeth in pain.

"My leg . . . !"

Malik's hand still clutched her ankle, grinding her shin into the sharp edge of the sill and the broken glass encrusted there. Blood spilled out onto the metal frame from her torn flesh.

Brady wrapped his hands around Malik's wrist, hoping to shake him loose or squeeze the tendons into submission. The man's hand was as unyielding as a shackle on Alicia's ankle. He leaned out, sure for a split moment that he would teeter too far and tumble right past Malik to join Apollo's corpse. He sank his teeth into the back of Malik's hand. He bit hard and sawed his teeth back and forth. Warm, coppery blood bubbled up into his mouth. Still gripping Malik's wrist, Brady tightened his bite. Finally, the fingers sprang open.

Malik swung away from Alicia's leg—dropping down, giving Brady a fierce tug as he took Malik's full weight. He leaned back, wiggling to get off the sill and into the room. Malik rose with him. He was twisting his wrist, trying to wrench free of Brady's grasp.

Is he trying *to fall?* Brady thought. *Could he still be delusional from the drugs?*

Malik raised his other hand toward Brady.

Grab my wrist!

Instead, Malik raked his black claws over Brady's hand. Brady growled in pain. Four deep furrows oozed blood. It ran down into Brady's grip, making it slick. He felt the bandages on his left hand tearing away, breaking free. He squeezed with everything he had.

Their eyes locked. A surge of repulsion and contempt made Brady see nothing redeemable in the creature whose life he held in his hands. Here was the man who had wrapped a wire around Alicia's neck and pulled her out a forty-ninth-story window. Here was the beast who had sent Apollo to his death, who had a connection to the attack on him and his son. This assailant was a cog in a machine whose purpose, as far as Brady cared, was to destroy him, his son, and his partner. Independent of that, Brady believed Malik's ranting during the Amytal interview was tantamount to a confession that he had slaughtered children.

And he's going to get away with it.

Without him and Alicia to take him in, press charges, and get an investigation under way, Malik would walk away from this hotel a free man.

His grip slipped from Malik's wrist to his hand. Only the tips of his fingers protruded from the top of Brady's clutch. Brady's damaged hand trembled in pain; he focused on keeping it pinched around Malik's fingers.

Brady closed his eyes. To let go would be murder. Not the way things were done. He squeezed even tighter; Malik's bones were crunching under his grip.

He felt Alicia grab his belt.

"Pull me back!" he bellowed. He felt the tug. His arm and hand muscles burned.

He's going to walk.

Not if he flies.

Malik's hand slipped through. One arm reaching up, fingers splayed, Malik plunged down. There was no fear in his eyes, only a hatred so fierce, Brady could still feel it boring into him after Malik disappeared into the shadows below.

He allowed Alicia to tug him away from the whipping wind, from the night that hungered for more sacrifices—he felt in his heart that it did.

He collapsed with his back propped against the climate control unit. Alicia sat hard on the floor beside the bed. The wind thrashed their hair.

He was looking at her, but all he saw was Malik falling, getting smaller and smaller.

What was I thinking? That he would walk . . . but not if he flies. Did I drop him? On purpose?

He could not answer. He honestly did not know.

After giving herself less than thirty seconds to catch her breath, Alicia rose. She used the bed to hoist herself up, groaning with effort. It was painful to watch. He held her injured forearm. Both of her shins were bleeding from being scraped over the sill and broken glass.

"We have to get out of here," she said. She stooped to retrieve her pistol from the floor, where it had fallen when Brady knocked it out of her hands. She put a suitcase on one of the beds, unzipped it, and pulled a lavender item from it. A fresh blouse. The one she wore was torn up the back. She walked to the bathroom door and turned back to him.

"Get Apollo's bag and medical supplies," she said. "Forget the EKG and IV stuff. We don't have time to pretend we were never here."

She paused, eyeing him sympathetically. She looked as weary as he felt. "We have to move fast, Brady."

She stepped into the bathroom but did not bother to shut the door.

53

After Karen died, Brady had thought the world was a dark place. He'd had no idea just how dark it could be.

They traveled awhile in silence. Images of the past six hours played in his mind like a horror movie trailer, whose fast flashes of fangs and blood and falling bodies were designed to rattle your senses. The attack on him and Zach; the assault on Alicia; the insanity of the truth-serum session with Malik, who had most certainly been a Satanist; Alicia's narrow escape from death; Apollo's forty-nine-story plunge; Malik's encore. Brady didn't know whether to try to sort it all out or to let it all go and not think of anything for now.

They had left the Marriott quickly, and not only to avoid hotel security and NYPD. Neither of them was convinced that Malik or the assassin who'd attacked his home were lone killers. If others showed up because of the commotion or simply to check on Malik's handiwork, they would try to pick up their trail. Brady was thankful he had been triply cautious getting Zach to the Oakleys'.

But leaving the hotel garage was another matter. They had taken his Toyota Highlander, since there was a chance whoever was after them did not yet know he had driven to New York. Still, someone could have easily spotted them and followed. So now he made frequent turns, occasionally doubling back and entering a parking garage just to immediately exit it— all the while winding farther away from Manhattan and the bloody mess they'd left.

They passed through Queens and Brooklyn, then over the Verrazano

Narrows to Staten Island, and headed southwest on Richmond Parkway toward New Jersey.

When she had finished redressing her wound with supplies from Apollo's bag, Alicia pulled out her laptop and began typing furiously. He knew it was her way of handling stress, to get it out of her head and into a word processor. In his peripheral vision, he saw light from street lamps sweep over her face, as regular as a heartbeat. Except for their similar height and slight frame, Karen and Alicia were polar opposites. His wife had been dark and mysterious; Alicia was blonde and pale, with expressions that made her appear as easy to read as a fast-food menu (Brady knew better). Karen often thought long and hard before gently explaining why she felt differently from Brady about a subject; Alicia never hesitated to air her disagreements. When something concerned her, Karen reached for her Bible; Alicia reached for her gun.

And yet, Brady felt something stir in his heart at the thought of Alicia sitting beside him, sharing this dark adventure. He realized that what he felt could be a profound gratefulness that she had not died tonight, as she could have—twice. He remembered the rush of protectiveness he'd felt when she told him of Malik's attack on her. This feeling was different. It was warm and comforting. Nothing approaching the emotions Karen had kindled within him, but it was the first time he'd felt anything like it since her death. It startled him. And gave him hope.

Her keyboard had fallen silent. He glanced over. She was slumped against the door, her eyes closed. He reached over and lowered the laptop screen.

"I'm awake," she said without stirring. Twenty seconds passed, then: "Barely."

"Need a Red Bull?" He'd seen her down three of the energy drinks in one long night of investigative fact-finding. He could use a couple himself.

"More like a Red Roof Inn. I'm beat, Brady."

"Say no more."

They needed time to think, to come up with a plan, to rest. He had heard that the best soldiers never passed up the opportunity to eat or sleep. They were both essential to peak performance, and in battle you never knew when you'd get another chance. And one thing that was painfully clear was that he and Alicia were soldiers in a battle for their lives.

He pulled into the first motel they came to, a Comfort Inn just out-side Baltimore. They were three hours and three states away from the Marriott room where crime scene investigators would find their fingerprints and DNA.

WITHOUT HAVING to ask, Brady knew she shared his desire to not be alone. This wasn't going to be one of those times when stress and the specter of death drove two people into each other's arms and beds, but he wanted to keep his eye on her, to be near her, and to know she was breathing the same air as he drifted off to sleep. He did not know if it was Alicia, specifically, he wanted to be near, or simply a comrade in arms. He suspected it was Alicia.

It would be the first time since Karen died that he had shared a room with another adult. He asked for two separate beds.

They parked in the rear, away from the main thoroughfare, and hauled their luggage into the room.

Immediately Alicia set up her computer gear on a chipped Formica table.

"Malik gave us some good intel," she explained. "I want to run it through NCIC. See what hits."

"Now?"

"Just a little bit," she said. "Half hour."

The sky was lightening and beginning to show through the sheers cover-ing the room's single window. He pulled the heavier drapes closed and went to discover how hot he could make the water in the shower. When he emerged twenty minutes later, the computer was dark and Alicia was lying fully clothed on top of her bed's covers, fast asleep.

WHEN BRADY awoke, his eyelids had gained ten pounds; they pushed painfully against his eyes and required every muscle in his face to stay open. His head and his hand competed for his attention, each throbbing with pain. A thick band of bright sunlight stole through an inch-wide gap between the drapes. Brady rose to remedy this breach.

Alicia had pushed the covers off her bed and slipped between the sheets. A lavender collar, bent up like a dog's ear and touching her chin, revealed that she had not bothered to remove her street clothes. She was on her back, her head thrown back, mouth open—the sleep of the truly exhausted.

The bedtime prayer he had uttered every night as a boy came to mind. *If I should die before I wake . . .*

What a thing to teach a child. He'd never liked that prayer.

The temperature in the room was stifling. He found that the air conditioner mounted through the wall under the window blew only hot air, regardless of its settings.

Alicia had left a bottle of ibuprofen on the bathroom counter. He popped four and went back to bed without looking at the clock.

THE HORROR of the previous night found Brady in his dreams.

"No! Can't you hear him? Can't you see it?"

"Yes, Master! I have the blood! I saved it for you!"

Brady rolled over, swiping at the sheets that gripped him like a hand. He sat bolt upright. His eyes strained against the sunlight streaming through the open curtains. Still, the nightmare assailed him.

"Alicia . . ."

"Where's Apollo? What have you done to him?"

Alicia was sitting at the room's small table. She saw that he was awake, and her hand shot to the recorder she had used during Malik's Amytal interview. The chaotic echoes of that event abruptly stopped.

"Sorry," she said.

Brady rubbed his face. His eyelids had returned to their normal weight, and his headache was gone. His hand pained him just enough to keep the injury in mind. "What time is it?"

She glanced at her watch. "One fifteen. I've been up for hours."

He groaned, threw his legs off the side of the bed, and sat. He stepped into his pants, tugging them up as he stood. He turned and caught Alicia watching him. She made no attempt to conceal her scrutiny. He played it cool. His shirt was on the back of her chair. He padded over, took the shirt, and slipped it on.

He put his hand on her shoulder. Her muscles were tight as cables. He began massaging her trapezoids. Karen had taught him to curb his impulse to brutally knead at the muscles and instead to gently coax tension out of them.

"You okay?" he asked.

"Last night," she said, nodding at the recorder. "I can't believe that's me."

Her head began rotating slowly on her neck. Her muscles were responding to Brady's fingers.

"Do yourself a favor," he said. "Erase that recording."

"I know the things I saw were hallucinations, but I can't shake the notion that there was something more to them."

He waited for her to continue. His attention moved to her deltoids, over the rotator cuffs.

She let seconds drift by, then said, "It's like I was peering into an invisible world, one that's always around us, but we can't see it."

"The spiritual world?"

"Yeah . . . something like that. Karma or . . . I don't know. I just think Malik was evil, and evil *things*—demons or bad energy or whatever—had been drawn to him, had *congregated* around him. I think I caught a glimpse of them."

Brady moved his fingers to the sides and back of her neck, careful to avoid the nick from Malik's garrote.

He said, "Lots of tribal peoples—Native Americans, aborigines of various countries—believe hallucinogenic drugs help humans commune with spirits. Timothy Leary tried to prove LSD breaks down our defenses, our conceptions of reality, and allows us to see the world as it truly is, with dimensions and beings we can't normally discern. He held that it was not the drugs that evoked a twisted state of consciousness, but our prejudices. That's why some people think small children are more aware of the supernatural than adults are; they haven't yet formed the prejudices that prevent us from seeing what's just beyond our five senses."

"What do you believe?"

For a few moments, he watched his fingers work. They found her trape-zoids once more.

He said, "I believe there are dimensions and beings at work around us that we can't see. The Bible says as much: 'For we wrestle not against flesh and blood, but against principalities, against powers, against the rulers of the darkness of this world, against spiritual wickedness in high places.'" He let her think about the passage, then added, "Whether we're ever supposed to see them in our time on earth, I don't know."

"I saw them."

He stopped his fingers and stepped around to look her in the eyes.

"Malik was talking some crazy stuff before you got a faceful of scopo-lamine. Maybe what you saw—"

"Was some kind of, what, posthypnotic suggestion?" She shook her head. "I don't think so."

He could tell that nothing he said would change her mind. She would work on what she believed she had witnessed until it became a mental tool she could use. Eventually, she would be a stronger person or do her job bet-ter because of the trauma she suffered last night. She was very Nietzschean that way.

"What I want to know," he said, trying to break the tension, "is what kind of movie would Malik find scary?"

She laughed softly, and he saw a bit of humor reach her eyes.

"*The Great Muppet Caper*?" she suggested, and they both laughed.

On the table, next to the recorder, her laptop was opened and booted up. Beside it was a short stack of printouts. A bold headline caught his atten-tion: "Vanishing Vikings: The Mystery of the Western Settlement." He dropped into another chair and picked up the top page.

"What's this?"

"Internet research," she said. "Something to do while you caught up on your Zs. You said the guy who attacked you looked like a Viking, right down to his clothes and choice of weapons, so I Googled *Viking* and *Norse* and *wolf-dog hybrids* and a few other terms. Seems that Vikings are all the rage these days. Hundreds of thousands of web pages dedicated to them.

Everything you ever wanted to know. Too much to sift through, so I went over to LexisNexis. You know it?"

He nodded. It was a database of articles from magazines, journals, newspapers. Very comprehensive. Having been published, the articles tended to be more thoroughly researched and better written than the average web site. As a graduate student, he'd tapped into the database regularly.

"That article is from the *Journal of Archaeology*," she said.

He began reading it silently.

The abandonment of the Western Settlement of Greenland in AD 1350 is one of the great mysteries of medieval history. Ninety families—there one month, gone the next, according to the records of Ivar Bardarsson, an Icelandic clerical official. In the spring of 1350, friendly Inuits brought word to the Eastern Settlement at the southern tip of Greenland that there was no one left in *Vesterbygd*—as the Western Settlement was known at the time. Bardarsson joined a group of men who went to investigate. They found dinner on the tables, kettles of stew over burnt-out fires, starving livestock in pens, but no people. Were they slaughtered by local Inuit? Did the particularly harsh winter of 1349–1350 drive them . . . somewhere? No one knows for—

"Where are you?" Alicia interrupted.

He told her.

"Okay, that's enough of that one. Here . . ." She pulled the stack of paper toward her and flipped through it. She tugged out a page and handed it to him.

"From the *Journal of Speculative Archaeology*."

"The what?"

"It has something to do with establishing theory based on known facts; I don't know. The writer is a professor in the Archaeology Department at the University of Ontario. Check it out. Just what I underlined."

This time he read out loud:

"'Far from the monastic cleric history books make him out to be, Ivar

Bardarsson was a ruthless "missionary of torture." He had a penchant for ston-
ing to death pagans who refused his efforts to convert them to Christianity,
even children as young as eight. So ruthless was he that in 1341 he was
exiled from Norway and sent to Greenland's Eastern Settlement, then
known as Osterbygd. There, under the guise of ombudsman of the Bishop
of Bergen, Bardarsson continued his practice of coerced conversion, under
penalty of death.

"'History does not tell us when Bardarsson first learned of the Western
Settlement, known as Vesterbygd, but when he did, he must have felt like a
child set loose in a candy store. For unlike other settlements, which were
largely Christian by this time, Vesterbygd was populated entirely by pagans.
When Erik the Red left Norway to settle Greenland in 984, Christianity had
already begun sweeping through his motherland. His ships bore both
Christians and pagans. To maintain peace in his budding new world, Erik
separated the religions. The pagans settled in Vesterbygd. Generation after
generation, Vesterbygd not only held on to its pagan beliefs, it became
fiercely anti-Christian. When the Norse, as a people group, converted to
Christianity, the violent passion it applied to plundering and conquering the
Saxons now turned to converting unbelievers. Indeed, Bardarsson's barbaric
conversion techniques were nothing more than a product of his heritage. To
the pagans in Vesterbygd, Christians were seen as a bloodthirsty people.

"'By the time Bardarsson set sail for Vesterbygd . . .'"

Brady stopped and looked at Alicia. "This guy's not trying to say
Bardarsson wiped out the Western Settlement, is he?"

"It's even stranger than that. Read on."

"'By the time Bardarsson set sail for Vesterbygd, he had been planning
the excursion for some two years. Word of his intentions reached Britain,
where it piqued the interest of a pseudo-religious organization called
Excubitor. This organization shared Vesterbygd's disdain for Christianity. In
a letter from the Archduke of—'"

"Just what's underlined."

Brady's eyes darted ahead. "'The group reached Vesterbygd ahead of
Bardarsson. It convinced the settlement's leaders to travel north, where
the organization's fleet would meet them in late summer. They made a

pact by which *Excubitor* would become their benefactor and help them preserve their beliefs and culture in exchange for their pledge of fealty to . . .'"

Brady read the words, then flashed his bafflement at Alicia. She smiled. He went back to the page.

"'Fealty to the coming Antichrist, who was prophesied to defeat Christianity and restore the world to Asetru.'"

"That's the Viking religion. I looked it up."

"But it's not even true. The Antichrist doesn't defeat Christianity."

Alicia shrugged. "Anything can be spun. He goes on to say he believes the people of the Western Settlement relocated to the wilds of the Northwest Territories, Canada, where their descendants are still waiting for the Antichrist."

"Does he have proof?"

"Some . . . In the 1890s, a guy in authentic Viking garb walked into Fond du Lac, Saskatchewan, claiming to have escaped a closed community way up north. The local newspaper interviewed him and took his picture, but by the time representatives of larger papers and universities showed up, the guy had vanished. The professor cites archaeological evidence that implies the same community of people kept establishing a village and abandoning it about once every generation to move deeper into the Territories." She shook her head. "I didn't understand half of it."

Brady looked at her a long time. Finally, he said, "So what you're saying is that the Pelletier killer came from this lost Viking settlement?"

She threw up her hands. "I don't know, Brady. I'm just doing research, and this stuff popped up. I think it's pretty interesting. Is it pertinent? I don't know. Is it a coincidence these Vikings are waiting for the Antichrist and all the Pelletier victims are linked by their interest in religion? I don't know. But let me show you one more thing."

His head lolled back.

"Just a few sentences, okay?" She found the printout she wanted. "Right here . . . 'The Vikings of Greenland and later of Newfoundland and Labrador were fierce and accomplished hunters. Their success can be credited in no small part to their skills as breeders and trainers of hunting dogs.

The first recorded crossbreeding of a gray wolf and a German shepherd can be traced to the village of Brattahlid in 1062. Within two decades, every Norse hunter in Greenland owned a wolf-dog hybrid, which was trained to bring down an animal or incapacitate it until the hunter arrived.'"

She looked up.

Brady said, "Wow."

Alicia nodded.

Lost in thought, he stood and headed for the bathroom. "I need a shower," he mumbled. Then he turned to her. "What are we supposed to do, find a Norse tribe that's been lost for seven hundred years?"

"Not necessarily. If the *Excubitor* is still their benefactor, maybe all we have to do is find it."

"An organization, probably *older* than seven hundred years?" Brady said. "No problem." He paused. "*Excubitor* . . . did you search the Net for that too?"

"I did. No hits, except for *Lanius excubitor*. It's a bird. Oh, and I found out *excubitor* is a Latin word."

"For . . . ?"

"Watchmen or watchers."

Brady nodded absently and strolled into the bathroom, still trying to get his mind around all she had laid on him.

———

WHEN HE came out, Alicia was cursing at her computer.

"Uhhh!" she said loudly and slammed her laptop shut.

"What?" Brady asked.

"We've been locked out of the system, out of the National Crime Information Center."

"What? Try my password—"

"I already did." She waved off his baffled expression. "I've had your password since the day we started working together."

"Of course. Who would've . . . ?" He sat on the edge of his bed. "They've connected us to Malik's and Apollo's deaths already."

She shook her head no. "Last night, after you'd been attacked, I asked you a question."

"Who knew where to find me."

She nodded. "The same person who knew I went to New York to pursue the Father McAfee lead."

"Gilbreath," Brady said.

John Gilbreath, head of the Bureau's laboratory and training divisions. The Evidence Response Team Unit was part of the laboratory, while profiling inexplicably fell under the banner of "training." Since the experimental team of which Brady and Alicia were a part was composed of personnel from both divisions, Gilbreath was their immediate supervisor.

She nodded. Her jaw was tight.

"Wait a minute," he said. He tried to envision their boss as betrayer, as murderer. The man was a go-getter with political aspirations, but did that mean he'd do *anything* to achieve his goals—assuming their deaths would somehow boost his career? Even with his education in psychology, Brady couldn't imagine how a person so seemingly together could hide this level of malice.

"Why him?" he asked. "I mean, anyone could have hacked into the Bureau's system and got my address. No computer is impenetrable."

"The person who knew where to find us had to know two things. First, he had to know where to find you at that precise time yesterday. So he not only had to have your home address, but he also had to know you were home from the investigation. Second, he knew I *wasn't* home. In fact, he knew I wasn't even in Colorado. But in New York, of all places. Finding one of us . . . okay, a hacker could do that. But both of us at the same time and with me in a new location? No, that's a combination lock that only one person has the right numbers to."

She saw that he wasn't convinced. She rose from the chair and began to pace.

"All right, Brady. For whatever reason, somebody wants to kill us. He needs to know where to go and when to go there, right? And just for argument's sake, this person is not Gilbreath. What does he do?"

"He taps our phones."

"Okay. You probably called Zach to let him know you were coming home, right?"

He nodded.

"When I called Gilbreath last night to ask him to let me pursue the McAfee lead, I was on the hotel phone. Did this UNSUB tap that too?"

"Maybe Gilbreath's line was tapped."

"At his home, to find *us*? That's a long shot."

"What about someone else in the Bureau?"

"Okay," she said, nodding appreciatively. "I can count on one hand the colleagues who probably know my address. You?"

"'Bout the same."

"So it's someone with enough clout to get into the personnel files. Now, when Gilbreath gave me permission to go, he said it was off the record for one day, just to see what I could uncover. He didn't want to step on any toes, so he didn't even tell the investigation's team leader what I was up to. You know how tight-lipped the Bureau is, even within itself. Who would he tell? The deputy director? That's who *he* answers to."

She almost had him. Almost.

"And remember, Brady, *I* didn't know I was coming to New York until after midnight on the day we were attacked. That's moving pretty fast."

Nudging him a little closer to her way of thinking.

"Let's say it's somebody totally outside the Bureau," she said, on a roll now. "The same person controlling the killer. To piece everything together— where and when to find us—he'd have to have access to the Bureau files and credit card processing databases and probably tap a dozen phones or so."

She stopped pacing.

"Or . . . ," she said, "he could be John Gilbreath and have all the information at his fingertips."

He nodded slowly.

"Look, he's the place to start. If it's not him, no harm, no foul."

"Okay," Brady agreed. "So what do we do?"

"We have to go see him."

"He leaves early on Fridays," Brady said. "If we leave now, we'll just make it."

"No," she said, a devious expression touching her eyes and her lips. "I have something else in mind."

54

John Gilbreath awoke suddenly at 12:37. Jaundiced light from a nearby street lamp filtered through sheers on the windows that flanked the bed. Jet shadows clung like putty to the edges of the room. Something had woken him, but what? His wife, Candice, inhaled loudly beside him. It sounded nasal, almost a snore. Not at all like the demure respiration he'd come to find so soothing on restless nights.

"Hon?" His gravelly whisper grated against the house's tomblike silence.

Another loud breath, this time the mother of all snores.

He shifted onto his left hip, propping himself up with an arm. His other hand fished forward, and he found Candice under their light quilt and cotton sheets. He could just make out the shape of her face in the dark. He shook her gently.

"Candice?"

Another shake, another snore.

Heart pounding, he spun and flicked on the bedside lamp, blinding himself for a mere second. And in that moment, a voice, strong and female, filled the room.

"She'll be fine."

He jumped, and a sharp noise escaped him—not a word, not quite a scream; something in between. His eyes darted around the room, settling on a pair of legs clad in beige slacks and protruding from the shadows in the corner. Someone was sitting in the overstuffed chair. Intended for late-night reading, the lamp was too weak to reveal the intruder's body and face.

Haltingly, he rotated his head away, then shifted his eyes to see his wife sprawled on her back under the bed linen, head cradled deep in her favorite down pillow. Her mouth hung open impossibly wide, and a thin line of drool glistened on her cheek. His nostrils flared, catching an odor . . .

"Midazolam hydrochloride," the voice said. "Kind of like chloroform, but a lot less dangerous. At least that's what the on-line PDR says."

"What is this? Who are you?" He reached for the nightstand drawer but stopped when a pistol emerged from the shadows. "What do you want?"

Alicia Wagner leaned into the light, watching him carefully. Of the three emotions that flashed over his face, the middle one was most telling. First, surprise: a natural reaction regardless of who she had turned out to be. Then fear: that mechanism of defense initiated when encountering someone who has a reason to harm you . . . such as someone you've betrayed. And last, indignation: the ruse.

"Alicia! How dare you!" His flesh was turning red from the neck up.

"I've come to ask you that."

"How did you get past the alarm system?"

"Oh, please." She put the gun in her lap.

His jaw found a posture of fiery anger, but he could not get control of his eyes. They darted to the gun, to her face, to the open bedroom door.

"What happened in New York?" he asked, a superior tone to his voice.

"Not what you expected to happen, I imagine."

"We got a call from NYPD. They wanted to know why your prints are all over a room from which two people fell to their deaths. Your prints and Brady's, for crying out loud! They found his service pistol too. He was supposed to be home in Virginia."

"Dead in Virginia, you mean."

"What are you talking about?"

"What's NYPD doing? What's the Bureau doing? Have APBs been issued?"

"For you and Brady? No! We don't air our dirty laundry to locals, not until we find out what's going on. We covered for you up there, said you and

Brady were undercover on something we couldn't discuss. That'll buy us a few days at best." He reached for the nightstand drawer. "Now let's get downtown and sort this—"

"Stop, John! I mean it!"

He snapped his hand back as though from a hot surface. "You can't do this, Alicia!"

"Who's after us, John?"

"I don't know what—"

"You would not believe the *thing* that paid me a visit at my hotel last night." She held up her arm to show him the bloody gauze. "He tried to kill me. You were the only one who knew where I was."

Gilbreath shook his head like a dog shaking water off its pelt. "That's New York; that's the way it is. Someone . . . a *mugger* must have followed you—"

"At the very same time, an assassin attacked Brady Moore at his house. Almost got his son too."

"What?" He looked genuinely stunned. "Is anybody . . . ?"

"They're alive. Sorry to break the news."

"I'm *glad* they're alive; of course I am!" His head jerked a millimeter as if grasping an idea. He softened his face. "Look, we need to jump on this right away. If someone's out there hunting down agents—"

"Shut up."

He froze.

"The attacks have something to do with the Pelletier killings."

Gilbreath's entire body spasmed—almost imperceptibly but enough to convey his surprise. His eyes locked on hers. He opened his mouth just to close it again.

"Tell me," she said.

He shook his head, breaking the gaze. "Nothing . . . no. I don't know anything."

"John . . ." A disappointed tone.

"Think what you want."

Her face hardened. She reached into the darkness beside her. Her hand returned with a cylindrical object about five inches long. Gilbreath watched intently as she raised the barrel of her semiautomatic pistol to it and began screwing it on.

"A silencer!" he barked. "You're an idiot, Alicia, threatening me with that!"

She understood. There was something about a silencer that instantly raised the stakes. It said "I mean business" more than anything else she'd done so far; more than breaking into his home, more than anesthetizing his wife, more than waving a pistol at him. As frightened as he may have been at finding her in his bedroom with a gun, he had never really believed she would harm him. This device changed that. It spoke of cold deliberation, of deadly intent, of wanting to kill and get away with it. That was precisely the reason she had brought it, and despite his angry words, she knew by the fear in his eyes it would work.

"Tell me," she said again, pointing the enlarged pistol at him.

He appeared transfixed on the silencer, hypnotized by it.

"Tell me, John, or you'll have to explain to your wife why she'll spend the rest of her life in a wheelchair." Slowly she panned the pistol's aim toward the unconscious woman.

John Gilbreath's mouth unhinged. His eyes moved from the silencer to his wife's legs and back to the silencer, as if calculating the trajectory of the bullet. For a moment she feared that he still would not talk, then he said, "I got a call two weeks ago about the murders."

"Two weeks ago? We didn't know about them two weeks ago."

"Somebody did," he said. He snapped his gaze toward the window as if he'd heard something. He slid the tip of his tongue over his lips but did nothing about the perspiration that had broken out on his forehead.

Alicia's breath caught in her throat, lumping there like a stubborn pill. "Either there's another Pelletier murder we don't know about—"

She stopped. Gilbreath was shaking his head no.

"Someone knew about the killings before they started?" Her mind raced through the implications. "Did the killer call you?"

"No, it was someone I know." He turned his head away. "In the government."

"What are you saying? Who called?"

"Jeff Ramsland. That's what he goes by, anyway. When I met him a couple of years ago, he said he was with Justice. Every now and then he'd appear at a high-level meeting. He'd never say a word, just listen and then leave. I got the impression he was an oversight officer, something like that. When he called, he wanted to meet. Haupt Fountains. You know them?"

She nodded. Geysers of waters shooting out of blocks of granite that were supposedly the oldest rock in the United States, three and a half million years old.

"Do you know why there?" he asked.

It took her a few seconds. "The water," she said. "The sound makes electronic eavesdropping virtually impossible."

"First thing he does is hand me a letter. Bureau letterhead. From the office of the director. Signed by the man himself; I've seen his signature a thousand times. Two sentences: 'Give this man what he wants. No questions.' As soon as I read it, Ramsland takes the letter back, puts it in his pocket. Then he tells me who he's with. At that point, he didn't have to. I had my orders. He did it to make sure I obeyed—to stress his authority and maybe give me a scare." Gilbreath smiled thinly. "It worked."

"Are you going to tell me?"

"The Office of Contingency Planning." He gauged her astonishment and said, "I see you've heard of it."

"Who in federal law enforcement hasn't? I started hearing the rumors a few weeks after I joined the academy. Some kind of government watchdog, waiting for flying saucers, alien contact, viable evidence of ESP . . . *The X-Files* was reportedly based on the rumors."

"But *The X-Files* got it wrong. The OCP is not some rogue FBI agent or two, stubbornly begging their superiors for funding and permission to investigate strange phenomena from a basement cubbyhole. It's the most powerful agency in the federal government. To remain secret, it has to be. It's small, so it uses the resources of other agencies. And to do that, its demands have to trump any objections those other agencies have. If it wants to appropriate a spy satellite to check out some djinni activity in the Sahara, it does it. If it needs a special forces unit to invade the home of some Oxford professor who claims to have found the staff of Moses, it picks up the phone and gets it. With impunity and without scrutiny. The CIA can't say no, NSA can't say no . . . I hear even the president can't say no. If it wants to close down an investigation, it can. If it wants to see a file, you send it over."

"Over where?"

"No one knows. Everything's electronic these days."

"You've had dealings with it before?"

"Not directly. I've been told to send files to anonymous e-mail accounts and to change direction on a case a time or two—at OCP's behest, was my understanding."

"Sounds ripe for abuse."

"An acceptable risk, considering its work."

"*Work?* UFOs . . . Bigfoot . . . ?"

"Extrasensory perception—everybody knows about the government's interest in that. But even ESP is insignificant next to *other things* that might be out there. The world's strongest nations have long believed in the power of religious artifacts. *Raiders of the Lost Ark* wasn't so far off the mark. No one cares if the artifacts' power comes from God or if they were found by men in ancient times to have natural power and used to propagate some religious belief. The power is what's important, not where it comes from. The OCP has funded expeditions looking for the ark of the covenant, the staff of Moses, the true cross of Christ. It watches for the Antichrist, the so-called beast—"

"Whoa, whoa," she said, stopping him. "The Antichrist?" She thought about the religious iconography in the Pelletier victims' houses, Malik's satanism, the mysterious symbol branded on the victims and on Malik's back, the rumors about the reason an entire Norse colony vanished.

"Sure, why not? If he makes an appearance, he's going to be mighty powerful. Don't you think the world's only superpower would want in on that? Or at least get a heads-up to defend itself?"

"But . . ." She felt as though she'd followed the white rabbit down a hole. "How could a government agency *watch* for the Antichrist?"

"It watches for signs, prophecies fulfilled. The OCP reportedly has affinity relationships with all kinds of like-minded individuals and organizations.

I've heard one of its operatives meets regularly with theologians. Spends a lot of time at the Vatican. Where better to get intel on religious stuff?"

Alicia felt dizzy. Nothing Gilbreath had said was proof of anything, but somehow she knew she'd seen the shadow of the beast they were pursuing. It sometimes happened like that. A sliver of circumstantial evidence that, when added to all the other circumstantial evidence, made a cohesive whole that felt as solid, as *right* as a murder weapon with fingerprints and video footage of the crime.

The Vatican. Again.

She blinked and saw Gilbreath eyeing the pistol. She had let it slump in her hand. She snapped it to attention.

"So what did Ramsland want from you? No questions asked?"

"To know when we got on the Pelletier case—beheadings in Utah, Colorado, and New Mexico."

"Pelletier hasn't struck in New Mexico."

Gilbreath raised one knowing eyebrow. "At the time, he hadn't struck *anywhere*. I asked Ramsland, 'What beheadings?' He said, 'You'll find out.'"

"So when the reports started coming in, you sent Brady and me?"

He lowered his gaze—ashamed? "As soon as I could justify it." His voice had lost a measure of strength, of self-righteousness. "I took Ramsland's request to be an order to put agents on the case."

"And with the Crime Scene Digitizer's ability to help local law enforcement, and its need for further field tests, you were able to get us out there sooner than you could otherwise."

He nodded. "Before we could establish official jurisdiction."

"Then you let Ramsland know?"

"Yes."

"How did you make contact?"

"A phone number." He rushed to respond to her next, unasked question: "But it's disconnected now. I tried calling today after I heard about New York. I have no way of contacting him again."

"You told him we went out to offer assistance?"

"I told him you and Brady were on the case. I didn't think he cared about semantics."

"And that was the last time you spoke to him?"

Silence. He looked at his wife.

"John, what did you do?"

He pulled in a deep breath, let it out.

"He called again, asked where you were staying in Colorado. I'd already pulled you off the case, because the evidence of interstate serial murder allowed the Bureau to step in with a real team. I thought . . . I thought . . ."

"You thought that's what Ramsland wanted, more bodies on the case." She watched him readjust himself on the bed. *Squirming*, she thought. "But he wanted us, Brady and me."

"I let him know you were following a lead in New York. He wanted to know what you were doing, where you were staying. He said 'they,' so I knew he meant Brady as well."

"And you gave him Brady's home address." She felt nauseated.

He lowered his head, then looked her in the eyes. "I sent him your personnel records."

A bolt of light, startlingly bright, cut through the sheers of the window on Gilbreath's side of the bed. Alicia's mind had just registered this intrusion when she saw Gilbreath leaping toward her, hands grasping for the gun, face skewed into a mask of white-hot fury. Instinctively, she pulled the gun away, then swung it around in a blurring arc, clubbing him in the temple. He crumpled before her. She vaulted over him and hit the wall beside the window as the light panned away.

A quick look, then another.

Cops. Gilbreath had found a way to trigger a silent alarm. Or she had not been as smart defeating the alarm as she had thought. Either way, she was in big trouble.

55

There was something funny about the police cruiser in front of Gilbreath's house . . .

Cautiously, she peered through the curtains again, this time long enough to assess the situation.

A private security car. Parked at the curb. One man standing behind the hood, watching as another operated a spotlight mounted on the passenger-side door. The beam hit the second bedroom window, again filling the room with the stark intensity of an autopsy table.

Had Gilbreath known? Had all the talk been nothing more than a stall tactic?

Last year, rising incidents of false alarms prompted the Alexandria Police Department to institute a policy of billing property owners for calling them unnecessarily. As a result, security companies stopped reporting every suspicious event; now only "positive triggers," such as breaches in door and window monitors and the activation of panic buttons, warranted 911 calls. Alicia was certain she hadn't tripped a positive trigger. Gilbreath must have had the home's security system programmed to send a coded signal period-ically—every twenty to thirty minutes, most likely—to the monitoring company, reporting its continued functionality. Disabling the phones, as she did to gain entrance, must have prevented the last signal from going out.

She caught movement in her peripheral vision.

Gilbreath—moving in fast.

Her gun hand was quicker: his face came dead-center on the pistol's silenced barrel. He jolted to a halt, cross-eyed on the weapon.

"God help me," Alicia hissed between clenched teeth, "I'll do it! Now back away. Back away! On the floor! Down!"

He dropped to his knees. She planted a foot against his upper chest and shoved him onto his back. He landed with an "Oomph!" and froze like that, only his eyes tracking her movements.

From the shadows of the chair she retrieved her canvas bag of breaking-and-entering tools, all purchased at a local hardware store. She moved toward the door, then suddenly stopped. She swung around and stepped on Gilbreath's neck, hard.

"Are these guys at OCP so spooky that you would deliver me in a body bag to them?"

Through clenched teeth, he hissed: *"Yes!"*

"The Bureau's out of it? We can't come in?"

His face was turning the color of an eggplant.

"Not if OCP wants you dead."

"How do we know it's OCP and not someone else with ties to it?"

He didn't answer. His eyelids were beginning to droop. She eased up on the pressure her foot was exerting to his neck. His eyes came back.

"You don't," he said. "Look, the OCP doesn't act alone. It watches. It exchanges information. If it wants you dead, you can bet someone else is behind the initiative."

She glared at him in disgust. Then she spun out of the room, pulling the door shut. She attached a travel gadget that locked the door in place.

From his side, Gilbreath yelled, "This is bigger than you or me, Wagner! These guys deal in otherworldly phenomena! Something's happening! Something's coming! *Alicia?*"

A crash inside.

She smiled at the thought of his finding the gun he kept in the bedroom closet and the one between the mattresses without bullets. Later, he'd have to fish both ammo clips out of his downstairs toilet bowl.

Another crash. She suspected he had yanked the nightstand drawer all the way out. Going for the cell phone. Oops, no battery.

He bellowed unintelligibly, and she wished she had time to savor his fury.

As she descended the stairs, staying close to the wall to prevent creaks, the pounding at the front door started. She slipped into the kitchen seconds before a flashlight beam cut through the narrow foyer window to illuminate the staircase. She heard the upstairs door rattle, then fall silent. She was betting on Gilbreath's reluctance to sic these rent-a-cops on her. Besides the humiliation of being bested, the incident would draw too much attention from the press. Best handled internally. How he conveyed that from his locked bedroom was his problem.

Gilbreath's house was spacious and contained a separate breakfast room adjacent to the kitchen. At the round table, she plucked the "silencer" from the gun. Fashioned from a toilet-paper tube and covered with black electrician's tape, it weighed next to nothing. A fat-barreled fountain pen jutting from one end held it firmly to the gun and provided the sobering sound of grating metal when "screwed" into the barrel. A perforated black cap from a juice bottle made up the business end. The thing would no more silence a pistol shot than would holding her finger over the barrel. But it had scared the tar out of Gilbreath, so it had accomplished its intended purpose. Several times, she had feared that he would recognize it as a fraud, and batting him with the gun had nearly sent it flying. Now she wanted to leave it for him so he'd know how she duped him. A small concession for what he'd put her through. She set it on the table and slipped out the back door.

Alicia was halfway to the fence when a pounding flood of rain dropped from the sky. She squinted behind her to see a light coming around the side of the house, igniting the silvery pellets of water in its path. She scaled the six-foot cedar fence at the rear of the property and dropped over.

56

Brady's wife had always been appreciative of God's custodial wonders, and through her, he had come to marvel at them as well. But on this night he did not like the rain at all. It drummed against the SUV's roof with deafening fury, like the pounding feet of a million tiny soldiers marching into battle. Almost immediately, his head began pounding too. He reached into his breast pocket, found two painkillers he'd stashed there earlier, and swallowed them dry.

Parked on a dark residential street in the affluent section of Alexandria, the car straddled the property line of two backyards. If either homeowner noticed it, each would assume it belonged to a guest of the other. Or so he hoped. Several other vehicles dotted the curbside, the nearest only a few feet behind the car. John Gilbreath's big colonial was four blocks east. He wanted to be closer, but Alicia had insisted that distance was the key to getting in and out unnoticed.

He glanced nervously at the glove compartment, where earlier he had shoved over $16,000. Back at the hotel, after convincing him they had to find out what John Gilbreath knew—and do it with surprise and stealth—she had asked him how much cash he could get his hands on.

"We need to fund our own investigation," she'd said.

"A couple grand?" he'd asked.

"We may need to buy a different car, not new, but dependable."

"Five?"

"Worse comes to worst, we'll need fake IDs. I know where to go, but good ones are expensive. We'll have to keep moving, chasing down leads, staying in motels. We won't be able to use credit cards after today. Too easy to trace."

"How much?"

"I can put in eight," she'd said, her eyebrow arcing up inquisitively.

After some thought, he had agreed to match her contribution. On one hand, it seemed like an awful lot of money; on the other hand, how much was survival worth?

He shifted in the driver's seat and glared at the water streaming over the windshield, obliterating everything beyond. He would switch on the windshield wipers but didn't want their movement to catch someone's eye. If he moved his head around, he could catch fleeting glimpses of the wet world outside: leaves and branches (dark chaos upon dark symmetry), a parked car (appearing to shiver instead of merely shimmer), a tall wooden fence (shaking off beads of water in violent tremors as a shadowy figure bounded over it from the other side).

Before he could grasp the image, a palm slapped against the passenger window, Alicia's face swimming into view behind it. Brady hit the electric door lock button, and Alicia clambered in, breathless and drenched. Bending low, she shook her head vigorously in the foot well. Brady thought he saw her look at her hand in profile. It reminded him of his high school and college days, when kids would do that to see if they'd consumed enough alcohol to give them the shakes. Then she snapped into a proper sitting position, pushing her heavy hair back from her face. Incredibly, she was smiling.

"Well!" she said.

Still stunned and relieved by her sudden appearance, Brady managed to ask, "How'd it go?"

Her smile wavered before she caught it and held it together. He suspected she was forcing light into one seriously dark place. Whatever had happened had really shaken her up.

A visible wave of exhaustion washed over her, slumping her shoulders, softening her face. "Gilbreath's the one. The man is very weak and very bad. And as we suspected, we're on our own."

Brady was about to prompt her for more, thinking about the gentlest approach, when he sensed movement outside the car. A street lamp a block away cast a ghostly aura in the blackness, and he thought someone had passed under it.

"Did you see something?" he asked.

"No, what?"

She peered out the windshield as he cranked the car to life, flipping on the headlamps and wipers. Raindrops raced through the beams, but nothing else moved. Illuminated now were trees, bushes, fences, other vehicles, a freestanding garage up ahead on the right: all superb hiding places.

"I'm not going to say it was nothing," he said, hitting the button that locked the doors. They looked at each other. "When people do that, it always turns out to be something." He half-expected her to contradict his pop culture wisdom with some professional axiom—"To the hunted, everything appears to be a hunter," or the like. When she didn't, he put the car in gear and made a U-turn, bouncing over the curb on the other side of the road. After a mile of pavement had stretched away, he said, "Where to?"

She showed him her teeth. "How do you feel about Rome?"

He glanced at her. "As in Italy?"

"You do have your passport, don't you?" Bureau agents were required to carry them when they traveled, even domestically; but Brady had started this odyssey from home.

"In the glove compartment," he said. "But do you think we can use them? What'd Gilbreath say about an APB?"

"Nothing's been issued yet. He may get around to putting one out on us, but not until he's covered his tracks, and certainly not before his wife recovers from the Midazolam. He's not going to want to explain what I was doing in his house."

"So we get out of the country before anyone knows we're gone."

She thought for a moment. "Just to play it safe, let's use a smaller international airport, one well away from here and one without an FRS." For several years, Facial Recognition Systems had been making their way into larger airports; they made spotting fugitives as easy as scanning a photo and letting the security cameras watch for a match.

"Harrisburg, Pennsylvania, is a couple of hours away," he suggested.

She checked her watch. "Probably can't get a flight till morning anyway. Let's do it." She slapped the dash. "Get this steed moving. We've got places to go and people to see."

"Italian places, Italian people," he agreed, trying to match her high spirits. He realized it was sugarcoating to help them swallow a frightening and bitter pill, one that might prove lethal.

"Viva Italia!" she chimed.

PART iii

ITALY AND ISRAEL

Evil that disguises itself as good is far more insidious, far more dangerous, than the vilest evil we can see.

—Cardinal Roberto Ambrosi

Oh, what a tangled web we weave,
when first we practice to deceive.

—Sir Walter Scott

57

Brady stood at their flight's baggage carousel in Leonardo da Vinci Airport, gazing at the hanging strips of vinyl that covered the opening through which their luggage would soon come. Alicia had insisted on bringing her laptop and the CSD: not only did they contain her Pelletier notes and video walk-throughs, but "You never know what will come in handy," she said. She had decided that a few CSD pieces—like the heavy printer and floor-analyzing boots—were unnecessary; they'd left them, along with her pistol, in the back of the Highlander at the airport. They had each purchased a change of clothes and had combined their personal belongings into a single rolling suitcase. And any second now, it and the CSD bag would glide though those vinyl strips to meet them.

Alicia nudged him. She said, "Looks like you're zoning out. You all right?"

He pursed his lips. "Just tired."

That was a lie. Rather, he was filled with doubt about their actions and concern for his son. If he could have been certain that traveling to Italy to confront Father Randall would bring them closer to stopping the attacks on him and Alicia, he would have possessed a stronger sense of purpose. If they had concrete evidence to analyze and discuss, he would have felt better, less adrift. As it was, by the time they reached the Harrisburg airport, they had brainstormed over the scant evidence they had and exhausted alternative action plans.

They'd considered taking their case to a Bureau field office; Brady liked New York because of its size and reputation for snubbing procedures and orders emanating from headquarters. Alicia had reminded him that their evidence against Gilbreath was circumstantial, and if his story was true, nobody would or could stand up to OCP.

What about the Pelletier killer? Brady had asked. Was there any sense in tracking him down? They had few clues and fewer resources. Brady figured there were ways to draw him out, using themselves as bait. But without backup, a positive outcome to an encounter with him was anything but certain. Even if they could capture him, so what? Would he know more than Malik? You never knew until you asked; that was the nature of investigations. More than anything, they amounted to a process of elimination and an accumulation of seemingly insignificant facts. If capturing or killing him could have guaranteed an end to the killings and assaults, of course Brady would have insisted on trying. But certainly the Viking, as they both now thought of him, was only a marionette. The puppeteer would simply send in another puppet, maybe bigger and badder than this one, though Brady could not imagine such a thing.

They had gone round and round, fielding any idea that popped into their heads, no matter how ridiculous. In the end, they had agreed that tracking down Father Randall was the best course of action. Both Father McAfee and Malik had pointed to him. They knew where to find him—at least as of yesterday, if Alicia's call to the Vatican had yielded accurate information. They'd know soon enough if they'd chosen the right tree to bark up or not.

An amber light over the carousel flashed, an alarm sounded, and the conveyor belt started moving. A few seconds later, bags came riding in.

———

AT CUSTOMS, the CSD helmet in its oversized bowling ball bag caused a measure of commotion. Several immigration officers led them to a back room, and Brady figured their adventure was over before it had started. But then Alicia proved that her ability to surprise him had not run dry. With all the flair of a flamboyant Hollywood-type, she explained that she was a documentary filmmaker and the strange device was a cutting-edge camera— *which,* Brady thought, *is not far from the truth.* She even donned the helmet and gave them a demonstration. That sufficiently impressed the officials, who slapped them on their backs, asked if they knew Francis Ford Coppola, and released them from customs.

They stepped into a cavernous hall. Straight ahead, a glass wall revealed the organized chaos typical of busy airports—shuttles, cabs, private cars, harried people, all with their own agendas but each determined to leave as quickly as possible.

"Rental car or taxi?" Brady asked.

Before she could answer, a small man in need of a haircut and a shave appeared before them.

"Avete bisogno di un tassì?" He looked eagerly into their faces. "English? You need cab, no?" He reached for the CSD bag slung over Alicia's shoulder.

"No," she said sharply. "We're fine, thank you."

He squinted at her with distaste, then bowed his head in resignation and darted to another couple emerging from the customs lines.

"Rental it is," said Brady, taking a step toward a wide corridor lined with rental agency booths. Alicia caught his elbow. She nodded toward the wall of glass.

"Let's use taxis until we know how long we'll be here and where we have to go."

"But I thought . . ."

"Not from him," she said. They both watched as the cabbie strode by, laden with a grin and three heavy-looking cases. The couple they'd seen him approach happily followed.

"At the Harrisburg airport, I logged on to some travel web sites," she explained. "One of them said unlicensed touts at FCO often rip off or outright rob unsuspecting tourists. And sometimes they do worse. It said to use only the white cabs, and their drivers are required to stay with their cars."

He looked impressed. "What's FCO?"

She looked around. "This airport. We're not in Rome yet. We're eighteen miles southwest, in Fiumicino." She spotted a clock and adjusted her watch.

He did the same, moving the hour hand forward six hours to just past noon.

"Let's find some lockers and a currency exchange. Then we can go straight to the Vatican, find out what Father Randall has to say." She spoke his name contemptuously. "Unless you need a rest first? We could find a place to crash . . . ?"

He opened his mouth to object when he saw the glint in her eyes and realized she was teasing him. She knew he wanted—*needed*—to pick up the pace as much as she did.

"I might be able to summon a little more strength," he said.

58

In silence, they watched vehicles go by and buildings grow taller and closer together.

"Look," said their cabbie, pointing. "The Coliseum. Real name is *Anfiteatro Flavio.* Built AD 72. Very old."

The words were flat from overuse. Brady suspected they were prompted by the quest for a larger tip rather than by any real pride in the city.

Alicia put her hand over Brady's as it rested on the seat between them. "I always thought I'd see Rome under happier circumstances," she said quietly. "Have you been here before?"

Brady took his time answering. He thought about his wife and the vacation they never took. When Karen was little, her father had been an air force navigator with the Fifty-seventh ARRS—an air rescue squadron— stationed at Lajes Field in the Azores. Back then, officers and their families could hitch a ride into Europe on any air force plane heading that way. Karen's mother took advantage of the free shuttle service, and Karen's most vivid memories were not of the glassblowers of Majorca or the pigeons of St. Mark's Square in Venice, but of the nauseating trips in the jump seats of dim and drafty fuselages. She told Brady she wanted to "do Europe right" someday: a first-class cabin on the Eurail from Lisbon to Barcelona, Paris, Berlin, Vienna, Geneva.

"And winding up in the most romantic place of all, Rome," she'd said, all teeth and sparkling eyes.

"I thought Paris was the city of lovers," he'd said.

"Oh, pooh. Paris doesn't have the Coliseum, the Spanish Steps, Bernini's Fountain of the Four Rivers."

"What about the Eiffel Tower, the Louvre, Notre Dame?"

"Quirinale Palace, the Pantheon, St. Peter's Basilica." She moved close to him, breathed into his mouth.

"Arc de Triomphe." He searched his memory for Paris attractions. She'd always been smarter than he was, with a memory like a hard drive. If the title of Most Romantic City depended on his naming the most sites, Paris was doomed. Besides, how could he think with those incredible dark eyes locked on his? "The Seine!"

"Trevi Fountain, Campo dé Fiori."

"Uh . . . Disneyland. There's one in Paris, isn't there?"

"Via Veneto." She whispered it seductively.

"Now that sounds romantic."

"Nothing but shops. It's the Rodeo Drive of Rome." She smiled coyly.

"Great. We can start the bankruptcy paperwork when we get our passports."

"I'm not *that* greedy. A second mortgage will do nicely."

Karen had pressed her lips against his, run a hand through his hair, and he'd forgotten about Paris. Later that night he decided that he really would take out a second mortgage to give her that trip. But he never did, and they never went.

Alicia's hand felt unnaturally hot on top of his. He wanted to pull his hand away. And he wanted to leave it right where it was.

"No, this is my first time to Rome," he said. "Let's stop."

"Stop? Why?"

"Driver, take us to a restaurant."

"Ristorante?" He pointed at an approaching McDonald's. "Hamburgers?"

"No," answered Brady. "A sit-down restaurant." He glanced at Alicia before adding, "With a bar, a lounge."

The cabbie nodded and flicked on his left-turn signal to change lanes.

Alicia was staring at him, concern etching a line in her brow, crow's-feet at the corners of her eyes.

"Nerves," he said weakly. "Aren't you hungry?" They'd had a full meal on the plane, but that had been hours ago.

"I'll wait in the cab," she said, an edge in her voice betraying her disappointment or impatience, probably both.

The taxi bumped over a low curb into a half-full parking lot on the side of a stuccoed restaurant with green-and-white-striped awnings. After the taxi stopped, Brady studied the building but did not exit.

"Signore?"

Brady didn't respond. He was there because he and his son and Alicia had been attacked and nearly killed. He wanted to do right by them, but he was tired and fatigued, and remembering Karen's desire to see Rome had constricted his heart. He was a criminal psychologist who had gone on administrative leave for four months after the death of his wife and was afterward put on light duty, nothing too taxing. He had not asked for it and his superiors had not discussed it, but everyone understood that he wasn't ready for the 110 percent effort the Bureau expected of its agents. He had been starting to believe he would never be ready for that level of performance again.

The drinking—he knew, somewhere deep inside he knew—not only dulled the pain of missing Karen, but helped him forget that he wasn't handling her absence very well. Her death had proved to be a double blow: the wound it caused and the revelation of his inability to heal. So now he ached for his dead wife, and he was on foreign soil, hunting a killer he didn't know, trying to protect the only other people in the world he cared about—a duty he felt incapable of performing.

On top of all that—because there was always something "on top of all that," something to further complicate complicated lives—Alicia had been giving him signs that she wanted more from their relationship. And he found his heart responding, hearing her heart's call and yearning to answer. Of all the times . . .

He filled his lungs, then tried to expel his tension with the air. He turned to her.

"I know I . . . uh . . . I think I just . . ." He pushed his lips tight. He eyed the driver, scanned outside. The taxi had stopped not far from a busy sidewalk. Beyond the cab's windows, the world seemed overbright and harsh and anything but private; not the environment in which Brady wanted to unload his thoughts.

He touched the driver's shoulder. "Sir, could you give us a minute?"

"Huh?"

"Alone, just for a minute? Could you step out?"

The driver laughed sharply. "You go," he said with a nod.

Alicia reached into her blazer pocket, peeled off some bills from the wad of Euros she'd gotten at the airport, and thrust them at the driver.

"Will you just please step outside?" she snapped. "Keep your hand on the door handle, if you want. Just . . . please?"

He grabbed the cash, examined it, grunted, and climbed out.

Alicia faced Brady with patient expectancy. Then she looked away to take the pressure off.

"I think I just gave him about a hundred bucks," she said and laughed.

Brady smiled. The respite was short, but it managed to relax him the way a stiff drink might have.

"Look," he said. "I feel like I'm not doing well. I'm out of my element, and even when I was in it, I wasn't all there. I know I've let my wife's . . . I've held on to grief longer than I should have."

"Brady, you don't have to—"

"I do. I have too many negative emotions churning inside. I feel overwhelmed, ready to shut down. And that's the last thing you need from me right now. I think if I can drag some of this out into the light of day, I'll be able to think more clearly."

She nodded.

"First, yes, I grieve for my wife, for my loss of her. It's an open wound that won't heal because I haven't let it heal. I keep picking at it and reopening it. I don't know how to leave it alone, to keep it from oozing and bleeding all over the rest of my life. I'm not fixing that right now, okay? It just is."

Her eyes softened. There was no pity in them, just acceptance.

He went on. "I'm scared to death, I mean, paralyzed-scared for my son. I keep seeing his face when he was looking up at me from his hidey-hole and that killer was at the top of the stairs, rattling the door handle. Those dogs. Was he only after me, or both of us? Is he still looking for Zach? Do the people who control him have the resources to track Zach down?" He shook his head. "But here I am, five thousand miles away . . ."

"Brady . . ."

"I know. I know. This is where I need to be to help him. But what good am I? I mean, really? Look at you. You're gung ho about this. You see what needs to be done and you do it. You're the one who wanted to pursue Pelletier even before the attacks on us, even when our responsibilities on the case were done. I just wanted to go home. You went to talk to McAfee. When the storm hit, thought to call in Apollo."

He caught her grimace and added, "His death wasn't your fault, and where would we be without the information he extracted from Malik?"

He paused a brief moment.

"You confronted Gilbreath. You set our course to here, to Rome. You . . ."

"Brady!" She shook his shoulder.

He looked at her, surprised.

"This might be your turn to vent," she said, "but I'm not going to let you sit there and flog yourself. Even if this is Rome." She smiled. "I hear what you're saying, okay? You think you're damaged goods and you're not pulling your weight. You . . ."

She was angry, unsure what to say. She punched him in the arm.

"Are you dead? Is Zach dead? You didn't freeze when a monster—a monster and his hellhounds!—came after you. You protected yourself and your son. Look at your hand. You grabbed an ax! You held on! And you would have fought if he hadn't run away. *He* ran away, not you."

She shook her head. More quietly, she said, "Am *I* dead? You didn't freeze when I went out that window. You saved me." Her voice cracked on the word *saved*. She took a deep breath. "All right, I wanted to continue the investigation and you wanted to go home. That's because you have somebody to go home to. You have someone who loves you and needs you, and you're determined to live up to your responsibilities to Zach. That's honorable. That's noble.

"I have my work. Brady, *this* is my life. I've dedicated myself to it the way you have to your family. Of course I want to stay on an investigation.

Of course I'm a little more decisive about the direction of a case, about a course of action to get to the end. This is all I've done for years, while you were pursuing a different field of study and making a home and having a family. Does that make you deadweight now? No, Brady, it doesn't!"

She had worked herself up. He thought she might hit him again.

Slowly, a smile bent his lips.

"With a little Wite-Out, we can take my name off my degree and write in yours."

"If that's another way of putting yourself down, I won't have it."

"No, I just mean you have an incredible way of cutting through the crap. A shrink would have required a dozen sessions to do what you did in two minutes."

"Did I lance your emotional boil?"

He cringed. "See? And yes, I do feel better. But there is one other thing." He lowered his eyes. "You and I. I mean, it's obvious . . ."

The driver's door opened. "We go now, yes?" the cabbie said, starting to get in.

Alicia shot up to the back of his seat and pushed him back out.

"No! Go count your money!" she yelled, then leaned over the seat, gripped the door, and yanked it shut. She fell back onto the rear cushion with a smile. "What's obvious?"

"I think . . ." He gave her a hard look. "Do you have feelings for me? Feelings that maybe go beyond . . . partners . . . I mean . . . ?"

"I do. But that's okay. I understand you aren't—"

"I feel the same," he said, cutting her off. "I think. I've caught myself comparing you to Karen. That's unfair, I know, but that I was doing it at all made me realize I had some feelings . . . you know?"

Man, why did he make everything so difficult?

She gripped his hand and squeezed.

"It's good you mentioned this," she said. "Now we can let it go. Let's not think about it or worry about it or play games while we take care of this Father-Randall-Pelletier-near-death-experience thing. Whatever happens, happens. Okay?"

Now *that* was like Karen, he realized. Decisive but accepting of the world the way it was. Karen's strength had come from knowing there was a God in control. Conversely, Alicia was one of those people who had a well of strength that came up from somewhere they didn't examine very closely; it didn't matter to them where it came from, as long as it was there when they needed it.

Keeping his eyes on him, she rapped her knuckles against the window glass. When the cabbie opened the door and plopped down on his seat, she said, "Where've you been? Let's go!"

59

Forty minutes later, the cab pulled to the curb on Via della Conciliazione. Brady didn't see much, except what looked to him like ancient apartment buildings, scrupulously maintained. Then he climbed out and looked over the roof of the cab. Across the boulevard and beyond two ornately decorated buildings opened a massive courtyard—the Piazza San Pietro. From its center rose an Egyptian obelisk at least a hundred feet high, originally moved there to commemorate the Circus of Nero. Past it, on the opposite side of the plaza, was St. Peter's Basilica, fronted by columns, its facade topped by statues of saints, and its famous dome, designed by Michelangelo, rising behind them.

"Signore!"

The cabbie's call made him realize he had been standing in the open door, transfixed by the sight. He closed the door, freeing the cab to roar away. Alicia was already jogging across the boulevard, as if responding to a siren's call. Brady followed.

The court was elliptical. Colonnades extended from the cathedral steps, then swooped around like arms embracing the souls in the plaza. There were perhaps a few hundred people milling in it now, but it felt vacant, able to accommodate thousands more.

Alicia tapped him on the arm.

"There's an office or something marked *L'ufficio informazioni*." She pointed beyond the southern colonnade at what could have been storefronts but whose signage indicated Vatican offices and assistance stations. They entered the information office and waited while a man behind a counter explained details about tours through the Vatican Gardens to a group of elderly and extremely hard-of-hearing American tourists. After the last loud "What?" had been answered and the group shuffled out, Brady approached the man.

"We're here to see a priest who works in the Archives."

"The Archives or the library?" the man asked, using the volume he had adopted for his previous inquisitors.

"Is there a difference?"

"*Sì.*"

Brady raised his eyebrows at Alicia.

She said, "Father McAfee said 'Secret Archives.'"

Brady returned his attention to the man. "The priest we're here to see is—"

"Two doors down," the man said, turning away from them.

"I'm sorry?"

"The business office." He pointed east.

The business office looked like a low-budget travel agency, with a couple of old desks and chairs for waiting visitors. Only one desk was occupied, by a kid Brady would card if he tried to buy alcohol. He wore a cleric's collar over a black short-sleeved shirt. There was an LCD monitor and keyboard on his desk, but his head was bent over a ledger. He was scrutinizing columns of tiny numbers, pencil in hand. His hair was black, cut short, and parted on one side. Gelled into place. He looked up with a bright smile.

"*Mi dica?*"

"Do you speak English?" Brady asked.

"Of course. What may I do for you?" His English was flawless.

Brady asked to see Father Randall.

"What is the nature of your business?"

He and Alicia had already decided to be as honest as possible—up to a point. Mentioning a murder investigation might create more walls than doors. He explained that they were following up on a burglary at a Catholic church in the States and needed to speak with Father Randall about it.

"You traveled to Italy, investigating a burglary?" The young priest was as baffled as anyone would be at hearing Brady's ludicrous story.

"There may be some ties to other crimes," Brady said.

"What agency did you say you're with?"

"We're not here in an official capacity. The priest at the burglarized church is a friend."

The priest nodded, as if this information put everything into perfect sense. He turned to the screen and keyboard on his desk.

"The father's name again?"

He hesitated. He didn't want to get Father McAfee in trouble.

The priest looked up. "Who is the man you wish to see?"

"Oh. Father Randall. Adalberto Randall."

He typed the name on the keyboard and watched the screen. Brady thought he saw a flash of concern tighten the priest's face, then it was gone. Brady leaned forward casually to get a peek at the screen. The young man pushed a key, and Brady had time to see the words disappear. After a second of gray, a photograph of St. Peter's filled the screen. Just as well. He couldn't read Italian.

The priest opened a drawer and withdrew a yellow form the size of an index card. Across the top, in a large scrawl, he wrote the date. More writing under that, smaller, sloppier. He retrieved a small key from his pants pocket, unlocked the center drawer of his desk, and pulled out an embosser. Placing the form in the jaws of the embosser, the young man squeezed tightly. After the drawer was locked again and the key back in his pocket, he held the form out to Brady.

"This pass will get you to the secretary of the Archives. He can help you further."

"Can't we go directly to Father Randall?"

The priest whipped a colorful map onto the counter and pointed at it with a pen. "Let me show you. Go past the Leonine walls, here, and through the Gate of Saint Anne. You will see an arched road. Take it past the *Osservatore Romano* building to the Court of the Belvedere. On your left, you will see a stairway. Take it to the top." He tapped the tip of his pen against the map and pushed it across the desk. "And so."

"And so," Brady repeated. "Thank you."

Before they reached the door, the priest called to them.

"You will have to show the pass to several guards on your way. Do not deviate from the route and you will be fine. God bless you both."

Outside, Alicia turned to Brady. "What happens if we deviate?"

"We won't be fine, I guess."

60

Brady had been to Las Vegas three times on Bureau business. Each time, he had marveled at the scale of the hotels. They were, as Zach would say, *gi-normous.* One could walk for five minutes through a single game room without stopping or moving circuitously. They housed Olympic-sized pools, Broadway-sized theaters, Disney-sized rides. The gold lion in front of the MGM Grand gave Brady a kinked neck. He could never decide whether the town was a monument to greed and gaudiness or the result of men remembering what it was like to build sand castles and Lego structures.

Walking through Vatican City, he realized the vision of the Vegas architects was too small. And too austere. He felt dwarfed by the statues, columns, fountains. The buildings cast a false twilight, as the mountains did in Vail. Every building he saw boasted museum-quality ornamentation: statuary, relievos of great moments in history, stained glass, and towers. It gave him a headache just imagining the treasures stored behind their walls.

Three pairs of Swiss Guards stopped them on their way to the Secret Archives. After the last pair had inspected their pass and let them continue, Brady said, "If I had a fifth of the masterpieces they have here, I'd have SWAT teams protecting it, not rent-a-cops."

"Don't let the dandy uniforms fool you," Alicia said. "I know a guy on the Bureau's Hostage Rescue Team."

He nodded. "Best SWAT team in the country."

"They are. Anyway, this guy says a few of them are heading to Switzerland to train with the Swiss Guard. And I say, 'What made the Swiss ask for help?' thinking some major hostage crisis opened their eyes to the need for better training, you know? He says, no, the Bureau guys were going to be *trained by them*. Apparently, they're the best in the world, every one of them. Mossad and SEALs and . . . *Samurais* all rolled into one."

Brady looked back at one of the guards, dressed in the traditional uniform of bright orange and blue bloomers, matching shirt with puffy arms, and a blue beret. He gave her a half smile. "Tell me you're joking."

"Dead serious," she said. "As you said, think of the priceless masterpieces they have here. And the pope. What a target he is." A few dozen steps farther, she said, "'Course you can give them a hard time, see what happens. Don't take my word for it."

They were heading across a cobblestone court toward an intersection of pathways, where a sole Swiss Guard stood with a halberd. Brady imagined the damage a weapon like that could wreak in proficient hands.

"I've always appreciated the tranquillity of sleeping dogs," he said.

"Exactly." She slapped his arm with the back of her hand and pointed. "I think that's it."

On their left, a wide flight of stone steps rose past an oversized marble statue to a second-floor landing and heavy wood doors. Alicia charged up the stairs, but Brady paused long enough to learn that the statue was of a guy named Hippolytus. The rest of the inscription was in Italian or Latin or Shelta, for all he knew. He wondered if Hippolytus was as wise as he looked here, gazing into the distance, a book in one hand.

Brady caught up with Alicia just inside the doors, where yet another Swiss ninja had stopped her. Brady presented the pass, and he let them by. They were in an anteroom. Above another set of double doors, a marble sign spelled out *Biblioteca Apostolica Vaticana* in relieved letters. A single door on a different wall bore a wood sign: *L'Archivio Segreto Vaticano.*

Even Brady understood that. He held the door open for Alicia, saying, "It says 'secret' on the door. How secret is that?"

They moved down a corridor toward a man sitting at a desk. The corridor was wide, arched, and constructed entirely of stone, except for large windows in one wall, overlooking the courtyard they had crossed to get to the library stairway.

Alicia leaned toward Brady. In a hushed tone she said, "For a thousand years, all the records stored here were off-limits to anyone except the pope and a handful of scholars, researchers, and archivists, all in the employ of the pope. It wasn't until 1881 that Pope Leo XIII opened about half of them to a limited number of serious scholars and theologians. Even today there's what's called the 'Hundred Year Rule,' which mandates that most new documents may not be examined by outsiders for a century." She showed him her teeth. "You need to read more, Brady."

They stopped at the desk. It was roughly the size of a car. Its baroque flourishes could have been carved by Michelangelo. Even so, it was a chunk of cut wood compared to the room that opened behind it. The ceiling and every wall was painted by the hand of some Late Renaissance master Brady had probably never heard of. But the style was unmistakable: rich colors, forced perspectives, fat naked or near-naked people so lifelike you expected them to start sweating. The ceiling was high and arched. The floor was paved in marble squares, too large to be called tiles. On both sides of a central aisle, heavy wooden cabinets, like armoires, stood like statuary three feet from the side walls and from each other. At the far end of the long room, open double doors revealed a similar room beyond, and then another and another, as far as Brady could see.

"*Sì?*"

Like the kid in the business office, the man behind the desk wore a cleric's collar, but he was old enough to be the other's grandfather. He was pudgy, with jowly cheeks and bulbous eyes. Balding. Brady thought he'd make a good Friar Tuck in a Robin Hood movie. They went through similar greetings and explanations. This time, however, Father Randall's name brought no reaction at all.

"May I see identification, please?" the man asked. His accent was much heavier than the younger priest's. Brady had the thought that English was—as foreigners charged, particularly the French and Latinos—becoming a universal language, at the expense of indigenous tongues. New generations were learning it earlier, and eventually they would speak it before their traditional language. He felt a vague shame for being part of the world's linguistic bully.

He fished his wallet out of his pants pocket. "Personal IDs or credentials?" he asked.

"The two, please."

He handed over his driver's license and FBI identification card. Alicia did the same.

The priest picked up the phone, punched in a three-digit number, and hung up. A moment later, the door they had used at the end of the corridor opened. The Swiss Guard who had checked their pass marched toward them. Their IDs in hand, the priest stood. He muttered, *"Momento,"* and walked away, through the beautiful room, out the far door, and off to the right. The guard stopped at the entrance to the room, turned his back to the wall, and solidified into a mannequin-thing. He wasn't armed, as far as Brady could tell.

"What's going to happen now?" Brady whispered.

"There's a very real possibility that they'll check with the Bureau." Alicia stopped. Her eyes scanned the fabulous room as she thought.

"And?" He realized she had never been in a situation like this before either, but she had a mind not for the way things were supposed to work, but for the way they really worked, in the real world.

"And if the Bureau wants to, it could probably convince either the Vatican or the Rome police to detain us until they can come get us."

He glanced at the phone on the desk, then at the Swiss Guard.

"We should have gotten fake IDs."

"Place like this wouldn't give nobodies the time of day," she said matter-of-factly. "The bogus people on fake IDs are nobodies. They were designed to be. Maybe they won't check. And maybe there are no red flags on us yet."

"And maybe whoever's behind the Pelletier killings and our attacks self-combusted at breakfast this morning, along with that Viking freak and his dogs."

"Now, now." She stepped close to him, gripped his forearm. "It's a risk we had to take. Otherwise, we should have stayed home."

They stood at the desk a long time. Nothing on its surface interested Brady: a keyboard, an LCD monitor displaying the same St. Peter's screen saver, a few loose pens, a notepad with nothing written on the top page, and a newspaper, *La Repubblica*. What appeared to be the sports section was unfolded in front of the chair.

Occasionally a figure moved past the doorway in a far-off room. The place was preternaturally silent, as though it had learned to be noiseless over the long years of its existence. There were chairs along the corridor wall opposite the guard, but both Brady and Alicia were too anxious to sit.

Alicia leaned close to Brady.

"I'd like to get on that computer," she said quietly.

"Good luck."

"I wonder what would pop up if I typed in Randall's name."

"Does it matter?"

"You never know."

He looked at the guard. His eyes were on them.

"Think you can distract him?" she asked.

He gazed at her, eyes flat.

"Really," she said. "Just run though the room and keep going. Bet he'll tear off after you."

"You'd sacrifice our chance of talking to the person we came here to see for a peek at a computer screen that's in a language you don't understand?"

He turned away, strolled to a corridor window. A few minutes later, he heard the guard bark sharply.

"Ma'am!"

He turned to see Alicia on the other side of the desk. Her hand darted out and touched the keyboard.

The guard came away from the wall, his hand going behind his back for something.

She held up her hands. "Whoa!" she said and came around the desk.

The guard stopped.

"I'm sorry," she said demurely. "Bored, you know? Can you . . ." She gestured over her shoulder. "Can you find out what's taking the father so long?"

"No," he said. He backed into his position by the wall. His hand appeared, wrapped around a walkie-talkie. The guard raised it to his lips, depressed a button, and spoke softly in a foreign language.

"Hey, what?" Alicia said. "There's no need for that."

She glanced at Brady. He shook his head.

The guard finished his communication, made the walkie-talkie disappear behind his back, and settled into mannequin mode. Brady walked back to Alicia at the front of the desk. The door at the end of the corridor opened, and another Swiss Guard stepped through.

"Uh-oh," she whispered.

He marched toward them, halted, and took a back-to-the-wall stance beside his brother-in-arms.

Brady heard Alicia let out a breath.

"What'd you see?" he asked.

"A log-in dialogue box. User name and password fields empty. I couldn't get on if they let me try for an hour, not without my hacker tools."

"So we wait," he said.

She made an impatient clicking sound with her tongue. She dug in her purse, pulled out a pack of Camels, and tapped one out.

"Ma'am?"

It was the first guard. He was shaking his head at her.

She turned to Brady. "I'm going outside for a smoke."

The guard spoke up again. "No smoking on Vatican grounds."

"Anywhere?"

He shook his head.

She made the clicking noise again, opened her purse, and dropped the cigarette in.

61

They waited another forty-eight minutes by his watch. They were staring out the windows at the priests and nuns and businesspeople passing through the courtyard below when they heard the click of leather soles on marble, echoing slightly. When he turned, Brady realized the echo was actually a second pair of shoes. Following the priest who had taken their identification was a taller man, also about fifty. His face was lean and muscular, the wrinkles tight, not flabby. His eyes were expectant, piercing. He carried himself gracefully, almost floating across the floor, the way dancers do even years after their last curtain call.

The first priest lowered himself into the desk chair with a sigh, as though he'd spent the time away in heavy labor. He handed Brady's ID cards to him, Alicia's to her.

"Gracie," he said without looking at them. He was bent over the newspaper in front of him.

Brady and Alicia took in the other man. He had positioned himself beside the man in the chair. His hands were clasped in front of him. A thin smile creased his skin and made deep dimples.

"Father Randall?" Alicia asked.

"I am Monsignor Vretenar, vice prefect. Let us talk, *per favore.*" He motioned for them to come around the desk, then turned and walked toward the far door.

Brady and Alicia fell in step behind him. Finally, activity. Brady peered over his shoulder. The guards were not following, but they were watching.

When they reached the center of the chamber, Monsignor Vretenar faced them.

In a hushed tone he said, "Why have you come here?"

Brady spoke for them. "To speak to Father Randall."

"Why?"

"He may have some information about a case we're working."

"May?"

"He does. How much, we won't know until we speak to him."

"What is this case?"

"A burglary at a church in New York City."

The man shook his head. "That does not seem—"

"The burglary may be related to a murder," Alicia interrupted. "Several murders, in fact."

The monsignor's eyebrows rose slightly. This news surprised him, but he was either an expressionless man or very good at keeping his thoughts off his face.

"And Father Randall is . . . implicated?" he asked.

"He's involved," Brady said.

"How?"

Alicia said, "He asked for a priest's private files, supposedly for the Archives. After the priest refused, his files were stolen."

"Father Randall *is* an archivist, but he is not a thief."

"If we could just talk to him ourselves . . ."

"This priest, was he murdered?"

"No, but we believe the killer got his list of victims from the stolen files." Alicia quickly brushed her hair behind an ear. Brady could tell she wanted to shake this guy, yell, *"Help us!"*

"Monsignor," he said, "one of the would-be assassins mentioned Randall's name."

"In what context?"

They did not want to get into that.

Monsignor Vretenar read their silence perfectly. A thin smile bent his lips, then he chuckled.

"What's funny?" Brady asked.

"I am sorry," the monsignor said. "You should have told me you were fans of *The Da Vinci Code*!"

"I beg your pardon?"

"Agent Moore, Agent Wagner," he said condescendingly through a smile, "there are no killers here, no secret societies, no conspiracies. You are looking for the wrong man. I am sorry you traveled so far. *Per favore.*" He gestured for them to leave.

"Now wait a minute!" Alicia seized his arm. "This isn't funny, and this isn't fiction. You are harboring a man who is somehow involved in at least five serial murders. Somebody is trying to kill us. Me. Agent Moore. They attacked his nine-year-old son! Why won't you—"

The two Swiss Guards were on them. One stepped between Monsignor Vretenar and Brady. He pushed Brady back and took a stance that said he was ready to whale on him if he even blinked in a threatening manner. Brady raised his hands chest-high, palms out. Alicia grunted, and he turned his eyes to her. The other guard had her in an *uchikomi* hold—her left wrist twisted behind her back and yanked up between her shoulder blades, the elbow of the same arm held down. All cops knew it, had practiced the maneuver as both cop and perp. It hurt. And it instantly pinched off any fight left in the person receiving it.

Alicia was sucking air between clenched teeth, her right arm frozen up in a position that suggested she wanted to grab her shoulder. Her bandages were in plain sight, maroon spots just under the top layer of thin gauze. At least the guard had seized her undamaged arm.

"Come on now," he pleaded. "That's not necessary."

"Isn't it?" the monsignor said. "Miss Wagner?" He waited until their eyes met. "Is it necessary?"

She paused. Brady half-expected her to spit on him. He was relieved when she shook her head tightly.

The monsignor nodded at the guard holding her. He let go.

Alicia pretended to shake him off. She rubbed her shoulder. Her lips were pressed together so hard, they were turning white. Brady knew she didn't trust herself to speak.

"Agent Moore," the monsignor said. "Did your informant provide you with a description of Father Randall? Did you get a . . . I believe it's called a composite sketch?"

"No."

"Get a description. Have a sketch artist render it, or whatever you do these days, with computers and all. Fax it to me here." He produced a business card and held it out. Brady took it. "If there is any resemblance to *our* Father Randall, we will talk again. I will not hold my breath."

After a beat, the monsignor said, "Can I trust you to find your own way out, or do you need an escort?"

"Monsignor Vretenar," Brady said, "we came a long way. My son is in danger."

"So you require an escort?"

Brady glared at the so-called man of God. How could Karen have been so warm and compassionate and this man be so heartless? Didn't they serve the same God? He spun around and strode for the door at the end of the long corridor. The priest at the desk was still hunched over the newspaper, as if there had been no yells, no guards running past his post. He heard Alicia directly behind him, but before he hit the door, her footsteps stopped. He braked as well, knowing what was coming. He did not turn around but simply waited.

With the lungs of an opera diva, she bellowed the monsignor's name and followed it with a long string of obscenities, words Brady imagined were new to the men and women and putti painted on the walls of the many rooms in earshot of her litany. Most likely, she was holding up a middle finger for good measure. Her voice was still resonating against the marble when she brushed past him and pushed through the door.

"Let's go," she said.

He paused. Did not hear the rush of booted feet. He pictured Monsignor Vretenar holding back the Swiss Guards with a touch, a shake of the head, and maybe a comment like, "A troubled young lady. Let her go."

How gracious.

62

He caught up with her at the bottom of the outside stairs. She was glaring up at the immortalized countenance of Hippolytus because there was no one else around to glare at.

He reached her, said, "You all right?"

"No! *No!*" She jerked her head down in frustration. "What a pompous . . . What haven't I called him yet?"

"I think you pretty much covered it."

She smiled thinly, rubbing her shoulder. "My right arm's filleted and my left one gets wrenched out of the socket. I'm going to be a quadriplegic before we're through." She took him in. "You all right?"

"No," he said honestly. Someone had poured lead into his body, just popped off his head and poured it in. His heart felt cloaked and heavy, his stomach compressed. If he didn't move soon, his feet would meld into the stonework under them. He shuffled off toward the arched road from which they had reached this courtyard.

Alicia fell in beside him. "Let's find a place to crash," she said wearily. "We'll come back at 'em tomorrow. There's got to be somebody over that jerk we can talk to."

"The pope," Brady said.

"Somebody else. He said he was the *vice* prefect. We'll get to the prefect. Or someone in personnel. Doesn't the Vatican have its own police department? Maybe they'll be helpful."

"You're an optimist."

"And you're a pessimist. So what? Let's get this job done. Do you want to go back home empty-handed?"

He stopped. They were on the arched roadway, at an intersection. The way out was straight ahead. To Brady's right was a road to points unknown. On his left were an alcove and a stone bench. He sat on it, letting his shoulders slump forward.

"We can't go home. We have few clues and fewer resources. Whether he's bold about it or sneaky, Gilbreath won't let us go on with our careers. And as far as we know, somebody still wants us dead. Added up, it isn't much of a life, being on the run."

She sat beside him.

"All right," she said. "So this is going to take a little longer than we planned. We're investigators, Brady. This is an investigation. So we hit a brick wall. Let's back up and come at it from another angle. Someone knows this Father Randall. We ask around. Get a description. We'll go through the Vatican newspaper; I'll search the web. I bet we can get a photograph of this guy. Then we wait and watch. He has to come out sometime. Right?"

Brady was nodding. "We Malik him."

"What?"

"Nab him, make him talk. Find someone like Apollo to string him out, loosen his tongue."

"Something like that."

He sat up straight. "Sure. Why not? These guys think they can do anything they want without consequence. I'm the consequence. Call me Mr. Consequence." He grinned at her.

She didn't return it. Just examined his face. She glanced around, up at the arched roof over the road. "Brady," she said thoughtfully. "Lemme ask you a question."

"What?"

"Back in New York, when Malik fell."

"Yeah?"

"You had hold of him because I was hanging on to him, right?"

"I wasn't going to let you fall, Alicia."

"I know." She smiled. "But you had hold of Malik's wrist, to get him off my ankle. Then he fell."

He nodded.

"Brady." She paused. Eyes focused somewhere up the street in front of them, she said, "Did he slip? Or did you let him go?"

He did not move, did not speak. Slowly, he lowered himself so his forearms rested on his thighs, his hands dangling between his knees. Footfalls came from around a bend in the road. His eyes came up to see a priest with a briefcase. The man nodded a greeting. Brady nodded back, then watched him walk the rest of the roadway to the courtyard and disappear around a corner.

He turned to her. "I don't know," he said.

She touched his knee. "I mean, I would have tossed him out that window without thinking twice. But that's me, Brady. That's not—"

"Look," he said.

She followed his gaze across the road and down the intersecting street. At the apex of a lazy curve was a small chapel, its few ornamental carvings almost obliterated by time and weather. The stone had a porous appearance, as though it was turning back into sand and would crumble away at any moment. One of its tall double doors was open, and in the darkened entryway stood a man looking at them. He was dressed all in black and hunched over with age. He raised a hand and gestured for them to come. Then he faded back into the shadows of the chapel interior.

She stood.

"Coming?"

He lifted himself off the bench.

"If this guy tries to sell us a Jesus bobble-head doll, I'm going to punch him," he said.

They reached the chapel together and stepped in. Blackness after the brightness of the day. A row of candles flickered on a stone altar. A patch of diluted sunlight from the door fell against the wall behind the altar, faintly illuminating a large rough cross. Its beams appeared hacked into shape by an imprecise tool—*an ax,* Brady thought.

As their eyes slowly adjusted, the rest of the interior architecture and furnishings coalesced out of the shadows. Ten rows of pews on each side of a center aisle. Arched recesses for stained-glass windows, whose art was indistinct because no light shone through them; since the chapel's construction, the Vatican must have grown up around it, sealing it between larger structures. The floor and walls were blocks of stone, most likely granite by their dull grayness. There were no ornate carvings, no florid cornices, no sinistrorse vines or columns for them to climb. The chapel was incongruous with its setting and somehow absolutely perfect.

"Hello?" Alicia called.

"Come in, please."

The voice was strong, unhampered by age. Brady wondered if it came from the old man who had beckoned them or someone else. Shadows stirred. The old man appeared, standing in the second pew from the front. He gestured for them to sit in the pew behind his.

As they walked, he hoisted his butt onto the back of the first pew and stabilized himself by planting his black oxfords on the planked seat of the second. Brady thought it was the old man's long-preferred way of sitting and he was determined to do it that way until he could sit no more. He seemed frail, like a bird. But his head was large, equine. Sunlight caught his eyes. They were blue and alive.

He stared at them each in turn, a grim expression pulling down the corners of his mouth and his eyes. His hand fumbled in his breast pocket, pulled out a hand-rolled cigarette. At least that's what Brady thought it was; it might have been a joint. His hands were shaking—from age or fear, Brady couldn't tell—and it took him a good fifteen seconds to push the cigarette between his lips. From the same pocket, he fished out a lighter. Thinking of the time it took for the cigarette to find home, Brady reached out and took the lighter from him. He lit the tip.

Alicia had found the cigarette she'd been denied in the Archives, so he lit that one too. He dropped the lighter back into the pocket. The cherry flared bright as the old man pulled on it. He blew out a billow of smoke. Tobacco. Brady smiled, thinking about the old man toking up on the other stuff.

The old man waved away the cloud and said, "You're in too deep. You don't know how deep."

Alicia shot a stream of smoke out the side of her mouth. "Deep into what?" she said.

He plucked the cigarette out of his mouth and looked at it as if to see how fast it was burning. Holding it between his thumb and index finger, he waggled it at them. "This thing you're here for," he said. "Randall. Malik."

Alicia coughed convulsively. Her cigarette fell into her lap, and she swatted at it as she coughed.

Brady shot forward, clutching the pew back in front of him. "How do you know about Malik?" They had not mentioned his name.

Through coughs, Alicia managed, "Are you Randall?"

The old man spared a few seconds to get the cigarette back between his lips, then spoke around it.

"I am Cardinal Ambrosi, prefect of the Secret Archives."

"Cardinal?" Brady said.

"Oh, don't let titles trip you up, son. Old Man Ambrosi fits me just as well. And before we continue, I must apologize for Monsignor Vretenar. You scared the bejesus out of him. He didn't know how to handle your accusations. Nice fellow, normally."

Alicia ground out her cigarette under her toe and said, "We didn't accuse—"

"Sure you did, and rightly so. Correct?"

She nodded.

"You'll pick that up, won't you, when you leave?" He gestured at the butt her foot was still grinding into the floor. He scanned the room around them. "This is my favorite place in the world. Oldest Christian house of worship in Rome. Built shortly after St. Peter's crucifixion in AD 64, 250 years before Constantine built his basilica over St. Peter's tomb. Records indicate the structure was hidden by a wooden outer shell until Constantine legalized Christianity. A miracle it survived to shed its skin and show the world what it really was." He closed his eyes and pulled on his smoke. "Lot of Christians like that," he continued. "Hiding what they got inside, waiting for someone to come along and tell 'em it's okay."

He sighed contentedly, gazing around as someone else might take in the trees and birds and clouds from the vantage point of a park bench. Slowly his eyes swung back to Brady and Alicia. The grim expression had returned.

"I understand you are with the Federal Bureau of Investigation, here about some murders?"

Alicia said, "We're not here officially. We're on our own."

The old man's eyes flared in surprise. "How is that?"

"A long story. We should be supported . . . but we aren't."

"So it's just you two?" He sized them up, apparently unimpressed. He closed his eyes briefly. When they opened, it seemed to Brady some issue had been resolved.

"You must tell me how you came to be seeking Father Randall. The details. You must trust that my knowledge of your story is important."

Brady cleared his throat. "Cardinal Ambrosi—"

"Roberto. Please."

Brady inclined his head. "Roberto, when can we speak to Father Randall?"

"I am afraid that is impossible. He is away on business."

"Wait a minute. *Your* business," Alicia said, her tone sharply accusatory. "Father Randall works for *you.*"

He nodded. "He does, but not in a capacity that has ever affected you." He took a final pull on the cigarette, removed it from his mouth, and pinched the cherry between his finger and thumb. He appeared to feel nothing of the hot coal. "You see," he said, "Father Randall serves two earthly masters. The Holy See and our *antithesis*, if you will. He does not realize I know about the other."

"Antithesis?" Brady said. "I'm sorry, sir, but what are you talking about?"

"Your story first, please."

Brady studied the old man for a minute, trying to know him better by his body language. He made eye contact with Alicia and found her glaring at him. Her jaw was set, and she shook her head no.

"Cardinal . . . uh . . . Roberto," he said, "would you excuse us for a moment?"

"Of course."

Brady rose and gestured for Alicia to follow him. He led her into a shadowy back corner, feeling her eyes between his shoulder blades. When he turned around, she cocked her head stubbornly.

"I think we can trust this guy," he said quietly.

"No." Not quietly at all. Ambrosi was looking up at the ceiling and pretended not to hear.

"He could be the break we were hoping for."

"And he could be the person who wants us dead. He mentioned Malik; *we* didn't."

"If he wanted us dead, we'd be bleeding out on this chapel floor by now." He took a deep breath, rolled his head on his neck. "Look, somebody is already after us. What would it hurt to tell him what we've been through? If there's even the slightest possibility he can help in some way—maybe shed some light on some of the . . . *weirdness*—we need to risk it. We have nowhere else to go and nothing to lose."

Her face softened. She looked over her shoulder at the cardinal. He was now staring at his hands, clasped in this lap. She faced Brady and said, "You're the psych guy here, Brady. You deconstruct people for a living. Is it your *professional* opinion that he's on the up-and-up?"

He spread his arms as if to say, *I don't know.* "I can't psychoanalyze someone I just met, but there's something about him that inspired my trust. He's relaxed and direct. His posture implies openness, honesty. So yes, that's my professional opinion."

"That's good enough for me."

They returned to the pew. Cardinal Ambrosi watched them earnestly.

"Everything in order?" he asked.

"We think so," Brady said. Then, together, they explained their purpose in visiting the Pelletier crime scenes, the clues they found, and Alicia's reluctance to let the case go when the Bureau officially came on board with a full-fledged investigative team. Brady described going home, spending time with Zach, and the attack they only barely survived.

"Where is your son now?" asked Ambrosi.

"Safe. I think."

Ambrosi stared at him as though he knew something about Zach's safety Brady didn't. Or was Brady just being paranoid? He considered prodding the old man when Alicia spoke up. She described her meeting with Father McAfee, his research into hellish near-death experiences, Father Randall's request for his files, and the subsequent theft of them.

"Hmm," Father Ambrosi said, rubbing his chin.

"What?" inquired Alicia.

"I'm just wondering why Father Randall requested the files if he had the inclination and means to steal them."

"To avoid the risk of an investigation, of getting caught, especially if he expected Father McAfee to happily turn them over. He implied it's supposed to be an honor to have your private papers archived here."

"It is, and quite rare. But if, as you suspect, the files were used to create a hit list, why would anyone want to be known as the person who requested and received them?"

Brady realized there was something familiar and enjoyable about Ambrosi's fielding of ideas. It was the very thing division chiefs did to kick-start stalled investigations. Even large investigative teams occasionally needed a fresh perspective. He crossed his legs and put an elbow over the back of the pew. He thought of an answer to Ambrosi's question.

"Maybe he didn't know what it would be used for," he said.

"Or he didn't make the request at all," added Alicia. "Someone used his name, either to frame him specifically or simply to deflect attention from themselves."

Ambrosi nodded. "You said Malik hung around to torment the priest. Perhaps his orders were to kill him, to keep him quiet about Father Randall's request for the files. Malik was taking his time doing it, because he was evil and sadistic. It would not be the first time an underling stretched his authority in performing a duty and caused grief for his superior because of it."

Alicia said, "It's a common mistake of investigators, assuming everything that happened was planned. In the Pelletier case, for example. If he strikes one or two victims who never had a near-death experience, of course we would have to reconsider the possible targeting criteria and that maybe we're dealing with a perp who is intentionally trying to throw us off. But also we would have to be open to the possibility that he made a mistake. We tend to give criminals more credit than they deserve."

Ambrosi thought about that, then said, "How many times, however, do you suppose good guys have *underestimated* bad guys, their cunning, their resourcefulness, their capacity to commit evil?"

All the time, Brady thought. And he knew the reason: It is human nature to assume others are like us. Intellectually. Morally. Give or take small degrees. But the criminal mind, the mind that can conceive and commit murder, treads in dark territories the modern, civilized mind has long abandoned. Or has pretended to abandon by turning slightly away. Instead of believing killers have advanced intellects that enable them to commit crimes and escape capture, we tend to think killers are as intellectually faulty as they are morally faulty. Hence, we underestimate them.

Not that all killers are geniuses—not by a long shot—but Brady knew wise investigators remembered that genius is an intellectual phenomenon, not a moral one. As easily as it could create, it could destroy.

63

Ambrosi patted his shirt pocket. "Ah, I brought only one cigarette with me."

"Here," said Alicia, opening her purse, starting to fish through it.

"No, thank you, my dear. If it's not my beloved blend from Lecce, my lungs will rebel and explode. Tell me more of your story."

She told of going to the hotel, being attacked, subduing Malik. Here, she hesitated.

Ambrosi waited, wheels turning behind his bright eyes. Finally, he asked, "Did you kill him?"

"No," she snapped. Then, more gently: "Not directly."

"You did something . . . unorthodox?"

Brady understood her reluctance to admit bringing in Apollo. At the point at which she turned from calling the Bureau or the local cops after knocking Malik out cold, she had become a criminal herself. Kidnapping. Police brutality. Whatever law was violated by drugging someone against his will. And it had led to two deaths. Criminally negligent homicide, at least. He thought a case could be made for their actions, given the attacks and the apparent complicity of someone inside their own agency. But a lot depended on the evidence they could find to support their claims and on the outcome of their current pursuit.

And here they were, about to confess their crimes to a stranger. They had no reciprocal felonies to hold over *his* head. Unless smoking on Vatican grounds was a felony, which it very well could be. Despite his assurances to Alicia, they really had no way of knowing if the old man was friend or foe. He knew the principal players, Malik and Randall—was even Randall's *boss*. Still, he seemed genuinely concerned. More than that, they needed a friend who could give them more facts about the situation they were in.

Sure that Alicia wanted to think through this part of the story with Brady, he started to stand.

She put her hand on his arm. "It's okay, Brady. I'm all right with this."

Slowly at first, then with increasing urgency, she told him about Apollo, the nightmarish sodium amobarbital interview, Malik's assault on Apollo, and the tumble through the window: three went out, one came back in. Withholding Gilbreath's name, she conveyed that episode and their decision to come to Italy.

Sometime during the telling, Ambrosi had closed his eyes. He remained that way, perfectly still, for several minutes.

Finally, Alicia said, "Cardinal Ambrosi? Roberto?"

He raised his index finger: one moment.

Shortly, his eyes opened, and they appeared tired.

"I can't see that you had any other choice but to come here," he said, as if that concluded the matter. "Tell me, what can I say that will send you home, back to your lives in America?"

"What lives?" Alicia said. "Everything has been turned on its head. It's dangerous for us there."

"It's dangerous for you here. And it will become even more so if you continue your pursuit of the man responsible for the serial murders and attacks on you."

"What else can we do?" Brady said, shaking his head. "By hunting him down, we have a chance at survival, at living normally after this."

"You may be only hastening your deaths."

"So be it," Brady said, firm.

"So be it," Alicia agreed.

Ambrosi took in their countenances, their resolution. He shifted on the pew back, took in a deep breath, let it out slowly.

"What will you do if you find the man responsible? Will you kill him?"

"Yes," Brady answered without hesitation.

"Unless," Alicia said, giving her partner a quick glance, "in the course of tracking him down, we gather enough evidence to bring him down legitimately. We would need enough evidence to show that our behavior was justified and to hand over to the authorities so they can arrest him, wherever he is." She returned her gaze to Brady for agreement.

Brady considered her proposal, then gave a single nod. "The opportunity to kill him or enough evidence to exonerate us and bring him to justice—whichever comes first."

How strange that they had not articulated their intentions before. They had opted to act based on the assumption that pursuing the strongest leads was their only viable strategy. Under normal conditions, they would arrest or attempt to arrest the person they found at the end of the trail. Without the power to arrest, what were their options? Brady was comfortable with what they had laid on the table and secretly hoped for the chance to put a bullet through the guy's head. He only had to remember Zach's face looking up at him from the hidey-hole: tears rimming his eyes, lower lip quivering, terrified not of his own death, but of losing his dad.

As far as Brady knew, Ambrosi had never been in law enforcement, and he certainly wasn't an investigator or division chief, but he could have been one. He was adept at getting a person thinking.

"What did you learn from Malik?" Ambrosi asked.

"He was into"—Alicia skewed her face into an expression of distaste—"some sort of human sacrifice. He mentioned children, their blood on his hands. I think he was a Satanist."

"That does not surprise me," Ambrosi said.

"What do you mean?" Brady asked. "Did you know him?"

"Only by reputation. You see, I believe I know the man you seek."

Alicia nearly jumped out of the pew. "What? Who? Father Randall?"

"Not Father Randall. But finish your tale. Did Malik say more?"

In unison, they lowered their heads, trying to recall everything.

Quietly, Alicia said, "Something about a horror movie."

"What's that?" Ambrosi asked, leaning forward.

"A scary movie," corrected Brady. "He said that several times. 'Scary movie.'"

Ambrosi's lips stretched into a wide grin. The papery skin of his cheeks looked ready to split.

"What?" Alicia said.

"You already know the name of your nemesis."

"An actor in a movie?" Alicia said skeptically.

"Not 'scary movie,' my dear. *Scaramuzzi*. Luco Scaramuzzi."

Brady repeated it. Yes, with the accent and the drugs, that's what he was saying. Scaramuzzi. He was sure of it.

He said, "Who is he? I've never heard of him."

"No reason you would have . . . yet. A rising star in world politics. Charming, bright, full of ideas. But America is so big and self-interested, a foreign politician has to be higher up the ladder before Americans take note. He is the Italian ambassador to Israel. However . . ." He picked a piece of tobacco off his tongue, examined it, rubbed his fingers together to get rid of it. "For your purposes, it is what else Luco Scaramuzzi is—or thinks he is— that is threatening your lives: the Antichrist."

Alicia slapped her thigh. "I *knew* it was something like that . . . all the clues . . ."

"But the *Antichrist*?" Brady said, in the same tone he would have used if the old man had said Scaramuzzi was Santa Claus. "From Revelation?"

"See, you do know him. Do you know his story?"

"Uh . . . he's supposed to come from the people who destroyed Jerusalem, the Roman Empire. A political leader, ruling over nations. Very deceitful: he'll make people think he's good, when all along he's planning their destruction."

"He'd have to have a very charming personality to pull that off, don't you think?"

"I know something about him," said Alicia, surprising Brady. "'Out of the sea he rises, creating armies on either shore . . .'"

Ambrosi brushed his hand at her. "That's from *The Omen*," he said. "The author made it up. But those verses do a fair job of summing up Antichrist's goal on earth. Do you remember the rest?"

"'Turning man against his brother, till man exists no more.'"

"Yes."

"But how can anyone make any legitimate claim to the title of Antichrist until he starts fulfilling biblical prophecies about him?" Brady asked.

"Because Scripture is not the only place to find prophecies. True prophecy is God's revelation of things to come. Some of the most respected theologians in Christendom, like Augustine and Origen, believed that God continued to reveal the future to individuals, usually in dreams. Extrabiblical prophets do not refute the Bible as the whole and inerrant Word of God. Rather, they attest to our Lord's ongoing interest and involvement in our lives. Theologians often look to these extrabiblical documents for clues to God's will and what is to come."

The old man levered one foot off the pew, lowering it to the floor, then the other. He slid off the pew back and rubbed his rear end. "Come walk with me," he said. He shuffled around the first pew and went behind the stone altar.

When they joined him, Brady saw that the altar was hollow, with no back side. Directly under it, the floor had been removed, leaving a rectangular hole as black as a pool of oil. Ambrosi produced a flashlight and clicked it on. He shone the light into the hole, revealing stone steps.

"Come," he said. He ducked under the altar and awkwardly shifted and turned to fit in the narrow space. Situated sideways to the stairs, he moved down, one step at a time.

Brady was bigger than Ambrosi, so he took longer to wriggle into a position that allowed descent.

"This must have been designed for children," he said.

"It was made for anyone trying to escape capture should the chapel be discovered." Ambrosi's voice echoed from below.

Brady could see only the reflection of light dancing on gray stone walls. He took another step down, then reached up to help Alicia navigate onto the first step.

"Remember," came the old man's voice, "when this chapel was built, capture meant being fed to lions in the Coliseum while the rest of Rome cheered."

64

Ambrosi held the light on the steps until Brady and Alicia came off them. Then the flashlight swung around, revealing a passageway that extended beyond the reach of the light. It was so narrow, they had to walk single file, Ambrosi leading, Brady bringing up the rear. The air was humid and smelled faintly of wet earth. Their footfalls and scuffs echoed against the stone walls. When Ambrosi resumed speaking, his voice too came back at them, like a microphone's feedback in a large auditorium.

"The original tunnel led to a cave," he explained. "Since then, more passageways and rooms have been added. Escape routes, hiding places, archaeological digs. There's quite a labyrinth down here now."

They passed another corridor on their left. Brady could feel a slight breeze coming out of it. They kept moving straight. If Brady gauged it correctly, they were below the courtyard they had crossed to reach the archive stairs.

"Those extrabiblical prophecies I mentioned?" said Ambrosi, sounding a little winded. "There are some who look to them not for any virtuous reasons, but for clues to the identity of Antichrist."

"The prophets had visions of Antichrist?" Brady asked. He said *Antichrist* the way Ambrosi did, as a name without an article.

"Oh, yes. Some of them had visions of nothing else, poor souls. The Franciscan friar Roger Bacon, for example. He was tormented by dreams of the end times. His writings have provided some intriguing glimpses of this 'man of perdition.' He will be left-handed, bear a scar from a childhood accident, and have 'eyes the color of ash.' Bacon supposedly invented gunpowder—or at least improved upon the Chinese formula for it—in an effort to reconstruct Adamic science, which he said humankind lost during the Fall in the Garden of Eden. He said it was the only way to defeat Antichrist."

"Does Scaramuzzi have those physical traits?" asked Alicia.

"He does," Ambrosi said, nodding. "But even if he did not, he would find a way to turn the prophecies to his favor or discredit them."

Brady asked, "Is the Bible itself as specific in identifying Antichrist?"

"Specific, yes. But Scripture is more difficult to interpret because of its language. It sometimes sounds vague because God wrote it to last millennia, regardless of the culture pressing on the mind of the person reading it. It transcends time, geography, society."

"*God* wrote it?" Alicia questioned.

"God breathed His word into the men who did write it. That's the way He often works. Through us. Or through what we would call nature."

He stopped at an intersection of passageways and turned. The light bounced off the floor to fill his eye sockets with shadows. He smiled past Brady to Alicia.

"Scientists now say the parting of the Red Sea, which allowed six hundred thousand Jews to escape Egypt, was entirely possible because of a reef that extends from one shore to the other. Four miles of reef. They say if the wind had blown sixty-seven miles per hour, it would have cleared the reef of water for travel on foot. Imagine that. This way."

He took off down a different corridor.

After about ten yards, Brady said, "Who are these people watching for Antichrist?"

"They are the God-fearing souls who want to brace themselves for the troubled times the appearance of Antichrist promises. They are well intended, but I wish I could say to them, 'Just live for God and you will always be braced.' Then there are the intellectually curious, who will delight in seeing prophecy unfold, even if they have not cast their spiritual lots with one side or the other."

He stepped into a square room the size of a single-car garage. Corridors branched off into three walls. An opening in the fourth wall showed stairs bending and climbing out of sight. Ambrosi started up.

It was a wide, circular stairway, wrapping around a pillar of stacked stones. Up they went, around and around, until the cardinal stopped on a small landing. Beside him was a wooden door, whose deep grain conjured in Brady's mind a castle's drawbridge, heavy and old.

"We will continue up, but I thought you would like to see where you are."

He pulled back an iron bolt, and the door swung outward. A great rush of fresh air swooped in on them, carrying the fragrance of wood and pulp. Electric light filled the space. Leaning out with the door, Ambrosi made room for Brady and Alicia.

They were looking into a room that was identical to the rooms they could see from the desk of the archive secretary. In fact, through an open door opposite them were those very rooms. This room, however, was furnished as an office. Bookcases. Filing cabinets. And from behind a big desk, Monsignor Vretenar stared at them, his jaw unhinged.

Ambrosi said, "*Buona sera*, Monsignor Vretenar."

Vretenar dipped his head. "Your Eminence."

Alicia waggled her fingers at him like a schoolgirl.

Ambrosi pulled the door closed. He headed up the stairs.

In the gloom, Brady could barely make out Alicia's grin.

They followed the stairs up and around. Shortly, long slits in the outer wall admitted the sun, and Ambrosi switched off the flashlight. They reached another landing and another door. Brady noted, however, that the stairs did not continue. This was their highest point, their destination. Ambrosi unlocked the door with a key and pushed it open. They stepped into a large, round chamber. The only light came from slits in the wall, identical to the ones in the stairwell. It had a plank floor. The ceiling was high above them, beyond cobwebbed rafters. Metal hooks were affixed to the wall at head height; a gas Coleman lantern hung from each.

Ambrosi swung the door shut. Dust motes puffed into the air and swirled in the shafts of light like miniature galaxies.

"My tower," he said. "Would you mind?" He held out his lighter to Brady and indicated the lanterns.

Brady walked around the room, lighting each lantern. Five of them.

Two crescent-shaped tables sat on opposite sides of the room. Each was stacked high with books and loose papers. Under them were wooden crates packed with documents. Bookcases lined the walls where there wasn't a table, a window, or a lantern. In the center of the room was a peculiar table, the likes of which Brady had never seen before. It was large, stout, and shaped like a doughnut. In the open space at its center sat a high-backed chair, scuffed and old. Papers of all sorts filled the table's surface—maps, photographs, drawings, handwritten manuscripts, pages torn from magazines and newspapers; some were white and crisp, freshly printed, others were yellowing and crumbling with age. Only a two-foot section of the table was bare, where the work surface hinged up, allowing access to the chair.

Ambrosi noticed Brady's scrutiny. "I'm told this was St. Francis of Assisi's writing desk," he said. "It allows messy researchers like me a chance to spread our work out without being too far from any of it."

"What do you research?" Alicia asked, leaning over an ancient-looking document resting on the table. The florid script was foreign. In each of its corners was a highly detailed drawing of an execution: a person being burned by fire at a stake, a beheading on a tree stump, a body whose arms and legs were tied to horses running in opposite directions, and a person being hurled off a cliff by a hooded figure.

"Antichrist, of course," he said plainly.

They gaped at him.

"Yes, I'm one of those. The Catholic Church has always had someone in my position, because the church should be among the first to recognize the beginning of the end, don't you think? In fact, most religions and some large governments like your own employ scholars who watch and wait and study the texts in order to watch and wait better."

"What do they hope to accomplish?"

"To be on the winning team. To not be blindsided by a sudden shift in political power. To hedge their economies against the financial pull of Antichrist's interests. There are as many reasons as there are watchers. Scripture says this man will be like no other who has ever walked the earth. Eventually, he will even perform miracles, because Satan will possess him and give him power. Scholars have long accepted the idea that this man's presence will create a sort of gravitational pull on everything human. Religions and armies, whole industries and societies will flow toward Antichrist and orbit around him. It will start slowly but gain speed and force."

Brady said, "I understand the Bible enough to know the influence Antichrist exerts on the world is so strong it leads to Armageddon, mankind's final battle. I just never considered what that meant in practical terms."

"There are certain people who do consider it," Ambrosi said. "All the time, from childhood on. Rich, powerful people. Their organization—their secret society, if you like—was formed a thousand years ago. *Collegium Regium Custodum et Vigilum Pro Domino Summo Curantium.* Literally, the 'Royal Order of Guardians and Watchers for the Supreme Ruler.' Now they're known simply as the Watchers."

"Excubitor," Alicia whispered, looking at Brady with wide eyes.

Ambrosi's eyebrows shot up. "Yes, one of their early monikers. Where did you learn it?"

"There's a theory that the group spirited away an entire Norse village, called the Western Settlement, in the 1300s."

"Ah, yes . . ." The old man rubbed his chin in thought. He appeared to come out of a memory and continued where he'd left off. "The group accumulated more power and wealth than any other private entity in history. I don't know if the Catholic Church is wealthier; certainly, it is less powerful, if power is defined by political influence. The only thing the Watchers want, all they have ever wanted, through forty successive generations, is to hand over the Church's vast resources to the one true Antichrist."

"Why?" Brady asked, deeply perplexed.

"*Collegium Regium Custodum et Vigilum Pro Domino Summo Curantium* started as a religion in the 1100s. Trying to understand why people believe what they do is a futile effort, but the founding members had backgrounds in Satanism, Zoroastrianism, and primarily, a sect of Gnosticism known as Cathari. The Cathars professed adherence to Christian theology, but they believed the only way to achieve divine form and spend eternity with God, as God, was through the end of humankind. For this reason, they developed an unhealthy interest in Antichrist. Pope

Innocent III recognized the danger and in his wisdom"—Ambrosi shook his head—"had nearly all followers of the movement slaughtered. The survivors recruited several like-minded people of great power and wealth and formed the Watchers. Since Antichrist was identified in Scripture as the being who brings about the destruction of all humans, they got it into their heads that the most spiritual thing they could do was help him achieve his purpose. They figured that Antichrist's goals—as stated in prophecy—would require vast amounts of money and manpower and political influence. Most of them were already extremely wealthy. They pledged to build their fortunes and clout and to deliver these to Antichrist when he appeared, no matter how long the wait."

While speaking, Ambrosi had sauntered to one of the crescent tables, pulled a sheet of rolling paper from its package, creased it down the middle, and sprinkled in a line of tobacco, which he stored in a humidor. While a slight tremor still haunted his hands, they were much steadier than they had been in the chapel. Brady wondered again if there just might be something with more relaxing properties than tobacco in that "beloved blend from Lecce."

Ambrosi rolled the paper tight and sealed it by moistening the edge with his tongue. He felt for his lighter.

Brady realized he was still holding it. He walked over, lit the cigarette, and handed him the lighter.

The old man pulled in a lungful, savoring the taste. He blew it out and continued.

"Each generation reared its children to take their places as leaders in society and as Watchers. Some families lost their wealth and influence, and with a few exceptions, they were replaced by whoever at the time had the gold and could be converted to their ideology. Eventually this group of twelve became strong enough to ensure that none would lose their status. They learned to help each other through difficult times, staying loyal even if it took several generations for a family to bounce back. Each member of the current group can trace his or her heritage as a Watcher back at least eight generations. Through the years, there have been rumors of infighting. Aside from differing opinions about Antichrist candidates, the primary cause of contention appears to be that some Watchers are not content to relinquish their assets for mere ideological rewards. They want positions of power in Antichrist's cabinet—or whatever his body of advisers will be called when the time comes. Even so, every Watcher takes his duties very seriously."

"There are only twelve?"

"Twelve who sit on the Council of Watchers. The ones with the money and power. The order itself has tens of thousands of members. Each must pledge fealty to Antichrist and to the Council in his stead. In addition, they must give their oath to abide by a strict code of conduct. They must contribute to the coffers, according to their ability. They must protect the secrecy of the order. They must rear their children in the ways of the order."

"It's a cult," said Alicia.

"Very much so." Ambrosi removed his cigarette, looked at it, and then stabbed it back into his mouth. "The most valuable contribution each member makes is of his talents. And among their numbers are those with dubious skills. Spies. Thieves. Assassins."

He let these last words hang in the air like the slowly dissipating tendrils of smoke.

Alicia walked to one of the window slits and peered out. The sun was going down, bruising the sky with shades of purple.

She sighed, turned around. "Okay," she said. "There's a guy out there who thinks he's Antichrist, and there is a group of fat cats who have nothing better to do than wait for the Antichrist to come along and take their money." She glanced at Brady, turned to Ambrosi, and opened her hands. "What does any of this have to do with us?"

"Everything," Ambrosi said. "And you have to know it, if you expect to face your enemy and survive."

The cardinal's eyes sparkled in the lantern light. He was in his element, explaining what he had spent a lifetime learning. He moved slowly to a bookcase. As he walked, he crushed out his cigarette in his palm, then brushed it to the floor. From a sagging chest-high shelf, he pulled an eight-inch-thick leather-bound volume. Holding it in both arms as though it were a baby, he carried it to St. Francis of Assisi's doughnut table and thunked it down.

"Come, the both of you," he said, lifting the volume's cover. "Take the only weapon I have to offer. Knowledge of the Beast."

65

The pages were vellum, thick and brown and curling at the edges. A smell like fine leather and dust wafted off them. The words on the first page had faded into the darkening animal skin. Squinting, Brady could make out just enough to realize he was looking at Latin written in longhand. Centered at the top was the official name of the Watchers. Under that were a signature and a date—1564. The year Michelangelo died.

"This is a record of Watcher activity for the past five hundred years," Ambrosi said. "The first six pages were inscribed by my predecessor, fourteen times removed. There are two earlier volumes, but they are in the archive's climate-controlled vaults, each page preserved in a silk-screen sheath."

Neither Brady nor Alicia could read Latin or Italian, so the book's value to them was more theatrical than practical. Brady supposed Ambrosi could use it as a guide to the intelligence he should impart, but he seemed to know its contents by heart anyway. He hoped Alicia would not lose patience with the old man's flair for the dramatic. When he looked at her, she appeared entirely engrossed in the lesson, even following Ambrosi's gaze when it dropped to a page. Her investigator's heart knew the difference between the trivial and the requisite.

"A candidate comes to the attention of the Watchers usually through scouts, who recognize the fulfillment of prophecy in an individual. Some expected characteristics of Antichrist are nonnegotiable, such as his being a Gentile and a descendant of the Roman Empire. Others—left-handedness, that he will be in his forties when he comes to the world's attention—are open to interpretation. Most candidates are eliminated from consideration very early in the vetting process. On average, the Council of Watchers gets excited about a candidate no more than one time per century. Which means two generations could go by without seeing any serious candidates. However . . ."

Ambrosi flipped to the last written-on page.

"Wait!" Alicia said. "Go back."

He did, until she said, "Stop." On the page, surrounded by hand-written text, was a drawing of the sun with curving flames radiating from it and vertical lines filling the circle.

"What is that?" she asked, stabbing the drawing with her finger.

"You've seen it before?"

Brady answered, "It was branded into the murder victims."

Ambrosi frowned at the drawing. "Every Antichrist candidate designs a symbol for his kingdom. This is Scaramuzzi's; it is his swastika. It's patterned off a medieval crest for Antichrist and embellished by Scaramuzzi. The twelve flames coming out of the sun represent the twelve Watchers. The ten lines within the sun represent the ten countries that will form Antichrist's kingdom."

They stared at it for a moment, and then Ambrosi turned to a different page. On it appeared to be an organizational chart, with boxes and lines showing relationships and hierarchy. He tapped a rectangle labeled "Scaramuzzi."

"Every now and then a candidate fulfills enough of the prophetic program for the transference of assets to begin. Don't ask me what 'enough' means. That can include subjective criteria, such as charisma and intelligence. At that point, the Council votes on a candidate's probability of being the one true Antichrist. They give the candidate authority over their resources in direct proportion to the vote of confidence he receives. So a two-thirds vote of confidence theoretically means the candidate has access to two-thirds of the resources reserved for him."

Alicia snapped her head back, flipping the hair out of her face. "Theoretically?"

"If he uses his resources unwisely, the Watchers can take them back. In the cases I've studied, the candidate has always tapped them cautiously, sparingly. Still, it represents enormous wealth and power. In 1921, when he was voted Führer of the Nazi party, Hitler had a nine-to-three vote in favor of his being Antichrist. That fluctuated over time."

Alicia shook her head as if she had caught a whiff of strong ammonia. "Hitler? What happened to the Roman heritage?"

Ambrosi smiled at her disgust. "Hitler was born in Braunau-am-Inn, once part of the Holy Roman Empire and not far from Rome. Besides, anyone with a rudimentary understanding of Antichrist prophecy could blow holes in the cases of every serious candidate the Watchers ever considered. Usually the errors are only evident in hindsight. As is deception by the candidate. On top of that, there is the nature of prophecy itself. More times than not, it comes through dreams as symbols or allegory. How they are distilled into accepted prophetic visions is a story unto itself. Let us just say they offer a lot of wiggle room."

Alicia shook her head. "For all that money and power, *I'd* be deceiving and wiggling."

"You don't have the capacity to be so corrupt," Brady said. He thought about his own recent desire to be more so. "You'd have to be willing to slaughter innocents." He raised his eyebrows at Ambrosi. "Right?"

"Oh, I believe the candidate would have to eat children for lunch and their mothers for dinner. Psychosis is a job requirement. No, ordering deaths and bloodying his own hands would not bother Antichrist in the least. What would be bothersome, I imagine, is having the Council of Watchers over you. First, a treasure is splayed before you, but you can partake of it only sparingly. Next, a candidate with less than 100 percent of the votes is subject to the management and discipline of the Council. Like the ephori in Sparta: they had the authority to veto the king's decisions and even remove him from power."

Alicia said, "Has anyone ever received a 100 percent vote?"

"Never. I believe to get all the votes, the candidate would have to grow horns and spit fire."

Brady's attention went back to the organizational chart. Above the *Scaramuzzi* box were twelve boxes lined up next to one another. Four contained handwritten names; in three were pasted photographs the size of postage stamps. He pointed at them.

"The Council of Watchers?" he asked.

"The twelve disciples," Ambrosi said sarcastically.

Brady ran his finger over them, reading. "Vajra Kumar, Koji Arakawa, Donato Benini, Niklas Hüber. No other names?"

"It *is* a secret organization."

"What are these?" He pointed to pencil marks, an *x* or a check over each box. Of the four named boxes, only Niklas Hüber's bore an *x*.

"The vote, as far as I know. I believe Scaramuzzi has secured eight votes. If the votes in favor ever fall below seven, he's out."

"Out?"

"In every case, the candidate has died or vanished." He studied the chart as if concerned he'd forgotten something. After a minute, he said, "When, someday, the candidate does secure every vote, a great shift in power will occur. This box"—he touched *Scaramuzzi*—"will move up here." He dragged his finger to a spot above the Council of Watchers. "Antichrist will have complete authority over the Watchers and their—now his—resources. At that point, the power can never shift back except upon the death of Antichrist."

He covered the chart with his palm.

"Scaramuzzi has not achieved this," he said. "It's my guess he never will. Right now, he has only two concerns in the world: first, to keep the votes he has, and second, to change the minds of the Watchers who are against him. Every single thing he does is motivated by these two objectives."

"How can he change their minds?" asked Alicia.

"Continue to fulfill prophecy."

"I don't understand. How can anyone do that, unless he really is the person prophesied about?"

"Essentially, there are three ways to accrue 'prophecy points.'" Ambrosi smiled at the term. "The first is obvious: Do what's expected of you. In the case of Antichrist, it's to rise to political power, which Scaramuzzi is doing. To those who see him only as a politician, he's smart and persuasive and has some very intriguing ideas about Israel and the Middle East. He appears very peace-minded. He has to. Antichrist will become a world leader by virtue of a peace program. He is almost certain to win the Nobel Peace Prize."

"But peace is the last thing on his mind," Brady said.

"Except as a ruse to gain power. Eventually he will rule a federation of ten kingdoms, or countries. Most of us spectators believe this federation has already been established with the European Union, though it does not yet have a centralized leader. And it may not for a hundred years, but it's there, ready for him."

"The countries of the European Union have been independent for thousands of years," Brady said doubtfully. "Aggressively so. I can't see them arraying under a single leader."

"And twenty years ago, who would have predicted that they would agree to a joint economic program that required each to abandon its own currency for a shared one? At the airport, did you exchange your dollars for lira?"

"Euros," Alicia said, pulling the wad of bills out of her pants pocket. Ambrosi bowed his head, his point made.

"But that's different from a centralized government. Europe just hands its countries over to Antichrist?"

"All but three of them do, according to biblical prophecy. Revelation 13 and 17, Daniel 7. He murders three leaders to take control. The Watchers believe he has already claimed his first."

"An assassination of a leader? Who?" Brady could not believe he was engaged in this conversation.

"Santo Mucci."

"The Italian prime minister? That was, what, four years ago?"

"Five. Prophecy does not indicate that Antichrist will assassinate three leaders and immediately step into their positions. That's not the kind of person people would tolerate, let alone champion. Remember, during his rise, he is seen as a great peacemaker, a uniter, not a divider. To fulfill his destiny, his murders must eventually lead to his ability to rule the victims' countries."

"And Mucci?"

"Scaramuzzi was a grassroots leader in Italy. Prefect of Agrigento Province. But Mucci's party did not think much of his ideas. He was too liberal. And his personal style, his ambition, rubbed the politicos the wrong way. After the assassination, Parliament held an emergency general election, and Silvio Bertoni was voted in. He was and still is an adamant supporter of Scaramuzzi's. A Southerner like Scaramuzzi, and that matters very much here. He appointed him ambassador. It is quite possible that the Watchers have connections within the current regime to help facilitate Scaramuzzi's continued ascent. Make no mistake: he will be our prime minister, and it will be because of Mucci's assassination. One down, two to go."

"But I thought you doubted he was Antichrist."

"So what if he is not? If he pretends to be and he convinces the right people he is, do you think he will be much less destructive than if he were actually Antichrist? Scaramuzzi's machinations may not lead to Armageddon, but they will most certainly cause untold death and destruction."

"And he got the ball rolling by having Santo Mucci killed?"

"Oh, no, not *having* it done. He himself assassinated the man. Otherwise, the murder would not have aligned with the Antichrist prophecy. Scaramuzzi would not have received credit for it."

"Prophecy points," Brady said.

Ambrosi nodded enthusiastically. "Lots of them. It's what took him out of the category of potential candidate and made him a serious contender. As far as I can gather, the Watchers had not voted at that point. There was only strong interest. Within three months of the assassination, as it became apparent that the wheels he set in motion would favor him politically, he garnered seven votes. He was in."

"Wasn't Santo Mucci assassinated in Israel?"

"At the Italian Embassy building in Tel Aviv. Scaramuzzi had been setting up a base of operations in Jerusalem, where he knew eventually he would be. You see, prophecy says Antichrist will have a strong relationship with Israel, appearing to be its ally. What better way to establish those relationships than as ambassador? Not much is known about Scaramuzzi prior to this time. But I believe he was recruiting followers, workers to do all the various legwork someone with his ambitions requires. When he became the Watchers' best hope, he got access to *their* vast roster of . . . uh, craftsmen."

"The spies, thieves, and assassins you mentioned before?" Ambrosi's tale was convoluted and densely populated. Brady wanted to be sure he didn't miss anything or make the wrong assumptions.

"Among others, yes. Scaramuzzi's head of security is a vicious man named Arjan Vos. Former Israeli army general. Former Mossad agent. A brutal man, as well as a highly skilled killer. I believe he trained Scaramuzzi to commit the assassination. The Asia House, in which several embassies in Tel Aviv are located, was the perfect location. Not far from Scaramuzzi's secret headquarters. And far from his public headquarters, where I'm sure he had alibis arranged should something go wrong. And Vos would have known the building well, having been once assigned to that district as a Mossad agent."

Brady noticed the temperature had dropped since the sun's passing. He looked around and did not see any registers or radiator and wondered how the room was heated. He imagined it in winter, the old man hunched over an ancient scroll, a threadbare blanket draped over his shoulders and back, breath pluming from his mouth. Reading words a thousand years old about a man who would usher in the end of the human race, a man who at that moment could be plotting death to the strains of Vivaldi. An icy finger ran up his back.

Alicia leaned her rear back against the desk. She crossed her arms over her chest and said, "You mentioned *three* ways he could strengthen his position?"

"There is also the discovery of new prophecy—keep studying prophetic writings until you find something that resembles an event that has already occurred in your life. A near-drowning, the death of a sibling. Roll it out, let the theologians confirm it, and your credibility goes up a notch or two. The canon of Antichrist prophecy grows with every serious candidate."

Brady shook his head. "That's ridiculous."

The old man shrugged. He wiggled his fingers in his shirt pocket and absently kept them there as it dawned on him that he'd have to roll his next smoke. Shuffling to the crescent table and the humidor, he said, "Lastly, you could select an unfulfilled prophecy and intentionally fulfill it. There is a vigorous debate about whether prophecy fulfilled in this matter counts. No prophet has ever said that foreknowledge invalidates the vision. It is what it is. However, knowing that someone set out to fulfill prophecy just feels wrong, does it not? For this reason, candidates usually deny having foreknowledge of any recently fulfilled prophecies."

Brady was amazed that the control of so much wealth and power could rely on the murky logic and tenuous conclusions that seemed to govern prophecy. Something about it disturbed him on a fundamental level.

Ambrosi slammed the volume closed. He caught Brady's eye, then Alicia's. He held up his hands as if holding a beach ball to his chest, which he shook as he spoke.

"You must understand your adversary. Scaramuzzi possesses no moral conscience. He is under intense pressure. And his resources are virtually unlimited. He may not be Antichrist, but he is a beast. A volatile, violent, unpredictable beast."

He dropped the ball and intertwined his fingers over his chest, positioned for prayer. An invisible hand of sadness gripped his face. Everything about him frowned. "My apologies for what I am about to say, but you must know. I do not think you stand a chance in a face-off with him. Whether your battle is one of wits or wills or weapons, he is stronger. He is motivated."

"So are we," said Brady firmly.

Ambrosi nodded, but he did not look convinced.

"Father Randall," Alicia said. "How does he fit into this?"

Ambrosi let out a long breath. "Father Randall travels frequently. He acquires documents of importance to the Church for the Archives. He also corroborates details within our records with other documents wherever they may be found. For the past four years, only half the time he's away is he where he claims to be going. The other half is spent with Scaramuzzi, as his head theologian. He provides prophetic writings, documented answers to questions Scaramuzzi or the Watchers have . . . whatever they need. And he works with the Watchers' theologians to arrive at equitable solutions to debated points of prophecy. He uses our Archives, much of which is unavailable to anybody else."

"And you let him?" Alicia asked.

"He is unaware of my awareness. Just as he is unaware of certain taps on his phone line and computer." He winked. "If it got out that he was even unknowingly leaking intelligence about Scaramuzzi, the Watchers, and the prophecies that interest them at any given time, my information flow would end, and Father Randall's head would arrive in a box at the Vatican post office."

He looked tired. His gaze grew distant, and he rubbed his cheeks. Then he snapped out of the thought that had occupied him and said, "Now let's get you a notepad. There's more you should know."

"Like . . . ?" Brady asked. He really didn't want to hear any more about prophecies or nutcases with delusions of grandeur.

"Like where to find your prey. What he looks like. And—if it's something that interests you—whom to see in Israel for a firearm."

"Now you're talking," piped Alicia.

66

They talked long into the evening. At nine the door opened, admitting a stooped old woman with a tray of food and a decanter of wine for Ambrosi. Her eyes went wide when she saw Brady and Alicia. Ambrosi introduced her as Sister Abigail and asked her to fetch two more dinners for his guests. She took the cardinal's food away and thirty minutes later returned with plates of roast beef, baked potatoes, steamed baby carrots, muffins, and more wine. The aroma alone could have kept a dying man alive. Brady realized he was famished, and he could almost hear Alicia's stomach growling. Ambrosi made room for their meals at his desk and turned two crates on their sides for chairs.

During dinner, which Alicia raved on about to Brady's mumbled agreement, Ambrosi would not speak of Scaramuzzi, the Watchers, or Antichrist. Nor would he answer their questions regarding these subjects. He broke into a discourse of the marvelous things he was blessed to hold and read as prefect of the Vatican's Secret Archives: a bound volume of a handwritten original transcript of the trial of Galileo; a Hebrew codex describing a voyage by the Queen of Sheba to "an enchanted land of abundance and beauty called Sypanso"—probably Japan; seventeen letters from Henry VIII to Anne Boleyn, in which the king's professions of love rivaled King Solomon's in florid verse and sheer steaminess.

"A few years later, Henry's affection shifted to Jane Seymour, so he had poor Anne beheaded," he said. He took a draft of the Bordeaux and shrugged, as if to say, *What are you going to do?*

Eventually Ambrosi got around to inquiring about their salvation. He smiled broadly when Brady described his late wife's faith since childhood and how she had gently coaxed him into the fold, how he had become a staunch believer. Brady explained that C. S. Lewis's *Mere Christianity* had attacked and conquered his doubts on the level they were strongest, intellectually. After that he'd become involved in their church, eventually becoming a deacon. He attended Sunday school, a midweek men's Bible study, and could usually be found with a book about Christian living in hand. He didn't mention that all this had ended with Karen's death.

"You realize, don't you, that your wife did not 'coax' you into the fold?" Ambrosi said around a mouthful of muffin. "She may have been a catalyst in ways we cannot explain, but it was the Holy Spirit that brought you to Jesus."

Brady nodded. He wasn't willing to get into a theological debate with the old man. Once, he would have agreed with his point. What he thought now was that everything good that had happened to him since meeting Karen was Karen's doing. He had enjoyed the peace, good friends, and intellectual stimulation that had come from attending church and worshiping together with his family. Even the theological basis of that lifestyle—that God was loving and took care of His children—had proved to be false. It had been Karen who created what they had. Karen, not the Holy Spirit. Try telling *that* to a man of the cloth.

To Brady's surprise, Old Man Ambrosi smiled even more broadly when Alicia boldly proclaimed her agnosticism.

"Child, you will hear His call someday," he predicted. "Your uncertainty gives you a great advantage over those who believe themselves saved when they are not. So many people think they know God, when their relationship is with some false deity of man's devising. Sadly, they close their minds, thinking they are already home."

————

THEY STAYED in Vatican City that night, sleeping in Cardinal Ambrosi's apartment. It was a suite of large, richly appointed rooms, with plenty of space for guests. He told them they were the first "fresh blood" in the place since his sister had died seven years earlier.

Brady ambled around the living room, den, and library, marveling at the heavy, intricately crafted furniture. He didn't know priceless antique furniture from flea market knockoffs, but he would bet these were not from Wal-Mart. Each wall contained at least one classical painting in a gilded frame, illuminated perfectly by a brass picture light above it. Most were from the low and high Renaissance and were undoubtedly masterful reproductions: he recognized Raphael's *The School of Athens* and a Titian or Rubens—who could tell the difference? On a coffee table he found a mug of what looked like cold coffee; an ashtray filled with butts and ashes; and an eclectic assortment of publications, from the *National Catholic Reporter* to *TV Guide*. He nudged the stack to reveal the supermarket tabloids the *National Enquirer*, the *Star*, and one of like ilk called *Cronaca Vera*. He smiled, inexplicably relieved to see signs of humanity in this museumesque environment.

Strolling back into the living room, where Alicia and Ambrosi were conversing quietly in front of a lit fireplace, the cerise liquid in their wineglasses sparkling like rubies, his attention turned to two paintings hanging together over an ornate sideboard. These were decidedly different from the others; there was no sense of peace or philosophical musings about them, nothing sublime. The painting on the left depicted a man on a horse charging toward something. His beard flowed back behind him; his muscular arm held a sword up high. Above him, a figure, maybe an angel, unfurled a scroll. Beneath him, another horse and rider raged toward the unseen battle. This other rider appeared to be bursting from flames. The painting's hues of gray and gold gave it a stark quality that made Brady think of a dream coming to life—no, a *nightmare* becoming reality.

The second piece was more realistically rendered, in the chiaroscuro style that brought near-photographic precision to Renaissance paintings. It showed a battle—a slaughter, really: four warriors on horseback, hacking at and trampling cowering men, women, and children. The central rider was a black demon, wielding lightning bolts. Behind them, phantasmic creatures pushed forward with impatient bloodlust.

The first painting made Brady uneasy; the second made his heart ache.

Alicia and Ambrosi stepped up beside him, one on each side. They observed the paintings in silence, as they might have watched a brewing storm from a mountaintop.

After several minutes, Ambrosi said, "They're both called *Rider on a Pale Horse*. This one"—he raised his glass to the gray-and-gold horseman—

"is William Blake's. That one, Benjamin West's. From the four horsemen of the Apocalypse. Revelation 6: 'And I saw when the Lamb opened one of the seals, and I heard, as it were the noise of thunder, one of the four beasts saying, Come and see. And I saw, and behold a white horse: and he that sat on him had a bow; and a crown was given unto him: and he went forth conquering, and to conquer.'

"This is Antichrist," Ambrosi continued. "He has a crown because he is seen as a great ruler. He rides a white horse because the world hails him as a great peacemaker, a Christlike figure. But he is also an archer because he means to conquer mankind. He leads the other horsemen: war on a red horse, famine and pestilence on a black horse, and death on a pale horse. 'And I looked, and behold a pale horse: and his name that sat on him was Death, and Hell followed with him. And power was given unto them over the fourth part of the earth, to kill with sword, and with hunger, and with death, and with the beasts of the earth.'"

Silence moved in on them again. The paintings seemed to grow larger under their gaze, clearer and more vivid. Brady noticed in Benjamin West's rendition a lion running with the horses, snapping at a falling victim. He thought of the Viking's dogs.

"Scaramuzzi believes he is the rider of the white horse," Ambrosi said. "In fact, he rides the pale horse. He is not Antichrist, but death." He paused a moment. "I had these replicas made to remind me for whom I watch. And that the monsters who come in his stead are nearly as destructive, certainly as evil, as he will be."

Alicia shivered visibly. "They're awful," she said of the paintings. She glanced around. "Here, in such a lovely setting."

"I want no respite from the reality of Antichrist or his harbingers . . . except in prayer. As long as he, or they, walk the earth, there can be no true rest. I feel his presence in my tower; I feel it in my home."

Alicia turned to him. "But what do you do? Only watch? Record his activities?"

He smiled coyly. "We do what we can."

"But what is that? What *can* you do?"

"Help people like you, for one thing. Impart my knowledge. I realize it does not feel like it to you, but there are people in the world who attempt to disrupt and stop the Watchers' efforts and the Antichrist candidates when they appear. They continually hound media outlets to investigate, with scant results. They have, at times, even sent their own assassins. Often, they come to people like me for intelligence, to understand their adversaries. Unfortunately, those of us who oppose Antichrist are outnumbered and underfinanced."

"So people have come before us," Brady said, shaking his head in dismay. "We have no chance of stopping them on our own."

Ambrosi reached out and gripped his shoulder.

"There is always hope," he said.

THEIR LUGGAGE, what little they had, was stored in a locker at da Vinci airport, so Ambrosi gave them robes and took the clothes they were wearing. In the morning, the clothes were hanging in the bathroom, wrapped in a dry cleaner's clear plastic bags.

Over fruit, rolls, and orange juice on the apartment's terrace, Ambrosi chattered pleasantly. He told them that the restoration of Sandro Botticelli's frescoes on the Sistine's walls had been botched the previous year by the use of an inferior varnish. Now, a dark glazing threatened to obliterate the masterpieces. He was particularly excited about an acquisition for the Archives he would be brokering in the next few weeks—the death warrant issued by the Court of Rouen that allowed rabble to burn Joan of Arc at the stake in 1431, ostensibly for wearing masculine clothing.

Brady marveled at Ambrosi's ability to direct their thoughts away from the tasks of the day.

"IT'S SO beautiful," Alicia observed.

The evening before, she had used the terminal in Ambrosi's study to reserve seats on the first flight of the morning out of Rome to Israel's Ben-Gurion airport. Now the three of them had come outside to wait for a cab.

The building that provided the housing needs of Ambrosi and several dozen of his fellow ranking Church officials had once been a papal palace. A fountain as spectacular as Brady had ever seen splashed and gurgled beside them. It depicted Samson, his mouth stretched in a cry to heaven, pushing over the pillars to which he was chained. Standing behind him was a winged angel touching one of the crumbling pillars with a sword, implying angelic assistance in Samson's final act, which brought the roof down on three thousand Philistines. Water sluiced from the top of Samson's head and ran through grooves in his long locks of hair, making them appear to shimmer and cascade into a pool at his feet. His blinded eyes gazed at a white dawn breaking over the Vatican walls. In the bleached-blue sky, a smattering of cumulus clouds moved sluggishly under the weight of platinum linings. The air was crisp and just a little chilly. The trees and bushes and lawns were green, wet from an early morning sprinkling.

Alicia turned to Ambrosi.

"I don't know how to thank you," she said.

"Stay alive," he said, staring hard into her eyes.

She hugged him.

He extended his hand to Brady and said, "Don't be impulsive. Be smart. If it gets too hot, get out of there. Live to fight another day." He pulled a small card from his pants pocket and handed it to Brady. "As promised, a . . . *friendly* firearms dealer in Israel."

A white van with a taxi light on its roof came around a building and curved onto a wide cobblestone drive toward them.

Ambrosi gave Brady's hand another tight squeeze. "Expect anything, absolutely anything," he said. "Remember: volatile, violent, unpredictable."

"I'll remember," Brady said. He opened the rear door and helped Alicia in. He climbed in after her, slid the door shut, and gave Ambrosi a somber nod. The cab pulled away, bound for Leonardo da Vinci Airport.

———

BACK IN his apartment, Cardinal Ambrosi paused before an ornately framed mirror, supposedly crafted in 1841 by Justus von Liebig himself, the inventor of the contemporary silver-backed mirror, and presented to Pope

Gregory XVI to commemorate the pontiff's tour of the papal states. He scowled at his reflection and shook his head sadly. He ambled to a white telephone on a wall in the kitchen. He picked up the handset and held it to his ear. Elsewhere in the Vatican, a switchboard light glowed red.

When the operator answered, he said in Italian, "Send my car, please."

He listened and said, "The airport."

Another question from the operator.

"No, no," he said. "Ciampino Airport."

He hung up and went for the carry-on of clothes and toiletries he kept ready in the front closet.

67

Luco Scaramuzzi was at his desk in the Italian Embassy when his private cell phone began emitting the opening drumbeat of Basil Poledouris's score for *Conan the Barbarian*. He continued to scan his computer monitor. It displayed a list of non-Council Watchers scheduled to attend tonight's Gathering in Jerusalem. More than two hundred, and he hoped to have a word with each one. Nothing built goodwill like a big smile and a well-timed wink or slap on the back.

He picked up on the fourth bar.

"Yes?"

"Pippino Farago is alive."

The words were filtered through an electronic voice changer. Luco leaned back in his chair and crossed his legs.

"Really?" he said.

"He has contacted the Americans."

"Americans?"

"The two FBI agents. He has arranged to give them the file."

Luco's heart began to pick up pace.

"When?"

"Today."

"Where?"

"That was to be arranged later."

"Here, in Israel?"

"Yes."

"Why are you telling me?"

"You have many friends. I am but one."

"And how did you come by this information, friend?"

Silence.

"Hello?"

Nothing.

He clicked off, picked up his desk phone, and punched a button. Arjan answered on the second ring.

Luco said, "Find out where the FBI agents are. *Now.*"

He hung up. This was an intriguing turn of events. He tried to think of a reason one of his enemies would have placed the call and could not. Very few people knew that the Federal Bureau of Investigation had agents looking for him. And only he and Pip knew about the Raddusa case file, or so he had thought. He suspected Pip had found help in getting away from Arjan the other day. Perhaps the caller was one of those who had come to Pip's aid. But why betray him now?

Because he did not know until later the person Pip was running from, he thought. *And I am not someone people want to align themselves against.*

Luco *did* have friends. Many whom he was not even aware of. He was certain of it.

The caller's use of a voice changer concerned him. It meant that either he was someone whose voice Luco would recognize or he was an overcautious stranger. Luco laughed. If the roles were reversed and *he* wanted to convey a message about a powerful secret to Antichrist, he'd be overcautious too.

Ah, he was thinking about it too much. The call had been a gift. He should act on it accordingly.

An idea occurred to him. For all he knew, the caller was Father Satan. He had been wondering when and how Old Nick would appear to him— as prophecy said he would. The more he considered it, the more it made sense. The caller knew things he should not have, and he had offered the solution to Luco's most desperate concern. Friend . . . ?

"Father," he whispered.

Maybe this was a test. Yes, a test. If it were, Luco would not fail it.

68

From her seat next to a porthole window, Alicia watched Rome drop away. *Short and sweet,* she thought.

She regretted not finding Father Randall, but Cardinal Ambrosi's assistance had been a boon to their pursuit. In retrospect, his church-sanctioned mission to monitor global Antichrist activity was not surprising. Antichrist, after all, belonged to the realm of religion. As Ambrosi had explained, Antichrist's primary function was as Satan's emissary. His hatred for Jews and Christians, as well as his hunger for power and wealth, would eventually combust into the last great battle on earth. Believing that such a person might someday exist was a matter of faith. Whether by cultural influence or some innate understanding or who knew what, she believed it. Maybe it boiled down to cynicism: the world *deserved* an Antichrist.

Even if she did not buy into the Antichrist mythology, Scaramuzzi and his backers obviously did. And they were acting on their beliefs, which meant people were dying. And according to Ambrosi, Scaramuzzi's bloodletting was just getting started.

Brady leaned close to her.

"A hundred and twenty seats," he whispered.

"What?"

"I counted them. A commuter plane. Strange, don't you think, seeing that Israel is esteemed by the world's top three religions?"

"Brady, the Jews and the Palestinians are fighting. People are dying. It's not the best time to visit."

"That's the West Bank and Gaza."

"Hamas goes where the people they want to hurt are. That's Jerusalem and Tel Aviv. When I booked the flight on-line, a window popped up saying that the State Department had issued a travel warning asking U.S. citizens to defer travel to Israel. There was a link to the complete warning."

"Did you read it?"

She smirked. "What if there were no commercial flights to Israel at all?"

"I'd have chartered a jet," Brady said firmly.

"Of course I didn't read the warning."

She tried to imagine what it would be like living in a place as unstable as Israel. Knowing that any outing could be your last. Sitting in a café, sipping tea, hearing first the rumble of an explosion, then the scream of tearing metal, the shattering of glass, the rending of brick and concrete. Turning slightly to catch all of it tumbling through space toward you. Your brain refusing to acknowledge the sight or what comes next and thinking something ordinary and incongruous ("We'll need some bread for dinner tonight"). At the very last moment, you open your mouth to scream but never do. *Just imagine the dread mothers must feel every time their children go out,* she thought. The clamp of fear whenever the phone rings. Never knowing when or where or if terror will peel itself away from the shadows to engulf you.

She thought the feeling must be very similar to her own for the past three days.

A tone sounded, and the seat belt light over their heads went dark. Immediately, two men in separate sections of the plane stood up in the aisle. They were dressed identically, in black slacks, white shirts, and black jackets. They both wore yarmulkes. They raised their hands, palms out, and began rambling at high speed in an alien tongue. Slowly, they turned in circles, as if intent on exposing every inch of the interior and its passengers with an invisible substance radiating from their palms. Alicia saw that their eyes were closed. They were praying.

"Oh, that's comforting," she whispered facetiously. "What do they know about the plane that we don't?"

"That it's in God's hands?" Brady suggested.

She lowered the seat-back tray and positioned her laptop on it. After it booted, she called up the file she had started last night to store Ambrosi's information about Scaramuzzi and Antichrist. She and Brady had reviewed them at the airport as they waited for their flight. From this, they had developed a plan of action. It didn't amount to much, she knew. Still, she was all right with it.

When she had been working investigations, before the R&D stuff, she had a partner who'd been with the Bureau something like thirty years. Fatherly guy, tough as a railroad spike, smart as Alex Trebek. Jerome Moyers was his name, and he loved to turn his advice into proverbs. One of his favorites was, "Conducting an investigation is like panning for gold. You might scoop up a fist-sized nugget, but most likely you'll build up flakes until it amounts to something you can take to the bank." When Alicia complained about the legwork and phone calls and interviews that seemed to add up to squat, he'd say, "You're panning, girl. Just keep panning." And sure enough, almost without her realizing it, her team would have accumulated enough bits of evidence to take to the bank, which in their line of work meant a U.S. attorney.

Just as a survey of the clues and the options available had sent them to Rome, it was now sending them to Israel. They had believed Father Randall was in Rome. Instead, they'd found Cardinal Ambrosi, whose information gave them a new target: Luco Scaramuzzi. She'd still like to pin down Father Randall, but Ambrosi was convinced Randall would lead to Scaramuzzi anyway. If they were lucky, they'd run into both in Israel.

She and Brady had agreed to treat Ambrosi's suspicions about Scaramuzzi and the Watchers as fact. At least until they learned otherwise. On the surface, everything Ambrosi had said lined up with what they had already known: the person behind the murders and attacks possessed power and contacts, enough to track relatively anonymous FBI agents and arrange for their executions. The Antichrist story was flat-out weird, no doubt about it. But so were the grisly beheadings of so-called endears, to use Father McAfee's term; a killer who pretended to be—or really was—a Viking and used war dogs; a would-be assassin who tormented priests and freaked out about Satan and child sacrifices; and an FBI division chief who was afraid of a shadow organization that monitored the bizarre from an ivory tower in the nation's capital. Flat-out weird. All of it.

The first step in their POA was to gather intel about Scaramuzzi's current operations from ancillary players, working from the least likely to have information—area shopkeepers and the community at large—inward, toward the center of the knowledge circle, which was Scaramuzzi himself.

They would pattern their investigation on those conducted by the Bureau's organized crime task force: use surveillance to gather a list of players, then try to ascertain each one's role and level of authority, as well as his or her potential as a source of information and as a possible ally.

The POA would be in a constant state of refinement. With each new piece of information, with each new lead, the plan would shift and flex, sometimes dramatically. That was the nature of the beast they were riding. The only rule: Don't fall off.

Their objective was to gather enough evidence against Scaramuzzi to force Israel or Italy or the U.S. into taking action against him for one crime or another. If that didn't happen, they hoped to discredit him in the eyes of the Watchers. Ambrosi said a Watcher vote of no confidence always resulted in the disappearance of the Antichrist candidate. Brady had told Alicia he would accept either scenario. However, he had made it clear that should the investigation stall or should it become apparent that Scaramuzzi would likely get them before they got him, Brady would make a serious attempt to "put a slug in that scumbag's brainpan."

Go, Brady, she remembered thinking.

Their plan was weak, tissue-paper thin. Holes big enough to fall through. Full of ambiguities and what-ifs and enough optimism to get the whole planet off antidepression meds forever. But it was all they had— that or rolling over and letting Scaramuzzi kill them and anyone else he wanted to.

Alicia bit her lip and looked out the porthole window. Blue sky. Wisps of cloud.

What are we doing? she thought.

What we have to, came her answer. *What we have been thrust into doing.*

In the faint reflection of the plastic window, she saw herself smile.
Bring it on. Bring . . . it . . . on.

BEN-GURION WAS much smaller than da Vinci, less concerned with first impressions. No soaring ceilings, no modern art, no sunlight glinting off expensive stone and metals. It reminded her of the countless small airports she'd seen with her travel-obsessed mother. A place of embarking and disembarking, a few stores and eateries—nothing more, nothing less. There was a charm to its no-nonsense, no-frills practicality, not unlike a neighborhood bakery.

At customs, Alicia remembered that an Israeli passport stamp could prevent a traveler from entering certain Arab countries, and sometimes worse. It was what made the PLO hijackers of the cruise liner *Achille Lauro* target and murder American Jew Leon Klinghoffer in 1985. Ink in a passport. Israeli customs often accommodated fretful tourists by stamping a sticky-note that later could be thrown away.

She immediately became Alicia-the-filmmaker and initiated the inspection of the CSD helmet-cum-camera; they skated through without a hitch. Outside customs, she checked her watch against a wall clock, as she had done yesterday in Rome.

"Up an hour," she informed Brady. "2:23."

He fiddled with his watch and said, "Breakfast time in the States. I want to call Zach." He scanned for a pay phone.

"All right," she said. "I need to find a restroom. I'll meet you at the Hertz counter."

She shot off toward a corridor that looked promising. She'd walked a hundred yards and was about to backtrack when she saw a pictogram of a woman above a doorless portal. She strode in.

The room was vacant. She chose the second stall from the last. On the toilet, she slipped off her blazer and inspected her arm, touching the bandages gingerly. Her prodding yielded dull points of pain that fanned out like ripples in a pond. A few pokes produced bolts of electric agony that shot up into her shoulder and neck. Even her lower back ached with a kind of aftershock. Still, she prodded some more, as if daring the wound to torment her again.

Footsteps clicked on the tile. The person paused, then went into the first stall and latched the door.

Alicia collected her things and went to the sink. She splashed water on her face, wiped it off with rough paper towels. She kept looking at her arm in the mirror. The blood was soaking through more quickly now. She would have to change the dressing in the car. Maybe put a strip of duct tape over it to prevent the blood from leaking through to her blazer.

She sighed heavily and appraised herself in the mirror. Overall, not too shabby, considering. The cardinal's comfortable guest bed, the morning's long, hot shower and healthy breakfast, the clean clothes had all helped, aesthetically and emotionally. Now, if only they knew what they were doing and she didn't have a gimp arm.

She put the blazer back on, picked up her purse and satchel from the counter, and headed out. She rounded a wall, turned out the door, and ran directly into a man who apparently had been standing just outside the threshold. She took a step back.

"Excuse—," she started, then stopped. The man was grinning at her. He was movie-star handsome. Square jaw. Large dark eyes. Strong brow and nose. Olive skin that could pass for a deep tan. Where his facial hair would grow if it were not shaved, his skin was a shade darker. Very masculine, with boyish qualities in his eyes and smile.

"Alicia, Alicia, it's nice to meet cha," he said with a singsong lilt. His voice was seductive.

For a moment, she tried to place him. She could not imagine forgetting this man, but nothing came.

"I'm sorry, do I know—"

Someone stepped up behind her from inside the restroom. She felt a hand pull at the satchel. She started to turn, caught a glimpse of a man. Bald. Severe looking. She drew in a sharp breath, ready to yell an obscene accompaniment to the blow she was preparing to strike with her elbow. A hand came around from the other side. It pressed a cloth over her mouth. Her lungs filled with a sweet, pleasant tang.

An anesthetic!

She tried to jerk away. The hand held her head firmly against the chest of the man behind her. She moved her arms, flailing and striking and causing great damage. But a second later she realized her arms were not obeying. They hung limply. Her eyes rolled up, down—from the ceiling to the handsome man's face. His smile broke as he moved his lips to speak.

What . . . can't hear . . . gotta warn Brady . . . gotta . . .

Everything went dark.

69

After examining the pay phone, Brady used cash to buy a calling card from an exchange counter. He inserted it and dialed, prefixing the Oakleys' number with the 011 country code. The phone on the other end rang. He smiled, almost giddy with the prospect of talking to his son. On the third ring a woman answered.

"Kari?"

"Brady? Brady, how are you? Where are you?"

"Everything okay?"

"Oh, yeah. The kids are getting along wonderfully, as usual. The first day, Zach kind of picked at his food, you know? You could tell he was down. Taylor and Tommy kept trying to cheer him up. Yesterday was better. He started laughing with the others. Ate all his dinner. 'Cept his broccoli. He doesn't like broccoli?"

"No. Can you put him on?"

"Oh. They gobbled down their breakfast and took off. Down to the creek, I think. Something about building a fort." Pause. "I can go get him . . ."

Brady knew the creek was a good twenty-minute walk over some rugged terrain.

"No, that's okay. Are you expecting them for lunch?"

"You bet. Twelve thirty."

"I'll try back then. Don't let him take off till I call, 'kay?"

"I'll tie him to the chair," she said, laughing.

"Thanks, Kari. Talk to you then."

He hung up, but his hand would not release the receiver. He was glad for Zach's having kids to play with and a project to take his mind off things, but he craved speaking to his son. He closed his eyes and recalled holding him on the couch thirty minutes before they were attacked. He had been squeezing the boy so tight, he could feel his heart beat.

"*Hul khalast?*"

Brady jumped. A turbaned man in business attire and holding a brief-case stood to one side. He repeated his query, gesturing with his head at the phone.

"Sorry," Brady mumbled. He hitched the bags over his shoulders, turned the rolling suitcase around, and wheeled it away.

"*La termi!*" someone called.

He turned. The man at the phone was holding up Brady's calling card. He walked back, took it with a nod, and pocketed it. He followed the rental car signs to an escalator and rode it to the floor below. He found the Hertz counter, but Alicia had not yet arrived.

He waited behind a couple unsuccessfully bargaining for an upgrade, watched the people coming off the escalator in the distance, checked the time. The couple left, and he stepped up to the counter. The rental process took ten minutes, and when he turned away, keys, agreement, and map in hand, Alicia still had not shown up.

He rode the escalator back to the main level and walked to the spot where they had parted. He had not seen where she went. The restroom, she'd said. Was she sick? Could authorities have stopped her, detained her? Alicia wouldn't have allowed herself to be taken away without getting word to him—probably in the form of a mini-riot of broken noses and screams of pain.

He eyed the people and the services in the direction he had taken when he left her. Tourists trickled out of the customs lines, several stopping to wait for traveling companions. On this side of customs, three round pillars quar-tered the wide room like sentinels, protecting the rest of the terminal from arriving tourists until their presence in the country was approved. Brady's vision scanned past them, then went back to a man leaning his right shoul-der against one of the pillars. He was dressed sharply in casual clothes. Chocolate pleated slacks. Royal blue short-sleeved shirt that appeared tailored to the man's tapered torso. His arms were crossed, and he was looking directly at Brady. Smiling. The man nodded in greeting.

Brady looked around, saw no one else paying him undue attention. He headed toward the man, who came off the pillar as he neared.

"Do you know who I am?" the man asked.

"How would I—" And the next word froze in his throat. He did know. His stomach flopped over.

Expect anything, absolutely anything, Ambrosi had said.

"Where is she?" he demanded. He resisted the temptation to slam his fist into Scaramuzzi's smug face, to get him on the ground and bludgeon him to death with . . . *anything.* The CSD case. A shoe. His hands.

"Halfway to Tel Aviv by now," answered Scaramuzzi. He studied Brady's features, searching for something.

"What do you want with her?"

"Are you going to waste our time together with stupid questions?"

Brady glared. "All right. What do you want from *me*?"

"Let's go somewhere. I know a room."

He took a step. Brady grabbed his arm.

"Here's fine," he said.

Scaramuzzi nodded. "I want the file."

Brady's mind raced. *File? What file?* He kept his face expressionless. He needed time to think.

"How did you find us?" he said, stalling. *The Pelletier case file? A computer file? The video walk-through?*

"Same way we knew where the two of you would be three days ago. What your FBI knows, we know."

"If I give you the file right now, you'll release her, unharmed?" He patted his satchel with his fingers for effect.

Scaramuzzi cocked his head. "Very funny."

"You expect me to give you the file without getting her in return? You're as insane as I heard you were."

Scaramuzzi's eyes hardened. "Just get the file," he said. "When you have it, bring it to this address." He handed Brady a business card.

It was thick and silky to the touch. There was an Italian crest on it,

Scaramuzzi's name, and "Asia House." Under that, in small script, was an address in Tel Aviv. The card trembled in Brady's hand. He shoved it into his pocket. He wanted to say something, anything. Maybe, *I have no idea what you're talking about!* But he was afraid that would squash any hope of getting Alicia back alive.

Just stay alive and see what happens, he thought.

"Instead of doing it this way, we could have tailed you," Scaramuzzi said. "Killed all of you when you made the pickup."

"So why didn't you?"

"Pip's a little paranoid right now. Seems someone shot him in the head." He plunged both his hands into his pants pockets, rocked up on the balls of his feet, and came down again. He appeared completely at ease.

Brady remained silent. *Pip? Who is Pip?*

"Even *my* men couldn't sneak up on that old dog in his present state," Scaramuzzi continued. "No, better to let you go get what you need to get your girl back."

"What if . . . ?" Brady shook his head. "What if something goes wrong? What if I don't get the file?"

Scaramuzzi eyed him sharply, trying to figure Brady's game.

"Then the girl dies," he said.

Inside, Brady buckled. His mind flashed an image of his wife, Karen, as she appeared in the morgue. A wax figure on a stainless-steel table, her skin as white as the sheet that came up to her neck. But it was not Karen on that table; it was Alicia.

He wanted to grab Scaramuzzi and shake him and say, *I don't know who Pip is! I don't know what file you think he's going to give me! Or why he would give it to me! I don't know where to start looking or who to contact! Why don't you tell me to pull a violin out of my ear and play "Für Elise"? I have as much chance of doing that as I do of finding this head-shot Pip and his mysterious file!*

Brady tried to conceal his extreme frustration. He looked around at the tourists milling past, the counters and kiosks deeper in the terminal. He let his eyes linger too long on a pair of airport police, one laughing at something the other said.

"They can't help you," Scaramuzzi said flatly.

Brady snapped his gaze back to him, anger flushing his face, tightening his jaw. "Are you going to tell me you have entire police forces, entire governments in the bag? You can't. No one can. Maybe you don't know it, but there are people who can't be corrupted. If you were as powerful as you're suggesting, you wouldn't worry about what evidence we've gathered against you. You wouldn't be here."

Scaramuzzi let Brady have his say, then he replied, "My point is that Ms. Wagner would be so much fish food in the Mediterranean before authorities here realized they have no jurisdiction to search the extraterritorial Italian Embassy. *My* embassy. You've got six hours." He brushed past Brady, his hands still buried in his pockets.

"Wait," Brady called.

Scaramuzzi turned, raised his eyebrows.

"What is all this about?" Brady asked. "Why the murders in Utah and Colorado? Why did you try to have us killed?"

Scaramuzzi smiled, tight-lipped. He closed the gap between them with two steps.

"You weren't supposed to make it this far," he said. "Now that you have, your role has escalated. The pawns have become rooks. Congratulations."

"But why kill us in the first place? What did we do?"

Scaramuzzi scrutinized his face

"You showed up, Mr. Moore," he said. "That's all you had to do." He turned and strolled away, leaving Brady staring after him, slack-jawed.

Scaramuzzi nodded at people passing him, and they beamed and gestured in return. He was pleasing to the eye and exuded a pleasantness too scarce in this world.

Brady realized that the only way for true evil to flourish was to masquerade as good. Aggressive mimicry. In high school, he had written an essay on cleptoparasitic bees, which mimic the physical appearance and pheromones of other bees. In this way, the female cleptoparasitic—or cuckoo bee—infiltrates the host's nest and lays her eggs. When they hatch, they attack and kill the entire host bee population.

Brady had just met a human cleptoparasite.

He wanted to vomit.

70

Brady charged through Ben-Gurion Airport, the CSD bag and his case-file satchel bouncing and banging against his hips. He had left the new wheeled luggage, with its store of clothes, where it stood. Speed and agility were priorities now. He spotted Scaramuzzi and slowed his pace. He needed to stay a good distance behind him to avoid detection. He intended to tail him to his car, grab a cab, and follow him. What if he was holding Alicia somewhere besides the embassy? He might go there to check the arrangements, make sure she was secure.

Maybe she's in his car, he thought. One glimpse of her—struggling in the backseat, unconscious in the trunk—and Brady would flag down the airport police, make enough commotion to bring the Israeli army down on their heads. He doubted Scaramuzzi would risk killing Alicia in a crowded parking lot with Brady yelling to wake the dead. If he could rescue her—right here, right now, before Scaramuzzi got her on the embassy's sovereign soil—they would leave, just go home and strategize. Live to fight another day, as Ambrosi had said.

Excited by the idea, he moved too quickly. Before he realized it, he was within thirty feet of his target. If Scaramuzzi turned his head, he would see his pursuer. Brady stopped at a newspaper vending machine, pretended to read the front page through the display window. Scaramuzzi abruptly stepped around a wall and was gone. Brady darted after him. He was nearly running when he rounded the wall and was stopped by a set of stiff, outstretched fingers. They caught him in the chest and he went down, landing on his back. The wind burst from his lungs. He gasped for breath.

Standing over him was a man about fifty. Compact and muscular. Piercing eyes below a bald dome. His face was lean, corded with muscle. He pointed one of his iron-spike fingers at Brady. His straight, lipless mouth bent down. The warning was clear. The man strode away. His legs scissored quickly and precisely; his arms swung stiffly. A soldier's gait. A name from the night before came to Brady's mind: Arjan Vos. Scaramuzzi's chief of security. *Brutal* was the word Ambrosi had used.

People moved in to help. Concerned inquiries in languages he didn't understand. Vertical again, Brady scanned the corridor for Scaramuzzi and Vos—assuming that's who it was. They were gone. He could see that the corridor opened into a hall, beyond which lay the bustle of cabs and buses and private cars. He lowered the CSD case and the satchel to the carpeted floor. He unbuttoned the top of his shirt and pulled it open. Three oval bruises formed a little triangle over his sternum.

His eyes closed, seemingly of their own accord.

What now?

He was expected to pick something up from a man. The something was a file. The man was named Pip. That was all he knew. Had Alicia made arrangements to meet this man, without his knowledge? Unlikely, but it wasn't beneath Alicia to work secretly, independently, if she thought doing so was more expedient than involving him. How would she have learned about him? When did she have a chance to schedule a meeting?

Didn't matter. Whether Alicia knew about Pip or not, he wasn't Alicia. He had to assume Pip would not suddenly appear to him.

Someone shot him in the head.

So Scaramuzzi had Alicia, and he had priced her freedom higher than Brady could pay. He simply did not have the item Scaramuzzi desired. The only option available that he could see was to get into the embassy and get her out. He tried not to think of his chances.

Instead, as he picked up his bags and headed for the shuttle that would take him to his rental car, he thought of his adversary. Through their entire conversation, the man had kept his lips bent in a haughty smile. Brady had never met anyone so comfortable in his own skin, so unabashedly self-assured. He understood how this man could deceive people into believing

he was whoever he said he was, especially if the charisma merely underpinned
a program of claims and fabricated evidence.

A notion slipped into his mind, then was gone. It had been important,
but Brady could not coax it back into the light of his conscious thoughts.
What was it? The conversation with Scaramuzzi. Something wasn't right. He
tried to reconstruct the exchange.

"*Where is she?*"

"*Halfway to Tel Aviv by now.*"

"*Huna!*"

Brady looked up at the shuttle driver. "Huh?"

"A16," the driver said, nodding toward a blue Peugeot.

"Ah . . ." He clambered off, opened the sedan's trunk, dropped in the
two bags, and climbed behind the wheel. Started the engine. Cranked the
AC. Stared out the windshield, not seeing anything but his own dark,
chaotic thoughts.

They started with a single word: *Leave.*

He heard Alicia say, "*You have somebody to go home to. You have someone
who loves you and needs you, and you're determined to live up to your responsibilities to Zach. That's honorable. That's noble.*"

*If I stay, if I try to rescue her, I will die. What will happen to Zach then?
Leave. Alicia would understand. She would want you to do it.*

His hands were gripping the steering wheel so hard, they were starting
to cramp. Perspiration seeped from his palms, dripped onto his thighs. He
squeezed his eyes shut.

In response to Alicia's abduction, the confrontation with Scaramuzzi,
and the challenge to act, his hypothalamus had triggered his "fight or
flight" response. Adrenaline surged through his bloodstream, increasing his
pulse and respiration, routing less blood to the vital organs and more to the
muscles and extremities. His vision was sharper, impulses quicker. He was
more prepared, physically and psychologically, to battle an adversary or run
from the danger than he had been even two minutes before. He sat there,
cold air blowing on his face, and willed himself to calm down. Deep breaths,
in and out.

Leaving Alicia was *not* an option.

Because he was better than that. Because she deserved better than that.

If he left, shame would tear at him until he was nothing but bitter. This time and location would burn in his consciousness as the hour of his most tragic failure, as the place he ceased being a man, ceased being human. The driver who had hit Karen and left her on the side of the road to bleed to death had driven off because he was afraid, afraid his mistake would cost not only the life of an innocent jogger, but his own life as well. Jailed for vehicular homicide. Ten years to life.

How could Brady do worse, after cursing the killer of his wife for eighteen months? What level of hell would leaving Alicia earn him? With his efforts, she had a chance. Without him, she was dead.

His eyes snapped open. He let out a determined roar, one of those Iron John bellows from the deepest part of his soul. He was going to do this.

Priority one: Save Alicia.

Priority two: Take Scaramuzzi down.

He would give his life for the first, and hope for the second.

He shifted into reverse, glanced over his shoulder, and made the tires chirp. Shifted into drive.

"Zach, I wish I had talked to you," he said out loud. He checked his watch. Almost four hours before he was to call back.

Four hours. I can stay alive that long.

The tires chirped again as he slammed down on the accelerator.

71

Brady drove out of the airport complex and ignored the signs for Highway 1—westbound for Tel Aviv, eastbound for Jerusalem. He passed under the highway and continued south. Almost immediately, he was in the town of Lod, an ancient, expanding amalgam of sunbaked, sandblasted brick-and-plaster buildings and gleaming contemporary structures fifteen stories high. Here and there, palm trees arced out of the desert floor like Loch Ness monsters popping up for a gander. He remembered that it was here the apostle Peter was said to have healed a paralyzed man by speaking Jesus' name. He hoped it would prove fruitful for him as well.

He followed Ambrosi's directions on the card he had given Brady in front of the Samson fountain. He found Gidon Gertbu Street and turned west. Except for the predominance of Arabic hash marks that advertised each business, he could have been cruising a 1950s American heartland Main Street. Storefronts made of wood or whitewashed brick. Tall, square facades hiding pitched roofs. Several merchants had set up sidewalk displays of their wares—fruit, grain, what looked to Brady like used Tupperware. Up close, he noticed the paint peeling back like wood shavings and the cracked windows that had been repaired with yellowing tape.

Gidon Gertbu more closely resembled Main Street of the sixties, he corrected himself. When the first generation of youths—the same ones tapped to bloody the soil of Vietnam—realized they were not obligated to stay and tend their fathers' grueling fields. After the beginning of the end for small-town America, but before the boards went up over the windows and the old-timers stopped caring about the dried amaranths tumbling down their streets.

He rolled slowly, rotating his head, trying to catch the gist of each store's trade. Judging by the scarcity of the Western alphabet, the area drew few tourists. After two blocks, he saw what he wanted on the left-hand side of the street: a narrow store with a low rack of books on the sidewalk. On the front window, in white and red paint faded to near-nonexistence, were Hebrew or Arabic letters and the words *Yonatan's Used & Rare Books*.

He paused for a rusty pickup truck to pass in the opposite direction, then turned and parked in front of the bookstore. A bell jangled above the door, and he stepped into air fragranced by aged paper, dust, and something sharper, tangier, that Brady had smelled before but could not place. Bookcases with warped shelves, laden with volumes, lined a room the size of his kitchen back home. An old man sat hunched over a book at a counter directly across the room from the front door. He did not look up.

"Excuse me?" he said to the old man's pink and freckled head.

Slowly the man lifted his gaze. Wispy gray hair puffed out of his lower face. His nose was long and thin and severely beaked; he could have opened cans with it. His eyes, beady and close-set, scanned Brady up and down.

"Do you speak English?" Brady asked.

The man tossed up a hand dismissively. "Ahhh!" he said, as if chasing away a cat. He turned his attention back to the book.

Brady stepped closer. He did not have time for arrogance.

"Hey!" he said loudly.

The ugly bald head moved slightly as the man continued to read.

Brady was about to tap him on the shoulder—hard—when he remembered that Ambrosi had written an introduction or referral on the reverse side of the card that had guided him to this shop. He pulled it out of his pants pocket and laid it on the old man's book, directly under his eyes.

The man stared at it a long while. When he looked up, he was scowling. The hair around his mouth was bent into a deep frown. His eyes held so much loathing, Brady took a step back. The man's hand came up from under the counter. His fingers were bony, with chipped brown fingernails. He nimbly pinched the card with two of them and lifted it. Without a word he turned, dropped from his stool, and pushed through a curtain of beads that covered a doorway behind the counter.

Brady watched the beads swing in the old man's wake. They rattled like seashells in the surf. He had half a mind to follow. Instead, he stepped up to a table. The books stacked on it were all in Middle Eastern languages. He opened one old volume. Hand lettering filled the pages. A diary or a journal. He flipped through the pages. Sandwiched between scrawled paragraphs was a crude drawing of a face, half man, half bear—split vertically down the center. Now he wished he could read the hash marks.

The beads rattled. He turned to see the old man reclaiming his position on the stool. Once again, he stooped over the book. He no longer had the card.

Before Brady could say anything, a man in his late twenties came through the beads. He was handsome, with short-cropped black hair, black eyes, heavy eyebrows. He flashed Brady a winning smile, big white teeth. He practically skipped around the counter, opened his arms as though he expected a hug.

"You are welcome, my friend," the man said as though he meant it. His English was heavily accented.

"Thank you. I—"

The man held out his hand. Brady shook it.

"I am Avi," the man announced.

Brady nodded. He did not think tossing his name around was a wise idea under the circumstances.

Avi seemed to understand. After giving Brady a few seconds to introduce himself, he said, "Nice to meeting you."

Brady tipped his head. "I need—"

Avi interrupted him with raised palms and a sharp clicking of his tongue. He looked around quickly, possibly to make sure some customer dressed entirely in book-patterned clothing wasn't pressed up against one of the bookcases.

"Come," he said, gesturing with one hand. He went around the counter and through the beads.

Beyond the beaded curtain was a room stacked high with cartons. Several were open, and Brady could see books inside them. Two long workbenches appeared outfitted for specific tasks. One contained an assortment of bottles and clothes, a blow-dryer, a feather duster, needle and thread: repair and cleaning, he guessed. The other workstation was more obvious. Bubble envelopes, a postal scale, a postage meter, pages of labels. Hanging from the ceiling above the table was an enormous clear plastic bag of Styrofoam peanuts, pinched closed at the bottom with a clothespin.

"We ship world over," Avi explained. "Our mail order sells . . . uh . . . outsells our retail ten times to one."

"Books?" Brady asked.

Avi's grin stretched wider. "Mostly."

He opened a door, stepped through. The room they entered was barren by comparison. Floor-to-ceiling cabinets, doubtless made on the spot, lined one wall. Padlocks on all of them. A large workbench occupied the center of the room. Over it hung a bare bulb, lighted, with a metal coned hood and a coiled yellow tube—Brady recognized it as a compressed-air hose. A single metal chair was pushed back from the workbench. A tarp the size of a beach towel covered something on the workbench that could have been a model of a mountain range. The odd odor Brady had caught in the store was much stronger here, and he knew what it was: gun oil.

"Would you please . . . ?" Avi motioned toward the far side of the workbench. He put his fingers under the near side and hefted it. Only the top came up.

Brady lifted his end. It was heavy. He saw it was a board that had been laid over the work surface of the bench. Avi indicated two sawhorses near the back wall. They shuffled over to them, balanced the board across them. Avi lifted the tarp so Brady could see.

"What do you think?"

It was a huge machine gun. A tight grouping of six three-foot barrels jutted from an open metal box. Sprockets and screws lay all around it.

"GEC Minigun," Avi said with pleasure. "Seven-point-six-two NATO rounds. The barrel spins"—he twirled his index finger—"like a . . . a . . ."

"Gatling?" Brady offered.

"Gatling, yes! But with electric. Fires six thousand rounds in single minute. Something in front of you—no more. Okay. You take. Enjoy."

Brady just stared.

Avi laughed and waved a hand at him. "Ha-ha, no. Just kidding." He let the tarp fall over the gun. "For a very special customer. In South America. You don't want it anyway. Needs a helicopter or tank. Or Arnold Schwarzenegger." He laughed again. As he did, he hinged open the top of the workbench. It went a little farther than straight up, then stopped. The interior of the shallow box underneath was lined in black velvet, upon which was arranged an assortment of weapons—rifles, submachine guns, pistols, knives, swords, throwing stars, a crossbow, a compound bow, a recurve.

"What do you have in mind for?"

"Just a pistol."

Ave nodded. "Revolver or semiautomatic?"

"I'm used to a semiautomatic."

"Then same here." He picked up a big black gun. "Beretta 92FS. Sidearm choice of U.S. military. Nine millimeter. Thirty-four ounces, unloaded. Three-dot sight. This one with laser grip." He straight-armed it toward the wall, did something with his thumb, and a red dot appeared against the plaster. It danced around as he jiggled his hand. He flipped off the laser and set the gun back on the velvet. He selected another.

"Taurus PT25. Small weight, twelve ounces. Twenty-five caliber. Not best for takedown, but backup good." He showed how the barrel tipped forward. "Quick load."

He replaced it, considered the others.

"You know, anything will do," said Brady. He felt the seconds ticking away. "How about the—" His eyes stopped on a black cylinder. "Is that a silencer?"

"Sound suppressor," Avi corrected. He picked it up. "Very nice. The coils keep quiet twenty rounds before needing replace."

"What will it fit on?"

"I . . . uh . . ." He twirled his finger again, tighter.

"Turned?"

He shook his head. "Machined! I *machined* single barrel for it, so far, but very good, absolutely." He lifted a small gray semiauto. "Kimber Ultra RCP—refine carry pistol. Modeled after the Colt 1911, but smaller, smoother. Forty-five caliber. Big punch." He screwed the silencer into the barrel, handed it to Brady, butt first.

Brady pulled back on the slide to verify it was unloaded. He held it out as if he were shooting. Running the length of the barrel was a circular groove.

"No sights," he said.

"A 'sighting trench' takes place. Hard to learn . . . uh . . . get used to. No can focus on front sight. No front sight! Close-quarters action, it does not matter."

Brady thought of working his way into the Italian Embassy. Mostly offices. Some corridors, but he could avoid them. He nodded. "How much?"

"Two thousand, American."

Brady winced.

"Tell you something," Avi said. "I will put in a holster, box of ammo, and this . . ." He held up a gray-handled knife in a black sheath with two short Velcro straps dangling from it.

"I don't need a knife."

"You never can know," Avi cautioned. "This one go right here . . ." He slapped his ankle. "Very nice."

Brady appraised the handgun. He imagined pressing the extended barrel to Scaramuzzi's forehead.

"Throw in binoculars," he said, "and we have a deal."

The buildings of Tel Aviv began rising out of the desert after Brady had been on Highway 1 only a few minutes. They shimmered in the heat, seeming to form from the moisture in the air.

He thought about Asia House. Ambrosi had said it housed several foreign embassies. It was the site of Prime Minister Santo Mucci's assassination. To make that hit, Scaramuzzi had breached it, probably by exploiting the inherent weaknesses of buildings occupied by multiple tenants. Common areas would have the weakest security. That might have changed after Mucci's assassination, but five years was enough time for people to forget and for tightened procedures to loosen again. There would be metal detectors at the lobby doors. He held no delusions about getting the pistol into the building that way. He hoped a quick reconnaissance would give him new ideas about the gun and getting to Alicia.

Halfway to Tel Aviv by now.

Brady slammed on the brakes. The wheels locked. He managed to swerve onto the shoulder amid a streaking blare of car horns. He pressed against the seat belt, then dropped back hard when the Peugeot finally came to a shuddering stop. A second later gray smoke enveloped the car, reeking of burned rubber. It drifted on, dispersing in a light breeze.

He got it, what was bugging him.

Everything about Scaramuzzi was deceptive. He had mentioned Tel Aviv twice—by name and indirectly by implying that Alicia would be held at the Italian Embassy there. Just in case Brady attempted to do what he was going to do. Ambrosi had explained Scaramuzzi maintained a public headquarters and a secret one. He wouldn't risk tainting his reputation, his politi-cal rise by bringing an abducted FBI agent to his embassy.

He had taken her to Jerusalem, to his covert hideaway.

On the chance Brady showed up at Asia House with the file, Scaramuzzi's men could quietly murder him and take it; no need for Alicia to be there. Or they could make a show of killing him and claim he was a deluded assassin; even the Bureau might back them up on the deluded part. If Brady demanded to see Alicia before exchanging her for the file, Jerusalem was fifty minutes away; she could be sent for. Maybe Scaramuzzi had been planning on redirecting Brady to Jerusalem all along. Ambush him en route or do it leisurely on his own turf, but where public eyes weren't focused on him.

Brady saw a narrow opening in the traffic, cranked the wheel, and stomped on the gas. The Peugeot fishtailed around, cut straight across the road, and plunged into the shallow, grassy depression that separated the westbound lanes from the eastbound. The front bumper plowed into the ris-ing hill on the other side and tossed soil and sod into the air. It rained down on the sedan, sounding like a barrage of BBs. For five seconds, Brady's only view was of the shifting dirt that covered his windshield. He fumbled fran-tically with levers and buttons until the wipers engaged. Through the glass he saw sky, baby blue and unadorned. Then the Peugeot's front end crested the incline and plunged down onto the asphalt. A white vehicle, all grille and glass, was shooting toward the right side of the Peugeot. Its front end dipped sharply as the driver obviously tried to push the brake pedal through the floor. Brady caught a glimpse of an oval face with grotesquely round eyes and the black "O" of a mouth that he suspected was emitting a screech to put the tires to shame.

The Peugeot's rear wheels thumped onto the highway and immediately followed the front ones into the farthest lane. The white vehicle squealed past it, missing the bumper by a finger's breadth. Brady cranked the wheel and stomped the gas. The Peugeot whipped around, aligned itself with a white line, and shot forward. In the rearview, cars were braking hard and jutting off in all directions, trying to avoid the accelerating Peugeot and the stalled white vehicle, which Brady now saw was a utility van. The horns again, fading quickly as Brady brought the speedometer needle up to seventy kilometers . . . eighty . . . ninety.

The maneuver not only got him moving in what he was certain was the right direction, but it would help thwart or reveal anyone tailing him. He checked the mirrors and did not see any vehicles attempting the same U-turn he had made. No flashing lights either. Maybe his luck was turning.

Someone was inside her head, pounding mallets against the backs of her eyes. Her brain flexed against the confines of her skull. Her eyelids flickered, opened. Gray all around her, swirling, congealing into shapes. A dim bulb in a wire basket. Stone ceiling.

Alicia stared up at it, waiting for the throbbing in her head to subside. She was lying on her back, on something softer than the floor, but not a bed.

The air was chilly, damp. And the smell . . . One of the many trips her mother had taken her on had been to Limerick, Ireland. There they visited Bunratty Castle, built on the site of a tenth-century Viking trading camp. It had seen great battles between Irish chieftains and the Normans and English. According to the tour guide—an elfish young woman whose lilt had mesmerized ten-year-old Alicia—it was the most complete and authentic medieval castle in Ireland. The basement, which had at various times served as storehouse, armory, and prison, had been filled with the redolence of stone and something else. At the time, she could not describe it. Now, with that scent in her nostrils again, she knew what it was: antiquity, as though the walls had absorbed time itself.

"Aspirin?"

Alicia jumped. She snapped her head toward the voice. The man who had addressed her at the airport—

Alicia, Alicia, it's nice to meet cha.

—was sitting on a cot, watching her.

She sat up. The movement brought a fresh bolt of pain to her head. She closed her eyes, felt her own cot spinning beneath her. She took a deep breath. Her mouth was dry and metallic tasting. She opened one eye, then the other.

The man was perched on the edge of the cot, not three feet from her. He held out a hand, palm up, offering three white pills. In his other hand was a plastic bottle. He nodded at the pills.

"They're aspirin. Really. If I wanted to give you anything else, I already would have." His smile was confident and at the same time disarming.

She took the pills. He handed her the bottle. It was springwater, unopened. She drank half of it, then squinted at him.

"You're Luco Scaramuzzi."

"You're Alicia Wagner."

She surveyed her surroundings. An eight-foot-square room. Stone walls on three sides. Iron bars on the fourth. A door, composed entirely of bars as well, stood open. Eight feet beyond the bars was another wall. Dark openings left and right, as though the corridor was U-shaped with this single cell at the nadir.

"Where am I?" she said, eyeing the open door.

"My home away from home," Scaramuzzi said pleasantly. "We're among a mind-achingly complex labyrinth of tunnels. If somehow you were to get out of this little suite I've set up for you, the chances of finding your way out are zilch, particularly now. I'm having a little get-together. Lots of my friends milling around, just looking for ways to impress me. Dragging your corpse to me would do that."

He said it as nonchalantly as a bored waiter reciting the day's specials.

"So why haven't you killed me yet?" She glared at him, defiant.

"Your partner hasn't delivered Pip's file."

"Pip who? What file?"

Scaramuzzi's smile did not falter, but she saw a ripple of puzzlement cross his face.

"Pippino Farago. Of course, he would have used a different name, if any at all."

"To do what?"

"To contact you. To offer you the ammunition you needed to come after me. I'm not surprised *you* thought it would work, though Pip's naïveté is startling."

She stared at him, uncomprehending.

"And Brady is supposed to get this file for you?" she asked.

"In exchange for your life. Who said heroism was dead?"

She sized him up. Athletic build. Broad shoulders, narrow waist. His short sleeves showed off toned arm muscles. He outweighed her by eighty, a hundred pounds, all of it muscle. Still, if he was like most workout freaks, his build was all form, no function. Did he practice martial arts? Was he adept at hand-to-hand combat? What she knew about him didn't cover his fighting skills. But Ambrosi had said he had prepared for years to step into the role of Antichrist. In his place, she would have trained to handle physical as well as intellectual threats. She should assume he knew how to defend himself and attack an enemy.

"Too bad you did not include information about your contact with him in your notes," he continued. "It would have saved me a lot of trouble." He clicked his nails against something on the cot beside him.

She saw he was resting a hand on her laptop. Her heart bounced into her throat. What had he found out? She had typed up everything Ambrosi had told them. Had she exposed Father Randall as the inadvertent mole he was? If he was helping Scaramuzzi, did she care? Certainly, losing that link to the inner machinations of Scaramuzzi's circle would be a devastating blow to Ambrosi. Worse, her notes gave Scaramuzzi plenty of reasons to go after Ambrosi, either out of revenge or to eliminate a foe with too much knowledge.

"Ah, well," he said, lifting the computer, tucking it under his arm as he rose. "Maybe it's here somewhere, yes? I had only a little time to browse in the car on the way here."

"Where is here?"

"Under Jerusalem, the Christian quarter." He glanced up and around, as though at the splendor of a cathedral. "A fine place to die, really." He stepped out of the cell, swung the door closed. It clanged loudly and echoed. She heard an electronic beep.

She got to her feet. The floor tilted under her, and she sat again. Her head had taken on the weight of an anvil. She lowered it into her hand, then propped her arm on her thigh.

"Why us?" she said without looking.

"Agent Moore asked the same thing," he said. He sounded amused.

"What did you tell him?"

"That the two of you showed up."

She lifted her head to see him. "What does that mean?"

He watched her through the bars a long moment. Then he glanced around furtively, as though contemplating or listening. He touched a keypad that was apparently set into the front of the door. Metal and stone were still as impenetrable as they were a millennia ago; not so for ancient locking mechanisms. It beeped three times, then the bolt within thunked. Scaramuzzi came back in and took his place on the cot opposite hers. He leaned over, closing the gap between them.

"From your notes, I gather you understand the somewhat fragile nature of my relationship with the Watchers." His voice was low, conspiratorial.

She nodded.

"Even among the Council, I have enemies, those who expend considerable resources and energy to discredit me." He shrugged. "I appreciate that their efforts are part of a process designed to ensure that only the rightful heir claims the inheritance with which the Watchers have been entrusted. But I think the safeguards have been refined over the centuries to the point where not even the one whose rise to power was foretold could get past them."

"And you are that one?" she said. She managed to keep her cynicism out of her tone.

His eyebrows went up. "Of course. Jesus Christ was who He said He was, as well, but nobody believed Him either. At least not enough to save Him from crucifixion. Don't you think if He had tried a little harder, He could have convinced more people, the people who mattered?"

"The Pharisees?"

"The Pharisees," he agreed. "The ones who were supposed to be watching for the Messiah. And they blew it. They didn't recognize Him." He shrugged. "Naturally, I don't want the same thing to happen to me."

"You being Antichrist?"

He gave her a small bow.

"So you're trying to convince them. How?"

"By bringing them evidence. Some prophecy previously overlooked that I fulfilled. Just as Jesus fulfilled prophecy and performed miracles to prove who He was."

She was finding it harder to remain composed. "What miracles have *you* performed?"

He appeared disappointed, a teacher whose student wasn't getting it.

"None . . . yet. Are you familiar with Antichrist prophecy?"

"I'm learning."

"'And he performed great and miraculous signs, even causing fire to come down from heaven to earth in full view of men.' Revelation 13. That's me, my future. I can't wait."

He's serious, she realized. It was in his eyes. He wasn't acting or lying.

"What does that have to do with us, Brady and me?"

"Where Jesus went wrong was always having an audience. No one ever stumbled onto Him in a field alone levitating sheep." He shook his head. "Uh-uh, He had to feed the five thousand and raise Lazarus with a mob of mourners outside the tomb."

When he didn't continue, she said, "And . . . ?"

"And because He always had an audience, His miracles looked planned. Staged with the intention of impressing the crowd. That's what the Pharisees thought, I'm sure. I have the same problem. I need to convince my Council, but the very act of my bringing them evidence undermines that evidence."

"They need to find their own proof," Alicia said, summarizing.

"Exactly. Either of my being who I say I am—which is not such an easy task, since almost all the prophecy is already on the table and everyone knows about it—or of my *sincerity.*"

"They have to know you're not scamming them."

"I knew you were smart, coming as close to finding me as you did."

She risked voicing her thoughts: "So being insane is better than being a con artist?"

Didn't faze him. "An insane person couldn't function under the intense scrutiny I'm under."

"An insane person could function better. No pressure."

"Then we should all be insane. Barring that, proof of my sincerity would go a long way toward securing my colleagues' confidence."

"Okay."

"What better way to do that than their finding out I acted on a prophecy for my own selfish motives? Not for show, because it was hidden from them."

She shook her head.

"I have a marvelous theologian who finds prophecy that fits my life. He also works with the Council's theologians. He gets a peek at what they're working on. A few months ago, he came to me with a prophecy they'd stumbled onto. From the prophetess Priscilla, I believe: 'The one who carries the flames of the pit shall lay down the man of sin.' Apparently, in Priscilla's time—the first century—'carry' was a euphemism for memory or 'having seen.' 'Lay down' means kill. Of course, the pit is hell, and I . . . well, I am the man of sin."

He smiled at Alicia's skewed expression. "Prophecy is like that. Exegesis. Every word analyzed—by itself, in textual context, in historic context, in relation to other known prophecies. It's a wonder anyone understands anything about it or that theologians ever reach a consensus. For the Priscilla prophecy, the Council's theologians are in the process of trying to find corroboration in prophetic writings and analyses—from Montanus and Tertullian, for example—and the symbolic language of Daniel or John. As it stands, the prophecy can be translated as: 'Antichrist will be killed by someone who has seen hell.'"

"Hell? How can—" Then she got it. At least a part of it. "Hellish near-death experiences," she said. "You're killing people who claimed to have seen hell in a near-death experience. Because of a prophecy no one is sure about."

"The prophecy will be confirmed. They nearly all are, those that have reached this level of investigation. But even if it is not," he said, "it will have suited my purpose."

"I don't understand," she said.

"The Council needs only to think that *I* believed it and that I attempted to act on it covertly, without their knowledge. They would logically assume that my action was not predicated on impressing them, but on protecting myself from a prophesied threat. Therefore, I must truly be who I say I am. Or at minimum believe it myself."

"Making you either Antichrist or insane, but not a con artist."

"I can't tell you how much easier my job will be once *that* is out of the way."

She tried to follow the scheme from beginning to end. As she encountered obstacles, she slowly articulated them.

"But the plan would require their finding out what you're doing, without you bringing it to their attention—even while you try to conceal it from them."

Scaramuzzi nodded. He watched her working it out.

"A lot of attention, media attention," she said.

His lips stretched wolfishly.

She said, "Which even serial killings don't guarantee anymore. But which the killing of the FBI agents investigating the case would." Her eyes snapped to his for verification.

He faked a shiver and said, "Oooh . . . smart. I had to attack quickly, before your team caught my man in the field."

"Your killer." Her voice was hard, sharp.

"The sensational murders of two FBI agents would concentrate unprecedented attention of the case they were working, the serial killings. The NDE link would come out."

"Do your Council members know about the prophecy yet?"

"No, their theologians only bring them new prophecies when they've been confirmed, or when my theologian presents something they need to independently corroborate. And that adds to the appearance of my trying to operate under their radar."

"But one of the theologians would undoubtedly hear about the murders of endears and—"

"Of who?"

He didn't know the term. He had not spoken to Father McAfee the way she had. He had only used him to develop a hit list.

"Endears," she said. "N-D-E-ers. One of the theologians would hear of their murders and report the 'coincidence' to the Council, who would investigate and find you."

"That's one line of communication. Redundancy improves the probability of success. I also made sure to use your country's Office of Contingency Planning. The OCP was founded by one of the Watchers' forebears. We enjoy a very . . . *symbiotic* relationship. They too would contact the Council about the deaths of two agents they recently assisted in locating. The Council would, as you said, find me behind the killings and determine that I must be genuine if I am attempting to destroy the one prophesied to destroy me."

"And doing it covertly," she added, still trying to comprehend the complexity of Scaramuzzi's plan—and its sheer wickedness.

"They, of course, would talk me out of continuing such a blind assault on so many people. When King Herod heard that magi had come to honor the birth of the prophesied Messiah, he ordered the death of all boys two and younger in Bethlehem and its vicinity. An atrocious slaughter, and for nothing; Joseph and Mary fled to Egypt with the baby Jesus, and Herod missed his target. The wise way of handling this newly revealed prophecy about me is to wait until enemies show themselves, then find out which one or ones died and were resuscitated."

Talking as if it were true.

He continued: "I'll have to convince the Watchers my judgment was clouded by passion and concern. A small blow to my reputation for managing the resources they've entrusted to me. A small price for the confidence in me it buys."

"So Brady and I were just flares to light up the serial killings? And the killings were staged to make you appear concerned about a prophecy?"

Scaramuzzi squinted in thought. Then he nodded and said, "Yes."

He stood. Conversation over.

Alicia wanted to hurl herself at him, to get her hands around his neck and not let go until one of them was dead. A wave of nausea and dizziness kept her down.

He stepped out and shut the door. It clanged and beeped. His smile said he was enjoying her dumbfounded anger.

"Don't feel bad," he said insincerely. "People die all the time for more frivolous reasons. Whole battalions destroyed trying to take a hill because some general thought the maneuver sounded impressive, something he'd read back in his war-college days."

He walked toward one of the corridors, stopped, and turned back to her. "At least *you* know why you have to die."

13

The binoculars were cheap and underpowered, but from the roof of the Gloria Hotel a block away, Brady could make out the identifiers Ambrosi had described. A sloping drive on the south side of the Latin Patriarchate. A wall shielding it from the activity in the seminary's front yard. Immediately to the right of the drive was the Old City wall, rising up, then dropping off into rubble and trees before Jaffa Road and modern Jerusalem took over the terrain. The drive was very private and nondescript; it could have been a utility-access alley, which is what most of the students and faculty probably believed it was. From his five-story perch, Brady was able to view straight down the drive to where the pavement leveled out. He could not see the metal door Ambrosi said was there, leading into a walled-off portion of the seminary's basement and the tunnels underneath. The seminary building was constructed with yellow-gold Jerusalem stone. It was a handsome finish, but its rectangular shape and small, evenly spaced windows gave it the appearance of a prison.

He watched as a figure walked down the drive from the seminary's main parking lot. It paused at the bottom, pulled open a door. When it shut, the figure was gone. The pause meant the door was kept locked.

Brady scoped the vicinity. The drive terminated in a concrete wall roughly ten feet high, which brought the top of the wall to ground level. Bushes overhung the edge.

Leaving the binoculars behind, he pocketed a few pebbles from the roof and descended the stairs to the lobby. He bought a pack of gum from the hotel's gift shop and nodded to the front desk clerk on his way out. He walked briskly up Latin Patriarchate Street until he was in its parking lot. Moving casually, he made it to the last row, twenty yards from the drive's entrance. Elms as tall as the four-story seminary shaded the entire south side of the lot.

He felt cloaked in shadows, but he knew from his own surveillance it was a false security; pedestrians under the trees were darkened but completely visible. A minivan pulled into the lot. He pretended to search his pockets for keys as it cruised past slowly. It pulled into a slot a dozen vehicles closer to the seminary's main doors. Three young men in their early twenties climbed out. They were dressed identically, in dark slacks, white shirts, black ties. They headed for the doors, never glancing Brady's way.

When they were gone, Brady walked to the far side of the drive. He stepped over a dying bush and stood between the drive and the Old City wall. The drive dropped away as he headed for its terminus. He could see the metal door now. Wide and black, with rivets. Heavy looking, like a vault. A keypad was mounted to the stone beside it. Five, six feet.

He reached the drive's back wall. The Old City wall angled in, arcing past the rear of the seminary. The ground here was sodded and trimmed with billowing bushes. The drive was wide enough to accommodate a truck, which would doubtless back down to unload freight. With a quick glance around—no one watching—Brady dropped to his knees, then to his belly behind the bushes. He reached back, touched the butt of the Kimber pistol in a belt holster at the small of his back. At least it had not fallen out: Avi had given him the only holster he had that was open at the bottom so the silencer could slip through, and it fit the Kimber poorly. He opened the pack of gum and stuck two pieces in his mouth.

He waited. Five minutes . . . ten . . . He examined the bandages wrapped around his left hand. They were frayed and dirty and bore a heavy stripe of brown blood over the palm. He closed his hand, opened it. No pain, just pressure, as though a string were wrapped around it too tightly. Still, he was thankful that he had damaged his left hand. His right was his gun hand, and on a *good* day he wouldn't bet on his marksmanship. He *had* nailed Malik—in the shoulder, when he had been aiming center-mass, but hey, the guy was dead and he wasn't. A thought to hold on to as he went forward.

Footsteps on the drive.

Brady pulled back. He parted the branches. Two men coming down the drive, one carrying a box. They were conversing—something funny by their smiles and chuckles—but Brady didn't know the language. They stopped at the door, and the empty-handed man punched a code into the keypad. Too quick for Brady to see. The man pulled open the door and held it until his companion walked through. Then he followed and the door began shutting slowly, as Brady had seen it do through the binoculars. A hydraulic door-shutter attached to the jamb and top of the door made sure the door latched after each opening, but it took its sweet time.

Brady rose to a crouch, stepped over the bushes, grabbed hold of the top of the wall, and swung himself down. He dropped to the pavement, landing on tiptoe. Two seconds later, he had his chest and cheek pressed to the wall beside the door, which had fifteen inches left before it was sealed.

Voices came through the opening. Close.

Brady pulled two pebbles from his pocket, held them to his mouth, and pushed the gum onto them. He kneaded the wad, satisfied at its size and the firmness the pebbles gave it. Without looking, he slipped his hand around the edge of the doorjamb.

No yells . . . yet.

He used his pinky to locate the recess for the door's latch. Stuck in the wad. Retracted his hand.

If a light on the inside confirmed the successful closing and locking of the door, and if the people using it were disciplined enough to watch for it, well, then he'd be up a creek. Security systems were only as effective as the people using them, however, and time begot complacency. He was counting on that now.

The door shut. Didn't click, didn't beep.

He waited thirty seconds. When he pulled on the handle, it held firm. His stomach clenched. He tugged. With a quiet *snick*, the door opened. He quick-peeked around the jamb, saw no one. He stepped in, holding the door with his foot. No keypad on the inside, a press bar on the door. It was designed to keep people out, not in. He dug the gum and pebbles out of the bolt slot, tossed the wad outside.

The room was dim, lighted only by an exit sign over the door. He waited for his eyes to adjust. Musty odor in the air, and rust. Slowly, a room the size of a convenience store came into view. Concrete and stone. An old, monstrous boiler, a matching furnace, and assorted other equipment hunkered like stealthy beasts in the shadows on the far half of the room. Closer to him, crusty paint cans, wooden crates, and lawn tools appeared to have come here to die. The setup reminded Brady of an attraction at Disney World: very well staged. However, nothing lay between him and a door set in the left-hand wall. It was also metal, but rusty and dented. A breaker box was set into the wall beside it.

He went to the door, felt around the edge. A tight seal, despite its appearance. Behind the breaker box door, he found a keypad, its rubber buttons lighted from behind.

A rumbling, as much felt as heard.

He stepped back, thinking the old door was about to burst open. Then he realized the sound was coming from the other door, from outside. The squeak of brakes. A truck had come down the drive. He hurried to the boiler, stepped behind it. The darkness was complete here. The outside door opened wide. The sunlight was blinding. The hazy silhouette of a man filled the opening, then backed away. A chain rattled. Doors creaked on their hinges, banged against the truck's metal sides. The whirl of a small motor—a hydraulic lift.

A single sharp sound that made Brady's skin tighten on his muscles: a bark, deep and vicious.

A man snapped, "Freya!"

Brady backed farther behind the boiler. He squatted down, closed his eyes. No reason he should come to the conclusion he did, but he knew, he simply *knew*: They were here. They had followed him.

Clanging, banging outside.

The same sharp voice: "Careful!"

A muttered apology.

Brady rose and peered between two pipes.

The man walked in, at first only a stocky figure backlit by the sun coming through the opening. He strode to the breaker box, opened it. Brady could make out the knit wool shirt, the fur shawl over massive shoulders, the long, stringy hair. His head turned as the inner door clicked open. An ice cube formed in Brady's heart, chilling his blood. The Viking.

Another man came in, pulling a metal cart. Its wheels clacked over the threshold. The cart carried four dog kennels, the kind used to transport large dogs in airplane cargo holds. Plastic, with holes in the upper halves of the sides. Chrome-plated grille doors.

The light faded as the door slowly closed.

The dogs began growling. One barked. The others joined in. In seconds, they were snarling and snapping and yelping as though fighting over a downed animal.

The Viking held up a hand to halt the man pulling the cart. He looked in at the dogs and pushed his finger into one of the door grilles.

"Er eitthvað að?" he said.

He turned to face the boiler, took a step forward. He stopped, slowly panning his gaze over all the equipment.

"Rats," the man said with an Italian accent. The word came out "Rrrratsa." "Sometimes cats get in, chasing 'em."

The Viking did not move. After fifteen seconds, he looked back at the dogs, which were still in a frenzy.

"Hættu ?essu!" he said. Four sharp syllables.

The animals immediately quieted. One whimpered, then it too fell silent.

Again he faced the boiler. He whispered, *"Er einhver hér?"* Louder, he said, "Give me a flashlight."

The other man, frustrated: "I don't *have* one. *Affrettarsi!* Arjan is waiting!"

The Viking walked forward. Brady carefully lowered himself to the floor until he was flat against it. He edged his body close to the base of the boiler. It was gritty and greasy and smelled like burned meat. He wiggled farther in, willing himself to meld into the metal. He thought of the promise he'd made on the way to the Oakleys'—Zach's words: *"And you won't let that guy and his dogs get you. Okay?"*

Okay, Zach. I'm trying, buddy.

Footsteps. The Viking stopped at the back wall. He looked into the long space behind the equipment, scanning over Brady. The man squinted, moved his head around. It came to Brady that the man was considering stepping into the space, walking along the back wall behind the equipment, just to be sure. He thought of the pistol and wondered how much movement he could get away with. Why hadn't he drawn it earlier? His hands were fisted under his chest. He slid the right one out . . . slowly . . . leaves change color faster.

"Olaf? *Affrettarsi!*"

The Viking—Olaf?—grunted, turned, and stalked away.

"Let's go!" he ordered.

The front wheels of the cart banged over the next threshold.

Brady rose and peeked between the pipes. A faint light radiated out from the passageway beyond the rusty door. The rear of the cart was sticking out. The Italian pulled it slowly, in little stops and starts.

"*Vaffanculo!*" he snapped.

Something was preventing the cart from rolling smoothly.

"Move," the man called Olaf said from deeper inside. "I'll pull it in." Suddenly the cart lurched forward. Its rear wheels bounced over the threshold. The door began closing.

Brady slipped out from behind the boiler, ran softly to the door, pressed up against the wall beside it. He looked. A low-wattage bulb hanging from a wire cast a dingy luminance onto the walls of a room, roughly hammered from the hardpan. Thirty feet from floor to ceiling. The door lay high in the wall, near the ceiling. An expanded metal catwalk slanted gently down from the door, stopping at a doorless exit from the room. Rails on each side kept users from tumbling off the catwalk. The cart's steel wheels were not turning, but sliding over the grated walkway, protesting loudly.

The kennels kept Olaf and the Italian from Brady's view. Which meant he was equally shielded from them. Crouching, he crossed the threshold onto the catwalk. One of the dogs started a low, sustained growl. Brady slipped over the edge and held on, dangling high above the floor in case one of the men looked back. He heard the door click shut above him. His damaged hand began throbbing, then throwing out electric currents of pain. Perspiration beaded on his forehead. A drop slid into his eye. He closed it. His other eye witnessed a dark rivulet run from his palm to his wrist, where a drop grew fat and fell. It splattered on his forehead.

He heard the cart's wheels come off the catwalk, one pair at a time, and felt the walk rattle with relief.

"Take it," Olaf said. The word echoed faintly.

Wheels squeaked away, fading.

Brady hoisted himself up and onto the catwalk. He wiped his brow with his forearm. Grimacing, he saw the bandages over his palm were soaked red. He turned to face the tunnel, and his heart skipped a beat. Carved deeply into the stone above the entrance was a large sun symbol—Scaramuzzi's swastika, Ambrosi had called it. Residing at the mouth of Scaramuzzi's lair, it could have been a warning. With cold resolve, he drew the gun and pulled back on the slide until he saw the brass of a bullet in the chamber. He flicked off the safety. Filling his lungs, he headed down the catwalk toward the tunnels.

74

Right or left? The stone floor left no clue of previous foot traffic. No scuff marks or disturbed dirt. Along the ceiling in both directions was a wire with lighted bulbs spaced too far apart to adequately illuminate the tunnel. The slightest sound reverberated off the walls, making it impossible to discern the direction of its source. The distant rumble of the cart he had watched enter could be coming from either direction.

Brady went left.

The tunnel had a gentle downward slope and curved lazily one way, then the other, as though the workers making it had continually veered off course and corrected. Brady's steps were too loud in his ears, broadcasting his presence and inhibiting his own ability to listen for approaching footsteps or noises that would help him find his way. After failing to tread more quietly by tiptoeing and slowing his pace, he removed his shoes and carried them with two fingers of his left hand.

About a hundred paces in, he came to a passageway branching off to the right. He peered around the corner. After a few feet, the surfaces of this new tunnel disappeared into opaque blackness. Air breathed out from it and cooled the perspiration on his face. He looked farther up the lighted tunnel. Just more of the same.

Lights or a breeze? he thought. *The lights are there for a reason. But doesn't a breeze indicate an opening, maybe an air shaft ventilating an occupied section?*

Brady liked that logic best and stepped into the dark tunnel. The slope here was steeper, forcing a quicker gait. He held his pistol near his face, pointing up—a position known in law enforcement as a half-Sabrina, after the favorite pose of Kate Jackson's character in *Charlie's Angels* (she held her gun in *two* hands, and thus a *full* Sabrina). This allowed him to cock out his elbow and skip it against the wall, keeping himself oriented in the lightless tunnel. Occasionally the wall dropped away where other passageways met his. Sometimes he would sense a change in the nature of the breeze and discover a passageway on the other side. He always paused at these openings and attempted to discern new odors or sounds or light emanating from them. Each passage seemed as anonymous as his own did, so he continued without turning.

Finally, he realized he was able to see the most negligible aspects of the tunnel: the faint shape of jutting stone, the darker shadow of an intersecting passageway. Light, however faint, was seeping in from somewhere. The tunnel curved and the darkness gradually eased into twilight. He followed the curve and stopped. A hundred yards farther, the tunnel opened into a lighted room. He fought the urge to run. Instead, he approached cautiously, as close to the wall as he could get without brushing against it.

The room was not bright, as he had thought; it only seemed to be, compared to the sightlessness of the tunnel. A few feet from the room's entrance, he swept his eyes across the visible portion, switched to the other side of the tunnel, scoped out much of the rest. He quick-peeked around the area closest to him, left and right, then stepped in. The light source was a bulb under an aluminum hood up high in the center of the room. The ceiling arced up on stone ribs to a height of about thirty feet. The room was an octagonal chamber. Each wall contained an arched portal into a dark passageway. The sound of faint hammering drifted from at least one of the passages, but he could not tell from which. Voices, hauntingly indistinct, rose and fell in volume but even at their loudest were no more than a wind's whisper. Maybe they were nothing more than his own pulse in his ears.

Brady felt his strength sag. He sighed and let his shoulder slump. He was getting a sense of the task ahead. Not Alicia's actual rescue; merely the finding of her. There seemed to be miles and miles of tunnels, branching in every direction. The probability of finding the precise passage to Alicia seemed infinitesimal.

He paced the circumference of the chamber, hoping to pick up a clue as he passed each portal. He returned to the center of the room and realized he did not know which passage he had come from. Going back to each one, he found three that sloped up; any of them could have been the one he had used to get there. Of the remaining five—three had flat floors, two sloped down—he chose one at random. He placed a pebble in the threshold. He checked his watch. Too bad it wasn't one of those adventure instruments, with a compass.

He walked straight for four minutes and found a passage lighted by a string of bare bulbs. He had no idea whether this was the same tunnel he had entered first. He followed it, ignoring other tunnels, some lighted, some black as paint. The tunnels he passed varied widely. Many were narrower— the worst would have required shuffling sideways through them. Several were broad alleys but no more promising than the others. Some boasted finely finished surfaces, either polished to a sheen or ornamented with intricate trefoils, columns, and arches; others appeared hacked out with crude tools. A pool of water filled the floor of one roughly hewn tunnel. Brady assumed the different designs and levels of completion reflected the subterranean ambitions of various sovereignties throughout the ages.

Twenty minutes after leaving the octagonal chamber, he came to another one, identical to the first. Though he had made only one ninety-degree turn, and the passageway had bent only slightly, he checked for the pebble he had left. He didn't find it. This time, three of the passages were lighted. He chose one of them, deposited two pebbles—one to mark where he'd been and one for where he was going—and trudged on.

Tunnels everywhere. He got the sense that at times there were tunnels running parallel to one another, a handbreadth of stone between them. He suspected the rise and fall of the tunnel floors allowed them to go over and under one another. The maze played with shadow and sound as if they were pliable things outside the boundaries of physics and reason. Corridors that appeared short took five minutes to traverse. A tunnel that appeared to extend forever could as likely stop at a wall hidden in the gloom, forcing him to backtrack. At times, voices came to him from intersecting passages. Usually the words sounded foreign, but once he was certain he recognized the word "sincere" and the phrase "two of a kind." Each time he headed in their direction, all sounds—even the occasional clank or hammering he was getting used to—would evaporate, and he was left yet again wondering which way to go.

He was crossing a short conduit between two lighted tunnels when a new sound froze him solid. A single bark. Immediately it became a cacophony of yips and snarls. Loud . . . close . . . coming around the corner. Then they broke apart, like mist in a crosswind. Brady glared at the corner, visible only as a line between gray and black. He blinked, suddenly uncertain that he had heard anything at all. The dog sounds had come and gone too quickly to be real. But how could he have imagined them? Were the tunnels messing with his mind *that* severely? He caught a whiff of an animal odor, zoolike. He shook it off and continued. What else could he do?

He encountered four more octagonal chambers and returned once to a chamber he had already visited. He kept walking, turning, listening, sniffing the air. How could so many feet of corridor exist without some of it revealing the passage or presence of humans?

Like space, time as well broke its bonds in these caverns and corridors, hidden from the world. Shortly after setting out from an octagonal chamber, he checked his watch and was shocked to see that fifty minutes had evaporated. Leaning his back against a dark wall, he rested, giving himself ten minutes. Pushing off to carry on, he realized only three minutes had passed.

He lost all sense of direction and distance. He could be inches under the cobblestones of Old Jerusalem or unfathomably far below. He felt he had an equal chance of being under the Dome of the Rock or Stonehenge. Slanting floors, soaring and plunging ceilings, widening and narrowing halls, shifting shadows, unstable temperatures, intermittent breezes, unreliable sounds— he swayed as the dim tunnel he was standing in shifted and rotated around him. He reached a hand out to the wall, but that didn't help, and he sat down hard. Objective vertigo. He closed his eyes. Now it felt as though it was he, not the tunnel, spinning round and round, slowing like an amusement park ride. He took a deep breath.

When he opened his eyes, he was in a tunnel, as motionless and solid as tunnels were supposed to be. This was hell, he decided. Lost in a labyrinth with Alicia's life hanging on his ability to find her.

Using the wall for support, he rose to his feet. He walked on, not really believing that he would find any life down here, let alone Alicia. He would wander until he collapsed. Eventually someone would happen along his bones and brush them into a dustpan.

He saw a lighted opening on his left. As he approached, his already-sunken heart found room to sink lower. He stopped in the threshold and looked up a sloping catwalk that ended at a metal door, twenty feet above the stone floor.

It can't be the same door, he thought.

His knees threatened to buckle under the weight of defeat. He dropped his shoes, slipped into them, and crouched to tie them. His pistol dangled from his trigger finger at his side as he staggered up the catwalk, not caring that it clanged and thumped beneath his feet. He saw the spot where he had hung from the catwalk to avoid detection. He stopped at the door, held his palm to it, as if his will alone could make it a different door. He pushed against the bar and the door opened.

The basement under the Latin Patriarchate. Brighter than it should have been. The outside door was open, closing slowly. A man stood at the open breaker box door, staring at Brady. In his thirties, he had long, hay-colored hair, pulled back into a ponytail. A face that had stopped more than a few fists. At least six feet six, the man was bulging and muscular, a walking bicep.

Whether Brady's expression gave him away or the man knew everyone permitted on the premises or he had been alerted to Brady's possible presence—he immediately recognized Brady as a trespasser. He scowled fiercely and snapped, *"Was machst Du denn hier?"* German, Brady thought. The man grabbed at Brady.

Brady backpedaled, bringing up the pistol.

The German stepped through the door, his eyes going wide when he spotted the gun. He swung a beefy fist at Brady's arm. It rammed into the silencer like a baseball bat. The gun flew out of his hand. It hit the wall and disappeared below the catwalk. A few seconds later, it clattered onto the stone floor.

The German drove Brady back down the ramp, swinging, punching . . . a right, a left . . . nonstop, insane.

The purpose of fighting is to win; there is no possible victory in defense. The sword is more important than the shield.

Advice every law enforcement trainee knew by heart, because his instructors repeated it incessantly. Its unlikely source was the writer John Steinbeck, imbuing battle smarts to the Knights of the Round Table in his novel *The Acts of King Arthur and His Noble Knights.*

Brady lowered his head and charged, slipping in between swings. His head cracked against the man's sternum. His arms encircled a muscular torso. A blow fell on his back, crushing. He punched, a sharp jab to the diaphragm. It thumped as if he'd struck a sack of flour. He shot his other fist forward, forgetting its injury until pain like a metal wire shot up his arm and exploded in his shoulder. A fist came down on the back of his head. The quickest flash of blackness preempted his thoughts, like a film jumping its sprockets, then catching again. He recognized consciousness as a drowning man finds air, and he held on to it with everything he had.

The German grabbed a fierce handful of hair and yanked him up. Warm moisture tickled his scalp: sweat or blood, Brady didn't know. Holding Brady's head in his left hand, the German's right fist reared back, shot forward. It connected with his jaw, smashing it sideways. He heard a *crack!* He'd have gone down if the man were not suspending him by his hair. The fist pulled back again.

I can't take this hit, he thought with absolute certainty.

Out of instinct, Brady's hand lunged out. His middle and index fingers protruded from his fist like talons. They struck the German's eyes. Brady felt softness under his fingertips, then hot liquid. The man screamed, a roar of pain and fury. He released his grip on Brady's scalp.

Brady stumbled back, rocking, dizzy.

The German continued to roar, holding one hand to his face, waving the other around to fend off another attack. He smeared blood on his cheek, blinked, and glared at Brady with a single bright eye. The other socket was a gooey mess. Rivulets of crimson streamed from it.

Brady stared back in horror.

His opponent took advantage of his hesitation. The German stepped forward and in a single movement grabbed the back of Brady's neck and plunged his head into the catwalk railing. His chin took it full-force. He felt the skin split between bone and steel. The viselike hand holding him forced his face off the rail and pushed his neck into it. Immediately he felt his windpipe crushing against it, denying the passage of air.

As if through a fog, he remembered a move and executed it: knife hand—straight and hard—backward like a pendulum into the German's groin. Breath burst from the man's lungs. He bent at the hips in pain, but the pressure on Brady's neck did not ease. Brady brought his elbow up into the German's nose. He heard a soft snap and a gurgling bellow.

The man stumbled back, and Brady could breathe again. The air rushing into his lungs felt like cool water dousing a fire raging in his chest. He rubbed his throat, turned around, rolling on the rail.

The German—his face glistening red—lunged at him. He clawed at Brady, trying to get his arms around him, his head oddly cocked back. Brady realized the man was maneuvering for a head-butt. The German would aim the top of his forehead at the delicate bones in Brady's face. It was a powerful, even deadly blow when delivered properly, and this guy looked like he'd had enough practice to pummel an army into submission.

Brady's thoughts turned hot and white and unintelligible, the blast-furnace confusion of rage and panic. He delivered another groin shot, this time with his knee. The German crumpled. His head slammed against the catwalk at Brady's feet.

Brady, expecting to deliver a series of blows, stumbled over him and went down. He was staring at big, worn work boots. Before Brady realized what was happening, he took a kick to the chin. His head snapped back, but he got the gist of what it meant to street-fight: any way possible, in any position you found yourself. He began kicking with everything he had in him. He squeezed his eyes closed, trusting his feet to find their mark. *Kick! Kick!* The German matched his blows and added punches to Brady's thighs and hips. Each one sent a starburst of red-hot agony up his body into his head. He could not take much more. He grabbed at the man's flailing boots, pulled them close, hugged them tight. He got a knee under him and *pushed.*

The two entwined men rolled, hitting the catwalk's railing. Brady pushed harder and wiggled over the edge. They tumbled off the ramp, rolling through space.

Brady pushed and pulled and spun to position himself on top. They landed on their sides. Air exploded from both of them. Brady rolled away. As he did, the German punched him in the stomach—weakly but with enough force to send a wave of nausea through him. He rolled farther, lifted himself onto knees and elbows, heaving for a breath. Saliva and blood poured from his mouth. He felt something hard in there and spat. A tooth hit the stone. His tongue told him it was an upper cuspid, what Zach called vampire teeth. He closed his eyes.

This guy's going to kill me, he thought. *This is it. Right here, right now.*

His opponent was bigger, better fit, and had the obvious advantage of fighting experience. Brady was sloppy with both his blocks and his attacks, because he had never been in a fight before. A couple of academy classes, which he had suffered through, trying to imagine how he'd put a suspect in a carotid restraint hold or land a power punch studying crime scene photos and slipping inside a killer's mind.

Still, he had not done too badly so fa—

The boot caught him in the ribs. He tumbled over.

Stupid! he thought.

Never stay down. Never take your eyes off your opponent. Two principles of fighting that he had forgotten as soon as he'd heard them.

He brought his knees up, curling into a fetal position, protecting his organs. He saw a dark object on the floor, far away: the gun. The next kick slammed into the side of his calf. The blow's energy disbursed across his leg, and he remembered . . .

He blocked a kick, yanked up his pant leg, unsnapped the ankle sheath, and withdrew the knife Avi had given him. Without a moment's thought, he plunged it into the German's leg.

A howl filled the room. The man staggered back. Brady yanked out the blade, pushed forward and plunged it into the man's other leg. He came down like a sheared redwood.

Brady pushed away and stood. Pain in his side flared, competing with violated nerves all over his body. For a second, he watched the German howling and groaning, holding first the wound in his right shin, then the wound in his left. Blood—black as oil in the gloom—spread and smeared under him.

Brady staggered back, collided with a wall. He slid around, only dimly aware of the rough stone surface grating against his bruised back. Hit a corner and kept moving. Under the catwalk. When he was near the pistol, he stepped away from the wall and picked it up. He walked to the German, now writhing in relative silence. He pressed the silenced barrel into the man's cheek.

The German's one good eye rolled up to him. He bared his teeth.

Brady pushed harder, straddled him, and sat on his chest. He leaned close.

"Where is she?" he said, breathing hard.

The German's eye narrowed. Calculations turned and tumbled within it. Brady knew he didn't have much time before the man would make his move. He shifted the barrel to the underside of the man's chin, where it would be harder to dislodge in a swift move.

"The girl," Brady said. "Came in with Scaramuzzi or Arjan Vos a couple of hours ago. Where is she?"

The man turned his head, spat out bloody saliva.

"I know nut-ting of a *gull*," he said contemptuously.

Brady shoved the barrel up. The man's face scrunched in pain.

"Scaramuzzi, then," Brady said. "Take me to Scaramuzzi."

The man laughed. He shook his head. "*Nein! Nein!* No one will lead you to him. Betta to die by your hand than his."

He believed him. Whether it was fear or unreasonable loyalty, instilling either was consistent with Brady's understanding of Scaramuzzi's character and method of dominance over his followers.

Rapidly, he pulled back and swung the flat side of the pistol into the man's temple.

The German had time to express surprise. Then his head jerked sideways and blood spurted from a laceration, but he did not pass out. He snapped his gaze to Brady and hissed angrily.

Brady hit him again, *hard.*

The German started to rock. He grabbed Brady's shirt, tried to block the next strike, but his arm went wide.

Brady slammed the gun into his head again and again. Finally, the German slumped, unconscious. Brady held the gun high, ready to continue the pummeling. Blood poured from the head wounds, but he was alive; Brady could feel the man's breathing under him. His own breathing was labored, from exertion and what he thought were fractured ribs. He lowered the gun, shaking his head. Knocking someone out was nothing like they showed it on TV.

He stood and lumbered to the foot of the catwalk. Slowly, feeling every flex of muscle, every bending joint, he holstered the pistol at the small of his back. He thought about retrieving the knife from the German's leg and decided against it. He considered the labyrinth, just beyond the room's threshold. He considered the metal door at the top of the catwalk, leading to the seminary's basement and out to Jerusalem. He stood there a long time, feeling his wounds, both physical and emotional.

He started walking. Up the catwalk. To the exit.

He MANAGED to navigate the few hundred yards to the Gloria Hotel without collapsing or drawing unwanted attention. His careful shuffling, slumped shoulders, tattered and dirty clothes undoubtedly gave him the appearance of a drunkard—rare in Old Jerusalem but not enough of a rarity to bring authorities or conversion-minded Samaritans. He entered the hotel through a back door and wound up the staircase to the third floor. He knocked on a door at random, and when no one answered, he kicked it open. Inside, he propped a chair under the door handle. He climbed onto the bed like a man easing into cold water and lowered his head onto a pillow. He pulled himself into a tight ball.

And he wept.

16

Hope is a merciless tormentor.

It's the sound of trickling water to parched lips. The prospect of love to the unlovable. A miracle cure to the parents of a dying child. It holds up victory over the inevitable and beckons us to crawl farther over slicing shards, all the while pulling back, remaining just out of reach. It makes agony out of mere pain by pretending a different outcome *could have been*. It laughs at mankind's embrace of it after millennia of disappointment.

Brady had to let it go.

He was not going to make it home. He would never see Zach again . . . or hold him . . . or watch him become a man.

Because he would not leave Alicia, and he had no chance of defeating Scaramuzzi's subterranean maze to find her.

He ached everywhere: the top of his head, his gums, jaw, shoulder, ribs, hand, arm, legs . . . heart.

He craved the dulling effect of whiskey, just a swig or two. He swung his feet off the bed and sat up. The room was clean but simple. No refriger-ator, no minibar. Just as well. If death was going to take him, he wanted to see its face straight on, nothing clouding the experience. The way Karen must have faced it. He'd spent God knew how many hours considering her last moments. He did not know if she saw the car coming, saw it not make the turn, realized it was going to hit her. Or if it had struck her without warning. Running, feeling her muscles working, the impact of the ground on her feet, the pulse in her chest, her neck, maybe pacing her gait to MercyMe on the Walkman—when Brady had checked, it was stopped toward the end of "I Can Only Imagine"—then . . . *nothing*. Blackness . . . God . . . whatever. Still, Brady believed something had come before, whether she saw the car coming or not. Maybe it was only a split second—feeling the air pushing a few inches ahead of the bumper or even the percussion of the metal itself. In that brief time, she had known her life was over. *What was her final thought?* he often wondered. It drove him nuts to think it was a terrified mind-scream or a pleading *Noooooo!* He liked to believe she'd said, *Bye, Brady . . . bye, Zach . . . love you guys.*

Zach.

He eyed the phone on the nightstand. He had to make the call. It was his turn to say good-bye.

He would enter the labyrinth with the intention of finding and rescuing Alicia. But he knew he stood a better chance of winning the Virginia lottery on a single ticket. No, he would not be leaving those infernal tunnels again. That was okay. Scaramuzzi had won. At least Brady was going out on his own terms, not as a coward, but doing the right thing.

He was so *tired.* Sore and tired and defeated. Death would be a relief. The hardest thing about it was leaving Zach. But what kind of father would he be if he left Alicia and could not face himself in the mirror? What kind of father could a self-loathing drunkard be? Zach was better off with Kurt and Kari Oakley. They were happy, healthy people. He would grow up being loved and taught strong values.

He read his watch: he was already almost two hours late calling him. He fished the new calling card out of his wallet and set it on the bed. He uncradled the handset, heard a dial tone, dialed nine. The tone stuttered, then held steady. He punched in the calling card information, followed by the Oakleys' number.

Before the first ring finished, Zach answered.

"Hey, kiddo," Brady said, trying to sound upbeat.

"Dad! I've been waiting for you."

"I'm sorry. Something came up."

"That's okay. Where are you?"

He paused. He did not want Zach to think his father had lied to him right to the very end. "You won't believe it," he said. "I'm in Israel."

"Where Jesus lived? Holy cow! What are you doing there?"

"You know that bad guy? We tracked him to here."

Zach didn't speak for a moment. "Did you arrest him?"

"Not yet."

"Is it dangerous?"

"Yes, but I'll take care."

"Remember your promise?"

"And you won't let that guy and his dogs get you. Okay?"

Brady squeezed his eyes shut.

"I do; 'course I do." His throat felt on the verge of rupturing. "But listen . . . if something *should* happen . . . if—"

"We made a fort!" Zach blurted, interrupting.

"Zach, I want you to hear me, okay? There are things I want you to know."

"I already know." Speaking too fast, wanting his dad to shut up about *something happening.*

Brady searched for words that would capture his son's attention without terrorizing him.

Before he found them, Zach said: "You love me. And Mom loved me. And I'll be all right with Uncle Kurt and Aunt Kari. And we'll all meet again someday . . . in heaven."

"Son, I—"

"But I don't *want* that to be where we meet again!" He was nearly yelling. Brady could hear the tears he could not see. Zach sniffed. "Mom's already there! That's enough! No more! Not you!"

Brady could hear Kari in the background, sounding concerned, comforting. There was a bumping sound, something muffled. He expected Kari to come on the line, asking what he'd said to Zach to make him hysterical. Instead, Zach's whispered words floated into his ear.

"You promised."

"Sometimes, things are just . . ."

"You promised."

Silence.

He did; he promised. He did not want to leave Zach. And he *could not* leave Alicia. His chest ached with the intensity of an open wound, but it had nothing to do with his physical injuries.

"Zach?"

"Yeah?"

"Can you hold on just a minute? Okay? Hold on . . ."

He set the handset on the bed. He pressed his palm over his mouth and paced to the corner of the room.

This was too hard. Saying good-bye.

He pictured Zach, holding the phone to his ear, listening intently, his heart wedged in his throat.

He loved his son's voice, always had. It was small and innocent. From the time he was in first grade, Zach had read to him. Every day, Brady looked forward to those twenty minutes.

And why was he thinking this? Why now?

He heard Zach reading to him, from Dr. Seuss to . . . more recently . . .

The words filled his mind as though his son were in the room, saying them then and there.

Dylan Thomas. Zach had selected the book of poetry from the school library. Brady had thought it was a little mature for a fourth grader, but Zach read it. And he had asked intelligent questions as well as making astute observations.

His favorite was: "Do not go gentle into that good night. Rage, rage against the dying of the light."

"That's about death, right?" Zach had asked.

"That's right. It's about not letting death take you without a fight. Love life enough to shake your fist at death and say, 'Oh, no, you don't!'"

"Did Mom do that?"

"Oh, yeah, she loved life." He had pulled Zach close. "Sometimes the fight is short and sometimes we lose it, but life is always worth fighting for."

Had he said that? Yes, and even then, after Karen's death, he had meant it.

Fight. Don't give up.

He strode to the bed and picked up the phone.

"Zach?"

"Dad?"

"I made you a promise, and I'm going to keep it if there's any way I possibly can. I have to do something very dangerous. There's no way around it. Somebody's life depends on it. But I'm going to be careful, and I'm going to fight anybody who tries to hurt me. Okay?"

"I just want you back."

"I want to come back. I love you, son."

"Love you too."

"See you later." And that was the truth. One way or another, it was. He cradled the phone.

Hope. You again? Well, welcome back.

Despair is a merciless tormentor.

It prevents your mind from finding a way out of dark places. It had told Brady his task was hopeless, and he had believed it. But he saw now that it wasn't.

He knew precisely how he was going to conquer the labyrinth and find Alicia.

11

It was a few minutes past ten when he pushed through the Gloria's back door into the hotel's rear parking lot. The sun had sauntered away two hours ago, allowing a soft, black blanket to settle over the city. Spots of light from street lamps and porch fixtures radiated against the yellow and red rock of low buildings and the gray of cobblestone, which had been set in place thousands of years before electricity's assault on man's circadian rhythm. He climbed into the Peugeot, fired it up, and burned two semicircles of rubber onto the asphalt. The car bottomed out as it bounded over a curve and into an alleyway that ran behind the hotel, parallel with Latin Patriarchate Street. His head banged against the roof—just another pain. He ached all over: some areas throbbed, others shot daggers through him. He gritted his teeth and ignored his body's pleas for relief and help.

He steered toward the seminary, remembered seeing a five-and-dime in the other direction, and veered in a wide U-turn. The Peugeot's right wheels thumped onto a curb, then off again. A couple, walking hand in hand, backed onto a manicured lawn, though Brady had not brought the vehicle anywhere near them.

Up a block, then into the tiny lot in front of the store. Half-expecting the resistance of a dead bolt, he *yanked* the door open. A brass bell rattled and flew off its hook. It landed in a display of olives, tinkling in protest before lying still. A boy about Zach's age stopped sweeping the floor to behold Brady's entrance.

"Sorry," Brady said. A quick glance around showed him a store packed with every conceivable touristy desire. "Aspirin!" he called out to the boy, who dropped the broom and zipped down an aisle. Brady followed and grabbed the first bottle he saw with the words "pain reliever." He ripped off its cellophane seal, uncapped the bottle, and dumped its contents into his mouth. He crunched on the pills and began swallowing the chalky pulp. He strode to a glass-doored cooler, pulled out a can of something, and poured it into his mouth. Aspirin paste loosened from his molars and the roof of his mouth and flowed down his throat. The carbonated beverage he'd selected foamed at the back of his throat and bubbled up into his sinuses. He held it in and swallowed it back.

Grimacing, he found the boy watching him, gape-jawed.

"Duct tape?" he asked, croaking the words. He gulped from the beverage can, asked again, "Duct tape?"

The boy turned his body without taking his gaze off Brady and walked to another aisle.

Brady found the tape and took a roll. He almost snatched up a flashlight and then realized he would not need it, not this time. On the way out, he dropped a handful of bills and coins on the counter.

He was in the seminary's front parking lot thirty seconds later. It was nearly deserted at this hour. He killed the engine in a slot not far from the drive leading to the labyrinth entrance. No light guided travelers down the ramp; it was dark and almost invisible. Watching for pedestrian traffic, thinking he'd rush through the first basement door after someone opened it and coerce his way through the second, he sat in the car and stripped off his shirt. He pulled out a length of duct tape without tearing it off and wrapped it tightly around his torso, where his ribs felt bruised and broken. He wound it around again and again, until he was encased from navel to mid-sternum in a stiff cast of vinyl. He climbed out of the car and bent and twisted until he'd formed enough grooves in the tape to give him some flexibility.

He opened the trunk with the key and in the glow of a small light saw his hope: the bag containing Alicia's CSD. He tugged it out, opened it on the asphalt. In the bowl of the inverted helmet, he found a metal box the size of a modem. This was the computerized brain of the CSD, he knew. It would mount like a belt buckle at his waist. Another box was the device's hard drive, for recording crime scene walk-throughs. He could not care less about chronicling the next hour, but he did not know if the CSD required information stored on the hard drive to function properly, so he hooked it up. He pulled out the helmet and discovered an assortment of attachments stored in the case around and under it. After some experimentation, he found a spot on the helmet for everything. He turned the now-heavy contraption in his hands and nodded; it coincided with his memory of it on Alicia.

His heart leaped when he could not squeeze into the CSD's gloves and armbands, which contained buttons that controlled the helmet's lighting and heads-up display. Finally, he wriggled into them, ripping only one seam. He hoped the vest, which acted as wiring harness and accessory mount, and the helmet were not as customized to Alicia's smaller form as the gloves and armbands were. He slipped them on with no problem.

Reassured, he pulled off the helmet. He returned the CSD bag to the trunk. He leaned through the Peugeot's front door and retrieved the Kimber and the duct tape. He taped the grip of the gun, played out a foot of tape, and wrapped the end around his right wrist. He squeezed the strip of tape between his wrist and the gun into a tight cord. He held out his arm, watching the gun dangle. With a snap of his wrist, the pistol was in his hand. He would be able to operate the CSD controls without fumbling with his weapon.

Donning the suit reminded him of every place the German had punished him, even through the dulling effect of the analgesic. He stood erect and drew a deep breath. His lungs were tight under his taped torso, but the sharp pain from his battered ribs was no longer a distraction.

Leaving the car keys under a floor mat, he shut the door and the trunk lid, picked up the helmet, and trudged down the drive. In the eight or nine minutes it had taken him to tape himself and suit up, no one had approached Scaramuzzi's lair. He wondered if the place closed down at night, or if the organization it housed limited its errand running to daylight hours to reduce the chance of detection.

At the metal door, he hoisted the helmet and lowered it over his head. He seated it into the O-ring that rested on pads over his shoulders. Blackness. No displays, no lights indicating the status of the device. He remembered that the faceplate was opaque; the suit had to be powered up to activate the pixels that allowed the wearer to either see through the face-plate or view other images, depending on the CSD's settings. He didn't understand the technology, but Alicia had tried to explain it to him once. He recalled her saying the vest contained two battery cells, located above each kidney. Alicia had said that each charge was good for five hours of heavy use. She had charged them after the Ft. Collins walk-through—he remembered working around the charging unit as he made piles of crime scene photos and reports in Alicia's hotel room. But he had no power and no CSD.

Don't give me this! he thought, instantly on the brink of panic.

He wiggled the helmet, shifted it around. He felt it slide easily in the groove of the O-ring. He rotated it, felt resistance, pushed harder. There was a *click* as it snapped into place. Light flickered in his eyes, and he was look-ing out through the helmet's faceplate. Instead of darkness, however, he could see the metal door and the stone bricks around it and the keypad box as well as he had in daylight. He recognized the day-for-night quality from the laptop display of Alicia's walk-throughs. Spending as much time as he had with those walk-throughs, he knew the high-tech gadgetry he now con-trolled—a DNA MEM microchip for rudimentary microanalysis of biolog-ical material left at a crime scene, infrared for thermal imaging, infrared and deep-ultraviolet laser to see . . .

His mind jumped from the academic to the practical. He flipped open the keypad box beside the door. Same design as the keypad on the inner door: rubber, lighted from behind, laid out like a telephone's numeric pad. He glanced at his left forearm and positioned the fingers of his right hand over the CSD's controls. He focused on the keypad once more. His index finger touched a button on the suit. A white-hot light blasted against the keypad and wall and bounced back into his face; the concave screen in front of his eyes dimmed to compensate. Instinctively, he snapped his head around to survey the upward slope of the drive. Bright as day, but he knew it wasn't optically adjusted to allow him to see in the darkness: he had acti-vated the helmet's intense halogens. Anyone within sight would think a bonfire was blazing beside the seminary. He pressed down with his index finger again. The lights dimmed away; the screen reverted back to day-for-night mode.

He waited without moving for a full thirty seconds.

Then he saw the flashing blue lights, flittering on the trees, against the wall of the seminary, growing brighter by the second.

F ather Randall sat at a small table among the street vendors and their carts.
Even at this late hour, the vendors displayed their wares, hoping to catch
the tourists whose body clocks had not caught up with local time. All around
him hung colorful scarves, quilts, and rugs. He particularly enjoyed watching
the flicker of the lighted cloth stars that more closely resembled Chinese
lanterns than novelties from the Via Dolorosa. Gentle violin chords drifted
from the open doorway behind him. His friend Nissim Ben-David's daughter playing, becoming quite adept. He sipped from a china cup of milky
almond tea—his favorite treat in all the world. It always calmed him, and this
evening, he needed calming. In the past few days, Luco had become a loose
canon, ordering Pip's murder and now, he understood, actually kidnapping
one of the Americans who'd come to investigate crimes in their country.

He set down the cup and glanced at his watch. He could spare only a
few more minutes in this tranquil environment. The Gathering would
start soon—with a pseudomass officiated by Luco himself. Randall felt a
headache coming on just from thinking about that atrocity. Beforehand,
he wanted to catch Luco to discover his intentions for the Americans. He
hoped they weren't as nasty as he suspected. He let his lids fall down over
his eyes. The music felt like a breeze on his cheek.

He withdrew his cigarette case from the inside pocket of his coat and
popped it open. He was selecting a cigarette when he glanced around at the
faintly flapping scarves and flickering stars. What he saw caused him to drop
the case. It hit the edge of the saucer, making the cup tip and pour hot tea
onto his lap. He bolted up, knocking his chair over.

He lowered his eyes to his lap and the disrupted tea setting for the briefest of seconds, but when he looked up again, Pip was gone. It had been Pip, Randall was positive. He had looked awful, his head heavily bandaged, his eyes sunken, his skin alabaster.

Randall hurried around the table and shuffled as fast as his aging legs could move him. Thirty feet—that's how near he had been, his face peering between lengths of hanging material. He reached the spot and saw that it was where an alleyway met the market street.

"Pip!" he called, though he saw no one who could be his friend. He raised his voice further: "Find me, Pip!"

His shoulders slumped. He looked back as his table. Ben-David's wife, Dalia, was righting the chair. His daughter stood in the doorway, violin and bow quiet in her hands. She watched him with concern. He waved, tried to smile. He started back, reaching for his wallet to pay for the tea and anything he had broken.

HER HEAD no longer ached, but her mouth still felt as if it had been lined with aluminum, and the water was long gone. Alicia sat on the cot, her head down in her hands, feeling the gloom of her surroundings pressing down on her. Her mind wanted to explore, to prod and grope at new information, and she let it. It was better than driving herself crazy looking for a way out of the cell. There wasn't one. The walls were solid—she had pushed and rapped on every stone, scraped her fingernail along every joint. The bars were firmly imbedded into the floor and ceiling, each a mere handbreadth apart. The door lock did not rattle or budge or so much as tease her with the slightest play. Oddly, she could reach the touch pad that unlocked the door, but she could not see it, and she had found that three incorrect entries caused it to beep shrilly for two full minutes before settling into silence again. She'd set it off three times, resulting in no visits from guards or jailers. The complete lack of attention to her was worse than vigilant scrutiny: it implied confidence in the cell's ability to hold her or the labyrinth's power to confuse—if a labyrinth did in fact exist between here and the exit; she had no reason to believe anything Scaramuzzi said.

One thing he had mentioned outright puzzled her: that Brady was to meet with someone named Pip to get a file Scaramuzzi wanted. He had intimated that this person had already contacted her and Brady. Was she missing something? When was this supposed to have happened? She sifted her memory for attempted contacts—pleading looks from strangers, cryptic messages on napkins, ringing phones left unanswered. Nothing came to mind. She had been joined to Brady's hip since they'd met up in the Marriott's room 4914.

No, she was certain nobody had attempted to contact them.

What kind of game was Scaramuzzi playing?

He was insane, no doubt about that. But in a sly-scary-charming-Hitler way. Crazy like a fox, was the saying. But that wasn't right either. This guy *really* thought he was Antichrist . . .

A thought hit her, and she did not like it one bit: *What if he is Antichrist? What if Ambrosi has it wrong?*

She could not remember his explaining *why* he believed Scaramuzzi was either faking it or insane. When he had scoffed at Scaramuzzi's professed identification, she had assumed he was correct, not because he was a scholar on the subject, but because of course Antichrist wasn't walking around on earth today, knocking off naysayers and scheming to rule the world. That was the stuff of bad movies. But if learned people, religious leaders, and even governments believed Antichrist would eventually appear, why not now?

Maybe they were approaching this the wrong way. What if . . .

She sensed eyes on her. She turned her head and nearly screamed.

A wolf stood inches from the bars, staring at her with yellowish-green eyes. It lowered its snout slightly, so its glare crossed a crinkled brow to reach her. A low rumble emanated from its husky chest. Its top lip quivered, a black sheath over white blades.

Alicia realized this was one of the wolf-dog hybrids that had attacked Brady and Zach and had assisted the Pelletier killer; if not this very one, then one like it. It was a war dog, trained to kill. She stood, took a step back.

The animal's rumbling grew louder.

Movement in her periphery drew her eyes. From the black corridor on the right another wolf-dog emerged. It stopped halfway out of the shadows. Another dog stepped around it, levering measured steps toward the first dog, never taking its eyes from Alicia's. Claws clicked against the stone floor.

The dog at the corridor stepped into the light, nudged forward by a larger presence: a man. He floated at the terminator between dark and light, like a man just under the surface of a murky pond. He had a heavy beard and what appeared to be animal pelts draped over his shoulders. Knitted shirt, dark pants, high boots.

The Viking. The Pelletier killer.

His eyes gleamed among the shadows. He shifted and came farther out of the corridor. A wooden handle protruded up from over his shoulder. Alicia was shaken by the conviction that this was the weapon he had used to behead Cynthia Loeb and the others. She imagined his reaching back, seizing the handle, and swinging it up and around, severing a head in one smooth motion.

As if sensing her thoughts, the way his dogs must certainly know her fear, he stepped forward, raising his hand to grip the ax handle.

79

Brady backed into the corner at the bottom of the drive.

The police cruiser slowed as it approached the seminary. Its flashing blue lights played on the wall and bushes above him. He remembered hearing somewhere that Jerusalem police left their strobes on at all times; he had in fact seen a few on his way in from the airport. He hoped the lawmen in the car had caught only a glimpse of the CSD's halogen moment and had come to investigate without knowing precisely where they should look.

That seemed the case when a bright searchlight flipped on from the road, panned past the head of the sloping drive, and as suddenly returned the darkness to the night.

The cruiser pulled away, pulling its blue lights with it.

Brady let out a breath he had not been aware of holding.

Back to the keypad.

Ready to reverse his action in case it again did something attention-drawing, he pushed the CSD control under his middle finger. His view turned red. He could detect faint specks and smears on and around the keypad. Under his little finger was a pinwheel, like the volume control on a clock radio. He gave it a tweak. The specks and smears disappeared. He turned the pinwheel in the opposite direction. They became splotches of glowing neon, too many of them to decipher any meaning. He spun the wheel back and forth but could not bring out only the markings that told the story he was searching for.

Frustrated, he pushed another control with his ring finger. The screen's hue changed to orange—and revealed to him the keypad buttons that had received the most recent attention. Three buttons . . . maybe as many as five. He rolled the pinwheel and two possibilities faded away, leaving three buttons, each superimposed by a bright orange glow, absent from the other nine. Two. Seven. Eight. When he'd slipped through this door earlier, the man who had opened it had caused the keypad to beep three times—a three-digit code. Three digits, three buttons: three to the power of three. Twenty-seven possible combinations. But that was if the same number could be used more than once, which would leave another number unused. The glowing buttons said the code required all three, reducing the possible key combinations to . . . He wasn't sure, six or nine. He could handle that.

He punched in two-seven-eight. Nothing. He tried the door anyway. Still locked.

Two-eight-seven.

Seven-two-eight.

Seven-eight-two. The locking mechanism on the door buzzed, and its bolt clunked as it shifted position.

He pulled it opened and discovered what he had hoped the CSD could provide: footprints, glowing bright orange on the floor. So many shoes had trod here, they formed a solid line two feet wide, as though a huge snail had passed instead of hundreds of humans. The outside edges of the line broke apart into individual prints, showing where people had veered off the straightest path to the keypad behind the breaker panel and the rusty inner door. He crossed the threshold and pulled the door closed. He caught himself stepping over the footprints, as though they were both tangible and distasteful. He saw his own footprints from his first visit circling behind the furnace and boiler. Larger prints marked where the Viking, Olaf, had followed, looking for him. But there were two sets of the larger prints heading to and from the equipment. Around them, and all over the basement floor he noticed now, were irregular dots the size of small fists. He felt his blood chill as he realized what they were: paw prints. Olaf had brought his dogs back to reexamine the area. Did that mean they had found the German? Had he awakened and informed his comrades of Brady's presence? Or was

it that Olaf was meticulous or so keen with his senses that he knew someone had been here?

Doesn't matter, Brady thought. He was going in. He would find Alicia,
despite an army of Vikings, wolf-dogs, German prizefighters, Satanists,
antichrists, or whatever else lurked in the tunnels beyond that rusty door.

As he moved his vision around, dizziness brushed over him like a breeze.
He took a step back and reached for the wall. It was nearer than he thought,
and he cracked his knuckles against the stone. Maneuvering solely by the
orange electronic graphics was disorienting. He had read that young recruits
with copious experience playing video games performed more efficiently in
the field. He understood part of the reason now. As electronics become an
increasingly important element of field craft, those who had learned to
understand three-dimensional landscapes from the two-dimensional and
limited-field-of-view graphics of computer monitors would have a distinct
advantage.

He took a step toward the inner door, felt no more vertigo, and moved
faster. At the second keypad, he found the correct code on his sixth
attempt. The snail had squirmed down the metal catwalk and, he could see
now, turned left into the tunnels. What must have been blood on the floor
below, where he and the German had brawled, seemed to shimmer like
orange phosphorus among a chaotic jumble of footprints, handprints, and
paw prints.

Brady snapped up on his right wrist and seized the pistol. He eased down
the catwalk, left hand on the rail, not trusting himself to navigate a slanted,
vibrating platform wearing the CSD. At the bottom, he took a deep breath.

This is better than the first time, he told himself, because he had to and
because it was true. He wasn't going in blind. He had a guide, lots of
guides—the footprints of everyone who had entered the labyrinth in the last
day or so and went directly to the occupied area. He peered into the tunnel,
first the way he had gone before, then the direction everyone else had
headed. The CSD display revealed greater lengths of tunnel than he could
see before. Tall shadows marked the branching passages that had loomed so
suddenly and mysteriously on his first foray.

He examined the controls on his forearm and used his pinky to push a

button etched with an icon of an audio speaker. A menu appeared, superimposed over his faceplate view:

TRANSCRIPTION PLAYBACK VOLUME—INTERNAL SPEAKERS
TRANSCRIPTION PLAYBACK VOLUME—EXTERNAL SPEAKERS
EXTERIOR SPEAKER—VOLUME
EXTERIOR MICROPHONE—VOLUME
EXTERIOR MICROPHONE—SQUELCH

He tickled a nub the size of a pencil eraser on the control panel, and a
cursor appeared, scrolling in response to his finger's movement. He selected
EXTERIOR MICROPHONE—VOLUME. A slide control appeared. He increased
the volume, only to have a high-pitched hum pierce his ears. He returned
the volume to its previous low level. He played with the squelch control but
soon realized it did nothing. He edged the volume up slightly, until he could
hear himself stomp his foot. The humming was barely noticeable, but the
CSD's audio problems presented a problem. A person with any level of
stealth at all would have no trouble sneaking up on him. He played with various menus and discovered a way to display the image captured by the rear-
facing camera in a small square low on the heads-up display. Not perfect, but
it did compensate a little for having poor hearing.

He trudged on.

Scuff marks and an occasional handprint in glowing orange marred the
walls. A vague sense of frustration hovered at the edge of his consciousness.
Then he realized it was in response to the ease of finding his way through
the tunnels this time versus the utter confusion and helplessness that had
plagued him a few hours before. He had to remind himself that the snail
track on the floor was invisible to the unaided eye. Perhaps he should have
thought to use the CSD before, but how could he have fathomed the
complexity of the maze he would encounter? And he had never used the
CSD—he had only analyzed the walk-throughs it produced—so it was not
a resource he readily considered.

He had it now, and it was working. That's all that mattered.

After a few minutes, he realized the maze was trickier than he'd imagined.

The majority of the footprints meandered through the most unlikely passages—two-foot-wide openings that resembled mere cracks in the earth; long
corridors of ankle-deep water; sharp turns into what must have appeared to
the naked eye to be shadow-filled recesses. He wondered how Scaramuzzi's
people successfully navigated the tunnels. He watched for clues, surface
markings, a pattern to the turns . . . nothing was apparent. He suspected
Scaramuzzi made some of his cohorts memorize the route through the
labyrinth and that the others required one of these guides. That would limit
exposure, even among those he allowed into his lair. Maybe guides traveled
back and forth from the entrance to the occupied area as regularly as a bus
schedule, leading anyone coming or going. Perhaps the room with the catwalk was the staging area for the uninitiated.

The more he thought about it, the more it made sense. Not just anyone
could lead a hostile party through the maze, even under duress. And chances
were good that a guide would always have companions—maybe by design or
simply because people constantly required passage through the maze. Brady
realized he had to prepare for a direct confrontation. He put his index finger
on the trigger of the Kimber—against Bureau policy, which specified trigger-
touching only to fire. The pistol's extraordinarily long barrel reminded him it
was silenced; shooting in the tunnels would not announce his presence to
everyone inside. He crossed his wrists in front of him, giving him quick access
to the CSD's controls.

It occurred to him that he was speculating about trivialities, and he
understood why: it kept him from thinking about what he would do upon
finding Alicia. For all he knew, she was in a cage hanging high in a mess hall
full of bad guys—if she were not already . . .

No!

He squeezed his eyes closed. He'd rather not consider the possibilities.
This was a case in which action depended on a good measure of ignorance.

Just do it. Fine for sneakers. Fine for him.

80

The wolf-dogs parted for the Viking's passage. They stepped aside without taking their eyes off Alicia.

Halfway to her cell, the Viking pulled the ax from behind him. Its head scraped against some metal, grating and ominous. He let it drop into his other hand so it crossed in front of him horizontally at the navel.

A glint of gold caught her eyes. A ring on his finger. She squinted at it and felt her stomach tighten. Rising out of the gold was a small sun symbol—she was looking at the very device used to brand the Pelletier victims.

Alicia backed up until she felt the cool stone wall behind her.

He centered himself in front of her cell, eyed her without emotion.

Had he been sent to kill her? Her eyes darted around, desperate to find a means of defense, then settled again on the ax. It was double-headed. Each blade flared out to an eight- or nine-inch span at its business end.

And she knew its business, the flesh and sinew and bone it had cleaved . . .

"Here you are," he said. His voice was smooth, deep, quiet. American-English with no accent.

"Yes . . . ?"

"I was told you were a danger to Mr. Scaramuzzi. You don't look dangerous to me."

"Let me out of here and maybe I'll change your mind."

The whiskers around his mouth rippled into a smile. He nodded and said, "That's better. But I thought you'd be roaming the tunnels. That is, after all, why they called me in, me and my trackers." He reached down and patted the side of the first dog she'd seen. It raised its head to look appreciatively at its master, then returned to its menacing posture.

"Sorry to disappoint you."

"My presence is not a complete waste. I understand Brady is here."

She was stunned to hear him use Brady's first name. As though he knew him.

She wondered if he had tried to converse with all victims. There had been no evidence of that. Only of swift and terrifying destruction.

"Is that what you do, kill for Scaramuzzi, guard him?"

"Whatever he requires."

"Why did he require you to go after my partner? Why his son? Why the five people you beheaded?"

The Viking considered her words. His face revealed nothing, but she caught something in his eyes that might have been sadness or melancholy.

"They stood in the way of *Ivaktar*, the Great Cleansing." He saw her puzzlement and continued. "The return of the way it was before."

"Before . . . ?"

"Before Christianity. Before all the bloodshed because of that single religion."

"Christianity is *not* a religion of death," she snapped. She may not know a lot about Christ or His followers, but she knew that much.

"The Crusades. The early explorers who tortured indigenous people not willing to convert. My own ancestors became hungry for blood in the name of Christ."

"People make mistakes. It's people, not religion."

"Religion is people," he said. "The European nations are steeped in Christian heritage. Christians founded America. Is your country peace-loving? Is this world the way you would like it to be?"

Of course it's not, she thought. In fact, she of all people held a skeptical view of human nature. She saw so much evil, it was difficult to conceive of a world without it. But was Christianity to blame? Or were the people who read Jesus' words and believed in Him responsible—at least partially—for keeping even greater evil at bay? Even as an agnostic, she was convinced the world was a better place because of peace-loving religions like Christianity, Judaism, Hinduism . . .

He seemed to find affirmation in her silence. He nodded once and turned away. A dog whined, and all three of them formed in a group behind their master.

"Wait!" she said. "Even if you're right, why do you think Scaramuzzi can set things right?"

"The Watchers believe," he said simply.

"They could be wrong."

"*I* believe."

She recognized the tone: a stubbornness based on a faith that could not be wholly articulated or explained. It was a conversation stopper every time.

"You said Brady was here. In the tunnels?"

"He was. If he still is, I will find him."

She smiled thinly. "Did you think he got past you and rescued me? Is that why you came?"

"I came because there are eighteen miles of tunnels to patrol."

"And . . . ?"

"My animals now have your scent. If you escape, they will find you."

He disappeared into the corridor. The dogs followed, claws clicking . . . clicking . . . until silence eased back into the cell and pressed against her like an insincere friend. She slid her back down the wall and sat. Her arm throbbed. It felt wet and gross. But all she could think about were those dogs and the Viking and the tunnels they were winding through, searching for Brady.

81

He had been walking for fifteen minutes when he noticed the limacine trail thinning into individual footprints, as others broke off to head down tributary passageways. He had expected to find a central room where the labyrinth terminated, a sort of lobby for Scaramuzzi's subterranean headquarters. Instead, it appeared that divergent passages led to different areas of his lair. How would he know which way they had taken Alicia? As anxious as he was to find her, he forced himself to move more slowly. He studied each footprint, looking for ones that might be hers—smallish, untreaded. At a junction, where an equal number of prints went in each direction, his heart leaped. Evidence of Alicia's passing: two inch-and-a-half lines, a foot apart, running along the center of the floor. He pictured two people carrying her, one on each side, hefting her unconscious body by the armpits, the toes of her shod feet dragging behind, leaving these twin tracks.

Excited, he followed the tracks and stepped into an intersection without his usual caution. A bright beam flared in his faceplate's monitor. The CSD instantly compensated for the glare, and he saw three men huddled together, one aiming a flashlight at him. It was shaking like a paint mixer. Their faces expressed sheer terror at encountering *I, Robot* in these tunnels.

The man on the left, a dark-skinned, muscular type in dirty coveralls, recovered first. His eyes narrowed in suspicion, then anger. He stepped forward.

Brady clicked on the halogens, blasting fierce white light into the men's pupils. They staggered back. He raised his pistol. One of the men stumbled, went down. The other two turned, tripped over their comrade, kept their feet, and ran. The downed man scrambled up and followed the others, bolting cockroach-quick. Brady held the pistol's grooved sight on his back.

Shoot, he told himself. The automatically adjusting optics of the CSD kept the men visible as they fled out of the reach of the halogens and deeper into the tunnel.

Shoot them all, or they'll bring reinforcements.

His trigger-finger tightened. Three pounds on a four-pound pull.

With a grunt of frustration he dropped his arm, took his finger off the trigger.

What he *should* do. What he *could* do. Two different things.

He switched off the halogens and hurried over the ground marked by two glowing-orange lines.

ROOMS BEGAN opening up, first on the right, then the left. Most were dimly lighted; all were empty. The drag marks continued past each one. The helmet began picking up voices and vague noises, footsteps maybe, or equipment being moved around. Static clung to every sound like lint, making individual words impossible to discern. Then two voices rose quickly in volume, emanating from an arched threshold twenty feet ahead on the right. An electrical charge buzzed through the words, but Brady could make them out:

A woman's voice, shrill and hued by an accent Brady could not place: "makes me nervous."

Man's voice, different accent: "Play your best and you'll be fine. Grab that, will you?"

Woman: "But the whole Council will be there. Doesn't that—"

Man: "Look, we're here for the One, that's all. Put your mind on playing your best for him and don't worry about anything else."

Woman: "Easier to say than do."

The man grunted. Footsteps. Brady turned and shuffled a few paces away, then realized the sounds were receding. He returned and peered into the room. No one. The man and woman must have left through one of the other exits. The floor was cluttered with cardboard boxes, wooden crates, music stands, and folding chairs. He darted past the opening.

He left the rooms behind. The corridor continued, long and straight, no lights. Alicia's drag marks were clearer than ever, marred by only half a dozen sets of footprints. He stopped cold. Paw prints, lots of them, and big boot prints. They streamed out of an intersecting passage, moved in the direction Brady was headed, and appeared to stream back the way they had come. He stepped past the passage, catching a glimpse of the empty alley and a far-off bend. His heart knocked against his chest wall. If she were dead, he would carry her out of this hellhole.

He tried to swallow and found he could not. A lump had lodged in his throat.

For crying out loud! he chided himself. *Get a grip! Get Alicia, get out of here, get home, and then fall apart. But not now. This moment has been reserved in time for me to rescue Alicia. Nothing else can happen. Nothing.*

Light . . . far ahead, a dot in the blackness—showing on the faceplate display as a yellow glow on the whiteness of the CSD's night-vision optics. As he approached, the dot grew into a room at the end of the corridor. He slowed his pace, stopped. Inching forward, he took in the room: stone walls . . . bars . . . a cell! He stepped fully into the room, and there was Alicia, at the rear of the cell, sitting on the floor. Her knees were up, her arms draped over them. Her head was lowered, letting her hair spill off it, hiding her face.

The posture, which conveyed defeat, was so alien to the Alicia he knew, Brady hesitated. Then she looked up, her eyes resigned to whatever new assault her captives had devised. The sad eyes instantly changed, becoming saucers of surprise. A grin transformed her face into something brilliant to behold. She bounced up but did not approach the bars.

"Brady?" she asked, hopeful but unsure. Her eyes narrowed. "Is Morgan there?"

"This is Morgan," he replied, stepping close.

The smile returned, twice as bright. She rushed to the bars, reached through, and grabbed his arms.

He let the pistol fall from his hand and dangle on its tether of tape.

She surveyed him up and down.

"The CSD! Brady, you're brilliant!"

"Let's get you out of there," he said. "This thing is amazing."

He sidestepped to the keypad, keeping his vision directed at her. He wanted to remember her like this—full of life and ecstatic.

"It's good to see you," he whispered, not caring if the helmet transmitted his words or not; saying them felt right.

"You too," she said. "What of you I can see."

It took less than two seconds for him to register the shift in her eyes. They flicked up to something over his shoulder, then became saucers again.

In the picture-in-picture view from the rear-mounted camera, he caught a blur of motion.

"Brady!" she screamed. It came though the helmet's internal speakers as a crackling squawk that crescendoed in a deafening *BOOM!*

HE CRUMPLED like an abandoned marionette. The helmet slammed against the stone floor. The left halogen light shattered; the top laser-guide snapped off and rattled away.

"Brady!" Alicia repeated.

A dent crushed one side of the helmet, too deep for him to have avoided injury.

Scaramuzzi stood over him, thumping a wooden baseball bat into the palm of one hand.

"When I heard there was a mechanical monster afoot in my tunnels, I was afraid my Louisville couldn't handle it." He chuckled once, as if to say, *Silly me.* "That's what you call this, right? A Louisville?"

"Brady?"

He didn't move.

Scaramuzzi said, *"Osservilo sopra."*

Two men who had been waiting behind him stepped around and squatted on each side of Brady. One patted him down. The other produced a knife and cut the tape Brady had used to tether the pistol to his wrist. The man appraised the gun approvingly. Alicia saw it bore a silencer, a real one, not the toilet-paper-roll variety she had used to scare John Gilbreath. The man slipped it into his waistband at the small of his back.

"*Niente,*" he said to Scaramuzzi.

Smiling charmingly, Scaramuzzi rotated on a heel. He disappeared into the left corridor, swinging the bat at his side as if he were an English gentleman and it was an unopened umbrella. The two men tugged at the helmet. One of Brady's arms and a leg flopped over.

"Brady?" she said quietly. Then, louder, to the men: "Turn it. Counterclockwise."

They stared at her, uncomprehending.

She pantomimed the instructions, and they pulled off the helmet. Brady's head rose with it and dropped to the floor with a sickening thud.

One of the men snapped a word at Alicia and pointed toward the back wall. She stepped back, scrutinizing Brady's slack body. The man punched a code into the keypad and opened the cell door. The other man lifted Brady's legs and dragged him in. His charge duly deposited, the man scurried out. The door slammed shut.

Before they were out of sight, Alicia was kneeling beside her partner, rubbing his cheek, looking for a wound. His face was black and blue in spots; there were scabbed-over lacerations, but these obviously had been inflicted earlier. His left cheekbone was discoloring into a yellowish tinge. Blood clumped on his left earlobe. When she wiped it away with her fingers, she saw the cut was round and about the same size as one of the helmet's internal speakers.

His head turned, and he groaned.

"Brady!" she exclaimed. "Are you all right?"

Stretching the groan into a noisy breath, he fluttered his eyes open. He said, "I'm not having such a good day."

She smiled and pulled him into a hug.

"Somebody hit me," he said.

"Scaramuzzi tried to knock your head out of the park with a baseball bat." She examined his eyes. Both pupils were the same size and not overly dilated or constricted. She made a peace sign in front of his face. "How many fingers?" she asked.

"Two, the same number of times I've been knocked flat today." He rose onto his elbows. "First, by Arnold Schwarzenegger's brother. Now, by Antichrist." He shook his head slowly.

"Do you know what day it is?"

"A bad day. A very bad day."

"Brady."

"Sunday . . . unless I was out longer than I think I was."

"About a minute. I don't think you have a concussion, but how you escaped it, I don't know."

"Guess your helmet works."

"It looks worse than you do."

He scanned the surroundings. "This ain't the Marriott."

She patted a cot. "Try it; you'll like it. Come on." She helped lever him up. He plopped onto the cot. She sat beside him.

He leaned into the wall, closed his eyes.

She wanted to ask him about his injuries, about the labyrinth, about his activities between the airport and here, but she appreciated his need to simply *settle*. Even the dimness of the cell could not hide the deepening discoloration of his cheekbone. Arteries in his temple and throat throbbed, slowing as he relaxed. She saw that his injured hand had bled through the bandages again. She squeezed the other hand.

After a minute, he sat up straight, trying hard to appear uninjured and unafflicted.

She told him about waking up to find Scaramuzzi in the cell with her and his reason for ordering the Pelletier murders and the attacks on them.

A spark in Brady's eyes flared, but he was too weary to effectively animate his outrage.

"So it was all a sham to make Scaramuzzi look sincere to his board of directors," he concluded.

"Smoke and mirrors with life and death," she agreed. She examined her gauzed forearm. She poked at a bloodstain, checked her finger; it was wet with fresh blood.

Brady shook his head. "I've squandered so many evenings contemplating the nature of evil. I thought I had stared it in the face. I thought I knew it." His frown deepened. "But I've been raging at an impostor . . . at . . . at the smoke instead of the fire."

"Scaramuzzi's the fire," Alicia said.

"I thought Karen's death was senseless. Some clown behind the wheel, either drunk or distracted or careless, swatted her out of existence like a fly. As much as that hurts, what Scaramuzzi is doing is worse." He raised his eyes to hers. "I've been in my own world, living in the past, mourning the present. I forgot about the real world, where the people I love live. And they're in danger from creatures like Scaramuzzi. If I'm the man my wife loved, then I have to let her go. She's in a different place now . . ."

His eyes drifted away, and Alicia knew he was speaking not only to her, but to himself. And to Karen and Zach and perhaps even to his God, with whom she had watched him battle for as long as she'd known him.

"I can't hold on to her and hold on to the others I love at the same time," he continued. "I wanted to be with her more than I wanted to be with them. Today, I decided I want to be with them more. They need me; she doesn't."

His eyes came up again. They were moist and red-rimmed.

She wanted to say something comforting but was afraid any words she had would come out wrong, so she just squeezed his hand.

"This isn't the end," he whispered. He was about to say more when a booming voice interrupted them—

"You're celebrities!"

Scaramuzzi walked toward the cell, his hands raised in mock greeting.

"Everybody's asking about you," he said. "Who are these enemies who invaded my home, they want to know. Who are these infidels? One person was particularly interested, so I invited him to meet you. I hope you don't mind."

He turned toward the blackened corridor and called, "Come, Father!" To Brady and Alicia he said quietly, "The poor man is ancient. He can barely walk."

From the shadows shuffled a stooped old man in black slacks and shirt, wearing a cleric's collar. He raised his head, and Alicia felt Brady's body stiffen, even as hers did the same.

"Special Agents Moore and Wagner," Scaramuzzi said, "meet my head theologian, Father Randall."

The old man locked eyes with each of them in turn. He raised a quick finger to his lips, then scratched a day's worth of stubble on his cheek.

Brady and Alicia looked at each other. Alicia helped Brady rise off the cot and step up to the bars. There, they stood face-to-face with the man they knew as Cardinal Ambrosi.

82

Cardinal Ambrosi—Father Randall—eyed them and nodded.

To his prisoners, Scaramuzzi said, "Father Randall asked me what you knew about me and how you got as far as my doorstep in just a few days of searching. I suggested he ask you himself."

"Indeed . . . ," Ambrosi intoned thoughtfully. His gaze had settled on Alicia. Trouble darkened his countenance, though he was trying to disguise it as curiosity. His eyelids fell slowly and opened again as if by great willpower.

"Don't be late for the Gathering," Scaramuzzi said quietly to the cardinal or priest or whatever he was. Turning his smile to Alicia, he said, "Be nice to him. He has friends in high places." He laughed, and Alicia realized he could have been referring to God or the Vatican or even himself; she suspected it was the ambiguity that pleased him. He gave Ambrosi's shoulder a friendly squeeze and strolled away.

The old man said, "Please, step to the back wall."

"What have you done?" Brady said, each word as hard and heavy as a stone.

"Please. You can't leave yet. It's too dangerous."

Alicia pulled Brady back. They watched the old man lean to the keypad, punch in a number, and yank the door open. He shuffled in and pulled the door shut behind him.

He shuffled over to Alicia's cot and sat. He sighed, deflating his shoulders and chest. He seemed smaller than Alicia remembered him from that morning. Frailer. She sat beside him.

Brady glowered. "Scaramuzzi's pawn," he said spitefully. "He sent you to trap us."

"No," Alicia said, squinting at Ambrosi's weary expression. "Scaramuzzi doesn't know something. He doesn't know who you really are."

Brady snapped, *"We* didn't know who he really was. Servant of Antichrist."

Ambrosi adjusted himself on the cot, slowly, carefully, using the time to gather himself. He cleared his throat.

"I had hoped for a different resolution," he said. "I tried to impress upon you how dangerous Scaramuzzi is, how volatile. I thought . . ." He shook his head, apparently at his own naïveté. "I thought with that knowledge and your desperation to save yourselves—and your son—you would not allow him to come close. I believed . . ." He lowered his gaze.

"What?" Brady said.

"I believed you would kill him first."

"That's what you wanted?" Alicia asked. "For us to kill him?"

"He is a dangerous man, the destruction he is capable of."

"So kill him yourself," Brady snapped. "You obviously have access."

Ambrosi tilted his head. "If I failed . . . First, I must find a successor. A priest who can carry on my work. Otherwise, who would watch for and stop future Antichrist candidates, and who would, someday, urge the faithful to hold strong against the schemes of the true Antichrist?"

"Shouldn't you have selected a successor about fifty years ago?"

He nodded. "I have had several. They grow bored and drift into different fields. God will send one to me when it's time."

"And until then, you send other people to do your dirty work," Brady said. He had gripped a bar to keep from collapsing. He stumbled to his cot and sat.

"You must understand," Ambrosi said, "when I realized what Scaramuzzi intended to do with the near-death experience prophecy, I attempted to call in the cavalry, so to speak."

Alicia said, "You told Father McAfee your name."

"With hopes of attracting the whole of your Federal Bureau of Investigation or Interpol. Instead . . ."

"You got us," finished Brady.

"I was working every angle I could," Ambrosi said. "I had befriended Scaramuzzi's closest confidant, Pippino Farago. He was a childhood friend of Luco's who became his personal assistant. I discovered that he possessed evidence that would prove Scaramuzzi is a fraud. I had nearly convinced him to turn it over to the Watchers. I was nudging him toward doing the right thing for himself and mankind. I arranged a meeting between him and a Watcher who would love nothing better than to end Scaramuzzi's reign. That's when Pip disappeared, four days ago."

"This is the Pip that Scaramuzzi thinks contacted us, and the file he thinks we have or can get?"

"Yes."

"Did you tell him Pip contacted us?"

"I did. I am sorry."

"But *why*?"

"To draw him out. You would never have come near him on your own. How could you kill someone you can't even see? The file is important enough to him, secretive enough, that he would never send his men after it. He would do it himself."

Brady said, "You set up this Pip guy to turn on Scaramuzzi and he disappears. You send us to kill Scaramuzzi and here we are, as good as dead. You're pretty lousy at this whole spy game thing, aren't you?"

Ambrosi smiled. "If you want to make God laugh, tell Him your plans."

Alicia moved her hand to his back and patted it gently. His face was kind when he looked at her.

"I only wanted to stop Scaramuzzi. Months ago, Pip was full of wine and complaining about how terribly Luco treated him. He said he wanted to stand up to him, give him his due. I reminded him Luco did not tolerate insolence. He scoffed at that, so I said, 'Pip, the man killed his own mother'—a story everybody knew. Pip laughed and said it wasn't true. I knew then that I could trap Scaramuzzi in the lie, make him look like a fraud to the Watchers. Nobody cared if he murdered his mother or not; I had to make them care. I constructed the matricide prophecy, and Scaramuzzi, in his eagerness to win over the Watchers, he bought it."

Alicia finished for him: "After the Watchers accepted it, with Scaramuzzi's approval, Pip would step forward and say Scaramuzzi had not really fulfilled the prophecy."

"Better than that. Pip came back to me and confided that he had proof Scaramuzzi had not murdered his mother."

"The file," Brady said.

Ambrosi nodded. "He must be stopped. Not because he is Antichrist; he is no more Antichrist than was Mother Teresa. But he is a very clever con artist, even more so now that he has deluded himself into believing he truly is who he pretends to be. He will not bring about the biblical Armageddon, but for hundreds of millions, he may as well. Imagine Hitler with modern weaponry—this is Luco Scaramuzzi."

Brady wasn't buying any of it. He said, "But because of your high opinion of yourself and your *calling* to watch for Antichrist, you're willing to sacrifice innocent people."

Alicia scowled at him. "I think he's right. What are a few people compared to the millions who could die if Scaramuzzi gets his way?"

Speak for yourself. He didn't say it. The only reason he would have said it was to be spiteful, because he agreed with her—and, he supposed, with Ambrosi. He simply did not like being used the way Ambrosi had used them.

Ambrosi lowered his gaze to the floor, whispered, *"Exitus acta paene approbat."*

Alicia gently touched his forearm. "What does that mean, Roberto?"

He met her eyes and bent his lips wryly. He said, "The end *almost* justifies the means."

That made Brady smile, but only a little. He said, "I understand what you tried to do, even though I don't agree with the way you went about it. And I appreciate your own commitment and risk, to have infiltrated Scaramuzzi's camp. But couldn't you have done something before it went so far, before the murder of five innocent people, before *we* almost died?"

"This may sound heartless, but wasn't it Napoleon who said, 'Never interrupt your enemy when he is making a mistake'? Scaramuzzi's operation in America was going to shine a blazing spotlight on him. Simultaneously, I thought that Pip's evidence against him would find its way into the Watchers' hands by this time. He would have been squeezed from all sides. I envisioned the Watchers taking him out, and the FBI or Interpol wreaking havoc among the Watchers, making it difficult for them to regroup or salvage the assets they had already invested in Scaramuzzi's world. I wanted to cause as much harm to them as possible."

Brady said, "Were you responsible for sending that Viking after me and Malik after Alicia?"

"Of course not. That was Scaramuzzi's plan moving along like clockwork. His intentions were to have you and Alicia murdered on American soil. The world press would have a field day over the slaughter of two federal agents—one of them killed in the exact manner of the crimes he was investigating. Within a day, the Watchers would know it was he who had ordered the killings, and he'd have the boost in credibility he was vying for."

Alicia spoke up. "You and Pip were close to Scaramuzzi, yet you were working against him all along, and Pip was about to betray him."

Ambrosi nodded. "That is the nature of deceit. Enter that world—that tangled web, as someone called it—and you never know whom to trust; you never know what schemes are working against your own schemes." He sighed heavily, then continued. "People wonder why villains seem so ruthless, so decisive in their cruelty. It's because they operate in an environment that punishes anything less."

Abruptly, he checked his watch and stood. "I must go."

"Wait," Brady said, rising from the cot. He staggered back, caught his balance, and drew close to Ambrosi. He grabbed the old man's arm, all bone.

"You can't leave us here," he said.

"If you escape now, I'll be exposed. I'll come back for you later . . . tonight."

"We may not be alive tonight!" He was pushing the words through clenched teeth. "We may not be alive in an hour! You got us here; you get us out."

Ambrosi laid a gentle hand on Brady's shoulder. "I will, but you must wait. Don't forfeit everything now."

"Forfeit? I've already—"

"Let him go," Alicia said. "He'll be back."

He leaned his head toward them. On whispered breath, he said, "Pip was not murdered, as I feared. I saw him today. I think he will contact me, and I will get the file. All is not lost." He reversed a step and nodded sharply, as if to say, *That's what we have done. We will win this war yet.*

He reached through the bars, felt for the keypad, and made it beep three times. The door opened and he stepped into the breach.

Brady said, "At least give us the combination. Just in case."

"Have patience, my son. I will not betray you . . . again."

Alicia raised her arm, crossing it horizontally over Brady's chest—a gesture, not a genuine attempt to stop him if he were determined to leave.

"It'll be okay," she whispered.

Ambrosi clanged the cage closed.

"But if you can get the file, you don't need us anymore," Brady said.

The old man pressed his finger to his lips.

He turned and shambled toward the dark corridor on the left, the one Scaramuzzi had taken.

"Today?" Brady pleaded.

"I pray it will be," he said without stopping.

"You *said* today, later today!"

At the threshold of the corridor, he turned and rested his hand on the wall.

"Brady, you must trust—"

The bat arced out of the darkness and cracked into the old man's temple. Flesh and muscle and bone split under the impact. Blood sprayed as if exploding from a balloon. Ambrosi crashed against the wall and crumpled to the floor.

"Noooo!" Alicia screamed.

Brady ran to the bars, rattled the door with all his strength. He swore at Scaramuzzi as the man stepped from the shadows, straddling the downed man, surveying his handiwork. A crimson ribbon streamed from the tip of the bat, drizzling on Ambrosi's black sweater.

The cardinal's lifeblood pooled out from his head, tracing the joints in the stone, rising to cover the stones themselves.

Scaramuzzi stooped and plucked something off the sweater. He held it up. It was a transmitting device, about the size of a dime, with two thin-wire antennae jutting from it like legs. For the first time, Brady noticed the white iPod earbuds nestled in Scaramuzzi's ears. Undoubtedly, the iPod was rigged to receive signals from the transmitter. He stepped closer to the cell.

"I *thought* the old guy was acting a bit peculiar lately," he said. "A shame, really. I liked him."

An unearthly rasp floated up from the floor: "It's . . . what . . . you'd . . . expect," it said.

All three of them looked to see Ambrosi propped up on his elbows, glaring at Brady and Alicia with wide-eyed wonder, an earnestness that made the hair on Brady's arms stand up.

"Oh, now," Scaramuzzi said, raising the bat.

"No! No!" Alicia hurled the words at him like stones. But they had no effect. Gripping it in two hands, he brought the bat down on the already misshapen skull. The sound reminded Brady of an overripe watermelon he'd once dropped, carrying it to the trash.

Alicia ran to the corner and vomited.

Scaramuzzi caught Brady's eye, pointed at the body, and said, "Could have been you."

He turned and disappeared into the corridor, the click of his heels fading with each step.

83

Alicia wept into her hands, raising her face only to curse Scaramuzzi. Brady sat beside her on the cot, rubbing her back. He held his fingers to his nostrils, preferring the odor of sweat and skin to that of vomit and blood. One good whiff of the air would have him adding to Alicia's mess.

"The old man amazed me to the last," he said, trying to distract her. "He just had to tell us what it was like." He cringed when he heard his own words. But he could not stop there; maybe there was hope of extracting his foot from his mouth. "What dying was like. 'It's what you'd expect.' He must have seen the pearly gates, huh?"

Alicia's convulsions trailed off. She sat silently, her hands covering her face. When she looked at him, her eyes were red, her cheeks wet, but it was not sorrow shaping her expression, but disbelief.

"I said the wrong thing," he admitted apologetically.

She stood, held out one finger, indicating, *Hold on a minute.*

She went to the cell door. She reached through and fumbled with the keypad. Three beeps sounded. The lock mechanism clanked, and the door snicked open an inch.

Brady rose. "What the . . . ?"

Her lips pressed together, and he realized she was trying to smile and hold back tears at the same time. He stepped forward and took her in his arms. Cheek pressed against his chest, she said, "'It's what you'd expect.' Not death, the combination. He kept his promise to you."

"But what was it?"

She leaned back to view his face. "Antichrist? A guy who thinks he's clever and funny?"

He shook his head.

"Maybe you just have to know guys like that the way women get to know them. Come on." She stepped through the door, averting her face from Ambrosi's corpse.

"You're not going to . . . ?" Then it dawned on him. "Six-six-six."

She smiled, thin and strained.

Shaking his head, Brady reached out and took her arm. "Let's get out of here."

They jogged into the tunnel on their right. Brady had used it earlier to reach Alicia; perhaps he could backpedal his way out. He didn't hold out much hope without the CSD.

"I've tackled these tunnels before," he told her. "I was lost for two hours."

"We have to try, Brady."

The passageways to the left and right appeared less hospitable than their own—impossibly narrow, flooded, emitting foul odors. Everything looked different not viewed through the CSD's optics. Finally, they came to a lighted tunnel and took it. Another lighted passageway on the right—Brady turned into it and stopped. Alicia turned the corner, bumped into him, and peered around him.

They were in a chamber of some sort, boxes and crates and bags stacked all around the edges. A man was bent over a box, applying shipping tape. He looked up at them.

"Hey!" he yelled. He dropped the tape dispenser and reached for the small of his back. He was too far away for them to rush him.

"Back! Back!" Brady said, reversing and pushing Alicia into the tunnel. He caught a glimpse of the man pointing a pistol. He moved out of the threshold as a loud report roared out of the chamber and rolled like thunder through the tunnel. Another sharp sound snapped behind him—the bullet had hit the wall near his head.

"Stop!" The man sounded American. He would be directly behind them in the tunnel within seconds.

"Turn!" Brady said. "Now!"

Alicia arced into a wide but jet-black passageway.

The gun fired again, and stone chips blasted off the wall, stinging Brady's cheek. He made the turn. *The man would be as sightless as they were here, but he'd probably shoot blindly into the dark,* Brady thought.

"Turn again," he instructed.

"I can't see anything!"

"Run your hand along the left wall. I'll cover the right."

Instinctually, each held out the opposite arm as well until they clasped each other's hands.

The pistol roared behind them: *Bam! Bam! Bam!*

Brady heard a slug zing past his ear.

"Brady?" Alicia called. Terror in her voice.

"Here!" he said and yanked her into the tunnel he'd found. It was equally lightless but narrower. They ran single file. If their pursuer fired into this tunnel, he could not miss.

The wall on the left kept pushing in on them as the tunnel bent right. Light drifted into view—an illuminated tunnel a hundred yards ahead. Suddenly, shadows flitted on the back wall of the approaching tunnel and shouts from a half dozen people drifted toward them. Brady braked hard.

"Go back," he whispered harshly.

"But the guy with the gun—"

"He's only one," Brady said. "There's a small army the other way."

He heard her spin and dash away.

"Alicia, wait!"

He darted after her.

"What?" she called back.

"Hold your arms straight out in front of you, head-high. Both of them. Run as fast as you can."

Their pace picked up.

"Get ready," he whispered behind her.

He heard the man's footsteps and breathing two seconds before Alicia collided into their pursuer. Both let out heavy grunts. Brady crashed into Alicia's back, using his weight and momentum to give her the advantage, in case her outstretched arms had not done the trick. They tumbled onto the floor of the tunnel, rolling and pitching. Brady was up almost before he was down.

"Alicia!"

"Here," she said, rising beside him.

"Where's—"

"I'm stepping on his chest. He's out."

"Get his gun."

From down low: "Can't find it."

He dropped to his knees, panning his palms across the floor.

Noises from other pursuers came to them. A flashlight beam skittered against the curve of the tunnel wall.

Brady's right hand hit metal, which danced away from him.

"Got it," he said. "Come on."

They reached the lighted tunnel where the man had first shot at them. Alicia turned left, away from the cell they'd occupied, far in the other direction. She slowed before a lighted portal on her left. She peered in. Nothing. It was a passageway similar to the one they were in.

"Straight," Brady said, and she did not hesitate.

Thirty seconds later, voices pranced ahead of the humans making them—Brady and Alicia were heading directly into another search party.

They spun in unison and jogged back to the lighted passage they had passed. They darted into it. The two groups of pursuers would meet in about twenty seconds and realize where their prey went.

"Take the next lighted tunnel," he said.

They passed three black tunnels before reaching one with a string of stingy bulbs tacked to the ceiling. Stepping into it, they slowed to a walk, which allowed them to catch their breath and listen for pursuers.

"Sound gets distorted down here," he told her. "It's really hard to pinpoint it."

"I noticed."

He looked at the pistol in his hand. Glock 21—same as the one he trained with and carried on the job, except this fired .45s. Its bullets were larger than the 9mm bullets he was accustomed to. He stopped and ejected the magazine. Empty. He pulled back on the slide: a bullet popped out. He slipped it back into the chamber.

"One bullet," he reported.

"Make it count."

A gunshot rang out, and a bulb above them exploded. They turned to see a woman with a rifle taking aim. She was at least a hundred yards away, past the tunnel from which they had emerged.

Brady and Alicia dropped to the ground. The rifle fired. The bullet gouged out a chunk of wall above Alicia's head.

The shooter walked toward them.

"Crawl as fast as you can," Brady said. He scurried behind Alicia, moving backward to keep an eye on their pursuer.

The woman took aim. Brady watched her close one eye. He raised the Glock and sighted down its barrel, aligning her head between two iridescent dots.

Three people burst into the tunnel from a side passage, between the woman and him and Alicia. Four more joined them. They seemed confused about which way to turn. Two spotted the riflewoman and dropped into a crouch as their own weapons came up on her.

"Hey!" someone yelled, and Brady thought it was Rifle Lady, ticked that a group of morons spoiled her shot.

He spun, saw nothing but Alicia's backside and the bottoms of her shoes. He scampered after her.

A chorus of voices rang out behind him, representing a host of nations: *"Erhalten Sie sie!" "Tiro! Tiro!" "Déplacez-le des secousses!"*

Someone fired a shot.

They rounded a corner and leaped to their feet. The voices bounced past them. The tunnel opened into a huge corridor or hall, at least three stories high and so long neither end was visible. Fluted columns lined both walls. Stone spandrels arced from the top of one column to the next in line, all the way down the hall. From as far as Brady could see in each direction, amber glass bowls, like giant contact lenses, hung from the ceiling by thick chains. Fire crackled in each bowl and cast the entire hall in a bright, flickering yellow glow.

Tall double doors were centered in the wall between each column. Alicia ran to one, tugged at it. It did not budge.

Brady tried a different door, same result.

They ran down the corridor, moving past each other, trying doors.

Voices reached them from behind and ahead.

"Look for another tun—," Brady called as the door he tugged came toward him with the shriek of a dying bird.

"Alicia!" he said, turning to find her. She was at his side. Together, they pulled the doors open.

"Come in!" bellowed a familiar voice.

At the end of a long, carpeted aisle, Luco Scaramuzzi stood behind a stone altar, beckoning to them.

"Ladies and gentlemen," he announced, "we have guests!"

84

In the corridor, their pursuers found them. Coming from both directions, two groups of at least a dozen people each, every one armed with a knife or pistol or rifle, converged on Brady and Alicia. They had no choice but to accept Scaramuzzi's invitation. They moved quickly into the room. It was a cathedral, intricately carved from the bedrock under Jerusalem. Even the pews on each side of the aisle were stone. Two hundred faces were turned to Brady and Alicia. They stopped halfway to the altar. The armed militia crowded the threshold behind them. Their voices faded as voices do in churches.

Brady rotated around, catching sight of armed guards on balconies in the four corners of the cathedral. Without hesitation, he raised the pistol and took aim at Scaramuzzi.

Breaths pulled in, firearms cocked. Several men in nearby pews rose to their feet, ready to spring.

"Wait!" Scaramuzzi called. He raised his arms like a televangelist healing his broadcast audience. He was wearing a white robe. The sleeves hung down like angel's wings. This mockery of worship—its location, its "minister"—felt *wrong* to Brady. It called to mind Hieronymus Bosch's depiction of black mass, and the thought sickened him.

"Who brings these persecutors?" he continued. "Is it my father? Is it Satan?"

Gasps and ripples of applause from the congregation.

"A challenge, perhaps? A test? Father, has my time of trial and triumph come?"

He glanced around the room. A smile creased his lips.

Brady risked his own glimpse of the crowd. They were transfixed, overwhelmed by the spectacle before them. Scaramuzzi was playing them perfectly. This was precisely the show they wanted. Regardless of the outcome, Scaramuzzi would spin it in his direction, and they would love him. The beast Ambrosi had described—with the malice of Hitler and the power of nations—was taking shape before their eyes.

An absurdity pushed its way into his mind: *Could Scaramuzzi have planned this all along?* Could he and Alicia have been prodded and herded to this place at this time, carried on a current of Scaramuzzi's design?

Keeping his arms high, Scaramuzzi stepped around the altar.

"You see, my beloved, these intruders *know* who I am. They recognize me!"

Brady called out, "Tell your guards to drop their weapons!"

Scaramuzzi nodded. "Of course." He made a vertical gesture with his hands, as though fanning the congregation. After some hesitation, weapons all around them clattered against the floor. The men in the balconies leaned their rifles against the balustrades.

"You see?" Scaramuzzi said calmly. "See how I embrace my destiny?"

All Brady could see was Scaramuzzi's head lined up in the pistol's sights. He felt the trigger under his finger.

Pull the trigger, he thought. *End it here.*

The end of everything: Scaramuzzi . . . Alicia . . . himself. He knew that before the gunshot blast faded away, the mob would be on top of them. They would tear the two of them apart.

He did not want that for Alicia. He did not want that for himself. He truly wanted to see Zach again. And he wanted to know what Alicia felt like in his arms.

His finger eased off the trigger.

"We're leaving," he announced and took a step back.

Scaramuzzi said nothing.

He wants us to leave.

He'd given his fans the drama they sought. He'd say his mercy spared his enemies . . . or his father, Satan, told him he had passed the test, that he had stood up to his enemies and survived . . . he'd tell them something that would solidify their faith in him and grant him more power.

Brady took another backward step. Alicia moved with him—close, her hand on his shoulder.

A latch clanked and a door off to Brady's right creaked open. Everyone's head turned, including Scaramuzzi's. Brady moved just his eyes and caught sight of three men standing in a doorway. The one in front was short and stocky, with bushy eyebrows and a full head of silver hair. He recognized him from Ambrosi's scrapbook—Niklas Hüber. The Asian man beside Hüber was . . . *Ah,* he could not remember the man's name, but his picture had been beside Hüber's. Behind them stood a tall black man. He had not been pictured in the scrapbook, but Ambrosi had said his information on the current Council of Watchers was incomplete. These newcomers quickly assessed the situation. Deep frowns etched into their faces as they focused their attention on Scaramuzzi.

"This test is mine!" Scaramuzzi's voice resonated in the big chamber. He gazed past the gun into Brady's eyes. "'And I saw one of his heads as if it had been slain, and his fatal wound was healed. And the whole earth was amazed and followed after the beast!'"

Brady's stomach tightened. He was quoting from Revelation. It was the passage that many theologians say describes a fatal head wound Antichrist suffers, from which he miraculously recovers, sealing his ascension to world power.

Is he suggesting I . . . ?

Keeping his eyes locked on Brady's, Scaramuzzi bellowed, "Listen to me, all of you! These intruders are sent from the father to demonstrate my power, my identity! Let them shoot me—"

The congregation erupted with shouts of "No!" and "We won't!"

Scaramuzzi continued: "Let them shoot me, for it is written that they will. And it is written that I will rise again. And all will know me!"

The noes turned into cheers.

"If they shoot, let them go. If they don't . . . kill them."

Silence.

"Agreed, my beloved?"

No one replied. He was asking more than many of them could promise. Shoot the savior and go free? Blasphemy!

"I will come back," explained Scaramuzzi, "and take my revenge. They are mine."

This the congregation understood. Applause and cheers welled to a deafening volume. Then it quelled, like a breaker rolling off the sand, back into the surf.

"So," he said softly to Brady, "fulfill my destiny."

Beside him, Alicia whispered, "Do it."

In his mind, he saw himself pulling back on the trigger, putting a bullet in this lunatic's head.

His finger was paralyzed.

This was wrong. Scaramuzzi was unarmed. Killing him this way was murder.

Shoot! he scolded himself.

Brady was not cut out for unprincipled action. He had been wrong to think he could do whatever it took, regardless of the law, regardless of morals. The end does *not* justify the means! Three days ago, when he had taken aim at Malik, he wasn't ready to re-cage the beast he felt stirring inside. Now he was.

The beheadings . . . Zach . . . the attack on Alicia . . .

He had every reason to shoot. Why couldn't he?

He had heard about soldiers who were well trained, both physically and psychologically, to kill, but found they could not—even as their enemies tried to kill *them*. What a time to find out.

"Brady?" Alicia whispered.

Brady saw Scaramuzzi's forehead glisten. A lock of hair was quivering. He was trying to play it cool, but his nerve was starting to crack.

"Do it," Scaramuzzi said, almost inaudibly.

Brady's aim lowered slightly. Centered between the sights was Scaramuzzi's neck . . . then his chest . . .

Someone gripped his wrist. Alicia, reading his thoughts. Her right hand rose and took hold of the pistol. She tugged and then *wrenched* it from his hand.

She aimed it at Scaramuzzi.

He squinted at her, and for a moment, the cloud of insanity seemed to disperse away from him. Sheer terror flashed on his face.

She fired.

A hole appeared above his left eye. A red mist burst from behind his head. Filigrees of gore instantly appeared on the back wall. Scaramuzzi snapped backward, falling on the altar. A second later he was back up, standing as though only by habit. A trickle of blood leaked from the hole in his forehead, pooled in his brow, and dripped onto the white robe over his heart. He teetered and fell forward. His head struck the floor with the *crack* of a sledgehammer. A dark halo of blood fanned out under his head, slow as syrup.

No one spoke. No one twitched. It seemed to Brady that no one breathed. They all stared at the body, at the dark pool, awed, waiting.

Alicia tugged at his arm, and he let her pull him backward up the aisle. He could not take his eyes off the still body. Then as he turned he caught the three Council members, the three ephori, watching them leave. Their faces were impassive, resolved. His gaze flicked up to the balcony, where the Viking surveyed the scene. Their eyes met, and Olaf stepped back into the shadows.

Alicia pulled him through the knot of militia crowding in the threshold. No one moved to stop them. She released him, stooped down, and exchanged her empty weapon for one of the pistols on the floor. She checked the magazine and the chamber, appeared satisfied, and strode away.

Over her shoulder, she called, "Coming?"

85

We need someone to show us the way out," he said. They were moving fast down the center of the huge corridor.

"Do you want to go back and ask one of those freaks?"

He glanced back. The group he thought of as the militia—but who were likely only guards or armed workers—had disappeared into the cathedral. What they might be doing, he did not want to know.

"This hall has to lead somewhere," he said.

When they arrived at the end, however, there were only three passageways, none of which appeared any more promising than the miles and miles of tunnels they had previously traversed.

"Pick one," Alicia said, impatiently bouncing the new pistol against her thigh.

Brady marched into one as though he knew what he was doing.

They hiked for twenty minutes and came to one of the octagonal rooms that Brady had become too familiar with during his first foray into the tunnels.

"Okay then," Alicia said optimistically.

"Don't get your hopes up."

He took a step toward a portal and stopped. Coming out of the shadows was a wolf-dog. When it reached the threshold, it stopped. Its head was lowered, and yellow eyes glared at him through wiry brows. A low growl emanated from deep within. One lip quivered, revealing thick, sharp fangs.

"Brady?" Alicia said quietly.

"I know . . . I . . ." Then he realized she had not spotted the same wolf he had. She was looking at another, standing in the threshold directly opposite. More growling came at them from a different direction. Slowly, they looked. A wolf-dog, smaller than the others but equally vicious looking, padded into place from deeper down a tunnel. Its claws clicked on the stone floor.

The Viking stepped up behind the third animal. His face was completely devoid of emotion. He was here on business.

He held an ax at his side, letting it dangle nearly to the floor. He stepped past the dog. He swung the ax up and caught it with his free hand, holding it at port arms.

Abruptly, the dogs growled and snapped, jerking forward as if by the sheer force of their anger.

"What'd you do?" Brady whispered.

"I moved my gun an inch."

"Well, don't."

"We have to do something."

"You can't get them before they get us."

"At least I can get *him*." She glared at the Viking.

Brady turned, squaring himself to his enemy. The dogs' growling became sharp barks.

"*Góð stelpa!*" the man commanded, and the dogs quieted.

Brady said, "Olaf . . . ?"

No response.

He was trying to think of something to say when Alicia spoke up. "Luco Scaramuzzi is dead."

"You know it's true," Brady said. "You saw."

Alicia continued: "You said you believed because the Watchers believed. They don't anymore, Olaf. They let us leave."

"You know the prophecies," Brady said. "He should not have died, but he did."

One of the dogs whined, apparently uncomfortable with inaction. The dog behind Olaf edged closer, inching around his leg.

Footsteps rumbled out of a tunnel behind Brady and Alicia. The

Viking's focus shifted to something over their shoulders. They turned to see light playing on the tunnel wall. A few seconds later, the man whose iron-spike fingers had stopped Brady at the airport—Arjan Vos—appeared at the opening. He gripped a large handgun.

His beady eyes took in the scene. A smile played at the corner of his lips. He held up a bloody palm, and Brady realized he must have examined Scaramuzzi's body, maybe cradled his head.

"Olaf!" Arjan snapped. "Get them! They killed Luco . . . they killed the master."

Olaf only stared.

Arjan raised his pistol, leveling the barrel at Alicia.

Olaf issued a sharp command. The dogs whipped around to face Arjan, whose eyes flashed wide.

"What is this?" Arjan said, seemingly to the dogs. He squinted at Olaf and instantly read the Viking's intentions. His aim shifted to the bearded brute.

The nearest dog sprang.

The gun fired, blasting a chunk out of the wall next to Olaf.

The animal clamped its jaws on Arjan's wrist. The gun flipped out of his hand. The other two dogs were on him. One bounded into his chest, going for his throat. Snapping and snarling, the third went for his free arm. He staggered and fell back into the dark tunnel. His screams turned into gurgling . . . then silence. Only the sound of the dogs' ravenous anger echoed back into the chamber.

Alicia and Brady turned away.

"Enough," Brady said.

Olaf called to the dogs: *"Hættu flessu!"* The animals quieted and padded into the room, licking pink muzzles. Cautiously, they resumed their positions surrounding Brady and Alicia.

Brady watched Olaf. His face appeared to ripple. The hairs of his beard shifted subtly. The wrinkles around his eyes grew more pronounced. A roulette wheel of emotions was spinning inside. Brady saw puzzlement, curiosity, anger. The feeling that finally settled on his face surprised Brady: a profound grief. He remembered the articles Alicia had dug up about the lost Western Settlement, how they had made it seem that honor and integrity had meant something to those people. It occurred to him that the Viking was not grieving for the loss of a savior as much as for the things he'd done in service to a fraudulent savior.

Brady said, "I'm sorry."

The Viking watched them for a long time. Finally, Olaf hoisted his ax over his shoulder and dropped it into a sheath.

He snapped out a word, and the dogs trotted to him and lined up behind his legs.

"What do you need?" he said.

"We can't find our way out," Alicia answered.

He nodded. He made a noise like a cough, and the dogs ran into the tunnel behind him. His head twitched slightly, a gesture for Brady and Alicia to follow him. He turned and disappeared.

Alicia leaned close to Brady. Her jaw tight, she said, "That's the Pelletier killer."

"I think you put a bullet through the head of the Pelletier killer."

"But, Brady—"

"The Viking was only a weapon."

"I could just—" She raised the pistol toward the tunnel.

They exchanged a look, and she sighed.

"I guess we'd never get out of here if I did that."

"I don't think so."

She squatted and set the pistol on the floor.

He held out his hand to her. She took it.

The Viking stayed a good distance ahead. When they sped up, so did he. When necessary, he stopped so they could see which passage he chose. The dogs swirled around his feet like phantoms.

"There's no way we would have gotten out," Alicia said after fifteen minutes. "No way."

A dozen turns later, they realized the Viking had vanished. They continued straight and found the catwalk that led to the basement door.

When they pushed through the exterior door, a breeze brushed their faces. The moon was full and high in the sky.

They ascended the ramp, hand in hand. At the top, they turned toward the trees and crumpled together in the grass.

"I shouldn't be happy," Brady said. "But I'm ecstatic, and I haven't a clue why."

"I do," she said. "You're alive."

She kissed him.

And the most amazing thing happened: he returned it.

EPILOGUE

Two weeks later

Zach and Brady stood side by side at the foot of Karen's grave. A breeze played with their hair and made the flowers they had brought wave at them from the headstone's built-in vase. Zach had his arm around his father's torso. He squeezed, reminding Brady that his ribs were still healing. As were various bruises, torn ligaments, and lacerations. It seemed his left hand would never be without bandages again. But he *could* run the fingers of his right hand through Zach's hair, so that's what he did now.

Zach looked up at him. "Do you think she's happy?" he asked.

"She's very happy. That's the way heaven is. No more tears."

They turned away from the grave and headed down the grassy hill to the car. Alicia was leaning against the Highlander's fender, looking great to Brady's eyes—legs crossed at the ankles, hair dancing around, a smile on her lips and in her eyes. Zach ran up to her.

"Wanna race me to the top of the hill?" he asked.

"Oh . . . I think another day. My poor ol' body's not quite there."

"You don't have to use your arm to run," he pleaded.

She padded her arm, which was crossed over her chest in a sling. "Arm . . . ," she said, then pointed at her leg, where gauze covered the wound she had sustained climbing back into the forty-ninth-story window. "Leg . . . face . . ." She touched her finger to her cheek. The deep bluish color had faded to yellow. "I can out-scar a gladiator."

"Least you didn't lose a *tooth*!" Zach said.

Brady smiled widely to show off the hole where his vampire tooth wasn't. Alicia shook her head. "How do you eat?"

"Liquids only," answered Brady. "I stick the straw right through the gap."

"Funny," she said. "Didn't I witness you gnawing away on a steak the other day?"

"Okay, watch," Zach said, completely bored with the conversation. He tore off up the hill.

Brady stepped up to her. "I have something for you."

"Really? I like gifts."

He reached into his pants pocket and withdrew something that he held up to her.

"A feather?" she said.

"A swan feather . . . a *white* feather."

She laughed and took it from him as if it were a rose. She twirled it against her face.

"The Bureau's not going to admit it, but you earned this . . . for your cap."

"Well, you earned one too."

"I don't know." He looked down at his shoes. "I couldn't pull the trigger."

"Brady." She seized his shoulder. "I told you before, that kind of thing is me, not you. I couldn't get inside a killer's head with a saw."

One hundred percent Alicia. He smiled and leaned against the SUV next to her. Zach had reached the top of the hill and was barreling back down.

He said, "If they let Gilbreath come back, I may have to find a new line of work."

He, Alicia, and John Gilbreath had been put on administrative leave, pending an investigation.

"They won't fire him," she said. "Too little evidence. But I hear they're talking about making him an assistant SAC somewhere far away."

"That's a demotion," Brady pointed out.

"They'll make it look the opposite. He'll know he screwed up, but no one will lose face."

"Too bad."

Zach skidded to a stop in front of them. He plopped onto the grass, threw back his head, and panted.

"Record time," Alicia told him. "Now let's go eat. I'm starving." She opened the passenger door, climbed in, and slammed it shut. Behind the tinted glass, she stuck her tongue out at Zach.

He returned the gesture, got a hand up from Brady, and leaned in close to him.

"I like her," he said.

"That's what you keep telling me," Brady said. "I like her too. And you want to know a secret?"

Zach nodded quickly.

Brady looked around, hunched low, and said, "She likes Olive Garden almost as much as you do."

"Ahhhh!"

Brady slapped his son on the rump. "Now get in the car!"

He did, and Brady made faces at both of them before walking around and climbing in.

ACKNOWLEDGMENTS

A long work of fiction is never the author's own creation, but born of everyone who shared the vision and shouldered the weight. I am eternally grateful to my family, who tolerated my obsessive and manic behavior—my sons Matt and Anthony, my daughter Melanie, and above all my wife Jodi. My mother, Mae Gannon, cheered me on even before I knew where my love of reading and writing would take me. My father, Tony Liparulo, prodded gently and wisely. My friends encouraged me in more ways than they know—particularly Mark Olsen, John Fornof, Mark Nelson, Jay McGuire, Bob Seeds, Tim Casey, Evangeline Edwards, Connie and Dwight Cenac, Jan Dennis, and Cheri Flores. I am grateful to the brilliant thriller writer David Morrell for the entertainment and education he provided through his many novels, and for his personal encouragement and counsel.

I extend my profound gratitude to the team at WestBow, especially Allen Arnold, Amanda Bostic, Caroline Craddock, Jennifer Deshler, Rebeca Seitz, Scott Harris, and Jenny Baumgartner, the best editor a writer can hope for. Thanks, also, to Pat LoBrutto and L.B. Norton for their invaluable advice. And to Joel Gotler, friend, visionary, and agent extraordinaire. "Where there is no counsel, the people fall; But in the multitude of counselors there is safety."

Available October 2006

FROM THE AUTHOR OF *Comes a Horseman*

ROBERT LIPARULO

germ